MODERNITY, FREEDOM,
AND THE AFRICAN DIASPORA

Modernity, Freedom, and the African Diaspora

DUBLIN, NEW ORLEANS, PARIS

Elisa Joy White

INDIANA UNIVERSITY PRESS
Bloomington and Indianapolis

This book is a publication of

Indiana University Press
601 North Morton Street
Bloomington, Indiana 47404-3797 USA

iupress.indiana.edu

Telephone orders   800-842-6796
Fax orders   812-855-7931

Manufactured in the United States of
America

Library of Congress
Cataloging-in-Publication Data

White, Elisa Joy.
    Modernity, freedom, and the African
diaspora : Dublin, New Orleans, Paris /
Elisa Joy White.
        p. cm. — (Blacks in the diaspora)
    Includes bibliographical references and
index.
    ISBN 978-0-253-00115-3 (cloth : alk.
paper) — ISBN 978-0-253-00125-2 (pbk. :
alk. paper) — ISBN 978-0-253-00128-3
(electronic book) 1. Blacks—Ireland—
Dublin—Social conditions. 2. African
Americans—Louisiana—New Orleans—
Social conditions. 3. Blacks—France—
Paris—Social conditions. 4. African
diaspora. 5. Community life—Ireland—
Dublin. 6. Community life—Louisiana—
New Orleans. 7. Community life—
France—Paris. 8. Dublin (Ireland)—Race
relations. 9. New Orleans (La.)—Race re-
lations. 10. Paris (France)—Race relations.
I. Title.
    DA995.D75W49 2012
    305.896—dc23

                              2011051854

        1 2 3 4 5   17 16 15 14 13 12

To my beautiful parents,
Reggie and Margaret, with love and gratitude

CONTENTS

ACKNOWLEDGMENTS

In the course of developing this book—a journey that spans a decade, three countries, and at least seven personal residences from the Atlantic to the Pacific—I have benefited from the kindness, commitment, insight, time, patience, and support of many wonderful people in various places, spaces, and capacities along the way. I am sincerely grateful for them all and what follows will no doubt neglect a few.

Thank you to Kim Butler, who expressed interest in this project in the early days and has been a beacon all along, and Robert Sloan, Editorial Director at Indiana University Press, for keeping the project alive and offering crucial critiques that pushed this work into its strongest form. Many thanks for the very helpful comments from the anonymous readers who approached the scope of the work with great care and consideration. Thank you to Sarah Wyatt Swanson for her careful preparation of the manuscript and Louis Simon for his gentle and fastidious copyediting.

I am particularly indebted to the many individuals in Dublin's anti-racism and immigrant rights communities for the numerous interviews, rich conversations, "hang out" time, friendship, and candid expressions of hope, doubt, joy, and pain. Thank you to the members of the Anti-Racism Campaign, Residents Against Racism, and the Anti-Fascist Action for the camaraderie, commiseration, and inspiration, from Mountjoy Prison to the pub. Special thanks to Rosanna Flynn and Mags Glennon for allowing me to lurk a bit and for unendingly demonstrating how the good fight gets won. Thank you to Pat Guerin for the useful updates, the proper politics, and the "good for you" Guinness over the years.

When working on a project like this, though there is certainly pleasure, it seems one mostly courts tragedy, stressful conditions, disaster, and sadness, or at least sniffs around in the aftermath. Thank you to the African Diaspora community of Dublin for showing me the meaning of perseverance and the drive to create something new in the world. Thank you to the individuals in the Paris suburbs who did not look askance at a wandering pregnant woman poking around for a whiff of the bad times. Equal thanks to the residents of the Lower Ninth Ward who were forthright and kind when yet another person came around to ask yet another question about the horrible events that had so changed their lives.

The initial Dublin field research would not have been possible without a grant from the Fulbright Program and my subsequent affiliation with the M.Phil. in Ethnic and Racial Studies Program (now Race, Ethnicity, Conflict) in the Department of Sociology at Trinity College Dublin (TCD). I am most especially grateful to Ronit Lentin for providing me with a space within the university community and, more importantly, the anti-racism and gender rights communities, as well as her scholarly mentoring, honesty, and continued support over the years.

I would also like to thank my mentors and advisors at the University of California, Berkeley, in the African Diaspora Studies Ph.D. program, who did not flinch at the idea of conducting research on the once-uncharted area of "Blacks in Ireland." I've particularly appreciated the conversations, feedback, and support from my dissertation committee members, Michel Laguerre, Waldo Martin, and Stephen Small, as well as the encouragement from Percy Hintzen, Ula Taylor, and the late VèVè Clark.

Thank you to Sean O'Riaian for providing the initial statistical data, back in the UC Berkeley days, that moved the project forward, and also for connecting me with the Ethnic and Racial Studies Program at TCD. I am also very grateful to the late Daniel Cassidy for graciously allowing me to audit courses in the Irish Studies Program at the New College of California in San Francisco and also connecting me with his niece, and my friend, Siobhan Leftwich, who also helped to expand the necessary and invaluable landscape of Dublin connections for me.

Thank you to Peggy Piesche and Fatima El-Tayeb for organizing the Black European Studies (BEST) conferences in Schmitten and Berlin, and facilitating the opportunity for me to participate in a vibrant community of Black Europe scholars. I am particularly grateful for the insights and comments brought forth by my co-members of the "Theorizing Blackness Europe-wide" working group during those exciting and intense few days of the first BEST conference. Thank you to Allison Blakely, Maisha R. Eggers, Terri E. Givens, Young-Sun Hong, and Sara Lennox for the productive conversations and healthy exchange of perspectives.

Mahalo nui loa to my colleagues (and some former colleagues) at the University of Hawai'i at Mānoa for the thoughtful feedback during our short-lived, but productive, faculty housing writing group: Hokulani Aikau, Jodi Byrd, Petrice Flowers, Ty Kawika Tengan, and Katerina Teaiwa.

A powerful caffeine-filled thank-you to Ken Kraft, owner of the Crafted Kup in Poughkeepsie, New York, for providing me with a summer "office" and the fine Woodstock Blend.

I am greatly appreciative of the many rich conversations, dialogues, passing comments, interventions, meditations, and intellectual considerations offered to me across diasporic, transnational, academic, and "real world" communities. At meeting halls, conference centers, wine bars, pubs, beaches, back alleys, and some combination thereof, the encouragement, positivity, and feedback brought forth by the following individuals have lifted this project well above its beginnings and provided immeasurable instances of inspiration. Many thanks to Maggi Morehouse, Barnor Hesse, Anna Everett, Abel Ugba, Chinedu Onyejelem, Trica Keaton, Katrina Goldstone, Tanya Ward, Fidele Mutwarasibo, Kensika Monshengwo, Bisi Adigun, Kate O' Flaherty, Caroline Ang, Conor Houghton, and so many others who can't be named here (but, surely, I owe you a pint, glass of wine, or fizzy mineral water straight-up).

Finally, heartfelt and passionate gratitude to my lifeline: my family. Thank you to my partner (and husband) Ian Fleet for his patience, research assistance, and love over the very long haul of this project. Thank you (and kisses) to my extra-special children, Declan and Oliver, for all the times they've endured the oft-heard expression, "Sorry, Mommy's working." Thank you to my parents, Reginald and Margaret White, for planting in me the joy of inquiry, the desire to see the world in new ways, and thoroughly indulging my lifetime of "dancing to the beat of a different drummer."

MODERNITY, FREEDOM,
AND THE AFRICAN DIASPORA

INTRODUCTION

Until quite recently when one considered African Diaspora communities, Ireland rarely, if ever, came to mind. But at the start of the twenty-first century, Ireland provided an opportunity to witness the swift beginning of a "multicultural" society in a formerly colonized, negatively racialized, and lesser-developed *Western* nation scrambling to catch up with its newly prosperous economy and relatively modern position in the global arena. Yet, in 2000 and 2001, just prior to the global ripple of the 9/11 terrorist attacks in the United States and the proclamation of the end of the "Celtic Tiger" (see McManus 2001; Hennessy 2001), Ireland was the site of the development of an African Diaspora community at a moment that was both crucial and unique; crucial in that the presence of the African Diaspora aided in the rapid transformation of prior notions of the Irish national and cultural identity, and unique in that Ireland's new global presence offered an unprecedented "social laboratory" in which to examine the persistence of race-based inequalities in perceived modern global societies.

Quite problematically, the modernity of societies is measured by the value of their economic success and related technological progress in the context of historical and contemporary industrialization and global economic markets (see Headrick 1988; Kiely 1998; Adas 1990; Bensel 2000). From the late eighteenth century to the early nineteenth century, representing a nascent form of the economic and cultural globalization that is now recognizable today, the theoretical construction of modern societies increasingly incorporated a notion of progress defined by industrialization that was also coterminous with the articulation of concepts of democracy, egalitarianism, and freedom (see Inkeles 1960; McClelland 1961; Kerr et al. 1962; Huntington 1996). And yet side by side with these

egalitarian values, these societies freely engaged in slavery and colonization. During the current period of globalization, the markers of modernity
continue to be those of technological progress resulting from economic
success in global markets. At the same time, as a result of the construction of international bodies in the early to mid twentieth century that reflected global commitments to egalitarianism, freedom, and democracy
(e.g., the League of Nations and the United Nations), the idea of modernity has become linked to notions of social progress that were made explicit in those eighteenth-century articulations of equality, but are still
unrealized.

Modernity is contingent upon ideological commitments to equality,
freedom, and democracy and the superficial manifestation of technological advancement resulting from economic success. I contend that technologically advanced societies that maintain social inequalities are not
truly modern at all. The fact that the economic success associated with
the implicit progress of modern societies was particularly contingent
on the exploitation and unequal status of individuals of African descent
(e.g., enslaved laborers in the United States and the Caribbean; exploited
workers and the pilfering of resources from colonial Africa) places Africans and individuals of the African Diaspora in the position of representing an active and implicit interrogation of modernity and its contingent dimensions of progress. How is it that technologically modern
societies remain socially retrogressive in their engagement with modern principles of equality and freedom? Ireland makes a particularly interesting case with which to foreground instances of retrogression amid
progress in the larger context of modern global societies.

As a society emerging (at least until the economic crisis that began in
2008) from economic under-development into the modern global environment by means of technological progress, but which retains pervasive
and highly conspicuous social elements or constructs that are more indicative of earlier periods of globalization, Ireland is what can be termed
a "retro-global society." "Technological progress" in this formulation is
shorthand for the perception that technological advancement and development are inextricably linked in representations of modern societies and modernity itself (see Kiely 1998; Adas 1990). The appearance of
"technological progress" tends to mask social retrogression or relegate it
to the realm of the epiphenomenal or anomalous.

Undoubtedly, the current period of globalization has involved major
shifts in social experiences (see Featherstone 1990; T. Friedman 1999;
Laguerre 1998; Robertson 1992; Sassen 1991, 1998). However, I am particularly interested in the persistence of an evolutionary logic and the way

that it continues to be operational in spite of "shifts and reversals" (Held et al. 1999: 414), particularly as concepts and experiences of globalization reflect a trajectory of social progress that is inextricably linked to notions of modernity. So, as we will see in the cases of New Orleans and Paris in part 2 of this volume, retrogressive acts or retro-global events or conditions are not limited to newly global societies. However, Ireland provides us with a narrow temporal period in which to examine the way that socially retrogressive events or conditions come to the fore. Furthermore, the persistent prevalence of socially retrogressive circumstances contradicts the popular assumption in Ireland that the Irish—a population historically subjected to British oppression, negatively racialized, humanitarian by reputation, welcoming to the point of a slogan, known for mass emigration due to famine and poverty in the homeland—would not engage in acts that enabled their own global subaltern status (i.e., racism, xenophobia, anti-immigration policies, institutional discrimination). Yet, the case of the substantial arrival of African Diaspora communities—individuals racialized as black—in Ireland powerfully exemplifies the way in which contemporary renderings of modernity are intrinsically flawed because of the structural antecedent of race-based social inequality.

TRUE BELIEVERS: FREEDOM, EQUALITY, AND DEMOCRACY AS INTEGRAL TO MODERNITY AND GLOBALIZATION

The contemporary experience of modernity remains linked to its Enlightenment roots in relation to the ideas of freedom, egalitarianism, and democracy. This is evidenced not only by the assertions of scholars who have historically praised modernity, albeit within the problematic context of a traditional-versus-modern dialectic (see Lerner 1958; Inkeles and Smith 1974), or individuals who launch more contemporary arguments in its defense (Habermas 2002; Coser 1991). But oppositional interrogations of modernity also acknowledge that the ideas of freedom, egalitarianism, and democracy are, as Avijit Pathak notes, "core values of modernity": "Modernity, its adherents argue, is invariably related to the spirit of freedom" (Pathak 2006: 13). He identifies these core values as "freedom, criticality, democratization, openness and optimism for the future" and further notes that they "seem to have become desirable ideals/ guidelines for the entire human kind" (Pathak 2006: 24). Pathak rightly cautions that while modernity's "core values have a liberating potential, its concrete practices may cause arrogance and violence" (Pathak 2006: 26). Nonetheless, he maintains that "irrespective of cultural differences, it is difficult to legitimate a civilization that does not adore these values" and that "no society that seeks to call itself modern can escape the moral pressure of these core values" (Pathak 2006: 24). In this volume, I am particularly interested in the ways in which the moral pressure becomes even more prevalent as individuals within societies embrace the notions of freedom, democratization, optimism for the future, and work to forge these core values or ideals when they are perceived as unavailable or un-realized.

To give another example: in her consideration of motherhood and domesticity in the context of modernity, Helen Crowley writes: "Ques-tions are . . . raised—both politically and theoretically—about sexuality, intersexual relations, mothering, childhood, old age, wealth redistribu-tion, individual freedom, and social control. These *social* questions are becoming a real testing ground of modernity and of its original promise of liberty and equality for all—women as well as men" (Crowley 2000: 361; emphasis in original). Again, there is a linking of modernity and the expectation or "original promise" of an underlying freedom and egali-tarianism.

In a different context, but still equating modernity with freedom and equality, S. N. Eisenstadt argues for a coexistence of differential expe-riences of modernity and the dethroning of a Western-centric locus of modernity: "One of the most important implications of the term 'mul-tiple modernities' is that modernity and Westernization are not identical; Western patterns of modernity are not the only 'authentic' modernities, though they enjoy historical precedence and continue to be a basic refer-ence point for others" (Eisenstadt 2000: 2–3). I contend that those earlier "Western patterns of modernity"—whether as "basic reference point[s]" or due to "historical precedence"—also persist in the contemporary de-sire to ensure that notions of freedom, equality, and democracy remain integral to modern socio-political arenas. Significantly, in his analysis of the emergence of protest as central to the modern political arena, Eisenstadt notes that "the themes and symbols of protest—equality and freedom, justice and autonomy, solidarity and identity—became central components of the modern project of the emancipation of man" (Eisen-stadt 2000: 6).

To reiterate, it is not that scholars such as Eisenstadt, Pathak, and Crowley view modernity as unproblematic. What is important to con-sider here is that their various discussions acknowledge that notions of freedom, equality, and democracy are inextricably linked to their own assessment of modernity's ideological impact on international and state-level discourse and policies, and throughout global social arenas. Even

in the process of breaking away from the earlier discourse and perception of a Eurocentric teleological modernity and its supposed benefits,
they are implicitly looking toward a new—presumably better—rendering
of the earlier experience of modernity; again, not necessarily going beyond modernity or eliminating modernity (if it were even possible) but
attempting to locate the "spirit of freedom" that remains as its core value,
but is for the most part globally unrealized.

It is also important to consider that more than a decade after Eisenstadt's discussion, the "themes and symbols of protest" to which he referred
were still being brought forth globally in the name of democracy and
freedom. This was particularly exemplified in the 2011 "pro-democracy"
uprisings in North Africa and the Middle East (see Abedin 2011; Sadiki
2011) as well as in the midwestern region of the United States in which
crowds protesting against anti-union legislation in Wisconsin—and in
other states—chanted "Freedom, democracy, unions!" (Davey 2011; Marlowe 2011). Also quite notably, upon the formation of the Libyan Republic
Interim Transitional National Council (LRITNC) in February 2011 during
the early days of uprisings in Libya, the council members launched their
website with the words "freedom, justice, democracy" under the LRITNC
name and included a statement reminiscent of the classic Enlightenment
text, the Declaration of Independence (i.e., "When in the course of human events, it becomes necessary for one people to dissolve the political
bands which have connected them with another . . ."). The LRITNC statement, excerpted here, reads:

> In this important historical juncture which Libya is passing through
> right now, we find ourselves at a turning point with only two solutions.
> Either we achieve freedom and race to catch up with humanity and world
> developments, or we are shackled and enslaved under the feet of the ty-
> rant Mu'ammar Gaddafi where we shall live in the midst of history.
> (LRITNC 2011)

In addition to putting forth the mission of "freedom, justice, and democracy," the council's statement links these concepts to progression and a
movement into modernity ("achieve freedom and race to catch up with
humanity and world developments") and to an explicit lack of freedom
("shackled and enslaved") if they do not choose progression.

Further exemplifying the link between modernity and the advancement of equality and freedom, in a thorough comparative sociological
study of "liberal modernity and its adversaries" Milan Zafirovski sets
forth as his main objectives:

[T]o posit and document that within modern Western civilization, liberal society as a rule has been and remains the social system or project of liberty, equality and justice, and conversely, its illiberal, including conservative, fascist and communist alternatives, systems of unfreedom, inequality and injustice [and to demonstrate that] contemporary civilization . . . since the 18th century Enlightenment and French Revolution . . . has essentially moved in the direction of liberal society and liberalism via societal liberalization, liberation and human emancipation. (Zafirovski 2007: 2)

His explicit assertion of "unfreedom, inequality and injustice" juxtaposed against the freedoms of "modern Western civilization" of course has a much broader reach, as expressed by advocates of non-Western-centric and non-Eurocentric modernities (Dirlik 2000; Eisenstadt 2000; Pathak 2006). Yet, while the Western is not contingent for modernity, "liberty, equality, and justice"—and I will add democracy and republicanism— continue to be clearly represented as necessities for the realization of modernity.

Ulrich Beck, Anthony Giddens, and Scott Lash advance the theory of a reflexive modernity or re-modernization that indicates the movement from the certainties of the first stage of modernity (class-contingent social order, nation-states, security) to a less certain second stage of modernity (risk contingent, globalization, digitalization) (Beck et al. 1994; Beck et al. 2003). Yet, even such a non-linear construction of modernity can still find room for the articulation of freedom and equality in social arenas. Noticeably staying clear of a more disjointed interpretation of current conditions, Beck and his colleagues reject theories of postmodernity in favor of a reflexive, self-monitoring modernity that must continuously acknowledge its impact (Beck et al. 1994). Particularly, Beck considers reflexive modernity in the context of a "risk society" which locates communities amid a shared experience of potential danger and insecurity (e.g., the global impact of ecological disasters, nuclear reactor meltdowns, etc.) (Beck 1992). However, I find that the concepts of a reflexive modernity and the related risk society also shed light on global social risks, such as racism and related social inequalities, and—in a reflexive sense—the self-checking and monitoring across communities that bring forth a global conversation about these inequalities in the context of modernity.

While the idea of reflexive modernity is theoretically compelling, it is also important to consider that its proponents are decidedly not interested in the trajectory of progress that has been so tethered to the "prior" modernity (Beck et al. 1994; Giddens 1990). This is worth addressing here to further highlight the distinction between the expectations of progress in modern industrial terms and progress in modern socio-political arenas, with the latter being of particular interest to the African Diaspora communities examined in this volume. Beck, considering "the social design of the consensus on progress in technology policy" in his *Risk Society: Towards a New Modernity,* explains: "[T]he consensus has its foundation in the harmonizing formula *technical progress equals social progress.* The assumption goes that technological development produces obvious use values that can literally be felt by everyone in the form of labor saving devices, improvements of life, rises in the standard of living, and so on" (Beck 1992: 201; emphasis in original). Beck, through his consideration of the risk society, sums up this disconnect between technological progress and its social imperatives by noting, "As risks grow, the prerequisites for the harmonizing formula on the unity of technological and social progress have been canceled" (Beck 1992: 202). Giddens, considering the early sociological theorists on modernity—Marx, Durkheim, and Weber—notes that in spite of their "pessimism" regarding modernity, Marx envisioned a "more humane social system," Durkheim thought that industrialization would lead to a "harmonious and fulfilling social life," and Weber, whom Giddens describes as the "most pessimistic" of the three, "did not truly anticipate how extensive the darker side of modernity would turn out to be" (Giddens 1990: 7). Particularly, Giddens's own reflections on modernity and progress exemplify the negotiation of these earlier discontents and, in another sense, the attempt to reconcile modernity's most problematic and contradictive aspects without embracing postmodernity. Forecasting a reflexive modernist approach, he writes: "The world in which we live today is a fraught and dangerous one. This has served to do more than simply blunt or force us to qualify the assumption that the emergence of modernity would lead to the formation of a happier and more secure social order. Loss of belief in 'progress,' of course, is one of the factors that underlies the dissolution of 'narratives' of history. Yet there is much more at stake than the conclusion that history 'goes nowhere.' We have to develop an institutional analysis of the double-edged character of modernity" (Giddens 1990: 10). The duality and, perhaps, duplicity of modernity or its "double-edged character" cannot be overstated, yet as I argue throughout this volume, the expectation that modernity—and modern societies—should bring forth progress persists and continues to reflect the assumptions of a "happier and more secure social order" that, as Giddens writes, must be qualified. It would appear that Giddens, publishing his thoughts in 1990, is in a rich conversation with late-twentieth-century postmodern theorists about progress (see Lyotard 1985; Harvey 1989; Jameson 1991), as we may look to Jean-François Lyotard for the "loss of belief" to which Giddens refers. Lyotard writes: "We can observe and establish a kind of decline in the confidence that, for two centuries, the West invested in the principle of a general progress in humanity. The idea of a possible, probable, or necessary progress is rooted in the belief that developments made in the arts, technology, knowledge, and freedoms would benefit humanity as a whole" (Lyotard 1985: 48). Undoubtedly, the "end of progress" analyses reflect this "decline in confidence" to which postmodernist Lyotard refers and, when considered by advocates of a reflexive modernity, engage the complicity of industrial progress in relation to current risks. However, I contend that the idea of progress and *belief* in progress can still be prevalent in reflexive modernist contexts and, more importantly, due to a variety of social circumstances there are very necessary interests in progress, progressing, and gauging progress that continue to be reflective of modernist terms and remain salient in contemporary communities. Furthermore, in spite of the problematic and untidy equation of industrial/technological progress with social progress, the desire for the achievement of social progress (i.e., freedom and equality) does not disappear, even when masked by or subsumed within the parameters of industrial/technological progress. Importantly, progress must not only be considered in relation to the moving *away* from traditional connections (e.g., church, kin, prescribed rituals, limited technologies) but also must explicitly refer to the moving *toward* social conditions that are, for example, not inextricably linked to social inequalities such as racism, discrimination, and ethnic bias.

Beck's analysis in *Risk Society* sees greater "individualization" as indicative of a "new modernity" resulting from the end of social classes as they "are emancipated from regional and particularistic restrictions and limitations" (Beck 1992: 99). This, Beck contends, is due to the equalizing impact of the mutual experience of global risks (Beck 1992). Particularly significant here is that he addresses social inequalities transmitted to the space of risks taken by "individualized" actors, stating that "[i]ncreasingly, everyone has to choose between different options, including as to which group or subculture one wants to be identified with. In fact, one has to choose and change one's social identity as well and take the risks in doing so" (Beck 1992: 88). However, Beck's "new modernity" also brings forth the reality that regardless of one's choices amidst the "risk society," social inequalities still persist as a result of *"ascribed* differences" (Beck 1992: 99; emphasis in original), which he describes as "race, skin color, gender, ethnicity, age, homosexuality [and] physical disabilities" (Beck 1992: 101). Considering the impact of these various ascribed differences, it appears that many individuals do not have choices related to "choos[ing] and chang[ing] one's social identity" at all. If anything, social inequalities seem to be a "carry-over" from what Beck, Giddens, and Lash consider the first phase of modernity. This, of course, leads one to question whether there is anything necessarily new about what Beck and his colleagues considered a new phase of modernity back in the early 1990s. Even some twenty years after the assessment and declaration of a new modernity, these lingering factors of social inequality cannot be easily dismissed and, as I argue here, also serve to prohibit the realization of any modernity—new, old, or in-between.

Current considerations of modernity must also address the relationship between modernity and globalization, as globalization is central to examinations of the role of modernity in contemporary society. Among myriad micro- and macro-level social, political, and cultural considerations, discourse on globalization includes theories of globalization as "replac[ing] modernization as a paradigm of change and social imaginary" (Dirlik 2000), globalization in tandem with postmodernity (Harvey 1989; Jameson 1991), globalization as a period of "high modernity" (Giddens 1990), globalization as producing a "global ecumene" represented as a "landscape of modernity" (Hannerz 1996), globalization "as a project of the second modernity" (Dinu 2007), globalization as producing various "scapes" from ethnic to financial sectors of modern societies (Appadurai 1997), and globalization as "the reigning ideology of late modernity" (Segesvary 2001: 5). It is here that I am particularly interested in linking the core ideologies of modernity—represented in notions of equality, freedom, democracy, and republicanism—as integral to the socio-political arenas of globalization.

When considering globalization and modernity, Arif Dirlik underscores the potential for globalization to extend the aforementioned non-Western-centric modernity, stating that the "discourse of globalization claims to break with the earlier modernization discourse in important ways, most notably in abandoning a Eurocentric teleology of change" and that "institutional arrangements informed by a Eurocentric modernization process are no longer sufficient to grasp and to deal with the world's problems" (Dirlik 2000: 5). Regarding the "Eurocentric modernization process," I would add that such an understanding of modernity is not "Eurocentric" solely because of the role of Europe in defining the parameters of modernity, but also due to the implicit exclusion of other communities that are either peripherally "of Europe" (i.e., within Europe but excluded from being "European") or not considered of Europe or Western at all when addressing problems of modernity. Thus, supposedly modern societies attempt to "grasp and . . . deal with the world's problems" without sufficiently looking within their own communities. This further indicates that globalization also must contend with American-centrism on similar terms, particularly regarding the situating of groups that are not racialized as white (limitedly read as "of European descent") outside of the purview of full American-ness. Dirlik goes on to state: "Globalization has an obvious appeal to a political left that has been committed all along to internationalism, equality and closer ties between peoples. . . . The emancipatory promise of globalization is just that, a promise that is perpetually deferred to the future, while globalization itself creates new forms of economic and political exploitation and marginalization" (Dirlik 2000: 5). Important for our consideration here, Dirlik brings forth the linking of globalization with notions of freedom and equality that have been integral to modernity, but also critiques their realization in the arena of progress as a "promise" not yet made; again we see the pessimism so neatly paired with the "end of progress" thesis. Even as modernity is "perpetually deferred to the future," as will be examined throughout this volume communities continue to remain invested in that future and work to progress toward it through an articulation of the "promise" (i.e., equality and freedom). In other words, they continue to believe in the possibilities.

Saskia Sassen, in her essay "Global Cities and Survival Circuits," argues that "[w]hen today's media, policy, and economic analysts define globalization, they emphasize hypermobility, international communication, and the neutralization of distance and place" and that "[g]lobalization thus privileges global transmission over the material infrastructure that makes it possible; information over the workers who produce it, whether these be specialists or secretaries; and the new transnational corporate culture over the jobs upon which it rests, including many of those held by immigrants" (Sassen 2004: 254). Sassen's assessment reminds us that without the social and cultural dimensions of globalization—without people—there is no economic globalization. This implicitly signifies the same for modernity and, to extend this, those core values that accompany it. So, in the discursive world of modernity—however its current form is considered—analysts, theorists, and scholars cannot escape the impact of notions of freedom, equality, and democracy. Even if these ideas appear to be failed ideologies which must be either reinterpreted, announced as moribund, or abandoned, these "core values" are still advanced at a micro-level by individuals who have not given up on them and require them for survival.

Malcolm Waters defines globalization as "a social process in which the constraints of geography on social and cultural arrangements recede and in which people become increasingly aware that they are receding" (Waters 1995: 3). While Waters acknowledges that globalization implicates the "expansion of European culture across the planet via settlement, colonization and cultural mimesis," he does not see globalization as an automatic default to Westernization, but does however contend that "every set of social arrangements must establish its position in relation to the capitalist West" (Waters 1995: 3). I find Waters's definition particularly useful here because the awareness of "social and cultural arrangements reced[ing]" implicates the rapidity of processes of globalization as well as the important role of perception in the human experience of modernity. I contend that it is the perception of a requisite lived experience of freedom and equality, which is inextricably linked to modernity, that creates friction or a disjuncture when individuals and groups find that they are barred from partaking of such freedom and equality; even as global societies—through policy doctrines, socio-political narratives, international documents, and discourse—maintain that these ideals are in reach. In this respect, I also find Giddens's explanation useful, as he defines globalization as "the intensification of worldwide social relations which link distant localities in such a way that local happenings are shaped by events occurring many miles away and vice versa" (Giddens 1990: 64). The three African diaspora communities examined in this volume are "distant localities" in conversation, as they share the collective expectation that freedom and equality—as advanced by the nations in which they reside—should be integral parts of their own lives.

In his late 1990s work, *The Global Age: State and Society beyond Modernity,* Martin Albrow begins by stating, "A sense of rupture with the past pervades the public consciousness of our time. It extends beyond national and ideological differences" (Albrow 1997: 1). Seeing a "postmodern" that has "never escaped modernity," Albrow explains that "despite all the 'new age' talk . . . the idea that we are still in some sense 'modern' is remarkably persistent. It indicates how successful the thinking of modernity has been in claiming any innovation as its own, even a 'new age'" (Albrow 1997: 1). So, Albrow brings forth a "global age" that, unlike his consideration of modernity, has "no inherent direction or necessary end-point" (Albrow 1997: 95). However, I contend that there remains an expectation of a "necessary end-point" for those who consider the terminal point of racism, discrimination, and other social inequalities. While it is not conceivable that one could actually *forecast* an endpoint, the desire for a particular outcome (i.e., the end to race-based inequalities) continues. Albrow also asserts that "[m]odernity holds its adherents in a double bind: it promises new futures and at the same time denies any possibility of an alternative to itself" and, therefore, he advocates for "moving on beyond both modernity and post-modernity and recognizing a new reality" (Albrow 1997: 1). However, I am also not convinced that the end of the "double bind" of modernity and the transcendence to "a new reality" necessarily eliminate the "modern" quest for a "new future" which—irrespective of the chosen terminology—still has an outcome or end-point. Such an end-point, for example, results in an equitable society devoid of racism. My point here is not to advance a utopian musing, but to emphasize that for communities that experience the adverse side of social inequalities, visions of a "new future" do not explicitly beg for any new alternative other than that which has been historically and contemporarily brought forth as a vital necessity (e.g., equality, freedom, democracy or, plainly, the end to racism).

The contemporary period of globalization also facilitates significant globality. Globality is not just contingent on interconnectedness via technologies but also the movement of people (and, as indicated by Sassen, not just corporate multinationals). Even more, there is an experiential dimension of globality that is paired with the movement of ideas, such as notions of freedom, equality, and democracy and the expectation that societies that experience globality would embrace these ideas. Roland Robertson has most notably contemplated globality (Robertson 1983; 1992), explaining that "'globality' refers to the circumstance of extensive awareness of the world," which he considers as "both the world in its contemporary concreteness and to humanity as a species" (Robertson 1992: 78). However, I find Wolf Schäfer's advocacy for a "lean globality studies" more useful for our consideration here. Schäfer, in a *Globality Studies Journal* article that works to define the approach or reach of the field of study, describes globality as a "local condition with four components—a globalization[1] or more, a geographical range, a state of interconnectedness and a state of consciousness" (Schäfer 2007: paragraph 32). He also notes that "globalization tends to propel everything under its influence from a lower to a higher degree of globality" (Schäfer 2007: paragraph 15). I maintain that the "core values of modernity" via globalization "propel[ling] everything" are expressed through globality and, reflexively, globality is only as effective as the freedoms that enable it.

I do not separate globalization from modernity, but view it as an integral part of the way modernity is experienced today. Thus, this volume considers the globality of individuals and societies, particularly in "global cities" (Sassen 1991), as part of modernity and, therefore, still operating within the context of the ideals of freedom, egalitarianism, democracy, and, particularly in France, republicanism. The conditions that accompany the contemporary period of globalization (and, implicitly, modernity) are at one pole lauded for the potentiality of a global liberal democracy and homogenization (Fukuyama 1989, 2006; J. Friedman 1999) and, at the other pole, significantly checked and challenged through interrogations of related global inequalities, Western / global north economic interests, cultural hegemony, and labor exploitation (Barber 1995; Segesvary 2001; Huntington 1996; Mander and Goldsmith 1996; see Held and McGrew 2007). It is not my intent here—even though it continues to be worth interrogating—to address globalization in an effort to examine whether global societies are at "the end of history" and moving into utopian capitalist renderings of a "liberal democracy" (Fukuyama 1989, 2006) or enmeshed in a "clash of civilizations" (Huntington 1996). However, I contend that, as with critical challenges to modernity, contestations of globalization—in all of its interconnected dimensions (social, cultural, political, and economic)—are not necessarily framed outside of the theoretical, analytical, or popular discursive context of freedom, egalitarianism, and democracy. This is not to dismiss the legitimate concern which Manfred Steger has aptly described as the neoliberal "assertion that free markets and democracy are synonymous terms" in the "globalist claim" that "[g]lobalization furthers the spread of Democracy in the world" (Steger 2001: 73). Furthermore, there is always the concern about the reduction of notions of freedom, equality, and democracy to mere platitudes. As the postmodernist Jean Baudrillard, finding himself in a France in which an opera house is built at the Bastille and contemplating the "reversal of history," caustically wrote: "Democracy itself (a proliferating form, the lowest common denominator of all our liberal societies), this planetary democracy of the Rights of Man, is to real freedom what Disneyland is to the imaginary. In relation to the modern demand for freedom, it offers the same characteristics as recycled paper" (Baudrillard 1994: 27).

However, my concern here is with individuals and groups—specifically African Diaspora communities—who have an interest in "real freedom" and, therefore, embrace democracy in the context of globalization but not expressly as a neoliberal project. In other words, globalization also facilitates a greater interrogation of the quality of democracy—and freedom and equality—experienced by communities within global societies that are considered catalysts for this "spread of democracy in the world" but are now forced to reflect upon their own engagement with these modern ideals.

When positing "multiple modernities" and envisioning a break from earlier renderings of modernity, Eisenstadt stated: "The undeniable trend at the end of the twentieth century is the growing diversification of the understanding of modernity, of the basic cultural agendas of different modern societies—far beyond the homogenic and hegemonic visions of modernity prevalent in the 1950s. Moreover, in all societies these attempts at interpreting modernity are continually changing under the impact of changing historical forces, giving rise to new movements that will come, in time, to reinterpret yet again the meaning of modernity" (Eisenstadt 2000: 24). This seemingly constant reinterpretation of modernity to which Eisenstadt refers also brings into question the unidirectional characterization of modernity. Even though modernity and globalization are not Eurocentrically teleological, as I have discussed here, there is still a persistent belief and expectation that societies should move toward a more extensive engagement with modernity in the arena of social progress (i.e., equality, freedom, democracy). However, there is also the consideration that there are potential reversals of modernity or "discontinuities" (Giddens 1990) and directional shifts in globalization or "deglobalization" (Hannerz 1996). In this volume, I consider such reversals to be "retrogressive" acts. As Dirlik has noted, "The euphoria over globalization, however, has served to disguise the very real social and economic inequalities that are not merely leftovers from the past, but are products of the new developments" (Dirlik 2000: 5). To add to Dirlik's assertion, I contend that even the "new developments" are a *legacy* of the past. While I am implicitly working to "reinterpret . . . the meaning of modernity" in the spirit of Eisenstadt's observation, I am also particularly interested in the salience of the association of modern societies with notions of freedom, egalitarianism, and democracy. Communities continue to hold out for the potentiality that the ideals of modernity will be realized through the creation of global societies that progressively advance rather than retrogressively eliminate freedom and equality. The perception of retrogression exists because the progress associated with global societies is undercut by the inability to meet the expectations of equality, freedom, and democracy that are the requisite core values of modern social and political arenas. In Jürgen Habermas's assessment regarding the life-world: "the project of modernity has not yet been ful-filled" (Habermas 2002: 13). Ultimately, this book is interested in the way that African Diaspora communities are at the forefront of requiring these global societies to come to terms with their disengagement from the ide-ologies that would otherwise make them modern.

FREEDOM AND THE "ANOMALIES" OF MODERNITY:
THE SIGNIFICANCE OF AFRICAN DIASPORA
COMMUNITIES IN DUBLIN, NEW ORLEANS,
AND PARIS

This volume takes as its point of departure Dublin in the first years of the current century, during a period of the first substantial African mi-gration to the city and nation. Dublin had already become the conspicu-ously "modern" locale it is today. Dublin city center is a bustling space of shoppers, students, musicians, sightseers, businesspersons, taxi queues, and double-decker busses. Internet cafés are always nearby, American fast food spots are filled with those in need of skinny chips and burg-ers, and pubs are packed with revelers who are as likely to be downing a Budweiser or Smirnoff Ice as a pint of Guinness. Tourists wander Dublin streets in search of remnants of a Viking past or more recent Joyceana. Traditional bands play a melodious "slip jig" that bounces out of the pubs and into the streets, while trendy bars with creative lighting play the lat-est electronica. Theatergoers enjoy the national venues and avant-garde performance spaces, car radios blast the latest R&B jams from America or the dance anthems from last summer in Ibiza and, in the hottest sec-tion of town, stag and hen partiers stumble along cobblestones dating back centuries to get to the wine bar, sushi restaurant, or hyped club of the moment.

Dublin is also a city with council housing (public or social housing), individuals on the dole, populations of people who will never attend third-level institutions or anticipate securing a job at a multinational IT com-pany, and a growing disparity between the haves and have-nots, creat-ing a group that was well aware—even at the peak of the "Celtic Tiger" economy and its neoliberal discourse—that the perceived progress of the nation was not their own.

Finally, Dublin is a city of immigrants, many of whom are not fully accepted in the city and nation; marginalized in a country mythically considered a place of *céad míle fáilte* or "100,000 welcomes." Once per-ceived as a homogeneous city, the streets of Dublin are now filled with persons of various ethnic backgrounds. Dublin may be considered culturally Irish, but as early as the year 2000, what that implied and whom that included was rapidly changing.

The second part of this book examines three events that exemplify the persistent and substantial role of African Diaspora communities in exposing the failings of would-be modern societies in the realm of social retrogression. Dublin, which informs the foundation of this study, will be further examined through the case of deportations of Nigerians from Ireland in the year 2005. That same year also presented highly significant events in New Orleans and Paris—Hurricane Katrina and the uprisings in the Paris suburbs—which yet again placed African Diaspora communities in the position of exposing socially retrogressive circumstances that inhibit the realization of egalitarianism, freedom, and democracy in modern societies. These three events challenged the saliency and success of modernity, as well as tested present-day understandings of freedom. The events in these three seemingly disparate sites underscore the significance of African Diaspora experiences in the context of modernity and a mobile, free, and egalitarian global society.

Dublin, New Orleans, and Paris are ideologically linked via the experience of modernity in the context of African Diaspora communities, even as their circumstances challenge differently formed and nation-specific renderings of socially progressive societies. That is, in Ireland, social progress must be discussed in relation to a precarious position in the nation due to asylum status that challenges the Irish reputation for humanitarianism. In the United States, social progress explicitly engages race and racism, which chafes at the rhetoric of American democracy. In France, notions of social progress rarely evoke "race" and, in effect, when racial discourse emerges, notions of assimilation and egalitarianism are disrupted. In each case, we see a lack of freedom emerging, suggesting the liberty that each society values is less than tangible for many, particularly individuals of the African Diaspora.

MODERNITY, FREEDOM, AND THE AFRICAN DIASPORA

See your Declaration Americans!!! Do you understand your own language? Hear your language, proclaimed to the world, July 4th, 1776—"We hold these truths to be self evident—that ALL MEN ARE CREATED EQUAL!! that they *are endowed by their Creator with certain unalienable rights;* that among these are life, *liberty,* and the pursuit of happiness!!" Compare your own language above, extracted from your Declaration of Independence, with your cruelties and murders inflicted by your cruel and unmerciful fathers and yourselves on our fathers and on us—men who have never given your fathers or you the least provocation!!!!!! (D. Walker 1993: 95; emphasis in original)

When David Walker published his appeal in 1829 he voiced the contradictions at the core of American society, inserting his concerns into an already established litany of the ways in which the institution of slavery was an affront to all that the American experiment promised. The language of Walker's appeal gives voice to the pain and frustration inherent in the arduous project of making free societies live up to all they profess; a project made manifest by the presence of African Diaspora communities. It is thought that Nat Turner was influenced by—or at least read—Walker's writings (see V. Thompson 2000). Notably, Turner had initially scheduled his August 21, 1831, resistance to occur several weeks earlier on July 4. Frederick Douglass, also foraging through the lapses of intellect and application meted out by American society in the face of the Declaration of Independence, remarked in his famous speech on July 5, 1852:

What to the American slave is your Fourth of July? I answer, a day that reveals to him more than all other days of the year, the gross injustice and cruelty to which he is the constant victim. To him your celebration is a sham; your boasted liberty an unholy license; your national greatness, swelling vanity; your sounds of rejoicing are empty and heartless; your shouts of liberty and equality, hollow mock; your prayers and hymns, your sermons and thanksgivings, with all your religious parade and solemnity, are to him mere bombast, fraud, deception, impiety, and hypocrisy—a thin veil to cover up crimes which would disgrace a nation of savages. There is not a nation of the earth guilty of practices more shocking and bloody than are the people of these United States at this very hour.

Go search where you will, roam through all the monarchies and despotisms of the Old World, travel through South America, search out every abuse and when you have found the last, lay your facts by the side of the everyday practices of this nation, and you will say with me that, for revolting barbarity and shameless hypocrisy, America reigns without a rival. (Douglass 1852)

The act of bringing the Declaration of Independence into question or planning an uprising against slavery on the Fourth of July suggests not only the symbolic means of appealing for independence or freedom but also a desire to bring the document into the full realization implicit in its Enlightenment roots and modern conception; that is, if modernity is equated with such notions of equality and liberty, then indeed America must adhere to its declaration (see Colaiaco 2007). But, the inability to do so in the face of the African Diaspora persisted, enabling a society rife with "fraud," "deception," and "impiety."

Alexis de Tocqueville, who visited America just short of twenty years before Douglass's speech, even as he lauded the American democratic project in his 1835 *Democracy in America*, clearly saw the contradictions inherent in a democratic society with slaves. Tocqueville, of course, separated equality from freedom in his analysis but envisioned "an extreme point at which freedom and equality would meet and blend" in which "men will be perfectly free because they are all entirely equal; and they will all be perfectly equal because they are entirely free" and, further implicating modern notions of socio-political progress, noted, "To this ideal state democratic nations tend" (Tocqueville 1835). Regarding the forced migration and enslavement of blacks, he wrote:

> When the Europeans chose their slaves from a race differing from their own, which many of them considered as inferior to the other races of mankind, and any notion of intimate union with which they all repelled with horror, they must have believed that slavery would last forever, since there is no intermediate state that can be durable between the excessive inequality produced by servitude and the complete equality that originates in independence.
>
> The Europeans did imperfectly feel this truth, but without acknowledging it even to themselves. Whenever they have had to do with Negroes, their conduct has been dictated either by their interest and their pride or by their compassion. They first violated every right of humanity by their treatment of the Negro, and they afterwards informed him that those rights were precious and inviolable. They opened their ranks to their slaves, and when the latter tried to come in, they drove them forth in scorn. Desiring slavery, they have allowed themselves unconsciously to be swayed in spite of themselves towards liberty, without having the courage to be either completely iniquitous or completely just. (Tocqueville 1835)

The conflict that is so clearly illuminated by Tocqueville when considering the European "violat[ion] of every right of humanity in their treatment of the Negro" paired with the fervent claim that such "rights were precious and inviolable" remains unresolved, not only in the realm of reparations discourse or other more immediate corollaries to the Transatlantic Slave Trade, but through subsequent race-based social and political inequalities on a global scale.

Tocqueville saw America through the relatively new republican lens of France, a nation that was undoubtedly working toward the implementation of its own ideals of egalitarianism and liberty. However, what is also important here is that in the United States and France we see a historical commitment to democracy, equality, and liberty either clashing or imminently clashing with the experiences of the African Diaspora. In the contemporary African Diaspora experience, across various nations, the proclamation of liberty or freedom is still lived through the specter of neglect, forcing the realization that the modernity, with its implicit notions of progress, is flawed in that it cannot account for the lack of progress in the areas of race-based oppression. More specifically, even factoring in the 2008 election of the first black U.S. president, Barack Obama, the full realization of liberty—reflected in all areas of social, civic, and political participation rather than doled out incrementally—is often unattainable for individuals who are not racialized as white.

It is with this in mind that we see the means in which, even in its twenty-first-century rendering, the African Diaspora—in all its diversity—still embodies the glaring reality that the modern notions of equality and freedom have yet to be fulfilled. Even two hundred years after the end of the Transatlantic Slave Trade, we see debate over the contradictory nature of embracing freedom while simultaneously restricting it for individuals of the African Diaspora; a continued debate about, in essence, the contemporary participation of individuals of the African Diaspora in these very same modern projects (Green 1997; D. A. Thomas 2004; Clarke and Thomas 2006). In the twenty-first century, we still have to consider whether certain black communities—in Dublin, New Orleans, or Paris—*inter alia*, are completely free or whether they forever remain in a liminal space carved out centuries before, now only modern in its technologies and policy language, yet functionally the same in its ability to delimit the lived reality of the modern project. As will be addressed in the examination of "retro-global" conditions in part 1 of this book, considering that modernity, in its contemporary rendering, is paired with the rhetoric of social progress I maintain that acts and events that contradict these democratic and egalitarian notions of modern social progress are *anti-modern* and *retrogressive*, thus negating the ideals that embody the preferred understanding of what modern societies should be.

Freedom, of course, can be articulated in numerous ways. At the birth of the United States we would have seen "freedom" or "liberty" constructed in contrast to slavery (Reid 1987). Slavery, at the time, could clearly be considered in terms of blacks in bondage or, in the British and colonial American usage, a more figurative engagement vis-à-vis the curtailing of rights by the monarchy (Reid 1987). Even if there was some debate over which form of slavery was considered the opposite of "liberty" or "freedom" in colonial American parlance (Reid 1987), it is clear that the bondage of individuals of the African Diaspora in the Americas was of concern. It is also clear that the lack of freedom for individuals of the African Diaspora in the context of a democratic and independent society was perceived as problematic enough for the constitutional mandate to end participation in the Transatlantic Slave Trade by 1808. This further underlines the early role of African Diaspora communities in advancing the lived realization of modern ideologies. As Eric Foner notes in *The Story of American Freedom,* in considering the War for Independence, the "most insistent advocates of freedom as a universal entitlement were African Americans" (Foner 1999: 32).

In contemporary terms, the articulation of freedom is even more nuanced, involving both the countering of the elimination of what Isaiah Berlin considered "negative freedom" or that condition of not being constrained by others and, even as Berlin saw the potentiality for totalitarianism, the experience of "positive freedom" and its relation to external actions (in spite of its implied relation to an internal experience of freedom) (Berlin 2002). Significant in the context of contemporary African Diaspora experiences, "positive freedom" indicates the importance of *substantive* freedom at our present phase of the modern project. Whether we consider the implications of what Armatya Sen and Martha Nussbaum consider "capabilities" in the experience of freedom (Nussbaum and Sen 1993; Nussbaum 1999), John Rawls's implementation of distributive justice in the project for equality of freedom (Rawls 1999), or Ronald Dworkin's linkage of resources with freedom and equality (Dworkin 2002), there is a keen correlation between life chances or opportunities and the lived experience of contemporary freedoms.

Considering the link between modernity and progress discussed above, the notion of development—despite its problematic value-contingent continuum of "undeveloped" to "lesser developed" to "developed status"—is also linked with progress. So, to fully and freely participate in the modern project entails the act of progression, which usually involves technology, governmental organization, and a movement toward social equality and human rights as agreed upon by international bodies. Societies that consider themselves at the culmination point on the path to progress and modernity—those who have successfully completed that metaphorical "march toward modernity"—have not truly arrived there until they meet the criterion of social progress as implied in contemporary notions of modernity, even if arriving at such a goal seems always beyond our grasp.

Armatya Sen provides a useful means of seeing the contemporary link between progress and modernity as it resonates with freedom in his analysis of "development as freedom" (Sen 1999). He contends, "Development requires the removal of major sources of unfreedom: poverty as well as tyranny, poor economic opportunities as well as systematic social deprivation, neglect of public facilities as well as intolerance or overactivity of repressive states" (Sen 1999: 3) and notably sees "freedom as the principle end of development" (Sen 1999: 5). It is the substantive freedom linked with notions of modernity vis-à-vis the current period of globalization that should be kept in mind as we examine those events in Dublin, New Orleans, and Paris that exemplify the African Diaspora role in exposing the flawed modern projects of societies that profess success.

The three cases to be examined in part 2 exemplify the role of diverse African Diaspora communities in providing "wake-up calls" in the context of the unrealized modernity of globalized societies that perceive themselves as democratic, egalitarian, and freedom loving. We see quite clearly that even as these societies have transcended the Transatlantic Slave Trade, colonialism, and *de jure* racism, they have yet to fully operate in the realm of a socially progressive "modern ideal." Again, there is a nation-based perception that—outside of what seems to be equated with a few "anomalies" (resembling "technical glitches")—these societies have achieved modernity and a place in the contemporary globalization project.

Importantly, the beginnings of an African Diaspora community in Dublin examined in part 1 of this book and the events of 2005 across African Diaspora sites considered in part 2 exemplify the rootedness and complexity of these "anomalies" of modernity. Ultimately, this volume's overall examination of retrogressive global societies becomes an exploration of ways in which individuals of the African Diaspora are not privy to freedom in twenty-first-century societies that are perceived as "free," making the anger and frustration expressed two centuries ago by Walker and Douglass all the more prevalent today; particularly as modern political rhetoric, national narratives, and popular discourse and media indicate a desire to eradicate contemporary unfreedoms.

NOTE ON RESEARCH

This book both examines and represents an interrogation of the realization of the goals of modern societies amidst egregious global social inequalities that continue to be paired with "race" and, particularly, individuals racialized as black. My aim is to capture a global dialogue about social progress that is under way which is precipitated by the lived experiences of African Diaspora communities, public discourse and policies, a range of media and media representations, and public and state-level initiatives that reflect, deflect, and challenge the social reality of supposedly modern societies. In this effort, an interdisciplinary methodological approach has served as the most efficient means of getting at the range of complex questions of modernity and society brought forth in this volume. The research draws on fieldwork conducted for my doctoral thesis while living in Dublin from September 2000 to September 2001, subsequent follow-up periods in Dublin at intervals in 2002, 2004, and 2007, and observations and interviews conducted during site visits to Paris in August 2006 and New Orleans in March 2008. Additionally, the considerations of the African Diaspora in Dublin, New Orleans, and Paris draw on examinations of global, national, and local public policies and initiatives, government documents and press releases, discourse and advocacy measures emerging from non-governmental and grassroots organizations, archival documents, broadcast, print, and digital news media sources and, among other materials, popular cultural media (e.g., film, music, zines, blogs).

Over a period of twelve months in 2000 and 2001, I conducted formal interviews (one-on-one interviews in pre-arranged locations) and informal interviews (in various gathering places and private spaces) with two hundred immigrants from the continent of Africa and observed approximately five hundred African immigrants in various social settings in the Dublin area that included: African-owned bars/restaurants, African-owned shops, African and international/interethnic weddings, private residences, celebrations, intercultural events, pubs, educational programs, and workshops. Thirty percent of the two hundred individuals interviewed formally and informally were seeking asylum. Seventy percent had a permanent or temporary resident status as a result of refugee status due to a successful asylum application, or had come to Ireland as an employee or student, or as a result of marriage to a resident or citizen and, in certain cases, a combination thereof.

During the 2000–2001 research period the population of African men was larger than that of African women and the percentage of interviews reflects this disparity. I interviewed 120 men between the ages of eighteen and forty-five and 80 women between the ages of eighteen and forty-five. The majority of individuals interviewed were between the ages of twenty and thirty years old, as the immigrant population consisted largely of younger adults. The informants represent a cross section of occupational statuses (including unemployed, informally and extra-legally employed factory workers, IT employees, students, entrepreneurs, businesspersons, office workers, proprietors, and retail workers). Half of the two hundred immigrants interviewed were Nigerian; another sixty were Congolese. The others were from Angola (11), Ghana (9), Sierra Leone (7), Liberia (4), Somalia (3), and South Africa, Sudan, and Ethiopia (2 each). I introduced myself to all those interviewed as a graduate student from the University of California at Berkeley conducting doctoral research on the African Diaspora in the Dublin area. I met most of the informants as a result of contacts made through my affiliation with the Ethnic and Racial Studies Program in the Department of Sociology at Trinity College Dublin, involvement in various anti-racism organizations, my presence at multicultural conferences and events, and connections with the larger African community made through my daily interactions in the city center area of Dublin's Parnell Street, an area with a substantial African population that was sometimes referred to as "Little Africa." I resided in the Parnell Street community for nine months and returned to a flat I maintained in the area for shorter intervals to conduct follow-up interviews and observations during a subsequent three-month period. After several months in the field, other informants came to know me through a column I wrote in the local "multicultural" and immigrant-focused newspaper, *Metro Éireann*, as well as through interviews and television work I did during the tenure of my grant in Ireland. The contacts used to recruit informants were also helpful in my integration into the larger Dublin community, which led to further opportunities to conduct the aforementioned participant observations.

My interview questions were open-ended and focused on experiences of "race," ethnicity, discrimination, adjustment to Irish culture, maintenance of African cultural traditions, social activities, and daily experiences of being an African immigrant in Ireland. The interviews were not recorded, as it became clear early in the research period that recording devices were awkward in many social situations and informants were frequently uncomfortable and guarded when being recorded. This was not surprising, considering that numerous informants held precarious positions within the state as they awaited refugee status or, regardless of status, feared that being too vocal about social conditions could lead to retribution. For obvious ethical reasons and out of utter respect for the many gracious individuals who let me into their lives, strict confidentiality has been adhered to and only pseudonyms are used to refer to informants who did not have public profiles (e.g., public officials, media representatives) and, in cases of confidential disclosures by individuals with public profiles, such individuals are described but not named. In lieu of audio recording, notes were taken and detailed reports of each interview were compiled afterwards. On numerous occasions, I had the opportunity to meet with formal interviewees again and continue earlier discussions in more informal interviews.

As an African American, I was widely accepted into the African Diaspora community and became a part of the Parnell Street community. However, my American nationality and academic status also placed me as an outsider within the predominantly continental African group. While being a woman afforded me an entrée into several male social circles, there were certainly social circumstances to which I would not be privy due to my gender. In addition, the women's circles tended to be closed systems and members were not immediately receptive to other women outside of their social units. Connecting with groups of African women during the initial part of the research period presented more of a challenge, as African women were more likely to avoid participation in public activities. I learned that some African women considered it socially unacceptable to assert themselves in male arenas. African women, particularly those without children, who were involved in social and activist arenas in the Dublin area do find a voice in this volume. Other African women with children were often isolated and housed in remote locations that prohibited regular visits to the African Diaspora community in Dublin. Furthermore, some African women preferred to remain in the safety of small close-knit groups in what was experienced as a potentially violent and less-than-inviting nation. I eventually connected with some of these women in the Dublin area through introductions facilitated by African women who were more active in the larger community, connections developed when accompanied by African men who were relatives of the women, and through trust earned during visits to asylum accommodation centers.

In some respects, being an American enabled my entrance into African circles because of an interest in African American culture, an interest most notably emerging out of the often skewed representations of African Americans in various media (particularly produced by the music and film industries). Ironically, the African perception of African American culture and identity often resembled the less racist assumptions presented by non-black groups. So, it is worth noting that while conducting my research among fellow members of the African Diaspora, I was also able to explore just how, in the eyes of Africans, African Americans are considered culturally "African" in some ways and culturally "American" in other respects. Nevertheless, the fact of my African descent resulted in my experiencing many of the same circumstances as other blacks living in Ireland (particularly objectification, racial epithets, and subtle forms of discrimination). Yet, the reality that I had a university affiliation, an American passport, and could always leave with few consequences (barring the detriment to my research project) set me apart from those individuals of color who felt they had no other safe option but to remain in Ireland.

The field research in Paris and New Orleans in August 2006 and March 2008, respectively, was conducted through visits to key sites related to Hurricane Katrina and the Paris uprisings to examine the aftermath of these events and to speak with community members, observe the devastation, and gather materials related to the examinations in this book. I introduced myself as a scholar visiting the locations to gain further insight about the events and circumstances experienced by individuals at the sites, as well as to examine the structural impact of each event. As with the Dublin fieldwork, confidentiality has been maintained through general references or pseudonyms where appropriate for individuals outside of the public arena.

REGARDING THE AFRICAN DIASPORA AND BLACK IDENTITIES

Since the 1990s there has been a significant focus on the function, form, and meaning of "diaspora" to scholars and its relation to historical and contemporary communities (Brah 1996; Braziel and Mannur 2003; Butler 2001; Cohen 1997; Edwards 2003; J. Harris 1996; Holt 1999; Van Hear 1998; Vertovec 1997). In this book, the concept of "diaspora" draws on the various considerations over the years, particularly beginning with its roots in "dispersion" from a homeland. Whether the flow from the homeland is due to economic pursuits, religious persecution, ethnic conflicts, famine, family reunification, or the Transatlantic Slave Trade is significant primarily because different reasons for diasporic experiences offer us insight into the way diasporas are forged and maintained; however, they are all diasporas. In my usage, "diaspora" functions as a means of explaining the phenomenon of a globally extended space or grouping of persons with a shared spatial origin and perceived affinity, whether through memory, maintenance of contact, or the replication of cultural activities beyond what all members consider to be their site of origin or homeland. In the case of the African Diaspora, it is also a shared experience of the racialized identification as "black" and the range of global circumstances related to their "blackness" that links its members. Though the scope of my study in the three locations primarily considers descendants of Sub-Saharan African communities and specifically groups that are racialized as black, the site of Paris presents a broader consideration of African Diaspora communities with a North African descendant population that self-identify as *Beur* (Maghreb descent) and, where applicable, are identified as such in this volume. Furthermore, while the experience of blackness may be site-contingent and there is a multiplicity of internal linguistic, national, ethnic, and cultural expressions within African Diaspora communities, the persistence of global anti-black racisms and their range of ramifications place African Diaspora communities—in all their diversity—in comparable positions of exposing social inequalities.

Through my examination of the three African Diaspora sites of Dublin, New Orleans, and Paris it is not my intention to essentialize or construct a monolith of an "African Diaspora identity" and, by extension, black identity. Quite to the contrary, this volume aims to highlight the diversity of the ethnic, social, cultural, political, and historical dimensions of African Diaspora experiences with a range of geographic, linguistic, and migratory histories as well as the diversity of African Diaspora communities within their respective sites. The Dublin community is primarily represented through a first-generation population from numerous nations throughout continental Africa. New Orleans, while inclusive of recent migrants, primarily contains African Diaspora communities that are descendants of migration occurring as a result of the Transatlantic Slave Trade and, therefore, descendants of individuals arriving directly from continental Africa or via the Caribbean at least two centuries ago. Paris is mostly inclusive of new migrants from former French colonies in continental Africa, citizens from French departments in the Caribbean and, resulting from significant African migration to France in the mid-twentieth century, generations of African Diaspora communities with a long history of presence in the nation.

While there are cultural expressions reflective of various spaces of continental Africa, some muted and others more explicit, that connect various African Diaspora groups—much like the examinations in Robert Farris Thompson's classic work on the African Diaspora in the Americas (Thompson 1984)—the communities examined in this book are *unsurprisingly* very diverse. However, to reiterate, what does link these African Diaspora communities is their racialization as black and the related legacy of oppressions that are rooted in supposed modern societies that would embrace egalitarianism and freedom at the cost of black equality and freedom. This racialization and its related legacy implicitly provide the impetus for the African Diaspora (e.g., migration due to enslavement, postcolonial political unrest, and the exploitation of natural resources by colonizing nations). This book does not argue that other diaspora, migrant, and negatively racialized communities in various locations are not calling into question retrogressive circumstances in modern societies. However, the emphasis is placed here because, due to a range of historical and contemporary events and conditions, African Diaspora communities are neatly positioned to interrogate the lived reality of the ideologies of modern societies and, as seen in the three sites examined in this volume, continue to do so.

PART 1.

THE AFRICAN DIASPORA IN DUBLIN

1

DECOLONIZATION, RACISM, AND THE RETRO-GLOBAL SOCIETY

The black presence in late eighteenth-century Ireland is often epitomized by the 1791 tour of Olaudah Equiano, the former slave turned abolitionist author and speaker. Equiano experienced Ireland positively and eventually published a fourth edition of his book, *The Interesting Narrative of the Life of Olaudah Equiano, or Gustavus Vassa, the African,* in Dublin (see Rodgers 1997). However, Equiano was not the only black person in Ireland; there was a small and little known population of blacks living in the country throughout the eighteenth century. Nini Rodgers, in her book *Ireland, Slavery and Anti-Slavery, 1612–1865,* notes the documentation of 167 "sightings" of blacks in Ireland throughout the eighteenth century (Rodgers 2007: 127). William A. Hart, in his groundbreaking article "Africans in Eighteenth-Century Ireland," notes that there were "about 160 separate references to black people in Ireland" in the latter half of the eighteenth century (Hart 2002: 20) and 188 references during the entire century, primarily of blacks living in Dublin (Hart 2002: 22–23). Considering that the references are mostly in newspapers and memoirs, which would not mention less conspicuously noted blacks, Hart estimates a population of between one thousand and three thousand blacks (Hart 2002: 21) and suggests that such numbers would place Dublin second only to London in the size of the black population among European cities of the time (Hart 2002: 22).[1] Most of these blacks were enslaved and free servants, seafarers, entertainers, and a plausibly more transient population, since "domestic servants [Africans] enjoyed a wide range of occupations and thus a varied social status" (Hart 2002: 27). Also notable, Hart suggests that slavery in Ireland "was nothing uniquely oppressive" in comparison to America and the Caribbean and describes the reaction in Ireland to "sexual relations between white and black," including matrimony, as "fairly relaxed" (Hart 2002: 27).

The black presence in nineteenth-century Ireland, particularly leading up to the American Civil War, is represented by the experiences of black American abolitionists. During a tour of the United Kingdom, Frederick Douglass visited Ireland in 1845. Writing to William Lloyd Garrison, Douglass observed that

> I find no difficulty here in obtaining admission into any place of worship, instruction, or amusement on equal terms with people as white as any I ever saw in the United States. I meet nothing to remind me of my complexion. I find myself regarded and healed at every turn with the kindness and deference paid to white people. When I go to church, I am met by no upturned nose and scornful lip to tell me, "We don't allow niggers in here!" . . . Thank heaven for the respite I now enjoy! I had been in Dublin but a few days when a gentleman of great respectability kindly offered to conduct me through all the public buildings of that beautiful city; and a little afterward, I found myself dining with the lord mayor of Dublin. What a pity there was not some American democratic Christian at the door of this splendid mansion, to bark out at my approach, "They don't allow niggers here!" The truth is, the people here know nothing of the republican Negro hate prevalent in our glorious land. They measure and esteem men according to their moral and intellectual worth, and not according to the color of their skin. (Douglass 1999: 19)

Predating Frederick Douglass's visit,[2] black abolitionist Charles Lenox Remond lectured in Ireland in 1841. During a November 1841 speech before the Hibernian Anti-Slavery Society, Remond described the Irish nationalist Daniel O'Connell as "a good and mighty man, who has put himself forth the undaunted and fearless champion of liberty and the rights of man in every clime the sun adorns" (Remond 1841). Upon his return to the United States, Remond carried an address signed by O'Connell and "60,000 Irishmen" requesting Irish American support of the abolitionist cause and amicable relationships with blacks (Quarles 1991: 133).[3] Remond's experience with Irish abolitionists such as O'Connell also highlights the distinction between Irish and Irish American relations with blacks during the period; the former seemed supportive and the latter more inclined to hostility. That praise of Irish abolitionists underscored the perception that anti-black racism was foreign to Ireland was aptly expressed by a quote attributed to black abolitionist William C. Nell: "The opposition of Irishmen in America to the colored man is not so much a Hibernianism as an Americanism" (*North Star,* Dec. 3, 1847, cited in Quarles 1991: 133).

Numerous other black abolitionists, including Nell, Henry Highland Garnet, William G. Allen, and C. L. Remond's sister, Sarah Parker Remond, made their way to the Emerald Isle. Allen lived in Dublin from 1850 to 1852 with his family,[4] and Sarah Parker Remond, whose presence offered a representation of black womanhood in Ireland, was very well received during her speeches before prominent audiences (see Quarles 1991; also see Midgley 1995). An account of Parker Remond's March 1859 speech before the Dublin Ladies' Anti-Slavery Association published in *The Liberator* describes her as having an "appearance [that] is remarkably feminine and graceful, coupled with a quiet, dignified manner, a well-toned voice and pleasing style of enunciation" and also notes her "impressive eloquence" (*Liberator* 1859).

While black visitors from the United States such as Frederick Douglass were welcomed in Ireland, it is their communication of the horrors of slavery and lynching beyond the borders of Ireland that particularly inspired the Irish to endear themselves to them and, for blacks, this treatment represented a stark contrast to nineteenth-century Irish American anti-black and racist behavior outside of abolitionist circles (see Nelson 2007). Furthermore, the fact of a limited black presence in the nation suggests a form of celebrity and spectacle around the sight of an individual such as Douglass—a great orator, an attractive man, *and* black— and elicited more curiosity than loathing.[5] However, whether black presence was represented by visits from African American abolitionists in the nineteenth century, the earlier eighteenth-century servants, seaman, and entertainers or, much later, continental Africans arriving in Ireland to pursue courses of study in the twentieth century, black individuals were mostly temporary phenomena, merely noticed as they were passing through Ireland rather than staying permanently. Even though blacks in twentieth-century Ireland described racist acts, such as fights, racial epithets, and bullying, and black children of single white mothers were often placed in orphanages (see Lynott 1996; Putterford 2002; McGrath 2006), throughout much of the last century, blackness and anti-black racism in Ireland were for the most part articulated through a sense of remoteness (see McVeigh 1998).

The increased black presence in the late twentieth and early twenty-first centuries effectively exposed racism in Ireland, making manifest a condition to which the Irish were, of course, never really immune. Yet, racism has coexisted with the Irish perception of immunity to it and, in some benign and not-so-benign ways, is inextricably linked to the national representation of humanitarianism and welcoming. This question of the Irish capacity for racism was brought forth by Robbie McVeigh as early as 1992. In his essay, "The Specificity of Irish Racism," he contends:

> To some extent, the existence of a long and proud internationalist and anti-imperialist tradition in Ireland has disguised other contradictory and reactionary strands in Irish politics and identity. . . . More recently, "Irish racism" has been theorized out of existence by the disingenuous use of the "racism + prejudice + power" equation to argue that Irish people, like Black people, have no power to be racist . . . I want to challenge the notion that Irish people cannot be racist. (McVeigh 1992: 31)

McVeigh launched this thoughtful challenge eight years prior to the significant migration examined in this volume and before the capacity for Irish racism would be truly tested. Equally prescient, McVeigh would later go on to consider the question of racism and proximity through his examination of Northern Ireland in the 1998 essay "There's No Racism Because There's No Black People Here." He explains:

> [I]t is not a requirement of racism that there be minority ethnic people in a given society for racism to exist. There can be racist jokes, for example, in an environment in which there are no minority ethnic people. The notion that there needs to be minority ethnic people before there is racism is dangerous because it inevitably suggests that the presence of Black people in a given society *causes* racism. This kind of analysis feeds directly into racist—and in some cases genocidal—practice because it suggests that the way to get rid of racism is to remove existing minority ethnic people from a society and keep others out. (McVeigh 1998: 13–14; emphasis in original)

Significantly, the remoteness and rarity of the Irish engagement with blacks prevailed up until the twenty-first century and intersected quite neatly with renderings of Irish philanthropy and humanitarianism toward black people vis-à-vis Catholic and Protestant charities. For example, generations of Irish while growing up in the twentieth century placed money in their church's "Black Baby" boxes to be sent to the "Black Babies" of Africa. This Black Baby box charity became a normalized means of engaging with blackness in the form of a remote neediness that was not so removed from the concern expressed for the needy slaves by Irish abolitionists and their supporters. Such a representation of black people would become increasingly problematic when contemporary blacks in the nation starkly contrasted the predominant perception of Africans as vessels of Irish charity rather than, say, university-educated professionals from Lagos. As McVeigh has so neatly put it:

> Irish Catholicism manifested elements of anti-Black racism in a specifically religious phenomenon. This is illustrated by the ubiquitous collections for "Black Babies" which, until recently, were a feature of Irish Church missionary appeals. These necessarily conditioned Irish Catholic people to regard Black people in a particular way—passive, helpless, to be saved by the proselytizing ambitions of the Church. (McVeigh 1998: 19)

Fundamentally, charitable outpourings and a shared experience of global ethno-racial and cultural oppression stood as proxies for a perceived Irish concern for blacks. Yet how were the Irish to reconcile the "Black Baby" monolithic—represented by the poster of a child with kwashiorkor or the smiling face on the UNICEF envelope distributed on an Aer Lingus flight—with the reality of diverse black identities (e.g., a Nigerian journalist, the middle-class Congolese businessperson, an African Irish student with a North Dublin accent)?

While I was gathering interview data during the period of significant African migration to Ireland, white Irish often remarked upon growing up in Ireland when it was rare to see a black person, particularly outside of cities. Even though encountering a person of African descent was not unheard of, it was certainly remarkable. Furthermore, throughout the twentieth century the racist stigma experienced by the families and children of relationships between white Irish and African nationals (see Lynott 1996; Putterford 2002; McGrath 2006) indicates a hostile relationship with blackness, in spite of the historic negative racialization of the Irish by the English and the impact of anti-Irish racism on the Irish Diaspora (see Ignatiev 1995; Mac an Ghaill 2000; Hickman et al. 2005). Yet I also became aware of the intertwining of the mediation of socio-economic status with earlier objectifications of the "black baby" and the excitement about encountering the "black other" (like Frederick Douglass). There was a new socio-cultural capital emerging for working-class white Irish women among their peers via their partnering with black men and having black children (i.e., possessing "black babies" of their own, represented both in partner and offspring). So, while black presence in twentieth-century Ireland can best be regarded as mostly transient with the occasional interethnic Irish offspring and the ubiquitous, yet intangible, faces of charity recipients, it is the substantial migration of the twenty-first century that brought forth a major experiential shift in the Irish social landscape. Quite simply and significantly, black proximity supplanted black remoteness.

IMMIGRATION AND THE NEW NATION

The Irish Free State (and later the Republic of Ireland) remained insular with limited immigration and became solidly defined as Catholic, white, and settled (the indigenous Traveller populations were seen as outside of what is considered Irish) (see Lentin 1998, 1999, 2000; Sinha 1998; Tracy 2000). The nation's first immigration policies, as presented in the 1935 Aliens Act and Irish Nationality and Citizenship Act, imposed restrictions on Jewish immigration while permitting free movement between Ireland and Britain, as well as the entrance of individuals from the Irish Diaspora (mainly from the United States, Australia, Britain, and Canada) (see Keogh 1998). Post–World War II Ireland, despite the Holocaust, was still not receptive to Jewish immigration and constructed policies that did not easily lend themselves to non-Catholic and/or non-white immigration. As Marshall Tracy explains in his study of racism and immigration in Ireland: "The debates surrounding the refugee crisis during the war years led to the Aliens (Amendment) Order of 1946 which created a hierarchy of immigrants. Nationals of: America, Belgium, Holland, France, Italy, Liechtenstein, Scandinavian countries, and applications for tourist visas were to have their applications considered favorably. Second preference was given to citizens of 'distant' European countries including Germany, Austria, and Greece, providing their 'business' was not contrary to Irish interests. The final group addressed were 'stateless persons', or refugees; this was reserved for Eastern Europeans" (Tracy 2000: 25). While Ireland accepted some "stateless persons," it did not join the United Nations until 1956 and was not required to follow UN guidelines concerning immigration. After joining the UN, according to the stipulations of the United Nations High Commissioner for Refugees (UNHCR), the nation accepted refugees from Hungary, Chile, and Vietnam, as well as members of the Baha'i faith. Tracy notes: "Ireland was reluctant to accept refugees and often had to be pressured by the UNHCR or by NGOs, and even then the numbers of refugees accepted were negligible.... However the 'pressure' applied to the Irish government by the UNHCR is a marked change and demonstrates Ireland's responsibilities in the larger global community. Interestingly, Ireland did not participate in UNHCR sponsored refugee programs from Africa in the 1960s, 1970s, or 1980s although there were other immigrant groups entering the country during this time" (Tracy 2000: 28). The reluctance to accept African refugees, to which Tracy refers, betrays the reality that even as Ireland's Catholics showed a charitable interest in aiding Africans, the larger Irish objective was to discourage African presence in the nation.

Ireland filed an application to enter the European Economic Community (EEC, now European Union) in 1961 and joined in 1973. This was advantageous for the struggling nation, as it received funds through the Common Agricultural Policy and Structural Funds that helped boost the economy. It is the result of EEC aid and the country's subsequent economic success in the 1990s that this relatively new state was transformed into an immigrant destination, forestalling its ability to remain isolationist as it engaged in international labor recruitment, and testing the notion of a "pure" Irish identity linked to the nation at its inception.[6]

DECOLONIZATION AND
THE RETRO-GLOBAL SOCIETY

The current pop-cultural usage of "retro" is an expression of "what's old is new" chic, meant to inspire consumption of the latest "back in the day" revision or corporate-generated nostalgia. My use of "retro" has a different emphasis. Certainly, encountering the social and political engagement with cultural difference and the daily negotiation of racism and discrimination experienced by the African Diaspora in Ireland makes a journey to the nation resemble a trip back in time. After all, until recently, Ireland was a place where seeing a person of color was still a spectacle for many. Black presence was somehow exotic and individuals racialized as "other than white" embodied the pain and joy of a changing nation. However, while the anachronistic elements of the technologically progressive yet socially regressive Irish society are conditions that inform my usage of "retro," they are not the totality of it. My use of the term "retro" is a means of articulating the impact of the Africans in Ireland in the context of global culture, postcolonialism, and the still incomplete decolonization of the Irish nation.

"Retro-global" identifies *a formerly lesser-developed, new global society that retains pervasive and highly conspicuous social elements or constructs that are more indicative of earlier periods of globalization.* As such, the concept has an application that extends beyond Ireland. It is an attempt to mark contemporary societies whose experience of modernity and membership in the global community expose an internal conflict with expressions of freedom and equality by a racialized "other" within that society. What makes Ireland so interesting is the way it has been adjusting to an African presence, which has in a sense marked the nation's

entrance into the global community, given the country's history of colonial subjugation and negative racialization of its people. In spite of its
prior subaltern position in the global hierarchy, Ireland's grasp at modernity and membership in the global community inherently involve complicity in the very projects of oppression from which its new status was
meant to distance it. The Irish treatment of its black population is not
simple hypocrisy, but it does implicate the errors of the larger projects
of modernity and globalization.

PROGRESS, RETROGRESSION, AND GLOBAL IDEALISM

In the contemporary period of globalization, as in the past, economic
advancement and the accompanying technological tools of advancement
represent "progress," an idea that is weighted in nineteenth-century discourse on civilization and its racialized, savage Others. Nevertheless, as
discussed in the introduction, the interest in progress, when articulated
as advancement in social and political arenas, persists and, importantly,
individuals racialized as "other" work for such progress. Furthermore, aspiring to progress (in terms of advancement) becomes synonymous with
aspiring to globality and, thus, moving away from globality signifies a reversal of progress. "Globality," again taking Wolf Schäfer's definition discussed in the introduction, is a "local condition with four components—a
globalization or more, a geographical range, a state of interconnectedness
and a state of consciousness" (Schäfer 2007: paragraph 32) and, considering that "globalization tends to propel everything under its influence
from a lower to a higher degree of globality" (Schäfer 2007: paragraph 15),
it is a result of a society's extensive experience of globalization. As noted
earlier, I do not view globalization as external to modernity, so within
the contemporary period of globalization—as within modernity—the
modern ideals of freedom, equality, and democracy continue to resonate within societies. Thus, meeting the criteria for globality becomes, at
the least, a superficial marker of social progress in global arenas because
of the expectation that the ideals—freedom, equality, and democracy—
would be commensurate with the realization of modernity during the
current period of globalization. Ultimately, the progress related to economic globality can starkly contrast with the progress in the area of
cultural globality, which delimits the overall globality—and, implicitly,
modernity—of the society.

Economic globality in Ireland is experienced through the awareness
of the presence of multinational corporations and the related fluctuations
in national employment opportunities, the currency shift from the Irish

pound to the Euro, the impact of global markets on local communities, and *inter alia* the international migration of workers. As with other components of globalization, economic globality has an impact upon the cultural globality of the nation, particularly resulting from the flows of in-migration. Cultural globality is experienced in various forms—including linguistic, culinary, and sartorial expressions—and is linked to the awareness of differently racialized groups and ethnicities who add to the cultural expressions already in the national community. Importantly, the acceptance of or resistance to cultural globality is experienced in social and political arenas (e.g., immigration policies, housing and employment restrictions, human rights concerns, racism and anti-racism) and these are the very arenas in which the ideals of globalization and modernity—equality, freedom, and democracy—find their actualization or failure.

In the case of Ireland, we see that resistance takes two common forms: (1) an overt assertion of one particular identity to which outsiders of color are considered a threat, and (2) the more subtle, somewhat passive (though not innocuous) form of resistance in which, due to the rapidity of change in recently global societies, prior (mis)understandings of the cultural and racialized "other" remain in place. Both forms of resistance represent a challenge to cultural globality within the society, disrupting the predominant, albeit always problematic, understandings of progress that are often predicated on utopian Western-centric one-world theories, as well as more tangible quests for social progress. The challenge is launched via resistance that supports and maintains *retrogression* rather than progression.

The "retro" in retro-global represents the point at which Western liberal notions of global progress are challenged by circumstances more reflective of earlier periods of globalization (see Held et al. 1999). This retrogression implicates the view that a nation's status in the global community corresponds to its progress, that it somehow exists on a continuum along which all societies find their place, leading up to the most valued spot in the continuum—the site of Western societies. The "retro" represents a disruption in global idealist discourse and forces reflection on predominant rhetoric regarding the success of modernity and globalization. Much like the uncontainable cultural and social interventions that encompass what Barnor Hesse terms "multicultural transruptions" (Hesse 2001), we see dormant social and cultural conflicts that challenge presumptions of egalitarianism emerge to form what can be considered a retro-global act, event, or condition.

It is a common critique that the West determines the trajectory of progress with its implicit project of modernity in non-Western societies

(Cooper and Stoler 1997; Gilroy 1993; Piot 1999; Said 1978). The contemporary presence of earlier notions of modernity and the related violence accompanying the discourse of civilization become even more apparent in the attempts of the last two decades to extract our present time from the past via a declaration of postmodernity, as we see that the modern still lingers. This lingering modernity, a project in itself that was meant to include the most reified notions of progress-as-civilization, was built on circumstances that would inevitably render its project unrealized. Quite simply, we have to consider how a modernity that aims for equality survives when its very notions of civility and civilization are predicated on vast inequalities, with its resulting dichotomy of winners and losers (i.e., the exploiters and the exploited). If anything, retro-global circumstances present a jarring reminder that contemporary conditions are forever paired with the failings of modernity and it is only a keen acknowledgment of these circumstances that will allow contemporary societies to truly separate themselves from anachronistic attitudes. If anything, retro-global conditions serve as proverbial wake-up calls, beckoning us to acknowledge that a mere declaration of a "meta" positionality does not eliminate the political, cultural, and social dysfunction at the center of our very own sense of modernity. As Paul Gilroy warns when considering the salience of "ideas about nationality, ethnicity, authenticity, and cultural integrity," we should be aware that "[a]ny shift towards a postmodern condition should not, however, mean that the conspicuous power of these modern subjectivities and the movements they articulated has been left behind" (Gilroy 1993: 2).

Of additional significance for our consideration here is that Gilroy, in his argument for a Black Atlantic cultural and theoretical framework, highlights the unique place of blacks in the larger project of modernity by noting the "icons of blacks that appear as signs of irrational disorder or as a means to celebrate the power of human nature uncorrupted by the decadence of the civilizing process" (Gilroy 1993: 45). He goes on to state that "[i]n either guise, blacks enjoy a subordinate position in the dualistic system that reproduces the dominance of bonded whiteness, masculinity, and rationality" (Gilroy 1993: 45–46). In fact, the subordination of blacks (and other groups not racialized as white) frequently calls into question the success of the project of modernity and globalization. This dilemma is not exclusive to Ireland. As we will see when we consider New Orleans after Hurricane Katrina and Paris in the wake of the uprisings of 2005, adverse social conditions serve as jarring reminders of the neglect of the utopian modern project and the equality and freedom it was meant to ensure. I argue that the "retro" elements of societies like those of Ireland, the United States, and France that represent themselves as beacons of global progress reveal the most contradictory and, therefore, problematic moments of modernity and contemporary globalization. In the case of Ireland we see the African Diaspora presence bringing into sharp relief inequalities, cultural misperceptions, and the mechanisms of power that were already extant.

"Progress" is of course a terribly weighted concept. Socio-cultural progress in the West has been attached to notions of the civilized and the savage, to the level of technological capability, and the like. Today it is further informed by a drive toward international or global peace. In this view, peace and all of its utopian implications is what defines a socially and culturally progressive society. Yet it can be argued that the civilizing project out of which our contemporary global society emerges is infused with racism and assumptions of the biological and cultural inferiority of various peoples of the world, an undoubted impediment to the realization of peace. Nevertheless, racialized "others," as demonstrated by African Diaspora communities in this book, continue to fight for the end of social inequalities on terms that reflect the acceptance of a society's ideological commitment to the values associated with progressing toward a global peace. The discursive mechanisms for social change—expressing the ideals of freedom, equality, and democracy—are embedded in the idea of global peace.

Contemporary globalization, in its more utopian rendering,[7] is meant to place us in an "advanced state"—economically, culturally, and socially (based on the seemingly unrealizable Kantian notion of perpetual peace: "the human race can gradually be brought closer and closer to a constitution establishing world citizenship" or, depending on your translation, a "cosmopolitan constitution" [see Kant 1991; Kant 1999]).[8] The social and cultural conflicts left over from a "less advanced" period suggest a "reversal of development" and are retrogressive actions which clash with things global. Modern notions of global social progress, even if problematically Western, place racism, sectarianism, and isolationism in the realm of retrogression.

It is apparent that "retro" acts of racial discrimination hinder progress toward the attainment of globally progressive projects. This is, of course, not a new idea and was particularly exemplified by international decolonization efforts over fifty years ago. The United Nations 1960 Declaration on the Granting of Independence to Colonial Countries and Peoples "*[s]olemnly proclaims* the necessity of bringing to speedy and unconditional end colonialism in all its forms and manifestations . . . the continued existence of colonialism prevents the development of international economic cooperation, impedes the social, cultural and economic development of dependent peoples and militates against the United Nations ideal of universal peace" (United Nations General Assembly 1960; emphasis in original). The social and cultural development required for "universal peace" at the root of the UN's existence only leaves room for condemnation of societies that aspire to "international economic cooperation" without the level of societal development required to achieve "universal peace." Economic progress is not the sole measure of development, then; development also involves meeting standards of social and cultural progress. The twist here is that concepts of social and cultural progress are being employed to counter the racist assumptions that fueled the notions of civilization that facilitated the colonizing project.

While I am skeptical of the idealist notion of "universal peace," particularly as it suggests a universalism which often privileges narrow renderings of Western cultural identities, it is still not difficult to see that global societies operate—at least institutionally—under the assumption that this is what we aspire to in all aspects of international discourse and exchange. The interest in "universal peace"—as the overarching ethos of the notions of freedom, equality, and democracy examined in this book—is particularly important in the areas of immigration, human rights, and anti-racism policies, as well as the detangling of histories of colonial subjugation, global social inequalities, and ethno-racial hierarchies that forestall its realization. As exemplified in the UN declaration, universal peace cannot be achieved without social progress. It cannot be retrogressively realized. In this respect, the idea of a retrogressive global or "retro-global" society becomes an efficient means of examining and articulating the circumstances in Ireland, and of the African Diaspora in the nation, convening at the intersection of competing postcolonial identities and, as will be considered in the next section, an incomplete decolonization.

INCOMPLETE DECOLONIZATION AND
UNRESOLVED RACIALIZATION

In *Postcolonialism: An Historical Introduction*, Robert Young notes that "[i]t is not only because it has not yet been fully decolonized that Ireland occupies a relatively minor place in postcolonial theorizing today. It is partly because, as so often, Ireland does not seem to fit the general pattern" (Young 2001: 302). However, Young places Ireland at the core of postcolonialism, further explaining: "Although among many postcolonialists Ireland tends to be regarded (as always) as a somewhat marginal case, in many ways its role has been central. . . . [T]he forms of revolutionary and cultural activism developed by the Irish against the entrenched self-interest of its rule by British aristocracy and bourgeoisie meant that it remained the standard bearer for all anti-colonial movements in the late nineteenth and twentieth centuries" (Young 2001: 302).

Young's neat placement of Ireland in the postcolonial discourse forces us to consider the circumstances that often led to its exclusion.[9] The possible prohibitive conditions are brought forth in Dawn Duncan's argument for the inclusion of Ireland in a broader conceptualization of the postcolonial that is not equated with specific racialized identities or extra-Western geographies. She states: "In the interest of opening the dialogue to include all people, regardless of place or skin color, who have lived under colonial constructs and who emerge from a postcolonial condition, we must rethink the danger embedded in the constricting racial definition that has been too easily accepted or assumed by postcolonial scholars" (Duncan 2002: 321). Duncan also argues for the "post" in postcolonial to not only refer to the "overly rigid interpretation" of the period "after the departure of the colonizers" but to directly reference the point of colonial insertion (Duncan 2002: 325). This would, of course, make postcolonial discourse inclusive of societies that are still enduring colonialism.

Duncan's approach not only acknowledges differential postcolonial conditions but highlights, particularly when considering Ireland's north and south, spaces of incomplete decolonization. As Young notes in considering critiques of postcolonial generalizations about colonial rule, "the apparent uniformity or diversity of colonialism depends very largely on your own subject position, as colonized or colonizing subject" (Young 2001: 18). This is significant if we consider Duncan's desire to see more articulations of Ireland's postcolonial condition, for we can extend Young's assertion to acknowledge that being racialized as white does not necessarily lessen the oppression for the colonized Irish. In addition, perhaps placing us back in the white/non-white binary of postcolonialism, as Duncan and others have noted, the Irish were not initially considered white at all (see Ignatiev 1995).

David Lloyd argues for a differential analysis of colonization which would include a discussion of Ireland's colonial subjectivity alongside other colonial experiences in non-Western nations. He notes that "[t]he apparent whiteness of the Irish is accordingly a frequent casual objection to the idea of Ireland being a 'Third World' or postcolonial nation. In fact, the doubt usually reveals to a considerable degree the anxiety 'white' subjects tend to feel in being identified with peoples of color" (Lloyd 2003: 51).

The anxiety to which Lloyd refers also reveals the impact and persistence of ethnic and racial discourses of modernity among those initially seen as peripheral to its project, as the Irish aversion to a racialized subaltern position vis-à-vis colonial status highlights the contemporary prevalence of whiteness as a significant global currency (in spite of global musings of egalitarian multicultural societies).

When we consider Ireland as other than a European nation (that is, a colony of a sovereign European nation, Britain, that still distinguishes itself from continental Europe) we also have to consider that this peripheral subjectivity is accompanied by a process of racialization that has historically placed Irish identity outside of the realm of whiteness. This is significant if we are to imagine the overt whiteness or, perhaps, counter-blackness of contemporary Irish identity serving as a "corrective" for the earlier equation of Irishness with a generic Africanness (Beddoe 1885; Stanton 1982; Curtis 1968, 1996).

Anthropologist John Beddoe, in his 1885 text *The Races of Britain: A Contribution to the Anthropology of Western Europe,* presents an "Index of Nigrescence" representing a scale ranging from individuals who have lower amounts of melanin in hair, eyes, and skin to what Beddoe describes as "those with a greater tendency to melanosity" (Beddoe 1885: 5). In addition to a higher rating of "nigrescence" found among the Irish, Beddoe also observes greater "prognathous," which he defines as "having prominent mouths" (Beddoe 1885: 10). Regarding Irish "prognathism," Beddoe writes:

> While Ireland is apparently its present centre, most of its lineaments are such as lead us to think of Africa as its possible birthplace; and it may be well, provisionally to call it Africanoid. . . . Though I believe this Africanoid type to have been of very high antiquity, it must be acknowledged that we have no evidence carrying its presence, in any of the British Isles, beyond the polished stone period. But the best authenticated ancient skulls from Ireland may have belonged to it. . . . These show the inclination to prognathism to be of remote date in Ireland, as well as the peculiar form of low straight brow that still prevails there, and which is connected with low, square, horizontal orbits. (Beddoe 1885: 11–12)

Beddoe's association of the Irish with African and black identities and his assertion that such traits were not prominent elsewhere in the British Isles ("beyond the polished stone period") is further underlined by L. P. Curtis, who writes in his classic *Anglo-Saxons and Celts: A study*

of Anti-Irish Prejudice in Victorian England: "How close was a prognathous and nigrescent Celt to a Negro? Such questions were implicit and
at times explicit in Beddoe's work; and the implicit answer was that not
all men in the British Isles were equally white or equal" (Curtis 1968: 72).

Jacqueline Nassy Brown's keen examination of blacks in Liverpool
takes care to establish the place of Liverpool, regardless of race, as a peripheral lesser-valued space outside of the predominant understanding
of Britain and Britishness (Brown 2005). It is no small coincidence that
Liverpool itself has traditionally served as a primary destination for Irish
out-migration, leading some to consider it an extension of Ireland itself. This distinction, undoubtedly, makes Liverpool a city in which Irish
otherness is transported to England, thus contributing to and fortifying
its place as "other" in the context of England.

The Irish were not only racialized as non-white but were, as some
have argued, racialized as black (Lebow 1976; Duncan 2002; Ignatiev 1995).
This leads us to consider whether the global progress so associated with
predominantly white Western societies, previously unattainable for Ireland and now a part of its Celtic Tiger identity, leaves Ireland in a position with more to lose than mere cultural integrity. That is, European
Union (EU) status guarantees whiteness (despite the historical and present reality of European ethno-racial diversity), and the resulting social
circumstances that place the Irish in close proximity to non-white post-
colonials serve as a reminder of the precarious whiteness that is an integral part of this non-Protestant, once "Africanoid," global ethnic minority (see Beddoe 1885; Curtis 1968, 1996).

We need only observe the conflation of economic concerns with
race and the masking of race by economic rhetoric in the discourse on
non-white migration to Ireland to see that socially retrogressive acts—
discrimination, race-based violence, anti-immigration rhetoric—protect
more than the national cultural identity: they reinforce the relatively new
racial identity of the "Irish." It seems to be imperative that the Irish history of out-migration be disavowed in the discourse on immigration
to contemporary Ireland as it is a racialized past to be forgotten amidst
membership in a new global club, a club, less flippantly known as the EU,
which includes reconfigured imperialist powers that would have less than
a century ago—during another period of globalization—questioned Ireland's place in Europe and, for that matter, its European-ness. Socially
retrogressive acts expose this concern, as they reflect the Irish society's
inability to keep pace with the changes that the old global nations have
contended with (if poorly) for decades.

In addition, to the north there is a constant reminder that the Republic of Ireland was a colony and, quite certainly, is not fully decolonized, placing the entire Emerald Isle in the company of Nigeria, Palestine, and other nations with historically unresolved postcolonial geopolitical conflicts. The illusion of stability is sustained by a national identity rooted in the myth of perceived homogeneity. Yet, as long as there is conflict in the six counties to the north, there is a signifier of the prior condition of colonial subjectivity. It is this incomplete decolonization that brings the "retro" into high relief in that the nation has been confronted with a culturally pluralist nation at a time when, despite economic progress, its very national identity is less than formed. If the 1920s represented the beginning years of the Irish sovereign nation, then the 1990s represented the beginning of an Irish global nation. However, the unresolved nature of the former leaves the latter more difficult to conceive even as it is already in progress in the early twenty-first century.

Also important for our examination here is the assertion by Lloyd that the subaltern position of the colonized Irish is not so far removed from other experiences of colonized subjects. This is highlighted in Wanda Balzano's essay "Irishness—Feminist and Post-colonial," for even as her focus is on Ireland, she could easily be discussing colonialism in Nigeria: "Colonial power tends to identify subject people as passive, in need of guidance, incapable of governing themselves, romantic, passionate, having a disregard for rules, barbaric. For all of these characteristics the Irish on one hand and women on the other have traditionally been both praised and scorned. Retaining the image of the relationship between Great Britain and Ireland as one between masculine and feminine, the metaphors most frequently used have been those of robbery and rape" (Balzano 1996: 92). If we agree that colonial practices are diverse, we also have to acknowledge that decolonization itself is equally diverse and the circumstances faced by individuals in postcolonial societies must certainly reflect a diversity of experience. Young makes this clear when he notes: "It would be a mistake to assume that postcolonialism involves a unitary theory espousing a single perspective or position. The cultural, historical, intellectual and political needs of contemporary black British men and women, for example, are clearly not going to be the same as those of activists in Nigeria fighting the exploitation and eco-degradation of the multinational oil companies" (Young 2001: 63). This is particularly poignant when we consider that the very activists to which Young refers, as well as others from the oil-rich and well-exploited Nigerian Delta, are represented in the new African Diaspora of Ireland, meeting at what we may consider a postcolonial intersection.

The Republic of Ireland has become a multi-diasporic site in a very short time period, with various forms of culture and identity merging to challenge previous renderings of "race," ethnicity, and nationality. In this current period of globalization Ireland has been thrust into the fast track of the global economy and is privy to the technological advancements, material accoutrements, consumerism, infrastructure changes, and cultural establishments which accompany this era. Yet, the rapid and recent transition from a nearly postcolonial, neo-nationalist, impoverished country depleted by out-migration into a site of a significant increase in immigration at the beginning of the twenty-first century has betrayed an inability to keep pace.

Is Dublin a global city with similar flows of capital and people that led Saskia Sassen to think of New York, London, and Tokyo as global cities? (Sassen 1991). Sassen's assertions that "many of the disadvantaged workers in global cities are women, immigrants, and people of color, whose political sense of self and whose identities are not necessarily embedded in the 'nation' or the 'national community'" and that "they find in the global city a strategic site for their economic and political operations" have a particular resonance in Dublin (Sassen 1998: xxi). The African Diaspora in Dublin is in the midst of developing "economic and political operations" and through this process its various communities are beginning to pose a challenge to prior socio-cultural formations.

Writing in the late 1990s, Sassen also noted that "dissecting the economics of place in the global economy allows us to recover non-corporate components of economic globalization and to inquire about the possibility of a new type of transnational politics, a politics of those who lack power but now have 'presence'" (Sassen 1998: xxi). The political "presence" of the African Diaspora communities of Dublin would eventually be assisted by granting refugees and asylum seekers the right to vote in local elections in 2004 (see UNHCR 2004) and yield the nation's first black mayor, Rotimi Adebari, of Portlaoise in 2007 (see DeFaoite 2007). Two years later, in 2009, among fifteen African immigrants running for local election across Ireland, three Nigerian candidates would compete in a County Council election in the northwest Dublin suburb of Mulhuddart (see Onyejelem 2009; Anny-Nzekwue 2009). Yet, in 2000 and 2001, during the early days of a significant black presence in Dublin—a period in which most of the African candidates of 2009 mark their arrival—one wondered how the disenfranchised could fare in a city in which numerous immigrants are not legally permitted to work, how non-Irish/

non-white immigrants would achieve political access in a nation that had yet to statistically acknowledge their existence, and why discussions around immigration were—and continue to be—focused on a small percentage of persons seeking asylum. How could a global city function and flow if the people within it were not able to do so? I soon determined that Dublin is not a global city at all. It is a *retro*-global city.

During my initial time in Dublin, it became quickly apparent that despite the presence of international foods, information technology, and global media, the Irish social, discursive, and theoretical experiences of race, ethnicity, and cultural difference were more representative of the mid-nineteenth- to mid-twentieth-century United States and Britain, with a smattering of social remedies derivative of 1980s discussions around multiculturalism and political correctness in the two nations. Ireland exemplifies a case in which the social progressiveness (often paired with utopian notions of cultural globalization) is experienced only superficially, as the nation struggles to rapidly work through socio-cultural conflicts and transitions that in any other period would have required decades. Ireland's history of oppression under British colonialism; the out-migration of its people during periods of severe economic stress; the perceived homogeneity of its population; and its cultural isolation—all have resulted in an anachronistic social experience of ethno-racial and cultural difference. One of the more pervasive "retro" elements of contemporary Ireland involves the response of the Irish to difference of race, culture, and ethnicity. While Dublin has all of the elements of a new global city, it is presently in a *retro-global* phase. As discussed in the introduction, and as will become further apparent in this volume, seemingly "global societies"— regardless of how recently so—are rife with retrogressive circumstances that undercut their representation as unequivocally modern societies because the contingent progress is lost at the moment of social retrogression. In this important respect, my labeling of Ireland as "retro-global" is not part of a reductionist or essentialist project, but serves as a means of presenting Dublin, Ireland, as a social laboratory in which we can "isolate" what is in actuality not isolated at all and examine the unfolding of twenty-first-century global acts of retrogression: the failings of modernity writ large and small, macro and micro.

African immigrants are forging diaspora, constructing new cultural identities, locating refuge, and seeking economic opportunities in the retro-global city of Dublin; negotiating "race," culture, identity, and difference amidst an Ireland that is perceived as economically progressive— due to the shedding of the global representation as an impoverished nation and firmly locating itself in the realm of global neoliberal projects—yet is simultaneously socially regressive. It is this grasping toward economic progress without social progress that negates all progress in relation to the overriding goals of modernity. To be considered here is that the arrival of a significant population of individuals racialized as black, many of whom are equally privy to the consumerist techno-social markings of contemporary global culture and represent a challenge to popular perceptions of immigrant identity, has exposed the latent racism and xenophobia of a deeply conflicted Irish society. Furthermore, the presence of a substantial black population in Ireland, a nation often perceived as homogeneous until the beginning of the twenty-first century, serves as an example of the formations of contemporary African Diaspora communities and the modes in which they are being forged, shedding light on the future renderings of such communities and the relevance of diasporic experiences in the early twenty-first century.

Theoretical concepts, of course, should have some resonance in the notable as well as mundane realm of lived experience. Hence, a retro-global society is constructed and maintained via the culture, identity, and expression of people. During 2000–2001, the African Diaspora communities of Dublin were frequently described as "emergent" or "emerging" because the newness of their presence rested on that line between an expected temporariness and a salient permanence. The racism and xenophobia notwithstanding, it was a time when there was the conceivable potential for the Irish—who knew British subjectivity, historically experienced their own negative racialization, and understood the story of diaspora—to take the opportunity to navigate the world of in-migration and cultural inclusion effectively enough to create a new society in a way that other nations had not. It was before Ronit Lentin and Robbie McVeigh in 2006 would importantly interrogate the embedding of racism in state policy in their aptly entitled book *After Optimism? Ireland, Racism and Globalisation* (Lentin and McVeigh 2006). Optimism was not yet dead and there was a period of possibility in a "social laboratory" called "Ireland" that something different just might occur.

STATUS, NUMBERS, AND THE "RETRO" REVEALED

The official status of immigrants determines their opportunities for mobility and economic success in Ireland and within the European Union. European Union (EU) nationals and European Economic Area (EEA) nationals are permitted to move freely throughout the EU and seek employment in any member state. For immigrants, there are more than a dozen classifications of status, ranging from travel and work visas to refugee and asylum status.[1]

The African immigrant population in Ireland includes businesspersons, IT professionals, entrepreneurs, service workers, and students. However, my interviews, observations, and the available statistics covering the period of this study indicate that the majority of African migrants entered the nation as asylum seekers. A high percentage are classified as seeking asylum, in part because, except for South Africa, Ireland has issued few work permits (see White 2009a)[2] or student visas to African nationals (compare 1,580 provided to U.S. students to that of 304 for all of Africa in the year 2000 [DES 2000–2008]).While entering on a tourist visa and overstaying the period would seem an option, it too has been curtailed by the difficulty in obtaining tourist visas and the limited option for visa-free travel from most African nations (except for Botswana, Lesotho, Malawi, Seychelles, South Africa, Swaziland, and up until 2010, Mauritius), particularly for those nationals with substantial representation in Ireland (e.g., Nigeria and the Democratic Republic of the Congo). Special status accorded to individuals wishing to start a business is rarely an option since it requires an investment in the country of IR£300,000 (€300,000 as of 2002). Further, the Department of Justice has consistently advanced policies that limit African migration to the nation, as in the case of a readmission agreement with Nigeria when Ireland had not conferred "safe country" status to Nigeria, which under Irish immigration law is a required designation before entering into such an agreement, and the fast-tracking of Nigerian asylum cases to facilitate rapid deportations (see White 2009a; White 2009b). Whatever the reasons for the limited number of business permissions, the reality on the ground is that the African population is little represented in business ownership, although there is a growing number of entrepreneurial endeavors. Overall, a significant proportion of African immigrants has been assigned a status (asylum seeker) that prohibits access to the workforce. After July 26, 1999, asylum seekers were prohibited from working and, if caught, would be fined £500 and/or receive a month of imprisonment[3] (see ICMS 2001). Still, even if they were not quite welcome, Africans continued to arrive in Ireland in greater numbers than ever before.

THE QUEST FOR DATA: AFRICAN DIASPORA COMMUNITIES AND CONTEMPORARY BLACK PRESENCE IN IRELAND

The rapidity with which African Diaspora communities changed the social landscape of Ireland was extraordinary. In 1992 the Irish Office of the Refugee Applications Commissioner (ORAC) recorded 39 new asylum applicants; by 2002 there were 11,634 new applicants (ORAC 2002: 2) with a substantial number of individuals from African countries. Of these, Nigeria held the number-one position in the "six most stated country of origin" list with 4,050 new asylum applicants, Zimbabwe the number-four position with 357 new asylum applicants, with an additional 4,349 applicants in the "other" category, which included unspecified African nationals (ORAC 2002: 6). By 2009, due to global economic crises and accelerated procedures that facilitated an increase in deportations—particularly of Nigerians (see White 2009a, 2009b)—the number of new asylum applicants was reduced to 2,689 (ORAC 2009: 6). In 2009 there were 569 Nigerians at number one in the "top five nationalities" list, 91 new applicants from Zimbabwe in the number-five position and, in the "other" category, 1,476 new applicants that included other African nations (ORAC 2009: 6). So, as asylum applications stayed at least over 7,500 (7,724 in 1999) per year between 1999 and 2003—with higher numbers in those years well above 10,000 new applicants—African nationals consistently represented the higher percentages of new applicants (see ORAC 2001–2003; USCRI 2000). For this reason, much of the narrative of the shifting social, cultural, and national identity of Ireland and the Irish can be understood through the experiences of African Diaspora communities arriving in Dublin at the dawn of the twenty-first century.

While the first years of the twenty-first century were a time of substantial increases in African immigration, there were no comprehensive data available with which to accurately determine the size of the black population in Ireland. To some degree it is possible to measure the size of this population by piecing together information gleaned from asylum applications and work permits. Official estimates were guesses at best (see P. Cullen 1997; Grennan 2000). For example, the Department of Justice Immigration and Citizenship Division's *Annual Return of Registered Aliens* and the Department of Enterprise, Trade, and Employment (DETE) work permit statistics for the years 1994–1996 included individuals from twenty-five African and six Caribbean nations (Dept. of Justice 1994–1996; DETE 1994–1996). While these documents presented the only available data, they were mere indicators of a larger black population. The work permit statistics, reflecting a time just before substantial in-migration, could not account for undocumented workers, African nationals from other European Union nations (no longer recorded as of January 1995), unemployed or informally employed students, blacks born in Ireland, and asylum seekers.

A January 2001 breakdown of the previous year's asylum applications listed Nigeria (3,041 applicants) as the country from which the largest number of applicants had come, surpassing Romanians (2,211 applicants) who held the number-one spot in 1999 (*Irish Independent* 2001; Ward 2001). In addition, statistics indicated that between January and September 2000, the Department of Enterprise, Trade, and Employment issued 18,000 work visas and work permits to individuals representing 118 countries (*Irish Independent* 2001), so it was conceivable that those statistics were inclusive of African nationals. While the available breakdowns included references to many of the non-EU nations represented, African nations (except for South Africa, which included a substantial white immigrant population) were subsumed under the category "other." During the period 2000–2001, there was no available tally of the number of Africans renewing or applying for new work permits.

In the absence of hard numbers, estimates of individuals of African descent living in Ireland ranged from 3,000 to 10,000. Statistics on asylum seekers offered data on the relatively small percentage of immigrants (16.2 percent) who were seeking asylum. It was also unclear how many of those individuals had actually left the system but were still in Ireland, or had given up and left the country, despite the threat of penalties (see ICMS 2001). Of course, not all of these were Africans, and it is not possible to determine how many Africans were among the other 83.8 percent (Lucey 2000b). Nor at the time did the government keep records of the number of student visas issued (Ward 2001),[4] which also included African students.[5]

Meanwhile, the National Consultative Committee on Racism and Interculturalism (NCCRI), along with other advocates for cultural and ethnic minority communities, lobbied for an ethnic origin question on the 2001 census on the basis that it would be helpful in serving the needs of new communities.[6] The state rejected it (see K. Moore 2002). The reluctance to include an ethnic category may appear to be a progressive move on the part of the government to thwart essentializing any group. But, in an Ireland that was not quite clear whether Irishness could be inclusive of other ethnic backgrounds, let alone blackness, the rejection appeared more reflective of a state-level inability to acknowledge shifts in the makeup of the Irish populace.[7]

By the 2002 census, "nationality" was added to the category known as "usual residence, birthplace, and migration" in the previous census of 1996. While the question yielded data on national origin, it still offered no means of accurately determining how individuals self-identified in the realm of race, cultural background, and ethnicity. As the NCCRI noted in a 2003 report: "The 2002 Census does not, however, provide a complete picture of ethnic diversity in Ireland because the ethnicity question, which is a separate question to nationality in the 2002 Census, was limited to a question on the Traveller Community. A separate question on ethnicity is required because there are many people from minority ethnic groups in Ireland who are Irish nationals and who would not be covered by the 'nationality' question" (NCCRI 2003: 2–3).

Four years later, the 2006 census compiled data on "ethnic or cultural background" for the first time, which included the "ethnic or cultural group" designation "Black or Black Irish." Reflecting the advocacy of the NCCRI and other organizations for relevant data, the Central Statistics Office explained the inclusion of a new question as follows: "Question 14—Ethnic Group—What is your ethnic or cultural background? The results of the pilot survey indicated that there was a high level of acceptance of the question from the public. The categories included in the question were developed in consultation with the Equality Authority, the National Consultative Committee on Racism and Interculturalism and Pavee Point [Travellers' Centre] along with relevant departments" (Irish Census 2006c).

The census recorded a total of 4,172,013 persons with 3,706,683 listed as "Irish" (including members of the Irish Diaspora now resident in Ireland) (Irish Census 2006a). The "Irish" figure also includes individuals of African descent born in Ireland prior to the end of *jus soli* citizenship rights in 2004 and 5,589 individuals born in Africa, which includes individuals racialized as black and others racialized as white. In 2006, 16,300 individuals stated their nationality as Nigerian and 16,677 individuals declared Nigeria as their place of birth. A total of 35,326 individuals declared an African nationality and 33,466 noted an African nation as their place of birth (Irish Census 2006a). The "Black or Black Irish" category includes 11,068 individuals identifying as "African" and 1,420 identifying as "Any other Black background" who were born in Ireland. The "Total Irish" category includes 11,440 in the "African" origin category and 1,546 in the "Any other Black background" category. This brings us to a total of 12,986 "Black Irish" and an overall total of 44,318 individuals identifying as "Black" in the Republic of Ireland; that is, a 1 percent black population in a nation of 4,172,013 people (Irish Census 2006b).[8]

Before this data was gathered, one wondered whether not counting individuals would be a determination of their worth or relevance in the larger Irish society and nation (i.e., if you're not counted, you don't count/ matter at all). It was as if accurate numerical data would somehow impede Africans from "passing through" the nation, pausing only to avail themselves of the Irish humanitarian endeavor and making a quick exit. The 2006 census, however, heralded a change. Now the Irish would need to consider that black populations would not only be permanently in the nation someday, but also identify as Irish. The data resonates even more when we consider the level of crisis in which Ireland found itself due to the presence of such a statistically small group. The African Diaspora community—a "hefty" 1 percent of the nation—not only became the manifestation of an inevitably changing society, but also forced a reevaluation of the Irish national identity, even as the nation showed its readiness to join the modern global community through retrogressive displays of racism, xenophobia, human rights violations, discrimination, and related acts of violence.

EXEMPLIFYING THE "RETRO": HOUSING, SPACE, DOCUMENTATION, AND INAUGURALS

The retro-global experience in Ireland emerges out of a combination of the cultural dimensions of globalization and the "retro" manifestations of Irish ethno-cultural biases and racism, all of which have an impact on the lived experience of individuals of the African Diaspora in Dublin. I will discuss four major areas that exemplify the experiences of African Diaspora communities during the early period in Dublin: (1) Housing, (2) Space or spatial location, (3) Documentation, and (4) Inaugurals.

Housing

A 2000 Irish study of 121 individuals not racialized as white revealed that 60.9 percent of a sub-group of Africans and Afro-Caribbeans[9] believed they had been discriminated against in "finding accommodation and dealing" with landlords (Casey and O'Connell 2000). Through interviews and informal discussions, I gathered accounts of individuals of African descent going to view accommodations and being told they were no longer available, only to find out through a follow-up phone call or visit by a non-black person that it was still available. Also, in 2001 discrimination against blacks increased as a result of steeper competition for accommodation as a result of a housing crisis precipitated by the rapid increase in house prices during the economic boom and the limited availability of affordable rentals and social housing (Memery 2001; Meylan 2001; Redmond 2001). This form of discrimination, no doubt, is in the realm of the "difficult to prove." It is racism at its most insidious because it is protected by the reality that, outside of deploying undercover investigators to catch landlords in the act, proof of discrimination is not easy to obtain.

The Equality Authority—established in Ireland in 1999 under the Irish Employment Equality Act 1998, the Equal Status Act 2000, and in accordance with the European Union Equality Directives (see Dobbins 2001)—investigates cases of discrimination (gender, race, marital status, family status, sexual orientation, religion, disability, age, and membership in the Traveller community) that, among other areas, includes housing cases. Of twenty-six cases related to housing discrimination brought to the Equality Authority in 2001, only four noted "race" as the reason for discrimination. The seemingly small number of race-related incidents reflects the underreporting of housing discrimination—and discrimination in general—because, as numerous informants imparted to me, they feared that their asylum applications would be rejected because asylum applicants were housed through a government scheme and were not permitted to rent accommodation.[10] Some immigrants who had resident status did not pursue legal action either because they did not trust the authorities or felt it was easier just to look for other housing. Rhonda, an immigrant from Liberia I interviewed, reported: "I went to five places one day. They were very nice and all. But, each one said they had someone interested in the flat and they would call my mobile if they changed plans. Now, why would [the accommodation office] send me there if each place was gone? Anyway, nobody called. I had to move in with a friend and I have the money to live in my own flat!" Yet, the most "retro" experience of housing existed in the realm of the Bed and Breakfast. In the tourist guides, we read of the quaint and friendly B&Bs of Ireland. In 2001, the website of the Irish Tourism Board, *Bord Fáilte*, beckoned visitors to: "Experience the Irish royal treatment in an old castle, or receive the warm family welcome in an Irish guesthouse or B&B." However, it is a very different story for the asylum seekers housed in B&Bs—as well as former holiday hostels—administered through the government Dispersal and Direct Provision schemes.

The Dispersal Scheme began in 1999 as a result of a concern that there would be a concentration of new migrants and limited space in Dublin where asylum applicants were initially housed (see Brady 2000b). There are forty-six centers under the aegis of the Reception and Integration Agency, established in April 2001, with a reception center in Dublin, an AC12 center (voluntary repatriation center for destitute EU nationals from the Accession States of 2004 and 2007, primarily from eastern Europe) also in Dublin, forty-two "direct provision accommodation centers" in eighteen counties across the country, and two self-catering accommodation centers, in County Dublin and County Louth (see RIA website http://www.ria.gov.ie/en/RIA/Pages/Reception_Dispersal_Accommodation). So, most asylum seekers are in direct provision housing spread out across the country. Before a revision in 2011 the accommodation stipulations for asylum seekers were outlined as follows by the Reception and Integration Agency (RIA):

- Your accommodation will be full board, i.e., bed, breakfast, lunch and dinner.
- As your accommodation will be full board, the only income you will receive from the state shall be a personal allowance of €19.10 per week and, if you have children and they are accompanying you, €9.60 per week for each child.
- Rent supplements are no longer payable to asylum seekers. Therefore, under no circumstances will you be granted any state supports to acquire rented accommodation. You must remain within the "Direct Provision" scheme until you are granted refugee status, leave to remain, or, if your application for refugee status is unsuccessful, until you are deported.

(Originally posted at the RIA website http://www.ria.gov.ie/ until 2011; now accessible at www.politics.ie and www.africadublin.com)[11]

The conditions above outlined on the RIA website represent the plan in its form ten years beyond the initial days of a substantial asylum presence. Yet, it is important to consider that the only difference is reflected in the conversion of the personal allowance from Irish pounds to Euros. Otherwise, the specific regulations remained consistent in form and continued to perpetuate the isolation, limited autonomy, and precariousness of status that have accompanied the life of a person seeking asylum in Ireland. Back in 2001, Frieda, a Nigerian immigrant who lived in one room of a hostel with her teenage son and daughter, discussed her difficulties with room and board:

> It is one room per family. I cannot make my own food, which is important because I have diabetes. I have submitted four letters from my doctor requesting independent housing. Some people have told me to take more sleeping pills to relax and relieve the stress . . . rather than just offering me new accommodation. My doctor says, "You can't keep taking sleeping pills. You'll be addicted. You need better housing." Most of us were not living bad. . . . We get £15 a week and £7.50[12] for each child. It's difficult. Kids want things. You can't say, "You're an asylum-seeker child. You can't have that."

Talia, an immigrant from Sierra Leone, viewed the accommodation process as "highly degrading" and pointed to the psychological effect it has on individuals who live in the nation, but are simultaneously cordoned off from it.

> We [asylum seekers] are so scared that we do not know when to speak to each other. Some people just have so much on them that they can't even speak to each other. They just walk with their heads down sometimes. And the woman who runs the B&B I'm in tells us, "You have to say please and thank you." We know that. We are not children. It is so degrading. I keep smiling and try to be happy. But, I am dying inside. I smile because I am the kind of person who tries to be happy. If you ask me how I am, I will always say that I am fine.

Talia's desire to present a "happy" face exemplifies the experiences of many asylum seekers that I interviewed who expressed a desire to not appear discontented with their circumstances for fear that such a re-sponse could in some way have a negative impact on their asylum cases. They would often endure near infantilization with the hope that, as one informant stated, "things will be better for us and everything will work out." A common phrase repeated on various occasions by a cross section of immigrants in the African community is "delayal [sic] is not de-nial," which sums up the hope behind the more difficult situations faced by asylum applicants.

The opposition against Direct Provision and criticism of the admin-istration of the Dispersal Scheme have been quite strong since its imple-mentation. The Irish Refugee Council (IRC) was at first supportive of the Dispersal Scheme in 1999, considering it a potentially "positive develop-ment; i.e., participative and consultative" (Irish Refugee Council 2001: 4). But, by 2001, the IRC recommended abolishing the Dispersal Scheme, particularly due to its combination with Direct Provision, which they described as a "discriminatory measure, which socially excludes asylum seekers from the local community, both physically and financially" (IRC 2001: 5). In considering refugee law and the legal framework that encom-passes Ireland's asylum policy, Claire Breen has argued for the abolition of Direct Provision on the grounds that the limitations on social welfare access for asylum seekers violate their right to housing, food, and health (Breen 2008). Furthermore, in February 2010 a report was released by Ireland's Free Legal Advice Centers (FLAC) concluding that individuals seeking asylum were becoming "institutionalized," calling for better over-sight of housing by the RIA, more options for self-catering accommoda-tion, an increase in the personal allowance to €65 per week for an adult and €38 for a child, and calling for an audit of the Dispersal Scheme and Direct Provision measures to ensure that they correspond with inter-national human rights treaties (FLAC 2009). Quite powerfully, the FLAC report called into question the curtailing of freedom and equality ex-emplified by the living conditions and related experiences of asylum seekers in Ireland: "Everyone has the right to be respected, to live free from discrimination and inequality and to enjoy certain basic and fun-damental rights. The direct provision system does not provide an envi-ronment conducive to the enjoyment or fulfillment of the most basic hu-man rights, including the rights to health, food, housing and family life. It also has negative repercussions on the right to education and the right to work as well as to freedom of expression, freedom of movement and freedom of association" (FLAC 2009: 8).

The concerns presented by FLAC have a particular impact on the "freedom" of future asylum seekers and, due to the large representation of African Diaspora communities among asylum applicants, the greater African Diaspora experience in Ireland. For example, a January 2010 Reception and Integration Agency Report indicated that out of a total of 6,339 individuals living in accommodation centers at the time, 2,279 individuals had been there over three years (RIA 2010: 22) and that 4,534 or 71 percent of the total were from continental Africa, including the following nations: Nigeria 1,729; DR Congo 393; Somalia 336; Ghana 248; Sudan 223; Zimbabwe 213; and Cameroon 178 (RIA 2010: 19–22).

The accommodations provided by the state for those seeking asylum contribute to the isolation of these new members of the population—particularly as they are sent to remote areas of the nation as part of the "dispersal" scheme and not permitted to secure employment—leaving them in a mode of limbo while waiting months and years to find out about pending applications. During my time in the field, African nationals awaiting asylum approval often described their housing circumstances as "enslavement," as individuals and entire families were struggling to reside in one room of a B&B and adhere to the meal schedule of the house. As one interviewee put it, "They tell us where to sleep and when to eat. There is no dignity here." This "lack of dignity" was the inspiration behind several cases in Dublin and other locations throughout Ireland in which asylum seekers, taking major risks considering their precarious status within the nation, organized strikes to highlight their concerns and better the conditions within their immediate terrain, the hostel (see Lucey 2006; O'Brien 2006).

While interviewing African migrants in Ireland, particularly those seeking asylum, the loss of autonomy continued to suggest a legacy of the loss of freedom experienced by African Diaspora communities in earlier centuries. I recalled a description of housing discussed in a slave narrative published in 1897. In *The Autobiography of Louis Hughes, Thirty Years a Slave; from Bondage to Freedom, the Institution of Slavery as Seen on the Plantation and in the Home of the Planter,* the former bondsman, Louis Hughes, writes: "There was a section of the plantation known as 'the quarters,' where were situated the cabins of the slaves. . . . Each cabin was about fourteen feet square, containing but one room. . . . There were in each room two windows, a door and a large, rude fire-place. . . . Sometimes a cabin was occupied by two or more families, in which case the number of beds was increased proportionately" (Hughes 1897). It would be a gross exaggeration to say that Hughes's description of the confining and oppressive space of the slave quarters finds its contemporary equivalent in Ireland, yet it is difficult not to see a modern corollary in the descriptions of life in the Bed & Breakfasts that housed persons seeking asylum in Ireland, particularly when it is not unusual to find parents and teenage children residing in the same room. At the time of my initial fieldwork, individuals could apply for larger quarters if a medical need could be proven. But, if housing was pursued on one's own or if one moved out of the B&B to stay with others, the stipend was revoked, as it appeared that such individuals did not need state support. However, by 2003, rent supplements would no longer be paid and it was firmly established that, barring reunification with a spouse already renting or the long shot of special consideration due to a medical condition, asylum applicants were not permitted to live outside of the designated accommodation center—under the Dispersal and Direct Provision Schemes—without risking the status of their application.

While Frieda and Talia may no longer be in the system some ten years later, the problem of "freedom and equality" persists for new generations of immigrants who will potentially experience protracted periods in accommodation centers and, even if permitted to remain in Ireland, must recover from months and years of life hobbled by the asylum applicant experience.

Space

In 2000 and 2001 the locus of the African Diaspora community in Dublin was the Parnell Street and Moore Street areas of the North Dublin city center in enclaves based on ethnic and racial affiliation. While numerous restrictions placed on African Diaspora communities of Ireland emerged in the context of immigration policies rather than the explicit isolation of the community due to ethnicity or race, because immigration—and, more specifically, asylum—became neatly paired with specific national and/or ethnic groups, it is analytically impossible to delink "race" from place when considering the ascendance of Parnell Street and Moore Street as African Diaspora spaces.

"Retro-spatiality"—defined as an explicit negation of progressive renderings of global multiethnic communities in which interaction seamlessly occurs—constructs and concretizes minority status, exemplifying what Michel Laguerre has termed "minoritized space." As Laguerre explained in his 1999 study: "Minoritised space is a space of exclusion. It comes about as a result of segregated practices that bar a group from participating on an equal footing in the mainstream affairs of the state. Two complementary effects occur from such segregation: minorities are excluded from majority space, and minorities have no choice but to live in a specific location—a marginal or peripheral space—assigned to them by the majority" (Laguerre 1999: 99; quoted in White 2002b: 258–259). The Parnell Street area, initially referred to as "Little Africa"—and occasionally "Little Nigeria" and "Little Brixton"—was both a celebrated space and one of derision. As Laguerre notes in *The Global Ethnopolis:* "At the bottom of the heap are those enclaves that have been inferiorized by the mainstream by being designated as 'little continents,' such as Little Africa in New York City. This designation came about during the colonial era at the peak of Anglo American discrimination against both slaves and free people of color as a way to further denigrate the inhabitants of these enclaves" (Laguerre 2000: 7; quoted in White 2002b: 257–258).

In particular, Moore Street was a precarious space. In one location, migrants opened up shops in stalls that filled a gutted-out department store. Permits were required to operate a stall in the space, which placed proprietors who were seeking asylum in the difficult position of not pursuing a proper permit because they were prohibited to work and, therefore, risking criminal sanction if found operating the business both without a permit and without resident status (see White 2002b). There was a sign in the building that read "no pictures are allowed in here" so as to prevent any documentation of illegally employed asylum seekers (White 2002b: 267). Equally precarious were the various African businesses along Moore Street, which included computer business centers, clothing shops, food shops, restaurants, telephone centers, and beauty shops, because all activity—regardless of one's status—occurred in the context of the impending demolition of many of the buildings for a project that would connect Moore Street with O'Connell Street. Nevertheless, in spite of the potential that they would soon have to relocate their businesses, many of the entrepreneurs considered Moore Street, as one Nigerian told me, at least a "good place" to "get something started" (White 2002b: 263).

Among the tenuous buildings on Moore Street was the multilevel space that housed the Pan African Organization, headed by executive director Gabriel Okenla, an asylum seeker from Nigeria. The organization was not officially affiliated with the political movement from which it took its name, but served as a community center and business training site. Okenla, part community spokesperson and part entrepreneur, was very well known in the African Diaspora and anti-racism communities. Numerous interviewees thought that he would someday be one of Ireland's first black public officials. However, Okenla's status in the state was also tenuous. His asylum application was rejected in 2002 and, amidst a scandal about his life in Nigeria before arriving in Ireland,[13] he was deported in March 2003 (see *Irish Times* 2006).

Jean, a chef originally from the Congo (also see chapter 5), rented a space from an Irish landlord and transformed what had formerly been a cafeteria serving traditional sausage, beans, and chips into a Congolese restaurant and night spot:

> The walls, incongruously, featured photos from the prior permutation of the restaurant space with enlarged photos of the White Irish women selling fruit in the street. As time progressed, photos of Congolese pop stars, Bob Marley, and Malcolm X were placed next to the smiling Irish Moore Street women; serving as a reminder that the space was in transition and very much representative of a clashing of two distinct spaces of experience within one place. The restaurant had certainly seen better days and it was often as if Jean were squatting in the location, as the heat became scarce in winter and increasingly the toilets were not functioning. However, he persevered with late night crowds who slipped in under the half-closed gate to join the social scene and wedding parties that went well past five in the morning. (White 2002b)

Jean's restaurant initially encompassed the first and second floors of the former cafeteria. He relinquished the second floor when his rent was raised and his landlord rented the upstairs area to a Nigerian restaurant. The Congolese and Nigerian restaurants would share both a kitchen and an equally precarious future.

By 2007, the Moore Street Mall, a 2,700-square-meter space with 31 units, described as "Ireland's first multicultural shopping center" with "an eclectic mix of first time and local retailers," opened at the corner of Moore Street and Parnell Street (Power 2007). The much less precarious space is located an escalator ride below ground level in a contemporary-designed building under a Lidl, the German supermarket chain, and a Jurys Inn, the popular hotel chain. The mall, billed as "Dublin's Most Colourful Shopping Experience," features a variety of shops run by Africans, Asians, and Eastern Europeans, including hair salons, electronics shops, clothing stores, as well as an International Food Court.

As late as 2009, as debate over the impending demolition of buildings persisted (see O. Kelly 2009), immigrant-owned shops continued to line Moore Street, some looking less temporary than in earlier years. Yet, Moore Street Mall, in the very fact of its permanence, acknowledged the permanent presence of immigrant, multiethnic, and multicultural communities in Ireland, albeit contained in the space of a "colourful" shopping area.

In 1998, a Nigerian man was arrested while renewing his "asylum-seeker identification" and faced deportation (*Irish Times* 1998). That same year, a Congolese man was charged with failing to carry ID (RAR Report 2000). In 2000 and 2001, I conducted numerous interviews during which informants described being asked by authorities to present their asylum card for what they considered to be no particular reason. In this respect, documentation is used to profile individuals of African descent regardless of their status in the nation. As Theodore, an immigrant from Gambia, complained: "I have a resident card. I'm a resident and they asked to see my asylum identification!"

So-called smart identity cards or biometric cards were being proposed in England and Scotland for asylum seekers in 2000 and 2001 and there was discussion and concern among anti-racism groups that Ireland would possibly be following suit. In October 2001, Scottish National Party MP Kenneth Gibson, bringing forth the "retro" dimension of the potential "smart" identity card, described them as no different than the "yellow star of David which persecuted Jews were forced to wear" in Nazi Germany (BBC News: Scotland, Oct. 31, 2001). Britain began issuing a "smart ID" to asylum seekers in January 2002 (see BBC 2002a). Shortly after, a British national identity card was also being debated, which led one proponent to assure opponents that the cards would not be "show on demand" and that there would be no "apartheid-style stop and search as part of this" (BBC 2002b). Such an assurance further underscored the potentially negative impact on asylum seekers who were already carrying such identification in Britain. Meanwhile, in Ireland the asylum ID cards continued to be a point of contention in asylum and civil liberties debates long after the government first considered them in 1999 (see Donohoe 1999).[14]

The UNHCR emphasizes that "[i]t is extremely important for refugees and asylum seekers under UNHCR's care to obtain identification cards. Without proper IDs, they run the risk of facing security problems or being exposed to harassment. Getting the cards should help to improve the legal protection of the refugees and asylum seekers" (UNHCR 2002). While it is well established that asylum and refugee identification documents provide the vital protection that accompanies the confirmation of one's legal status in a State (UNHCR 2002), in Ireland the identification cards or papers have become the focal point of a contentious relationship between authorities and asylum seekers and refugees. The card is used to single out individuals and justify arrests of those who do not have cards or papers readily available (see RAR Report 2000; Healy 2004), a practice reminiscent of apartheid-era South Africa. (In South Africa, the Department of Home Affairs regulated the classification of South Africans via the well-known three-tiered system of racialized identities: "White," "Mixed Race" or "Colored," and "Black." The passbooks were carried by blacks, who were expected to show them to officials when moving outside of the designated black "homelands." A black individual's movement beyond the "homelands" was recorded in the pass book, which also contained an individual's photograph and fingerprints.) In October 2004 a Nigerian man was arrested in Dublin for not presenting his asylum documents while en route to the hospital with a sick child. An article in *The Irish Independent* titled "Nigerian jailed for failure to produce ID papers" reported: "An asylum seeker arrested when he could not supply gardai with identification because he was rushing his baby to hospital was sentenced to two months imprisonment yesterday. Jay Ugi Imagbe (30), a Nigerian asylum seeker living in Clonsilla, Dublin, tried to get into a taxi to continue his journey to the hospital with his 21-month-old child, but was arrested by gardai, charged with obstruction, and spent two days in custody" (Healy 2004). Notably, the documents that asylum seekers carry in Ireland are technically not considered identification cards. They are Temporary Resident Certificates (TRC) issued by the *Garda* National Immigration Bureau (GNIB) that note on the back, "This is not an ID," lest there be an outrage-inspiring perception that it is something comparable to a passbook or worse. The TRC is used for access to the limited services for asylum seekers. When refugees and asylum seekers received the right to vote in 2004, the card became a permissible form of picture identification at the polls (see UNHCR 2004). The use of the TRC at the polls emerged after it was determined that even though asylum seekers could legally vote, their only piece of identification was not on the list of acceptable documents at the polls (UNHCR 2004). After this omission was rectified, the use of the TRC for voting represented a more progressive use of a form of asylum identification, which previously had been firmly in the realm of migrant stigmatization and racial profiling.

Inaugurals

The fourth major "retro" element related to the African Diaspora in Ireland is what I describe as "retro-inaugurals" or "the firsts." These "firsts" bring into sharp relief the newness of the African Diaspora site of Dublin and illustrate the rapidity with which the nation as a whole is moving through socio-cultural shifts and developing formal and informal cultural products and institutions that have taken longer periods to develop in other Western nations. Overall, the "first" representational presence of African Diaspora communities presents a palpable change in the social and cultural form of contemporary Ireland.

The "firsts" that emerge from within the community represent an assertion of a variety of cultural identities and reflect the desire for the community to address social needs. The "firsts" that emerge from outside of the community, while in some cases meeting the same needs as those internally produced, also reflect the state-level, private sector, and broader Irish populace's economic and social interests in acknowledging the community and deflecting racism. Through a range of modes, including media, politics, and pubs, these "firsts" reflect a changing Irish society driven and forged by African Diaspora communities.

Between September 2000 and September 2001, Ireland experienced the following "firsts":

1) The first public anti-racism protest by the African community occurred after a Nigerian teenager was beaten in a Parnell Street chip shop. Protesting police inattention to this and to prior racist attacks, demonstrators marched down O'Connell Street to the Fitzgibbons *Garda* Station (see Dolan 2000; RAR 2000).
2) The first television program produced about the changing face of Ireland, *Mono,* which had a Nigerian co-commentator, Bisi Adigun.
3) The first African community–oriented magazine, *Heritage.*
4) The first website for and about Africans, *AfricansMagazine.com*
5) The first African-owned "trendy" lounge and café bar, Forum.
6) The first black theater group, the Black Actors Workshop, which was started by a white Irish woman.
7) The first black cast member on a national television drama.
8) The first anniversary of *Metro Éireann,* the monthly newspaper founded in April 2000 by two Nigerians, Chinedu Onyejelem and Abel Ugba, focusing on issues of interest and concern in a multicultured Ireland.

Along with these firsts, we see the continued development of the nation's first centers of the African Diaspora community, Parnell Street and Moore Street—both lively spaces of African diasporic social interaction, commerce, educational training, and entrepreneurial endeavor even as they are spaces that serve to perpetuate the minoritization of African Diaspora communities.

These inaugurals indicated that, regardless of the presence of transnationals and other migrants who intend to return to their nation of origin, the existence of African Diaspora communities in Ireland would not be a temporary phenomenon. Also, several "firsts" served other ethnic communities in the Dublin area, as there were few spaces in which difference was not constructed as "other" but normalized. During an interview with John, one of Forum's two Nigerian co-owners, whose company "Tropical Group" was instrumental in the transformation of Parnell Street from an area of urban blight to its initial manifestation as a center of black Dublin life, I was told that a major impetus for starting the Forum Café Bar was that he "wanted it to be a place where people of different nationalities could come in and relax without having to worry about trouble." The sort of "trouble" John had in mind is evident in the statistics from the previously mentioned study in which, out of the sub-group of Africans and Afro-Caribbeans, 58.6 percent said they had been discriminated against in "gaining entry to pubs," 26.7 percent noted they had experienced "persistent verbal harassment," and another 26.7 percent noted they had experienced "actual physical violence" due to their race (Casey and O'Connell 2000). One interviewee, Keller, described his experiences with clubs outside of Dublin's African Diaspora community:

> I was in a club in Kilkenny and an Irish guy came up to me and said, "If you do not leave this club, I will kill you." I said, "Get away from me or I will beat you. I will beat you." Then, I went to the doorman and asked, "Are blacks not allowed in this club?" The doorman said, "Yeah, they are. Who said they weren't?" I brought the guy over to the doorman and the guy was kicked out of the club. You have to fight back because this way, next time, they will think twice before bothering someone.

A *Metro Éireann* reporter describing the international experience of the Forum Café Bar wrote:

> People are chatting more, there is a new sound of chatter, and the ambience is different. Something is happening. There is no way to articulate what this is. You only have to be there, in the Forum Bar on Parnell Street. (M. Browne 2001: 11)

But, if we were "to articulate what this is"—in the context of a retro-global city and society—the Forum Café Bar is what modern societies should offer: internationality, intercultural engagement, and multiethnic interaction. The Forum Café Bar was not only a "first," but also became a means of escaping the harsher realities of an Irish society unable to come to terms with its multiethnicity.

MODERNITY GRASPED AND OPPORTUNITY LOST

The presence of these four major "retro" elements of Ireland and Irish society indicates that while Ireland has enjoyed the economic dimension of globalization, it has been less than equipped to negotiate the social and cultural dimensions. Certainly, other societies contain "retro" elements that undercut the freedom and equality that is integral to modernity. Yet, Ireland represents a particularly effective evidential example of the way modernity continues to be simultaneously embraced and negated. The nation's experience of anti-Irish racism, colonial subjugation, and emigration brought about by severe economic hardships, along with its self-representation as a philanthropic and "welcoming" society, presented the potential for a more progressive engagement with the multiethnic and intercultural society precipitated by in-migration. Yet Ireland's success was neatly paired with the replication of global inequalities, suggesting that such inequalities are currently inextricably linked to so-called modern societies.

A superficial reading of contemporary Dublin would not lead one to conclude that overt discrimination, racial epithets, the presence of a nearly interned black immigrant population, and a blatant ignorance of cultural difference would be so prevalent at this point in its history. Surely, one would deduce, with all of the apparent characteristics of global cosmopolitan societies (e.g., advanced technology, multiethnic populations, gourmet restaurants, arts, cinemas, nightlife) Dublin would not be a society in which individuals *persistently* shout or write, as one sign painted on a north inner-city wall read, "Go home, niggers!" It is the enigmatically paradoxical instance of a society being *global*, but not quite modern. The often jarring realization that the "retro" is violently crashing into the "global" is an integral experiential part of black life in Dublin. To further convey the sensory dimension of a "retro-global" society, we may consider it the socio-cultural equivalent of whiplash.

MEDIA REPRESENTATION
AND BLACK PRESENCE

"Black" mannequins appeared in O'Connell Street department store windows in 2001. Also that year, Irish filmmaker Gerry Stembridge's film *About Adam* included African extras in the Dublin bar and club scenes. In 2001, RTÉ aired "Black Day at Black Rock," a satirical television film, also by Stembridge, which examined the reaction of a small Irish village to the arrival of asylum seekers as part of the "dispersal scheme." The comedy featured several negative critiques of racist viewpoints, including an anti-immigration character worried about villagers "bumping into big lips" and an old villager who exclaimed, "Any them blackies come near me, I'll give 'em a work-up" and then requested an ethnic food product (El Paso crisps) (White 2002a: 110). Meanwhile, a Nigerian artist[1] launched a website to address the specific social, cultural, and political needs of African Diaspora communities in Ireland. Also, among numerous other media activities, *Metro Éireann*, Ireland's first multicultural newspaper started in 2000 by Nigerian journalists, Chinedu Onyejelem and Abel Ugba, continued with its mission to cover news stories that reflected its motto, "Many Voices, One Ireland." This was the beginning of a significant African Diaspora community in Ireland and, as noted in the previous chapter, a time of many "firsts."

Various media may perpetuate "retro" and facilitate "global" aspects of a society. In Ireland the "retro" or retrogressive representations in various media reflect and serve a national story emerging out of social issues and constructs that are considered remnants of earlier periods of globalization (e.g., flagrant racism, cultural isolationism, homogeneous national identity), and the more progressive "global" representations in various media reflect and serve a national story that embraces the results of recent global processes (e.g., significant in-migration, cultural diversity, more inclusive national identity). The conflict between things "retro" and things "global" is omnipresent, blaring in the forefront or lurking in the background, often rendering any progressive expression of the "global" somewhat "retro" in the need to assert itself at all in the twenty-first century and any retrogressive or "retro" expression somewhat "global" because the strident need to articulate what is not embraced implicitly acknowledges the globality of the nation.

In 2000 and 2001, within a relatively short period, representations of individuals of African descent began to appear in the media-generated narrative of Irish experience, not only in the context of a community outside of Ireland (e.g., a film featuring African Americans, a magazine article on black Britain, a documentary on the Congo). The various media—including narrative fiction, radio talk shows, newspapers, television news programs, websites, theater projects, and comedy club performances—brought forth a constant flow of racist representations and the counter-representations produced to challenge them; an ongoing Irish narrative featuring appropriate and problematic renderings of "blackness" (see White 2002a). The tabloid and broadsheet newspapers often featured inflammatory headlines that criminalized asylum seekers and refugees, groups predominantly racialized as black. Headlines read: "Fake identity papers seized in asylum raid" (*Irish Independent* 2000), "New deal to curb asylum seekers' scam" (Brady 2000c), "Crackdown on crime gangs trafficking in bogus refugees" (Brady 2000d), "Judge tells asylum-seekers not to resort to crime" (*Irish Times* 2000), "State's Pounds 9M to Kick Out Bogus Refugees; Minister to make deal with Nigeria" (Bray 2001), and "Asylum Babies Scandal; Exclusive: 5,000 Nigerian women abuse legal loophole and give birth in Republic to get permanent residency" (Lane 2001) (see NCCRI 2002; NCCRI and Equality Authority 2003). Correspondence to the newspapers also included coverage of anti-immigrant and racist commentary, as exemplified by regularly published letters from Aine Ní Chonaill, the founder of the Immigration Control Platform (ICP). The ICP stance is "Ireland for the Irish" and, due to its dangerously racist anti-immigrant rhetoric, it is referred to as the "Neo-Nazi ICP" by the alternative media group Indymedia Ireland (see www.Indymedia.ie). In addition to newsletters and pamphlets, ICP media include a website that, among other items, contains Ní Chonaill's unpublished letters and a news archive with links to Irish newspaper articles on "sham marriages," "asylum scams," and other alarmist immigration topics (www.immigrationcontrol .org). Also during this period, websites containing racist material became common, particularly in the discussion forums of white supremacist and anti-immigration sites such as the self-described "community of white nationalists," Stormfront (www.stormfront.org), the National Socialists Are Us website (www.nsrus.com), and other internet sites reported to the National Consultative Committee on Racism and Interculturalism (NCCRI) (NCCRI 2002; also see N. Anderson 2001). Further exemplifying the use of relatively new media technologies for retrogressive acts, informants discussed receiving racist text messages on their mobile phones (e.g., "black bastard," "black nigger," and "get out nigger") and the NCCRI also received reports of similar racist texting incidents (NCCRI 2002). Even as media representations were implicated in the invidious misrepresentation and perpetuation of the exclusion of black communities in Ireland, media representations were also increasingly integral to the construction of a "multicultural Ireland" that required the inclusion of black communities.

While the spatial representation of the African Diaspora community was manifest in Parnell Street and Moore Street in Dublin, the various media representations of the African Diaspora communities, though mostly produced in Dublin, were disseminated throughout the nation; significantly contributing, therefore, to the social and cultural location of black communities in the nation. These representations were integral to the formation of the national understanding of the new African Diaspora communities, reflected the diverse efforts of the African Diaspora community to locate itself within a sometimes hostile Irish society, and replicated or reconstructed predominant notions about what Ireland—socially and culturally—happened to be or would become in the twenty-first century.

REPRESENTATIONS FROM INSIDE AND OUTSIDE:
CLASS, RACISM, AND COMEDY

In 2001 a Nigerian businessman launched *Heritage Magazine,* a publication that indicated the future prevalence of a middle-class well-educated African community in Dublin. As the publisher wrote in the inaugural issue, "We will forthrightly establish [an] excellent reputation and occupy our deserved market position" (Afoloyan 2001: 7). The very existence of *Heritage* at the time offered insight into the class distinctions within the African communities and the drive to represent black culture outside of the issues of asylum and immigration status in Ireland. The inaugural issue, which focused on African students, artists, and entrepreneurs, immediately facilitated the representation of black identities that transcended those created for Africans by members of the white Irish community. Unlike *Metro Éireann,* a weekly focusing on harder news and features related to social concerns, politics, and immigrant issues, or *Africans Magazine* that, in both a hard copy and short-lived website form, attempted to combine a range of political and human interest stories, profile pages, poetry, and recipes for a cross section of the African Diaspora community, *Heritage* was constructed as a monthly magazine that decidedly presented a middle-class representation of Africans in Dublin and consisted of light features about business professionals, social gatherings, and African successes in Ireland. The venture resembled the early *Ebony* and *Jet* magazines of the United States. The cover of the first issue featured a glamour shot of a Dublin student from Nigeria and the headline, "Exclusive: African students in Irish colleges reveal it all." The cover story read:

> If law student Ronke Adefolalu had decided to be a model, no doubt she would have found her way to the top. With her beauty and good carriage, this friendly Nigerian will carve a niche for herself in the fashion industry, if she chooses to go into it. She, however, shrugged off that suggestion, preferring the classroom to the catwalk.
> The 21-year-old Dublin School of Law level one student, who enjoys travelling, singing and watching movies, seems happy in Ireland. "Ireland is a very conducive place to obtain decent and good quality education," says Ronke. She enjoys studying in Dublin, and says that, unlike London or New York, it is a city without many distractions. (Afoloyan 2001: 10)

Heritage and other "firsts" offered an outlet for various taste groups and interests to emerge out of the non-monolithic African community. The diversity of the community was notably represented when the first issue of *Heritage* was negatively criticized by journalists in the African community. A Nigerian journalist told me, "It is not a good magazine. The stories are old. They did a story on Mary McAleese's [the Irish president's] trip to Uganda. That's old news. I did the story six months ago for [a local journal]." Yet, *Heritage* represented the beginning of other African Diaspora media that would address similar community needs, as would later be seen in 2006 upon the launch of the magazine *Xclusive* by Nigerian Peter Anny-Nzekwue. The monthly magazine noted in its mission that it is "Ireland's African only lifestyle monthly and the first and only African magazine to break into the mainstream Irish media market" and that it "celebrates African people and affirms Ireland's multicultural life" (*Xclusive* 2009). Yet, reflecting the "many voices, one Ireland" approach of the multicultural newspaper *Metro Éireann,* the magazine's eponymous exclusivity was also inclusive, as the mission statement also noted, "Our readers are African and ethnic minority people. But *Xclusive* is creatively packaged to appeal to everyone" (*Xclusive* 2009).

During the spring of 2001, a weekly television magazine program, "Mono," covering feature stories about multicultural Ireland (e.g., food, historical presence, businesses, entertainment, arts), premiered on the national network RTÉ. The program was hosted by musician and actor Bisi Adigun, a Nigerian, and Shalini Sinha, a South Asian Canadian who taught at University College Dublin at the time. Adigun and Sinha, who have in subsequent years achieved celebrity status in the nation, are both residents of Ireland, married to Irish spouses, and active in various aspects of the intercultural discourse in the nation. Informants at RTÉ described the development of the program as part of a "multicultural mandate" to reflect the changing face of Ireland. In addition, quite certainly as a part of this mandate, in 2001 I became the first black character[2] on the nation's only soap opera, "Fair City."[3] However, while the character I played, "Venus O'Brien," offered "blackness" to the nightly program, she was not representative of the African community. I played an American music industry representative of Irish and African *American* descent. In perhaps a more progressive nod, the character was involved with a white Irish character, albeit in the capacity of stealing him from his devoted white Irish girlfriend.[4] So, even as the interethnic relationship involved the crossing of the "color line"—often still difficult in twenty-first-century U.S. casting though not uncommon in Britain—the character, Venus, also perpetuated an eroticized blackness that not only represented an age-old fantasy of the licentious black woman luring the white man, but also metaphorically represented the national fears about what immigration would lead to: the white woman (Ireland and the Irish) will somehow have her power and identity usurped by the presence of the black woman (Africa and the African Diaspora community). Yet, Venus was a temporary character, set for the summer episodes, with no future beyond the seasonal story line and in that sense quite representative of the black individuals of the past who would pass through Ireland but never settle there. The "multicultural mandate" was not necessarily considered with longevity in mind; six years later, *Metro Éireann* reported that an RTÉ representative discussing the review of "outside-funded proposals" noted that "an Irish audience always responds better to an Irish face on screen" (*Metro Éireann* 2007). The statement led ethnic minorities in various media professions to wonder if they had been "programmed out" (*Metro Éireann* 2007).

A telling instance of the contemporary interconnection of cultural experiences in Ireland and the potential for a retro-global society to unearth new identity formations can be seen in the example of Samantha Mumba. The Dublin-born pop star is the daughter of an Irish mother and Zambian father. The seventeen-year-old Mumba was featured on the cover of the Irish entertainment magazine *Hot Press* with the headline: "Young, Irish and Black." In an interview with journalist Joe Jackson, Mumba observed: "The fact that I'm black, then when I open my mouth to talk and people realize 'God, she is from Ireland!'—that leaves people culturally confused! They don't know what to make of me. But, they remember the mix because it is so unusual. And the Irish population in America, have been brilliant, behind me 110%" (Jackson 2000: 20). Mumba also said that she considered herself lucky that she did not "encounter any kind of racism" growing up. Her experiences are dissimilar from those of earlier generations of black Irish children whisked off to orphanages rather than remaining with their white Irish single mothers (see *Dear Daughter* 1996; Putterford 2002; McGrath 2006). But, regarding her mass acceptance, it is not unusual for the Irish to accept their best and brightest who just happen to be black, as exemplified in the success of footballer Paul McGrath and rocker Phil Lynott, after enduring years of Irish racism (see McGrath 2006; Putterford 2002).

Mumba, however, was not as immune to racist attacks as she may have believed. In November 2000 the *Irish Examiner* reported on local comedian James Young's performance at a Dublin comedy club. According to the report, Young stated, "Samantha Mumba, now that's an Irish looking woman" and proceeded to do an impersonation of Mumba while dancing and singing the theme song from the 1960s television program *The Monkees*, "Hey, hey, we're the Monkees." It was reported that many audience members were offended by the "monkey" reference and days later Young apologized by saying, "The remark about Samantha being an Irish looking woman was meant to be a joke, reflecting the multicultural aspects of Irish society" (*Irish Examiner*, November 10, 2000).

I would like to take a moment here to consider Young's "Mumba" performance because it offers further insight and context both for other stories of racist representations and the efforts to present alternative narratives of black experiences in Ireland. Humor can function to articulate the place of blacks in Ireland, as it is utilized to mask, advance, or deflect a range of perspectives regarding their inclusion or exclusion. Recall Freud's discussion of "tendentious jokes" in *Jokes and their Relation to the Unconscious*: "Generally speaking, a tendentious joke calls for three people: in addition to the one who makes the joke, there must be a second who is taken as the object of the hostile or sexual aggressiveness, and a third in whom the joke's aim of producing pleasure is fulfilled" (Freud 1989: 118). It was comedian Young's presumption that the characterization of a beloved pop star as a performing monkey would be capable of "producing pleasure" that provides some indication of the transition that Ireland was undergoing at the time. In "Discourse and the Denial of Racism," Teun A. van Dijk notes that "even the most blatantly racist discourse . . . routinely features denials or at least mitigations of racism" which "suggests that language users who say negative things about minorities are well aware of the fact that they may be understood as breaking the social norm of tolerance or acceptance" (van Dijk 1992: 89). In a notable consideration of the Ku Klux Klan's racist jokes, Michael Billig discusses the duality of racist jokes and maintains that racist jokes "become both a means for saying the unsayable and an object of criticism" (Billig 2001: 270). Billig observes that a justification such as "'I was just joking' is both a claim to be doing something permissible (i.e., joking) and a denial of doing something criticizable, which is contrasted to the joking" (Billig 2001: 270). Considering that Mumba is indeed culturally Irish, it is apparent that the "multi*cultural* Ireland" that Young professed to be addressing in his apology or "mitigation of racism" was more an act of "saying the unsayable" about a multi*ethnic* and multi*racialized* Ireland. If the unconscious desire to express racist hostility emerged through Young's performance, it also indicated that Young did not expect the extent of disapproval that he experienced, suggesting that he presumed a racist climate in Ireland which would sustain such a joke or that he was ignorant of the potential for his audience to negatively judge racist discourse.

Freud also noted: "The greater the discrepancy between what is given directly in the form of smut and what it necessarily calls up in the hearer, the more refined becomes the joke and the higher, too, it may venture to climb into good society" (Freud 1989: 119). Freud's consideration of the changing form of tendentious jokes related to "smut" also finds application in the world of racist jokes. Negative reaction to a racist joke appears on that social continuum from least acceptable to most acceptable in "good society." There is no available data to determine whether Young's audience would have accepted a racist joke "higher" than that of the monkey joke, whether many individuals would have been offended in years before there was a substantial black presence in the nation, or how many in attendance actually derived pleasure from the joke. Yet, it is clear that, by telling the joke, Young inadvertently tested whether Ireland was actually changing as a result of its "multicultural" newness. The inconclusive results were the fact of the newspaper coverage of the offended, a forced apology by the offender, and silence from uncounted individuals who may or may not have condoned the joke.

A sense of the complexity of racist comedic representations in Ireland at the time can be gleaned from an incident involving a local free magazine, *The Slate*. The magazine was known for irreverent, albeit crass, humor. Yet, the line was never clear where the joke ended and the editorial reality began. A September 2001 issue on the R&B music scene in Dublin contains a photo of an African youth dancing and the headline "RnB in Dublin: Blacky music is taking over." The article states:

> As Dublin gets darker by the day, a new sound is spreading across the city like the proverbial clap in a rugby changing room. . . . The Slate gives you the 411 on this phenomenon and shows you how to be down with all those well-dressed black people. . . . In 1991 when there were no black people in Ireland things were a lot different . . . Dublin music tastes had about as much black shit going on as Jackie Healy Rae[5] addressing one of his Klan meetings down in Kerry.[6] (*The Slate* 2001a: 15)

The same issue featured what was called "Racist Crossword" (*The Slate* 2001b: 10). The crossword consisted of clues that can only be answered through the lens of racism:

> 29) Whites excel in mental attributes, blacks in _____
> 1) Yo Daddy, is a favoured phrase, but a black chap rarely knows his.
> 6) The foreigners and refugees have the hardworking Irish man over one of these containers.
> 10) Where black people live before going to prison.
> 28) A piece of an African woman's jewelry that may be bigger than her entire village.

The caption above the crossword, which featured swastika icons, read: "It's the Slate's all new themed crossword series—and the first one's on racism. Anyone who can complete the grid wins a job at Dublin Bus."[7] While the puzzle could be read as satirical, much like the aforementioned Mumba joke, its meaning is usefully explicated by Freud:

> A joke will allow us to exploit something ridiculous in our enemy which we could not, on account of obstacles in the way, bring forward openly or consciously; once again, then, the joke *will evade restrictions and open*

sources of pleasure that have been inaccessible. It will further bribe the hearer with its yield of pleasure into taking sides with us without any very close investigation, just as we ourselves have often been bribed by an innocent joke into overestimating the substance of a statement expressed jokingly. This is brought out with perfect aptitude in the common phrase *"die lacher auf seine Seite ziehen* [to bring the laughers over to our side]." (Freud 1989: 122–123; emphases in original)

The National Consultative Committee on Racism and Interculturalism (NCCRI) took note of *The Slate* in their October 2001–April 2002 report in the category of "Misinformation and the circulation of offensive material":

There were 18 phone complaints received by the NCCRI in relation to a student type magazine called "The Slate." The magazine was handed out free in outlets such [as] one well-known record chain, public houses and Internet cafes. Samantha Mumba and the mother of Phil Lynott also condemned attributed quotations in the magazine. (NCCRI 2002)

The reliance on hackneyed "retro" racial stereotypes presented in the guise of satire and irony rendered it difficult to determine who was on which side of the cultural debate at *The Slate*. Humor became a safe space for ambivalence and/or passively racist intentionality.

AFRO-STORIES AND AFRO-AGENCY

During the period examined here, the more high-profile African immigrant media productions in Ireland emerged in the medium of theater and were produced by white Irish artists. The productions concerned either African experiences or Africans interacting with white Irish individuals. The performances—or what I consider "retro-global" media projects—were self-conscious productions that explained the world beyond Ireland inasmuch as they introduced the "other" to the nation so that the Irish could grapple with issues that were once considered peripheral. The "retro-global" media projects often echoed artistic approaches to racial narratives apparent in the United States at least thirty years earlier. Simultaneously, the projects perpetuated notions of Irish humanitarianism and replicated the paternalism reminiscent of the historical savior of the "black babies" of Africa.

Three theater projects that opened in 2000 and 2001 represented a significant intervention in the overtly racist media produced by white

Irish and, in spite of their "retro" elements, reflected the more progress-oriented members of the white Irish populace who wished to address racism, explore cultural difference, and legitimately work toward the realization of a global modern society. These were *Limbo*, a play by Eithne McGuinness, Roddy Doyle's story "Guess Who's Coming for the Dinner," which ran in monthly installments in *Metro Éireann* and was later produced as a play, and white Irish actor Aoibhinn Gilroy's launch of the Black Actors Workshop.

Limbo tells the story of two immigrants, one a program refugee from Bosnia Herzegovina and the other an asylum seeker from Nigeria, and of their experiences with the immigration system via interactions with white Irish civil servants and immigration bureaucracies. The play highlights various contradictions within Irish society. One of the civil workers assigned to determine the outcome of asylum seekers is revealed as having been "an illegal in America," while another character describes a colleague who is sympathetic to refugees as "making up for the time she stole the black baby box" at the parish. Workers at the employment agencies and refugee center are no less indifferent, if not completely at odds with the work they must do to integrate immigrants into Irish society. One worker, doubting that immigrants will ever succeed, laments, "They're never going to fit in. They don't even drink!" Playwright McGuinness also alludes to a difference in the Irish response to immigrants based on gradations of skin color, which is expressed when the Nigerian, Paul, tells his Bosnian friend, Ahmet, "You can pass. I can't even get a taxi!" After receiving notice that his application for asylum was refused, a frustrated Paul pulls a knife on a caseworker. The situation is contained and due to a turn of fate Paul is not punished for his actions, thus facilitating a somewhat lukewarm, if not happy ending.

At the end of the *Limbo* production I attended, which was sponsored by the Irish Refugee Council, an African man rose out of the audience during the curtain call, went on stage, and hugged each cast member. Later on, during a conversation the man revealed to me that the play was so relevant to him that all he could do was thank the cast for getting "his" story out. Yet, some months later, during the casting of a second production of *Limbo*, I spoke to a Congolese actor who auditioned for the part of the Nigerian. He complained, "I don't want the part. When will we have any other plays to do? I don't want to say those lines [mockingly paraphrasing] 'Oh, I'm an asylum seeker. Oh, where is my welfare?' I hate that. When will we have any positive stories? Why does it always have to be about asylum?" The actor's complaint exemplifies the difficulty in using representations to address social problems related to a group that is so narrowly defined within a society. Even as the late McGuinness presumably intended to expose the life of Paul and Ahmet as a means of eliciting wider community support for migrants, the characters concretized the negatively viewed status of a specific ethno-racial identity. The play could be viewed as an extension of Irish charity in its effort to help the "victims" by representing their plight. The Congolese actor's quest for "positive stories" that did not always involve asylum posited a radical rejection of the "black baby" role in an Ireland that offered few other options for black representation.

Roddy Doyle's "Guess Who's Coming for the Dinner" is the story of a white Irish woman who is dating a Nigerian man. She brings him home to meet the family and the clichéd conflicts are ironed out through the vicissitudes of the occasion. Doyle's "retro-global" media project blatantly references the 1967 Stanley Kramer film "Guess Who's Coming to Dinner" with its near-flawless Sidney Poitier character, but Doyle's Irish family is less San Francisco posh than Archie Bunker's Queens. Nevertheless, the same issue is being explored: How to deal with the black "other" who enters the "white world" without stepping on too many toes? While the dilemma faced by American civil-rights-era liberalism was played out metaphorically in the home of the 1967 Drayton family, the predicament of immigration in twenty-first-century Dublin is presented at the Dublin dinner table. But unlike its more saccharin predecessor, Doyle's narrative pushes to the core of the conflict within the new Irish family: How to reckon with a perceived liberal openness, a land of *céad míle fáilte* (one hundred thousand welcomes), and the very real danger that too many years of isolation have rendered contact with outsiders problematic at the least and violent at the most?

I will consider an excerpt from the *Metro Éireann* print version here. In a chapter titled "Spuds," tension erupts when Stephanie brings her Nigerian boyfriend, Ben, to dinner. While eating, Larry, Stephanie's father, asks Ben, "What d'yis eat over in Nigeria?" Stephanie's younger brother, Laurence, responds, "Anything they can get." He is chastised and made to apologize "like [he means] it!" This leads the family into a discussion about Ben's experience with racial abuse in Ireland:

> "Does it happen often, Ben," said Mona [Stephanie's mother]. "You know?"
>
> "Yes," said Ben. "I'm afraid so."
>
> "All the time," said Stephanie. "He can't walk down the street without someone shouting at him."

"That's desperate," said Larry.

"And not just eejits like him," said Stephanie, pointing at young Laurence. "Respectable-looking people too. You know, like. In suits. And women with their kids."

"God," said Mona.

She looked at Ben, but couldn't find anything to say, nothing that wasn't empty.

"Well," said Larry. "All I can say is, on behalf of the Irish people, sorry. The Irish are warm, friendly people."

"Yeah, maybe," said Stephanie.

"Shut up a minute, love," said Larry. "In 1985," he told Ben, "when Live Aid was on, the Irish people gave more money than any other country in the world."

"So what?" said Stephanie. "That's just stupid."

"Shut up," said Larry.

He was getting annoyed with her. He was trying to get to the point, to everything he wanted to say to Ben—you're welcome but different; enjoy your stay, and stay away from my daughter. (Doyle 2000: 7)

Doyle challenges the notion that Africans should somehow be thankful for a smile after an attack or, in general, simply be happy to be in the nation. He presents a formally educated, articulate Ben (a Nigerian Poitier) and uses him to expose the ignorance within Stephanie's family, which mirrors that of the Irish nation regarding ethnicity, immigration, and cultural difference.

Larry believes that outpourings of charity such as "Live Aid" should speak for themselves and serve as testimonies to the goodness of Irish people. Yet Ben's very presence and Larry's own reaction to Ben offer the contradiction that looms over Irish society. The nation, like Larry, must reconcile the feeling of "Live Aid" with the feeling of "stay away from my daughter." In an interview on the "multicultural" television program *Mono*, Doyle explained that he could not write in contemporary Dublin without seeing current societal changes, but believed that even though he was writing a "Nigerian character because he is Nigerian, maybe someday a Black character will be written about because he is Irish" (*Mono* 2001).

In March 2001 the Black Actors Workshop was established by Aoibhinn Gilroy, a white Irish woman. As the first Irish theater group consisting solely of persons of color, it is difficult not to see the more "retro" aspect of the workshop, particularly when we consider that the first American black theater group, the African Company, was established in New York City in 1820. Yet, until the start of the twenty-first century, an all-black acting group was not something that could even be imagined in the context of the Irish experience. As Gilroy explained to me: "I was interested in starting something for blacks. My ex is an actor from Kenya. He has so much trouble getting work here. I felt that if there was a group where blacks could work maybe things would change."

The workshop began with three-hour meetings every Saturday at the Dublin City Arts Centre. The call for actors was placed in the monthly newspaper *Metro Éireann*. A core group of eight persons of African descent—from Nigeria, Liberia, the Democratic Republic of the Congo, and, due to my presence, the United States of America—filled out the group. Gilroy, a trained professional actor and first-time acting teacher, led the group in improvisational and Stanislavski-influenced exercises. The first assignment Gilroy gave to workshop members included a reading of a chapter of Stanislavski's *An Actor Prepares* which features an acting student, Kostya, working on *Othello*. The seminal acting text, written in the form of a diary, includes objectified constructions of Othello's "blackness" in the Russian acting student's attempt to fully grasp the character. Kostya states:

> This evening I intended to go to bed early because I was afraid to work on my role. But my eye fell on a cake of chocolate. I melted it with some butter and obtained a brown mess. It was easy to smear it on to my face, and make myself into a Moor, as I sat in front of my mirror I admired at length the flash of my teeth. I learned how to show them off and how to turn my eyes until the white showed. In order to make the most of my make-up I had to put on my costume, and once I was dressed I wanted to act; but I didn't invent anything new; I merely repeated what I had done yesterday and now it seemed to have lost its point. However, I did think I had gained something in my idea of how Othello ought to look. (Stanislavski 1989: 3–4)

As a scholar and participant, I pondered what it was like for my workshop cohorts, all black migrants in Ireland in their first formal engagement with the craft of acting, to ponder the chocolate-cake-faced actor "turn[ing] [his] eyes until the white showed." Yet, the problematic representations of blackness were not particularly important to the group members. For the most part, they enjoyed being exposed to Stanislavski's teachings and were even more excited by the prospect of acting. As one member noted early on, "I have always performed at home [Nigeria]. I gave speeches in competitions at school. I would like to work as an actor in Ireland. I think there's going to be work for us [blacks] here soon. It's coming soon."

Members of the group had pictures taken and gave their headshots to Gilroy, as she also planned to serve as an agent for the workshop members and had already received requests for black actors in various new projects. Soon members were auditioning for local plays, commercials and, in my case, a soap opera. Meanwhile, by the third month of activity, *Mono* had produced a segment on the workshop which was presented by the show's popular co-host, Bisi Adigun, and led to greater interest in the phenomenon of a Black Actors Workshop in Ireland. Shortly after, an informant at the Department of Foreign Affairs expressed interest in funding a travel project for the group to show the new face of Ireland. He explained: "We are concerned about the way Ireland is seen in the world. We would like to support a group that shows the diversity here. While we may not send such a group to an area of the world that knows nothing of Ireland, places like America and Europe would benefit from seeing a side of Ireland they did not know existed." The Department of Foreign Affairs had already sponsored other projects with a similar agenda, including the Celtic Traditional African Rhythm fusion band De Jimbe (the band of the aforementioned *Mono* commentator), which received partial funding to visit a St. Patrick's Day celebration in Queens, New York, in March 2001. When we consider the sudden high-profile presence of the Black Actors Workshop, it is clear that the project was much larger than an artistic endeavor, as it functioned as a new means of telling the story of the nation and provided an immediate challenge to prior representations of Irish artistic expressions.

The greater dilemma facing the Black Actors Workshop involved the dearth in available work to develop in Ireland. Echoing the Congolese actor's complaint, the workshop members expressed concern about performing immigration stories. One actor said, "I want to play a couple in love, a family, something like that, not some story about deportation and immigration." The group did not emerge out of the black community, as it was formed by someone outside of it. This circumstance, reflecting the white Irish paternalistic framework, suggested a future problem if group members were to assert interests that challenged the group leader's white Irish worldview and limited awareness of African and black cultural experiences. However, in the early days of the group, the approach to the workshop was more practical. Another member explained, "She [Gilroy] knows a lot about the business in Ireland. If we started our own group, we would have had no contacts. She can act as an agent and help us get work. So, it is a good thing."

Gilroy expressed an interest in "training the group to go out throughout Ireland and teach acting classes to other immigrants." The idea that there was a missing artistic outlet in the African communities of Ireland implicated the primary reason why the few projects developed about the African Diaspora in Ireland tended to focus on immigration and racism, rather than stories about families, lovers, and other not necessarily ethnicity-based conflicts. The stories of the nation are not seen as inclusive of non-white individuals outside of the issues of cultural difference and "race," as Roddy Doyle acknowledged: the Nigerian character in his story is represented because he is Nigerian rather than because he is Irish. Black characters in Ireland are seen as an anomaly in the national story, rather than integral to it.

The Black Actors Workshop existed because the members of the group were not able to find their place at the Abbey or Peacock (the national theaters). However, another issue that emerged was that of training. As a local actor of African descent noted: "The Black Actors Workshop has a lot of work to do. They need training. Otherwise, people will just think of them as crap. They're black, so when black actors are needed, people will come to them. But, people will still secretly think 'they're crap' and that black people do crap work. So, they're going to have to get better training." The actor's candid response also lent itself to several key questions about the group: Is this just objectification? Are black actors a type of spectacle or are they to be taken as seriously as any other actor in the nation? Also, bringing the issue of responsibility to the fore, how much responsibility do black actors in the group have to the African community as far as their choice of artistic expression is concerned?

In the fourth month of the workshop's existence, actors from the group were asked to participate in a multicultural corporate seminar, in which they would role-play situations related to diversity in the workplace. At other times the group had been asked to travel to schools to act out morality scenes about racism and cultural difference. There was some reluctance on the part of the group to take up these types of projects. "We will show Ireland who we are just by doing the work that we do," one member noted. Perhaps the interest in just "doing the work" is no different from that of any artist who would rather not represent the whole of a social group, yet it is also an indication that group members, ironically, did not want to be singled out for their blackness or African cultural interests, even as they staked their membership in an exclusively black project.

The interest of one Black Actors Workshop member in traditional Celtic dance certainly exemplifies how individual tastes cannot be neatly fixed into geographical spaces of origin. Betty, a Nigerian woman, studied traditional Irish step dancing and watched videos of Michael Flatley, the Irish American traditional dancer who developed *Riverdance* and *Lord of the Dance*. She took her first Irish step classes while staying in a bed and breakfast near the Northern Ireland border during the asylum-seeking process. Betty wanted to locate a dance teacher in Dublin who had worked with *Riverdance* professionals and stated: "I know I can become very good at it . . . like when I conducted the church choir in Nigeria and became known by so many people. I changed the rhythms and sang the words in very clear English. Michael Flatley took a type of dancing and made it his own . . . that's how you become famous . . . I want to do that. There is just something in me that says I will be very successful here." The optimism expressed by Betty and other members of the workshop is paired with the yearning to employ theater to transcend the limited identities available to individuals of African descent in Ireland. However, it would be at least six years before a formidable challenge to black representations in Ireland would occur in the world of theater, with the 2007 production by Bisi Adigun and Roddy Doyle of the J. M. Synge play, *Playboy of the Western World*.

The Adigun and Doyle version of the play featured the protagonist, Christy Mahon, as a Nigerian asylum seeker. In spite of the apparent contribution of yet another item on the list of immigration roles for blacks, the successful production worked to challenge predominant representations. In a review of the play, *Xclusive* editor-in-chief Peter Anny-Nzekwue asserts: "Unlike Synge's *The Playboy* that borders on the humanity of the Old Irish, Adigun and Doyle's *The Playboy* explicates the foibles of the New Irish, with its stereotypes. . . . But the strength and beauty of Adigun and Doyle's *The Playboy* is the way it challenges these stereotypes" (Anny-Nzekwue 2008). However, highlighting the difficult task of revising the predominant narrative of the black experience in Ireland, a review by Karen Fricker in *Variety* argues: "The major wobble is the reimagining of Christy not as a desperate member of the social underclass, but an affluent, educated young Nigerian. The writers may be trying to counter the prevalent Irish representation of black people as oppressed refugees and asylum seekers, but the explanations needed to make this new twist work are way too convoluted" (Fricker 2007). The Adigun and Doyle production represented a significant intervention in the predominant narrative of black identity in Ireland, as well as—due to Adigun's contribution—a break from the more paternalistic relationship with blacks and black subject matter. The production, through its twenty-first-century rendering of an early twentieth-century Irish classic, also firmly inserted the African experience in the historical narrative of Irish experience. Above all, the play facilitated a conversation about representation that became inclusive of the consideration of alternative black experiences and identities; one that began in the earlier days of black presence in Ireland and undoubtedly continues to be a pressing issue.

REPRESENTING ANEW

During a 1999 panel discussion on emerging Irish identities, Kensika Monshengwo, a resident from the Congo and representative at the National Consultative Committee on Racism and Interculturalism (NCCRI), stated: "There is a new group emerging which will be referred to as the 'new Irish.' These are people who do not fit the traditional stereotype of an Irish person. What do you call a ten-year old black girl born and raised in Dublin, who speaks English, Irish, French and Lingala fluently?" (Monshengwo 2000: 77). The vision of the Irish Congolese Francophone girl exemplifies the intersection of cultural identities that would lead to new Irish identity formations, as eventually evidenced in the 2006 Irish Census. The combining of identities occurring in Ireland at the very beginning of the twenty-first century also facilitated historical linkages with new and innovative points of reference. This was particularly exemplified in the pop music presence of Samantha Mumba, but even more in the international interest in Celtic-and-African-influenced music.

While groups like the Afro Celt Sound System and Baka Beyond were demonstrating African and Celtic links through their music, in the early 2000s the historically complex experiential links between West Africa and Ireland were expressed through the music of the Dublin-based band De Jimbe, which included white Irish musicians and one black musician, though occasionally other blacks participated. This is particularly exemplified in their song "Paddy's Lamentation," with its engagement of the Irish Diaspora experience and, somewhat by default, the African Diaspora experience in nineteenth-century America. The song's cross-diasporic and cross-historic references aptly exemplify the social and cultural complexity of the African Diaspora site of contemporary Ireland.

In 2001 De Jimbe released their first CD, which featured a photo of a multiethnic wedding party on the jewel box cover and a photo collage of

Irish resident immigration stamps inside the box. On the CD, De Jimbe present a rendition of the traditional Irish song about an Irish immigrant arriving in the United States during the American Civil War. "Paddy's Lamentation" is a track in which Afro-Cuban congas and bongos and an African talking drum are played along with flutes and traditional Celtic uilleann pipes while an Irish female vocalist croons the lyrics:

> There is nothing here but war
> Where the murdering cannons roar
> And I wish I was at home in dear ole Dublin.
> Well me-self and a hundred more
> To America sailed on
> Our fortunes to be making we were thinking.
> When we got to Yankee land
> They shoved a gun into our hands
> Saying, "Paddy, you must go and fight for Lincoln."

The phrase to "fight for Lincoln" is a veiled reference to the "draft riots" of 1863 which pitted Irish immigrants against free blacks in New York City. On March 3, 1863, the U.S. government enacted the Conscription Act, requiring the enlistment of men aged twenty to thirty-five and married men over thirty-five if the first class of men was no longer available. It was legal and quite common for wealthier men to hire substitutes to go to war for them. This inflamed already contentious class conflicts and helped to increase the growing friction between Irish Americans and African Americans. The former were a negatively racialized disenfranchised immigrant group that had not yet "achieved" whiteness (see Ignatiev 1995) and that believed they were being forced to die for an elitist abolitionist cause, and the latter, a population of free blacks in a subaltern position within a nation of enslaved Africans, who were subjected to a class and racial battle that was no fault of their own. By July 11, 1863, there were uprisings in the streets of New York. The "draft riots" are often described as among the bloodiest riots in New York City history, in which African Americans were beaten, burned, forced to flee their homes, and murdered by mobs of predominantly disenfranchised Irish Americans (see Bernstein 1990; Cook 1974; Herbert 1997; McCague 1968).

The traditional song lyrics, now in 2001 sung by a mixed African/Irish group over Afro-Celtic instruments, articulate a new experience of immigrant longing layered over an earlier immigrant experience, one black, the other white. Yet, the immigrant condition expressed is further problematized by Paddy's rejection of fighting "for Lincoln" because his lament is now, to some extent, a rejection of fighting for the ancestors of the Africans who now find themselves in Ireland singing, Africans who face a new curtailing of freedom through asylum-related immigration policies, as well as the loss of rights/choices because they are black.

On a track titled "Lagos to Lacken," a song recorded live at the Cobblestone pub in Dublin, Bisi Adigun, the group's only member of African descent, discusses what is described in the liner notes as "his experiences of Ireland's new cultural diversity."

Adigun states:

> "Bisi" is from Nigeria and I am from the Yoruba tribe in Western Nigeria. When people ask me, "Where are you from?" jokingly I say I'm from Cork. [audience laughter] And . . . rather than telling me "you don't look like you're from Cork," they say, "You don't have Cork accent." [audience laughter] . . . "Seriously," I say, "I'm from Nigeria."
>
> [They say] "Woah! How did you get here?" [audience laughter] And I just answer seriously, "I came by plane." [audience laughter]

In this speech—and often as the only African member of the African-and-Celtic-influenced band—Adigun served as an unofficial ambassador moving between communities, using humor to prod the audience into realizing how subtle and ignorant race-based assumptions can be. The Cork joke not only demonstrates how politeness veils other more racist beliefs, but also demonstrates Adigun's awareness of the specificity of regional identities in Ireland that often manifest as inter-county bigotry, a knowledge that serves as an indication that he cannot be easily categorized as a foreigner (i.e., other). Adigun, who is a resident in Ireland, challenges assumptions of what Irishness means and who gets to be considered of the nation, rather than someone just passing through. This begs the question: How many generations of individuals of African descent must emerge on Irish soil before the question "Where are you from?" ceases to be the assumed initial topic of conversation? Or perhaps, the question will remain, but the answer—"Cork"—will no longer elicit laughter.

The representations of blacks, by and for the diasporic community, tell part of the new story of Ireland. Yet, the extent to which these representations remain ghettoized, exoticized, and, overall, "retro-global" in form and function remains to be seen. It also remains to be seen whether the stories told in Ireland about individuals of African descent will eventually remind immigrants *and* Irish-born citizens alike of home (i.e., Ireland), in the sense that something uniquely Irish and, for example, Nigerian or Congolese, will merge into new representational accounts and visions of Ireland and Irishness. Perhaps these new representations will resemble what was described in Dublin's artistic culinary circles as "new Irish"; yet, not "new Irish" as a bit of spice in the spuds, but "new Irish" as an entirely original dish. Ultimately, whether through newspapers, magazines, music, or theater, the various media generated by the African Diaspora community—regardless of longevity—transcended overtly racist representations, provided a point of departure for more accurate or, at least, appropriate representations of the community, and contributed to the ongoing rendering of a new *modern* Irish society.

RACISM, IMMIGRANT
STATUS, AND BLACK LIFE

From September 2000 to September 2001, I lived in a one-bedroom flat on North Great George's Street, a classic North Dublin street that went uphill from Parnell Street, the main road of the African Diaspora community of Dublin at the time. As the street name suggests, it is a traditional block of homes built in the period of the Georges with colorful Georgian style doors and fixtures of the long-gone era of Dublin's oppressive Protestant elite.[1] My back window faced a narrow street that opened onto Cavendish Row (Upper O'Connell Street), near which I could see magpies resting on a building across from the back car park and, in the longer distance, the famous Gate Theatre. My apartment building was across the street from the James Joyce Center and the street was very well known, not because of the center or its Georgian beauty, but due to its famous resident, Senator David Norris, who was known for his leadership of the North Great George's Street Preservation Society, direct and witty newspaper columns, commitment to gay rights and other human rights issues and, as one Dubliner told me when she found out my street address, "festive" social events at his house.

It was at the foot of North Great George's Street that the vibrant area known positively and pejoratively as "Little Africa" emerged. The stretch of Parnell Street had fallen into rough times and blight, but was being transformed by its new migrant residents. A block to the east of North Great George's Street, Parnell Street becomes a road called Summerhill, which features numerous council housing (public housing) complexes. In the other direction, a block (minus an alley) to the west of North Great George's Street, Parnell Street intersects with the North Dublin thoroughfare of O'Connell Street. Three blocks east, on the other side of O'Connell Street off Parnell Street is Moore Street, where a transformation was also under way with the closing of many of the traditional Irish establishments that complemented and served the area filled with fishmongers and produce vendors working the market stalls. The businesses were no longer as viable in Celtic Tiger Dublin. They were also not compatible with the Dublin City Council (formerly Dublin Corporation) plans to renovate the area by demolishing some of the buildings to open up the Moore Street area to O'Connell Street where a large-scale plaza was planned.[2] As the older businesses closed in spite of the impending demolition of the spaces, they were rapidly replaced by African entrepreneurial sites, including food stores, beauty shops, restaurants, and business centers.

My life in Dublin was experienced as an "outsider inside." That is, I experienced my research role as that of a fluid "outsider inside" because of my ethnicity (African American), racialization (black), nationality (American), and status in the state (graduate student / researcher / Fulbright scholar). Depending on the circumstance, one or more of these facts of my presence in Dublin afforded me the opportunity to move fluidly among the various national and ethnic African Diaspora communities, anti-racism and immigrant support groups and non-governmental organizations, academic and state-level conferences examining immigration policy and multiculturalism in Ireland, and to participate in a range of social events and activities reflecting all of the spaces in which I, the "outsider," happened to be "inside." For example, on one particular day, I went to a morning conference on cultural pluralism at a hotel on O'Connell Street, interviewed a Liberian informant outside of an African beauty shop south of Parnell Street during a conference tea break, had a juice with a Nigerian journalist not far from Trinity College Dublin near Grafton Street in the late afternoon, attended a Fulbright reception at the American Ambassador's Residence in Phoenix Park in the evening and, afterwards, headed over to a Congolese restaurant on Moore Street to meet informants at a late night / early morning gathering. Additionally, as an individual racialized as black, the movement among locations constantly required my own negotiation of racial difference, racism, and xenophobia in Ireland. It is this range of experiences that enabled me to better comprehend the larger impact of the African Diaspora presence upon the city of Dublin and, by extension, the Irish nation.

SADYA

Sadya's Speech

I met Sadya at a meeting organized by the Anti-Deportation Campaign (a group consisting of members from various human rights and anti-racism NGOs in Ireland) at a Dublin city center hotel. After a panel of several speakers representing NGOs discussed the governmental attempts at deporting immigrants who did not have successful asylum applications and the human rights implications of imprisoning those who entered the country without sufficient documentation, Sadya was called to the front to tell her story to the crowded room.[3]

Sadya is Itsekiri, a Nigerian ethnic group in the Niger Delta region. The region is mostly impoverished due to years of oil industry and state-level exploitation and neglect of the communities, so few members of the ethnic groups in the Delta are represented in Ireland.[4] She said, "I left because of tribal conflict. I did not want to leave. Many people went underground. In June [2000], when my house was broken into and burned down, fearing for the life of my son [sixteen at the time of the speech] and daughter [nine years old], I sold my clothing business selling traditional wraps, and left for Ireland."[5] She left her partner and stepson behind and did not know if they were alright. She said that she had no place to hide and it wasn't safe in Nigeria. The money from the sale of her business and "what little possessions I had left" were used to arrange an exit from the country. She told the group that she was so frightened and stressed that she did not even ask where she would be sent. "I did not ask where. I just went." She gave a contact the money and headed to Ireland.

Sadya was very relieved when she got to Ireland and thought she would be safe. "I was told to take a taxi to the Justice office. . . . They welcomed me at the office. They seemed nice." Sadya told them her story, all she had gone through, and how she feared for her life. "I told them I could not stay in Nigeria because even if you go to another part of the country, you don't know who to trust and there are so many dialects that they would recognize if I was from another tribe." After telling them everything about her circumstances, she says, "I don't know what crime I committed right there because I was placed in the 'manifestly unfounded track.'"[6] She said she did not know what criteria they have for placing one in the "manifestly unfounded track." She and her children were sent to a hostel in Waterford. After a week, she received a letter for an interview. "I was interviewed by a woman," Sadya said. "I told her everything I knew." An "application refusal" was received in August 2000. She appealed and her appeal was turned down in October. Responding to the news that the Department of Justice, Equality and Law Reform believed a recent announcement made by the Nigerian government asserting that everything was safe again in Nigeria, Sadya exclaimed, "Of course, they're going to say that. What country is going to say 'It is unsafe here. Everything is horrible. Our people should stay away.'"[7]

In November, the community of Tramore in County Waterford rallied to keep her in the country. Dublin anti-racist groups also went to support the Tramore community as they rallied against her deportation. There was coverage on the popular Pat Kenny morning radio show on RTÉ. Sadya applied for a "humanitarian right to remain" and was still awaiting word at the time of her 2001 talk at the Anti-Deportation Campaign meeting.

Sadya told the crowd that she is living in one room with her two children. She receives the allotted 15 pounds a week and 7.50 for each child. Sadya ended her talk by saying, "These are human lives. We are not toys. We are humans. . . . My children want to know whether we are staying or not. I can't tell them anything. It's very hard."

A Meeting with Sadya

I made plans to meet Sadya at Joyceanne's, an African grocery shop on Moore Street. She phoned me on her mobile just after eleven A.M. and I walked over to meet her, as the strip of African shops and restaurants was not far from my flat in the Parnell and North Great George's Street area ("Little Africa"). She was just about to pick out some groceries when I arrived. Sadya introduced me to the owner of the shop, a Nigerian man in his mid-thirties, and she and I went to the back of the store to talk.

Sadya was wearing a fashionable, yet well-worn, white mini coat that she said she picked up at a thrift store for 15 pounds, her whole week's allowance. As we talked, she carefully picked out her groceries (cassava, rice, dried fish), which she planned to bring back to the hostel. She reminded me, "You cannot cook in the hostel." She explained, "The food is not very good at all and my daughter barely eats. The Irish food puts her off." She planned to cook some items at a friend's flat in Dublin and bring it back to the hostel, where there is a mix of people from numerous African nations (including Nigeria, Cameroon, and the Congo). She told me, "Everyone mixes together. The women sometimes go to a space downstairs and talk. . . . One of the women braided my hair." She pointed to the tight rows of hair neatly wrapped around her head.

Next Sadya told me that she did not think that the experiences of women are any different from that of men who are seeking asylum. "If you have a black face. It is the same." I asked her if men helped her with her children. She said, "No. But, I spoke to an African man at the meeting that night and asked if he would speak to my son. He's sixteen. I think he really needs a male to talk to. I ask him to tell me about his problems, but he says, 'Ah, Mom.'"

Sadya said that she had many friends in the African community in Dublin. "Everyone is friendly, very different from the Irish," she said. "In Nigeria, you can just go and visit anyone. You are always welcome. But, with Irish people it is different. . . . The African community is different. You can just visit anyone. Some people have independent housing, so you can stay with them . . . I have made so many friends."

While we were talking, a woman with a baby came in and, noticing Sadya, said, "hello" and asked if she was coming to her shop later in the day. Sadya said "hello" and told her she wasn't "coming in this week." Sadya told me the woman was from Studio Zee (a Nigerian-run beauty salon also on Moore Street). Sadya then said, "I try to look nice. It's the way I am. But, people think you're supposed to look bad if you're seeking asylum. I like to look nice. It makes me feel good." She told me about the mini coat (£15) and the scarf she had on which she bought for £1. She said, "In Nigeria, I had a home, a maid, a car . . . here I have nothing."

As we talked, a Romani couple came into the shop looking for potato flour. Sadya called up front to the shop owner and he directed her to look in the back of the shelf closest to us. She pulled a bag of flour out, but it was leaking. She told the owner and he said it was the last bag. So, Sadya, like an unofficial co-partner in the shop, instructed him to get an extra bag for the couple so that it wouldn't leak out.

Sadya said that she and her children were unprepared for the cold Irish weather and still had trouble adjusting to it. "When it rains, my son says he does not want to go to school. I send him out anyway. I cannot afford a raincoat. . . . Isn't that horrible?" She smiled and recalled that there was a time when, in Nigeria, "I would look at the telly and see refugees and I'd say, 'What? Refugees? Who are these people?' But, now it is different."

Sadya told me a story of a conflict her son had at the hostel. While seated at the dinner table, a Russian girl thought he called her a pig. He said he hadn't and was talking to his sister, teasing her because she doesn't eat much and at that time happened to be enjoying a hamburger. The girl's mother later told Sadya about it and Sadya told the woman her son's account of the incident. "But, the mother still argued. I told her, 'Let's not argue over children. They'll be playing together and we'll be' . . .'" She paused to make a mock expression of adults being distant and angry and said, "I don't argue over children." Sadya continued, "A day or so later the father came up to my son and shouted 'I'll change your life!' . . . I was angry that the father was yelling at my son. I asked him what he meant by 'change your life.' I told him, 'Maybe your English isn't good. What do you mean by that?' The father said it again." Sadya said she took it as a threat. "I wanted to call the police, but a friend said I shouldn't because it may get on my record that 'Sadya is always complaining, Sadya is hostile' and affect my [asylum] application. So, I didn't say anything." Her daughter and the Russian girl continued to play together. "I let them. It's not her fault what her father does."

When we first met, I asked Sadya what it was like for her to speak about her difficulties in front of so many groups and to have such a public presence in Ireland. She said that she would rather not be doing it. "It is not something I do at home. But, I have to. I don't want to be sent back to Nigeria."

Sadya would like to open a business in Ireland someday, preferably in County Waterford. She said her son does not like Dublin. "'Everyone looks so serious,' he says." Sadya studied to be a teacher in Nigeria but never taught because "in Nigeria, they do not pay teachers much at all." She said, "I only studied teaching because I was bright in school and it would have been embarrassing if I had not pursued higher education." But, she never really planned to teach.

THE KILKENNY HOSTEL

The hostel in Kilkenny, two hours from Dublin, which served as an accommodation center, was much like the one in which Sadya and her children were housed. I visited shortly after the residents held a food strike in an effort to lobby for more control over meal preparation.

After leaving the Kilkenny bus station, I headed toward the center of the medieval town, thinking I would see the hostel. I ended up at the tourist information center, where I asked a touristy question (Where are the medieval tours?) and a not-so-touristy question (Where is the hostel where the "refugees" are housed?). The woman behind the desk told me about a walking tour which would begin at half past one and said, "Oh, the Ormonde Hostel is right here." She brought out a brochure with a town map in it and drew a line on it guiding me to the hostel. She was very upbeat about the place and said, "There is a wall around it, you can't miss it." I later noticed it was listed in the 2000 *Let's Go Ireland* tourism guide with no mention of the current residents, as it had been published prior to the government dispersal scheme, when the hostel was merely reserved for budget holiday seekers in town for the medieval sites. I left the tourist center and headed toward the hostel.

I moved along the main thoroughfare of the small city, greeting Africans as they too walked the main road of the town and headed toward the hostel. I stood in the road and took a good look at the building. There was a wall around it, but the gate was wide open, leading to a large gravel car park with four vehicles in it and about ten black men standing around one of the cars. I went into the car park to get a closer look at the hostel, a very large building which I later found out had been a hospital. The men by the car looked at me. I said "hello" to all and headed into the building. There was a bulletin board in the lobby and the space had an institutional quality that still resembled the hospital check-in area it had once been. As I looked at the bulletin board, one of the men from the car park came up to me. He asked if I was looking for anyone. I told him that a friend of mine, Jimmy, lived there and had told me about the place. He was currently still in Dublin, but I decided to stop by anyway to see where he lived.

Patrice, the man I was speaking to, looked at me closely. His expression I initially read as suspicion, but I would later realize that it was really a language barrier. He was from the Congo and spoke better French than English. I asked him if he worked at the hostel, lived there, or was "in charge." He told me he lived there and, as a woman passed by, he asked her if she knew where "Jimsies" was. I said, "No, he is not here today. I just wanted to stop by anyway." She smiled a soft gentle smile and kept going. She had a self-conscious gaze that seemed to be a combination of shyness and embarrassment. Two other men came in and stood by Patrice, who asked them about "Jimsies." I explained that he was "Jimmy" and, again, that he was actually not there at this time. Patrice finally understood me and we started talking about life in the hostel.

A man walked by us and said, "The matter has been solved." Patrice explained to me that there had been a protest and mentioned a committee. I looked at a sign that said something to the effect of "I resign from the committee." There were similar resignations posted on the bulletin board and another one on the perpendicular wall. I asked Patrice about the committee and he responded, "They don't do a fucking thing. Only for themselves. You know? They do for them. You understand what I say?" I said, "Yes." He continued, "'Cause my English is not good. French is my language." I told him I understood. I asked who elected the committee. "They elect themselves," he said.

A Nigerian man, Christopher, came over to us. He was holding a copy of the multicultural newspaper *Metro Éireann*. Christopher pointed to a photo included in an article I had written and asked, "Is this you?" I said, "Yes." He said he liked the article, the way I said what was going on. He began to tell me about some of the conditions in the hostel and called two women (one of whom was nearly nine months pregnant) who had been hanging in the lounge just off the foyer to come over. He showed them my article and they appeared excited to meet me. The three of them told me about a one-day hunger strike that had just taken place. "We can't eat the food. It is for white people. We can't eat the white people's food," said the woman who was not pregnant. "It is the same thing every day. The same food day after day." Christopher said, "Ninety percent of the hostel did not eat. Now they are talking to us about fixing the problem." The same woman told me, "We said, 'Give us the money and we will cook our own food.'" Christopher explained that it was not until a few people were transferred to Kilkenny from other hostels that they became aware that some hostels had better conditions. "We did not know that in some places you could cook your own food," he said.

I asked Christopher about the committee that Patrice told me about. Christopher made a sound of disgust and said, "They don't do anything. Now they're all resigning." He told me that the only member who did anything was the pregnant woman I had just met. The pregnant woman later explained that they would have meetings and not tell her or not follow through on things. She was fed up with it. The woman who was not pregnant told me that there was a woman who had just had a baby two weeks before and the living conditions were not good. She asked if I wanted to meet her. Christopher also suggested I go meet her. "So you know we are not exaggerating," he said.

The woman took me down a long hallway and up two flights of stairs. We turned a corner and knocked on a door. She went in first and then beckoned me to come in. She introduced me as a journalist (something she had said before and I had corrected by telling her that I was doing graduate research). I explained that I was doing research and not a journalist. The young Nigerian woman, in her early twenties, lay on a bed with her newborn daughter. I asked the infant's name. "Faith," she said. Another African woman lay on the bottom bed of a bunk bed. A crib sat against the only free wall in the cramped room. They watched a chat show on a small telly. There was no room to move around. They told me they had a third roommate who was presently out. We chatted briefly about food. The mother said that the baby received IR£7.50. I did not want to invade what little space they had any longer and said "thank you." I made a joke about dreadlocking the baby's hair and left with my "guide," who kept thanking me for going up to see the woman. I returned and Christopher said, "You see how it is. I wanted you to know it was true." I told him that I knew this was happening and had not doubted him, then commented on how bad it was. I stood with the two women from earlier and another woman, along with Christopher. We talked a bit more about the conditions. They said the committee was made up of all nationalities and had been created to represent the issues of the asylum seekers because Amnesty International was investigating the conditions in the hostel.

HENRIETTA

Henrietta, a resident from Nigeria, works as an accountant at an IT corporation. We arranged to meet at an office building in the business park where she works. I chatted with the Sudanese security guard before Henrietta came down to collect me. She told me that the Dublin office handles accounting for all other offices, except New York. "I sometimes go to New York on business." She was dressed in IT casual wear, jeans and a top. We went up in the elevator and I waited in a break area while she got her purse. She explained that they used to have lunch catered in the office, but the caterers stopped coming. As I waited, I saw youthful white Irish employees gathered around the cappuccino maker.

We walked out toward the Clontarf promenade (a Dublin suburb near the business park) to look for a lunch spot. Henrietta told me things had been very busy at work because her boss was in New York and someone else was on holiday. So, she had extra accounts to handle.

Henrietta and her husband, Peter, who works for an international insurance firm, live in a Dublin suburb with their young daughters. They both worked in London before Peter's company transferred him to Dublin. She said, "Ireland is so racist . . . I told Peter when I leave here, I will not look back." They have been in Ireland for four years. Both daughters, aged one-and-a-half and three, were born in Ireland.

> The older one speaks with an Irish accent. Peter said we have got to bring them back to London so that they can speak properly. She does not understand Yoruba very well. I'll say something and she'll just stare at me. I think she got confused because before she went to the crèche in our apartment building, she had a child minder who was French and spoke very little English. So, I would ask her something in Yoruba and she would answer in French. . . . We also speak English to her. But, she is not understanding the Yoruba.

Henrietta does not want her children to grow up in Ireland. She lived in London for six years, where she studied "Financial Economics." She does not want to go back to Lagos because it "is too dangerous," but would like to go back to England. "When we go to London, it is like we have been freed from a cage." She continued, "There is so much racism here. The people are ignorant."

Henrietta said that while at a work-related dinner party, "A co-worker, who is Irish, told me, 'I'm Irish and maybe I shouldn't be saying this, but do not trust Irish people, Henrietta. They say one thing, but in their minds they have plans of doing another.'" Henrietta said that when Peter came over to Ireland to work for the insurance firm, "The racism was so bad. Every day there was a problem." She continued:

> People said "stick it out, it will get better." Peter was miserable. He had left his London job and couldn't go back to it. He thought of committing suicide. . . . It has gotten a little better. But, when we came in '97, people were coming up to you saying "why are you here?" and throwing and shouting things. . . . Still, when I go into a store, I have to think "what are these people looking at, what are they thinking?" When I lived in London, I did not have to think about my race every day.

Henrietta has a brother in London and his wife, who is from California, will not come to Ireland. "She says she would not come to Ireland for a million pounds because 'the women are not ladylike, they're loud, they curse too much, they drink too much' . . . I'm like 'what are you saying?' But, every time we go to London they say they'll come see us and they never do." Henrietta is concerned about putting her daughters through "the racism and life in Ireland."

> I worry about them now, when they're in the crèche. I don't know what they are going through in a day. My three-year-old says, "You are brown. I am brown. Daddy is black" and I'm thinking, "She is three years old, where did she learn this?" I say, "You are three years old, who said this to you?" She says, "Tanya." I say, "Who is Tanya?" She says, "My teacher." I say, "Oh no. I've got to get her out of there." Sometimes I fix their hair one way and it comes back another. I don't know what is going on there. When I pick them up, they're kissing them [makes excessive kissing and hugging gestures]. I say just give me my children. I'm thinking if they have to do all of that when I pick them up, what are they doing with my children during the day?

Henrietta said she has tried to make friends with many other Nigerians she has met in Dublin. But, she has little in common with them.

So, when I talk to them, they think you are trying to impress them. . . . There are Nigerian families on both sides of us and when we moved in one neighbor was so happy. She said, "Oh, you can watch my children when I work and I can watch yours when you're at work." So, I said, "Okay, when do you work?" She said from 7 to 11. I told her that would be a problem because I work from 8 to 6. She started asking questions, like "What factory are you working in? Do you do boxing?" I said, "No." . . . I couldn't believe it. She thought I was lying when I told her where I worked and gave her my office number. When a job for a receptionist came up, I told her about it. I told her to come in for the application because, I told Peter, I didn't want her to think, if they didn't call her, that I didn't turn it in. So, she came in and got the application and ran out of there, saying, "There are too many people. I couldn't handle that." . . . I asked her what she wants to do. She said, "computers." I asked if she had any experience. She said, "No." . . . Some of them want to live well and get social services. I have a friend from Nigeria. We studied together. She reads English and speaks four languages. I said, "You can get any job here. Like that." She said she does not want to have to pay the rent. . . . My neighbors, when I get up at five to take care of the children and go to work, they are asleep. When I come home, they are in front of the telly. What kind of life is that? I have daughters and I want them to see their mother working, making a life, not sitting around sleeping all day and watching telly.

Henrietta said that when she went back to work a month and half after her second child was born, "People said, 'Oh, Peter is a horrible man, making his wife go back to work so soon.' You know how Africans are . . ." She added, "Peter and I are partners."

MICHEL

Michel's father was a Minister of State in Zaire/Congo. But when Laurent Kabila came into power, he had to flee. Michel says he does not know the whereabouts of his father. Michel has a brother in Ireland and a sister living abroad. "She may be in France now, but we don't know." His mother still lives in the Congo. She sends him money regularly to supplement his direct provision of 15 pounds. He sometimes works "off the books." He speaks French and Lingala. Since coming to Ireland two years ago, he has studied English and speaks it very well. His asylum application has been rejected twice. At the time of our interview, he was awaiting leave to remain on humanitarian grounds.

I studied accounting at home. I wanted to go to school here, but asylum seekers are not accepted. I was up for work at the airport. They liked me so much, but I did not have the papers. . . . When [Laurent] Kabila first came in, I went to France. I had been to Paris ten or twelve times before on holiday growing up because my dad was a minister. So, I lived in Paris and my father wired me money. I spent the money until it ran out and I wired for more, and I found out that my father was no longer at home, that he was in hiding. My mother just heard word that my father may return home if everything is okay now [At the time of the interview, Laurent Kabila's son, Joseph, had recently come to power after his father's death]. When I ran out of money [in France], people advised me to apply for asylum in France, to say that I was a political refugee so that I could get money from the state. I did not understand why I had to apply as a refugee. I said, "I've been coming here all my life." A friend told me I should go to Ireland. He brought me over and helped me get settled here for the first two weeks after my arrival.

Michel says that he tries to get along with other Africans, but there are "sometimes problems."

Nigerians sometimes do not know you. They are not your friend. They say hello, but that is it. There are some people from the Middle Congo here [he is referring to what is now known as the Republic of Congo, on the western border of the Democratic Republic of the Congo] but they just say they are from the Congo when they come into the country. But, people from the Congo know that they are from the Middle Congo because their Lingala is poor. The people of the Middle Congo are not considered as worldly as those from the Congo. They go to Kinshasa for things they need. In Ireland, the people from the Congo speak French or English with them because their Lingala is so poor. . . . Most of the time, when you have ten or more people from the Congo together, they will speak Lingala. One-on-one they may speak French or English.

TEA WITH JACOB

Jacob is a resident from Angola. He works in the shipping department at the United Parcel Service (UPS). Jacob and I met up at the general post office and went to a café on Middle Abbey St. We ordered tea and coffee and began our chat. I thanked him for meeting with me. We started to talk about his experiences in Dublin. He asked if I was working today. I explained my research again and the work that I do. He said,

"You just go around interviewing people, talking to people?" I smiled, as it was appropriately reductionist and said, "Yes. That's pretty much it." He asked whom I worked for. I explained the university element again. It was as if he hadn't completely understood me before. I said I would do my research and then return back to the United States to write. He said, "So, you're a writer?" I said that I do write but explained that I was talking about my thesis writing. I explained the Ph.D. process.

I sensed that when I talked about the Ph.D. process, understandably, Jacob became more guarded. He would nod a lot and seemed to shut down, as if he were in an interview with an official. He'd look down a bit. I tried to downplay the work and just laugh and joke about it. I wanted to make it clear that we were equals. He still was not as forthcoming or flowing with information as many interviewees had been. He tended to speak in generalizations. I asked him if he had encountered racism in Ireland. He said, "Some people do." He paused a moment and then said, "My situation may be different. You cannot let it get to you. I just go on. . . . If you are black in a white country, a European country, you are going to have some problems."

Jacob, who was in his early twenties at the time, had been in the country four years. He studied marketing in Luanda then came to Ireland on holiday, liked it and decided to return to study marketing at a college just outside of Dublin. It is unclear what problems he personally encountered in Angola, as he was not forthcoming with specific information about his life there. His father is deceased. His mother and sister have visited him in Ireland. It was not clear whether they still lived in Angola. I did not care to push him for this information, as it was clearly a sensitive area of discussion. He told me he would be traveling to Germany to visit friends and his uncle in Hamburg soon. He would later say that he does not let many things upset him anymore because, "I've been through things that make some things not bother me." I tried to find out what pivotal event, if any, may have led to this life philosophy of shirking off most conflicts and deterrents. He replied, "In general, as people grow older they change. You do not think the same way you did when you were fifteen, right?"

I asked him what it was like being from Angola, a country that has been mired in civil conflicts since the 1975 independence from Portugal and what it was like to see only negative representations of his country. He said, "It is political. I do not like politics. I don't like to talk about politics. It is political." I asked if he meant that the way Angola is seen or what is happening there is political. His throat tightened and he became very choked up. He said, "There are problems. They are political. It is hard to talk about them. I don't like politics." I apologized for asking and said I understood if he didn't want to talk about it. I apologized again. He said it was okay and smiled.

I asked about his girlfriend. He said that he had a French girlfriend for two years, but she moved back to France a few weeks back. In line with his approach to life's vicissitudes, he said he did not mind that she left. "We were friends and you never know what can happen. You don't know where life will take you."

I was curious about his connections with other Africans in Dublin and he told me that he mainly socializes with other Angolans and Congolese. He said, "We speak French. We speak Lingala. We are the same people. We were separated because of French colonialism. But, we are the same people." I asked if he socialized with any Nigerians. He abruptly said, "No." I asked why that was. He seemed defensive, "Look, you see. I like everybody. I do not hate anybody. I just don't know any Nigerians."

While we talked, we discussed the internet and other technology. He had a new mobile phone and I asked him if he sent many text messages to friends. He said that he did and would send me one. He asked if I spoke French because he sends text messages in French sometimes. I said that I looked forward to the correspondence.

We talked about food a bit. Jacob lived in a Dublin suburb on the south side of the River Liffey, but he often came to the north side to shop in Parnell Street and Moore Street for African foods. He cooks cassava leaves at home. I asked about kwanga, the spongy starch I had tried in several predominantly Congolese settings. Jacob, as I had been told by others, said, "The women make the kwanga."[8] He said he makes some other dishes, more fish than beef because of "the trouble," referring to the mad cow disease which was then infecting cattle in the United Kingdom. He said that he does prepare some of the dishes traditionally made by women, but "I make them here because I don't have a girlfriend." He said the kwanga is shipped from Angola or the Congo fresh because it is difficult to make. I asked him if his former French girlfriend made African dishes. He said, "She cooked French food and I made some African dishes."

ARLENA

Arlena is a journalist from Sierra Leone. In 2001, she was awaiting a decision on her asylum application.

> I could not stay in my country. I knew that if I stayed, I wouldn't be able to write what I want to write. . . . My boyfriend died in an accident [in

Sierra Leone]. I didn't feel safe. It was a very difficult decision, but I had to leave. Life in Ireland is difficult because there is not enough being done about the racism and the violence. . . . I am very independent in Ireland, in a way that I wasn't at home. I lived with my family at home. Now I have to make a way for myself.

BOLA

Bola is a Nigerian resident. After her asylum application was approved, she began work on a temporary government employee scheme. She lives in a small flat in the north inner city of Dublin.

I came from Nigeria through Belgium to Ireland. I stayed in a B&B for 2½ years waiting word on my application. The flat I have is my first flat in Ireland. An Irish girl I know got it for me because I was having trouble finding one. They see you're black and then forget it. . . . I came here with a small bag and nothing else. Now, I have a computer, printer, television, and mobile phone. It is also a pleasure to be able to cook at home. When I lived in the B&B, I only ate cold cereals. I didn't like the food.

JEANNE

Jeanne is a resident from the Congo. She is applying to study at university in Ireland.

I waited a long time for asylum. A few of us would meet together and talk about what was going on in Ireland and the racism. We were like family, supporting each other. If someone got shouted at or hit by some white ones, we would help each other. When my application letter [approval] arrived in the post, everyone was so happy for me. But, after a while, it was like they thought I was saying I was better than them because I got my letter. I did not think that. But, people talk. So, it was good and bad when I got my letter.

RITA

Rita, a resident from Nigeria, owned a service business in Dublin. She had an Irish woman fronting it for her because "when they phone up, as soon as they hear the accent" the clients lose interest. So, the clients speak to the Irish woman who answers the phone and sits at the front desk. "They come in and they deal with her." Meanwhile, Rita says that she runs the entire enterprise in the background.

TERRENCE

Terrence is a resident from Liberia.

I work outside of Dublin. I have a car, so I get around. I would like to work for myself. But, I'm happy now. . . . Some people very close to me died back home. I've seen some very difficult things, you know. So, when someone says something stupid here in Ireland, you know, calls me "blacky" or says something like that, it just slides right off of me. I don't care. I've seen worse. I just smile a lot.

MEL

Mel is a resident from Zambia who had lived in Ireland for five years when we first met. She is married to a German and they have three children. They reside in the south city center, not far from a council housing estate.

I live in a tough part of Dublin. There is so much racism. I don't go out much, except to deal with the children, take them to school, buy things for them. People will shout at us "nigger, nigger!" or throw something at us and then look away, act like nothing happened. So, I don't go out much.

JUNE

June came to Ireland from Nigeria with her husband and three children. They were awaiting word on an asylum application. She had an informal business selling African fabrics and clothing. There was a period in which she was not seen as often in the community. She explained to me, "My husband was hitting me. My face was so ugly I didn't want to leave the house. I just stayed with the children. I was so embarrassed." June was reluctant to report the beatings because she did not want anything to have an adverse effect on her asylum application. A group of local Irish women helped her get the medical attention she needed and locate housing away from her husband. When her face healed, she began to get out more. "I tell you, it was just so embarrassing."[9]

DRINKS WITH MAX

I met Max, as planned, in front of the internet café on Parnell Street, just after 9 PM. It was a Bank Holiday weekend, so I figured I would catch up with someone I had not seen in a while. He came in from Maynooth (just west of Dublin in County Kildare), where he works in a factory. He and a mate rented a room there so that they would have someplace to stay when they were working the factory job (usually Monday through Wednesday). Max, a Nigerian asylum applicant, was still housed in a hostel in County Kilkenny. "You can't live off of the 15 pounds. It's nothing," he told me. So, he took the bus into Dublin and then transferred to another bus going to his job in Maynooth. If it was found out that he was not only working, but also had acquired alternative housing on his own, there would be serious consequences and more than likely lead to deportation.

We went to the East African restaurant upstairs at the Pan African Organization building on Moore Street to have a can of Guinness. Max discussed a range of problems he encountered on a daily basis and asked me to visit the hostel in Kilkenny:

> It is difficult around the hostel. The Irish give you so much trouble. . . .
> When I walk in the street, someone will say "Hey nigger" or they'll sing,
> "Who let the dogs out . . . whoo whoo whoo." I wish you could come talk
> to everyone at the hostel and walk through the town, so that they can
> see that black people can express themselves well. . . . African Americans
> cans have made it possible for an African to go to any part of the world
> and be respected. Like someone like you . . . when, for example, an Afri-
> can woman comes through the airport and is treated badly by officers,
> she may not be quick enough to respond to it. But, an African Ameri-
> can woman will defend herself and leave the officer feeling stupid. So,
> then, maybe next time the officer will think twice before offending a black
> person. Many of my friends, not just me, feel that African Americans
> have paved the way for Africans.[10]

A concert taped in Paris, featuring African dance groups, played on the video monitor with the sound down, while an East African CD played on the stereo. The restaurant was in a small room just off of a large hall where events are held and snooker is played. The room was dark and cozy with red lighting. It was early in the evening, about nine-thirty. Usually the restaurant did not become lively until 11 PM, with a late-night crowd eating and drinking. If there was a wedding, the celebration could start as late as midnight and go well into the next morning. On that night, when we entered there were only two white Irish women at a table sipping Bacardi Breezers while the owners stood behind a counter preparing food. Later, a larger group of four African men and two African women came in for drinks while food was being prepared for them.

Max and I ordered drinks at the counter and sat down. We talked about the "Where are you from?" phenomenon; the common Irish query that immediately signified the "otherness" of the interrogated. Max said, "Now, when they ask me 'Where are you from?' I say, 'What are you, from immigration?'"

Max received a text message on his mobile and went outside to make a call, where it was less noisy. He was gone a while, long enough for me to watch an East African band on the video monitor go through two sets. The stereo was now tuned to the video. The group sang in English. Women, dressed in colorful halter-tops and tight pants, performed American hip-hop dances that included some traditional African movement. Inside the restaurant, the party of six settled into their meals of Ethiopian meat and vegetable dishes and the two white Irish women had been met by their African boyfriends. They ordered another round of Bacardi Breezers.

Max returned and told me that a mutual acquaintance, Matthew, had been on the phone. A couple of months before, I ran into Max on the street and he told me that he wasn't in Dublin as often anymore because he used to stay at Matthew's flat, but Matthew was "trying to get married." At the restaurant, I asked if Matthew had gotten married. Max said, "Yes." I asked if his wife was Irish. He said she was Dutch. But, then he said that Matthew "was married to an Irish woman and now he is with a Dutch woman." I asked if they had gotten a divorce. He said, "Not yet." Then he said, "Well, he's working it out."[11]

I asked Max if he ever goes to the local internet café in Parnell Street where we met that evening. He became despondent and said, "I am not free here. I cannot do a lot of things here because of the system." He then told me that his family wanted him to return home to Nigeria. He had an interview for his asylum application eight months earlier and still had not heard anything. "Not even a letter," he said.[12]

RACISM GAINED, FREEDOM LOST

As these vignettes suggest, the African Diaspora experience in Dublin is infused with racism and is characterized by the loss of autonomy, limited mobility, and a dearth of control over the destiny of oneself and one's family. In Sadya's case, we see her struggling to offer definitive information about her asylum application to her children: "These are human lives. We are not toys. We are humans.... My children want to know whether we are staying or not. I can't tell them anything. It's very hard." Bola, upon leaving a B&B after two and half years, expresses joy in the simple act of cooking for herself in her own flat: "It is also a pleasure to be able to cook at home. When I lived in the B&B, I only ate cold cereals. I didn't like the food." The one-day hunger strike launched by the ad hoc committee of asylum applicants at the Kilkenny Hostel is a call for autonomy, an attempt to gain control of one's own nourishment and taste preferences. Even though the Kilkenny Hostel committee members were at odds with each other, the strike nevertheless represented a united effort to change overall living conditions in the hostel and to have some input in the direction of their own lives. Amnesty International's interest in the Kilkenny Hostel indicates the extent to which the concerns of asylum applicants who were fleeing human rights abuses in their homelands were linked to Direct Provision–related human rights violations in Ireland. The lack of autonomy and the restraints on human rights that are embedded in immigration policies are perhaps best represented in Max's statement: "I am not free [in Ireland]. I cannot do a lot of things here because of the system."

The loss of prior socio-economic status by immigrants requires them to negotiate their new, lesser-valued place in the social hierarchy. As Sadya, who left the Nigerian Delta region and a successful clothing business behind, notes, "In Nigeria, I had a home, a maid, a car ... here I have nothing. ... I would look at the telly and see refugees and I'd say, 'What? Refugees? Who are these people?' But, now it is different." Michel, the son of a former Zairian government minister, who had vacationed and lived in Paris, struggles to understand the conditions that require him to apply for asylum and that have reduced his horizons to the hope that he can at least secure factory work "off the books." These accounts also indicate a concern for the impact that racism and loss of class status will have upon the next generation, as seen in Sadya's attempt to find a male mentor for her sixteen-year-old, Henrietta's fear that her daughter is experiencing racism at the crèche, and the concern of the residents of the Kilkenny Hostel for a newborn baby in a crib wedged between beds in a closet-size room and the pregnant woman who took leadership of the ad hoc committee.

These stories also indicate that the experience of racism is ubiquitous in the African Diaspora community, regardless of migration status, gender, nationality, and ethnic affiliation. As Sadya notes, when considering whether the asylum experience is different for men and women, "If you have a black face. It is the same."[13] Sadya's observation highlights the importance of race and, specifically, blackness in the daily negotiations of life in Ireland. Henrietta says simply, "There is so much racism [in Ireland]." As a professional employed by an IT company, she and her family had more options for mobility and were able to seek temporary respites from Ireland to reduce the impact of racism in the nation. "When we go to London, it is like we have been freed from a cage," she says. "Ireland is so racist . . . when I leave here, I will not look back." However, Arlena, the journalist from Sierra Leone, found that she has greater independence in Ireland than she did "at home." Yet, she admits, "Life in Ireland is difficult because there is not enough being done about the racism and the violence."

It is also evident that mediation of the effects of racism is required when considering entrepreneurial and business prospects, as in the case of Rita, who has a white Irish woman fronting her business and answering the phone so that she will not lose potential clients when "they hear the [Nigerian] accent." The white Irish proxy is also used to circumvent discrimination in accommodation, as in the case of Bola, who has a white Irish friend secure a flat for her because potential landlords "see you're black and then forget it."

Individuals in the African Diaspora community find different means of negotiating racism and its impact on their lives. At one pole, we see the extreme impact of racism upon personal mobility. Mel laments, "People will shout at us 'nigger, nigger!' or throw something at us and then look away, act like nothing happened. So, I don't go out much." Her fear of encountering racism inhibits her free movement throughout her community. Yet, Jacob and Terrence, both at the other pole, represent individuals who deflect racism through an acknowledgment that they have experienced worse circumstances in the homeland. As Jacob, originally from Angola, says, "I've been through things that make some things not bother me." In addition, Terrence, reflecting on life in Liberia, explains, "I've seen some very difficult things, you know. So, when someone says something stupid here in Ireland . . . it just slides right off of me. I don't care. I've seen worse."

The condition of asylum, particularly Direct Provision, represents a severe hobbling of basic human rights, manifested in housing conditions, food allocation, and employment. However, in some circumstances, the asylum community offers some protection against the difficulties of racism in Ireland. For example, Jeanne's experience was bittersweet when she received asylum because she missed the camaraderie with other asylum seekers. "We were like family," she recalls, "supporting each other. If someone got shouted at or hit by some white ones, we would help each other." Sadya sought similar camaraderie throughout the African community in Dublin, making a distinction between the Nigerian and Irish communities: "Everyone is friendly, very different from the Irish. . . . In Nigeria, you can just go and visit anyone. You are always welcome. But, with Irish people it is different. . . . The African community is different. You can just visit anyone. . . . Some people have independent housing, so you can stay with them . . . I have made so many friends." It is also apparent that asylum restricts the extension of human rights because individuals are afraid to lobby for freedom from harm or seek justice for fear of retribution. This is apparent in June's reluctance to report spousal abuse and Sadya's refusal to report a threat against her son by another asylum applicant. "I wanted to call the police," admits Sadya, "but a friend said I shouldn't because it may get on my record that 'Sadya is always complaining. Sadya is hostile' and affect my [asylum] application. So, I didn't say anything."

The quotidian experiences of black Dublin at the start of the twenty-first century do not only implicate the inherent contradictions in Irish society, but exemplify problematic social conditions across seemingly modern global societies. Ireland represents an evidentiary microcosm that exemplifies the meting out of inequality and "unfreedom" in would-be modern twenty-first-century societies. Through the African Diaspora communities in Dublin, we see the experiential details of the lives of individuals who endure and thrive amid such inequalities and, undoubtedly, in spite of them.

A COMMUNITY
IN THE MAKING

The making of an African Diaspora community in Ireland involved, quite simply, the process of acting upon a group identity or several identities and the bringing forth of a presence within the larger representation of the nation. The experiences related in this chapter represent the further negotiation of status by this community through marriage and family, the desire to create a social environment that assists in the coping with racism and restrictions related to immigrant status, and the tensions implicit in divergent African Diaspora communities with different postcolonial histories, different reasons for migration, and different personal narratives. These stories also make clear the contrast between the perception that a migration to Ireland would present a positive opportunity to increase life chances and the harsh reality of public policies, social conditions, and inequalities that prohibit that realization.

TWO WEDDINGS

Edward and Nora

Edward, a Nigerian immigrant with a pending asylum application prior to marriage, and Nora, a German immigrant with resident status working in the call center of a major computer corporation, were married on a Thursday morning at the marriage registry on Lower Canal Street in Dublin city center. Approximately twelve guests attended the ceremony, which took place in a small brightly lit auditorium resembling a combination conference theater and contemporary church. The guests included Nora's mother and her mother's partner (both traveled from Germany), a German friend from Nora's workplace, Nigerian men with their partners (who were Irish, Dutch, Nigerian, and Chinese) and three small children of African and Irish parentage. Nora's friend stood as her maid of honor and Edward's best man was a close Nigerian friend whom he had known in Lagos before either of them considered making the journey to Ireland. Nora wore an elegant velvet dress and Edward a smart suit. All in attendance wore suits and dresses. There were no traditional sartorial expressions of either national background.

The reception took place from 6:00 PM to 11:30 PM at the Vietnamese Center on the north side of Dublin not far from the Parnell Street area. The center is a very "no-frills" place. The building is located in a council housing area and it costs little to have a meeting there; it has rooms on the upper floors where various organizations, such as the Anti-Racism Campaign, held meetings. The reception took place in a large room on the first floor, which usually served as a gym (or dojo) for Capoeira and Tai-Bo classes. The walls were lined with photos of Vietnamese martial arts masters, though the center serves the larger Irish community. At the time, one was more likely to see white Irish and recent immigrants in the center, but its genesis is rooted in the arrival of UNHCR program refugees from Vietnam in 1979.

Nora and a few friends spent the afternoon decorating the room/gym with balloons and covering the tables with colored paper cloth. Cans of Becks and bottles of Lambrusco Bianco (a sweet white wine popular at most of the African community events and sold at the African restaurants in Dublin) and champagne were on the tables.

Early in the evening, few guests had arrived. Four or five Nigerian men (friends of Edward) stood together and about five or six women (mostly Nora's German co-workers) also stood together talking amongst themselves. The separate groups formed because guests were greeting those they knew upon arrival, rather than constructing a purposeful nationality or ethnicity-based divide. This "lack of ethnic divide" became evident as more guests arrived, including many who were in interethnic partnerships and had multiethnic children. More interaction among the various ethnic groups occurred. Most of the fathers were Nigerian and the mothers were white (Irish and other European nationals). Approximately fifty-five guests attended. Just over half of the guests were of African descent.

Later in the evening, a Nigerian woman, Judith, arrived with a salad mixed with creamy dressing and two thermal coolers filled with two kinds of Nigerian rice dishes and baked chicken. Judith had recently started an informal catering business for African events. Two tables were put together for a buffet. Close male friends of Edward, following the traditional hospitality of the homeland, encouraged everyone to eat and would not sit down and eat until guests, particularly women, were served.

Nora's mother, Helga, and her partner, Oz, sat at the head table with Edward and Nora. Oz shot video with his digital camera. Several guests took still photos. The disc jockey, Lorin, a Nigerian, arrived late and took some time to set up his equipment. He works numerous events in the African community and was a party disc jockey in Nigeria. The music included a few Nigerian standards, but was mostly American contemporary R&B. Once Lorin set up his equipment, most of those in attendance danced, including the small children. Germans, Irish, Dutch, and Nigerians danced together.

The men in attendance were mostly Igbo (Edward's ethnicity), though there were Nigerians of the Yoruba ethnic group present. Timothy, who was in his late thirties and older than most of the men in attendance, described himself as the "chairman of the Igbo Community in Ireland."[1] Later in the evening, the reverence paid by other Igbo men and specific references made to Timothy suggested that he had royal links in the homeland. Timothy explained to me that the maintenance of kinship rituals and community are very important to the Igbo in Ireland. He then noted, "If I die, they know what to do with me. They know that my body must be sent back to Igboland."

The reception included the cutting of the cake and then ended promptly at 11:30 PM because the Vietnamese Center was set to close at midnight. Also, it was a Thursday night and some guests had to work in the morning. Others went to a local African establishment to continue the party. Nora and Edward were not going on a honeymoon. "We'll save money and go at a later time," Nora said. She had to work at the call center in the morning and Edward planned to be looking for employment once his resident papers came through.

Several months later, Edward and Nora had to bring a case to the Department of Justice, as they had not received papers acknowledging Edward's resident status in Ireland, despite his having married a resident.[2] "It is so frustrating. So much bureaucracy," Nora told me while showing me wedding photographs. She was seeking help from various NGOs. They had still not had their honeymoon.

Alain and Michelle

Alain and Michelle, a Congolese couple, were married at the marriage registry on a Monday and had the wedding party the following Saturday at a restaurant on Moore Street run by Jean (also from the Democratic

Republic of Congo). Though I had not yet met the couple, Luambo, a resident from the Congo, invited me to attend the wedding with his family.

I met Luambo around 10 PM in front of the Tropical Store in Parnell Street. He was smartly dressed in a classic French suit, clearly ready for a special event. We headed over to Moore Street. When we arrived, the restaurant was not very full. The tables were set up with white cloths and candles, and balloons were taped along the walls. Jean appeared in sportswear: a bright tracksuit with an oversized corporate logo T-shirt and cap. He had yet to change into his zoot suit, which he wears at special events. It was early. He greeted Luambo and me, and set up a table for us. We ordered cans of Guinness, which would have been quite unusual in an Irish pub where the pull of the Guinness pint is a careful ritual. However, outside of the more upscale Forum café bar on Parnell Street, the African-owned establishments were not set up for tap beers—the mainstay of Irish pub life. All the same, many African immigrants were well accustomed to drinking bottled and canned beers in the homeland. A video of interviews with different Congolese pop music stars played on a monitor in the corner of the space. I listened carefully and could make out some of the French amidst the Lingala.

More guests began to arrive. The majority of guests were from the Congolese community, with a few Angolans. As people arrived, they stopped at our table to say "hello" to Luambo. His friends, Max and Jay, sat with us. Later his sister-in-law, Isabel, arrived and then a sister-in-law-to-be (wedding scheduled for three months from then), Ann, arrived. They sat with us. Some of the women were very dressed up, some more casual. Isabel took off her coat to reveal a long white shirt over slacks. The shirt had homoerotic photos printed on it.[3] No one, though, appeared to notice it. The photos were nearly postcard-size pictures of very "buff" men standing together; one man alone and naked, waving a towel between his legs and a naked couple, embraced in silhouette. I later told Isabel that I liked her shirt and said, "Very suggestive." She smiled and thanked me. There was a language barrier, so the "suggestive" may have been lost.

Luambo jokingly said, "Isabel is my wife. I call her my wife," and said to Ann, "You'll be my wife, too." He then pointed to Jay and said, "When he gets married, his wife will be mine." It was Luambo's way of expressing his love for his extended family, but in addition to the polygamous implications, his references were actually more polyandrous (i.e., Jay's wife would have two husbands). Though, more than likely, such relationships would not come to pass in Ireland. While there is polyandry in the Democratic Republic of Congo (DRC) and, through various interviews,

I was aware that the social and familial tradition had carried over to Ireland, it was not overtly displayed or discussed.

Mostly, the wedding guests spoke in Lingala. "Sángo-níni" (formal greeting for "How are you?"). "Malámu, melesí. Na yo?" ("Fine, thanks. And you?"). Guests continued to pass by our table and greet Luambo (and then the others at the table). Luambo told me that everybody is friendly to him and comes to greet him because they know his father. "My father is very rich and has helped many poor people . . . so when they hear that Luambo, his son, is here, they want to say 'hello.'"[4] The head of the Congo Solidarity Organization in Dublin stopped by to say "hello" to us. I know him and have seen him at numerous events. He moved through many circles in Ireland and worked for the National Consultative Committee on Racism and Interculturalism (NCCRI). Luambo described him as a "big man."

The bridegroom Alain sat alone at the head table waiting for his bride to make her grand entrance. He sat for approximately an hour and a half before the music was set up and eventually the bride appeared. The tradition in the Congo is that the groom waits for long periods for his bride to arrive for the ceremony. Luambo told me, "It's a surprise! Oh, great, you are my wife! You are so beautiful!" Because Alain and Michelle were married at the wedding registry earlier in the week (and appointments are necessary, so the custom of the delayed bride would not work well with the Irish civil service), they continued the tradition at the wedding party. Eventually, Michelle appeared in traditional Congolese wedding dress with a group of women who danced her over to the table where the groom waited.

Around 1 AM, a meal was served. The food was traditional Congolese cuisine prepared by Jean and several Congolese women, who were also helping him serve from the large platters of food. Also, Pierre, a friend of Jean's, made some of the dishes. Pierre is a Paris-trained chef, originally from the Congo, who works at an upscale restaurant on the Dublin quays. They served salt fish, sea bass with a spicy onion and pepper sauce, plantain and kwanga (a popular cassava-based staple, which takes several days to prepare and resembles boiled potatoes with a harder and thicker consistency). While I enjoyed my kwanga, Luambo reached over and tasted my sauce. He said, "That's good sauce." Then, he took some from Ann's plate (she was sitting on the other side of him) and placed it on my plate. It was very common to share food in this way. Even though I did not know Ann well, there was an immediate familial-like connection, as we were all of African descent and I was a guest of the family.

The sound on the video monitor was turned down. The disc jockey sat in a cubicle of equipment spinning tunes and guests crowded the small dance floor. Hip-hop dancers moving through Congo streets could be seen on the video monitor. The disc jockey played dance music from the Congo which was mainly rumba (the Afro-Salsa hybrid that is very popular in the Congo) and soukous (the extremely popular rumba-influenced Congolese dance music that meshes Latin, Caribbean, and American music genres). Unlike the Nigerian events, no American or UK chart busters were played. But, most of the crowd knew the latest and classic Congolese hits and sang along. "I love this song!" Luambo shouted to me during a rumba hit. Guests danced the rumba. While mostly men and women danced together, there were still more men at the event than women, so some groups of single men danced together. For a while, I danced with a Congolese immigrant from Paris, Jacques. He had lived in France for three years before coming to Dublin to start a business with a cousin from the Congo. We had met before when he translated from French to English during an interview with his cousin. As we danced, Jacques said he was considering a permanent return to Paris. "They are too racist here," he said.

Later in the night (which was actually early in the morning), I noticed an African immigrant named Julius was at the party. I never found out his country of origin, but his accent and spoken English indicate that it is most likely an Anglophone nation. I first met Julius after a political event at the Wynns Hotel in the north city center. At the time, he was rather drunk and standing at the hotel bar talking and drinking with two white Irish men. He repeatedly told the Irish men that he was from San Francisco. I attempted to talk to him about San Francisco, as I lived in the Bay Area before going to Ireland and also did not meet many Africans in Dublin who had lived in the United States. However, it became clear that Julius had never been to San Francisco and that saying he was from the city was apparently, for him, a clever way of not answering that loaded question, "Where are you from?" So, Julius remembered me and came over to us at the Congolese wedding. While I was dancing the rumba with Luambo, Julius appeared on the dance floor and did a solo dance next to us. As he bopped around in a somewhat drunken way, Luambo asked him, "Where are you from?" A question automatically signaling the "otherness" of Julius. Julius said, "San Francisco. I am from San Francisco" and continued his dance. Luambo looked at me and said, "This guy is very drunk." Julius was definitely not part of the Congolese community. He was an African outsider, not fully accepted in this part of the diasporic community and, as I had seen him at other African circles and events, not fully accepted in other diasporic circles. This, of course, could have been related (the cause as well as effect) to his frequent intoxication and his San Francisco fantasy.

We were talking about weddings and I asked Luambo if he would ever marry a Nigerian woman. He said, "No, because they will hit you." I asked him to repeat what he said and, once again he said, "They will hit you." It was difficult to get a full explanation of this specific belief, but he did offer insight into his feelings about Nigerians in general. "Nigerians just want to make money fast. They love money too much." Luambo explained, "I like money. You need money to live. But, I will take it slow. Nigerians want to make money quickly with credit card scams or anything else that gets quick money. A Nigerian woman will marry you for money and not love." He then said, "Because of this need to make fast money, Irish people do not like Nigerians."

It was 3 AM, long after licensed drinking hours in Ireland. The window gates of Jean's restaurant remained down so that nobody could see into the space. Two white Irish couples entered and danced for a short time. It was not apparent whether they were crashing the event (which I have observed at other events with white Irish individuals in search of an after-hours drink or curious about African cultural events) or if they thought it was an open venue as opposed to a private party, particularly since they did not interact with any of the other guests. It is at times difficult to draw the line between private and public event in these settings. In the spirit of openness of the African community, Jean did not put a sign on the door stating the restaurant was closed for a private wedding party. Besides, the upstairs area, a Nigerian restaurant, was not closed (but had few customers that night).

The Irish couples were noticeable because the entire party (which included approximately sixty individuals), except for three white European guests, consisted of African immigrants. The other white guests were: one Irish man who was a friend of someone in the wedding and two Irish women in attendance with Congolese dates. One of the Congolese dates wore sunglasses throughout the event and sat posed as if he were a film star. (He was not a film star, just a young man interested in looking "cool.") The foursome drank bottles of the popular Lambrusco and Lambrusco Bianco throughout the evening. I watched as Jean served them. He placed wine glasses on their table and, with a bit of finesse, tore off the wrapping and removed the twist-off cap. He then poured the semi-fizzy wine as if he were a sommelier in a fine Paris restaurant.

There were four or five children who were under the age of four at the wedding party. Most slept at different points during the party, but some were brought on the dance floor and were still awake when I left around 5 AM.

On the way home, while picking up the Sunday morning papers, I ran into Pierre, the chef, at the Centra (a 24-hour convenience store chain) at the corner of Parnell and O'Connell. He was picking up cigarettes and getting ready to return to the wedding party. "It will be going on another few hours," he said. It was just about sunrise.

JENNIFER

Jennifer is a resident from Nigeria. She had recently married an Irish man and the two moved to Dublin from a small Irish town in the north of the Republic in County Donegal. She told me that she and her husband, who is white Irish, were starting a cleaning business with around ten workers to clean flats and office buildings. When we had our first interview, they had just created their first poster. She had a cleaning job at a computer graphics agency. "But, I have to work for myself. I can't work for other people." She told me she was upset with her husband, Ruari. "He was depressed after a twelve-year relationship with a 'crazy woman' ended. But, he still goes to see her. She's a drug addict. She throws glass. Threatens her children. . . . The woman is in a mental hospital." Jennifer said that her husband "is such a sweet guy" and that "he will drop everything to help someone and this includes this ex." She said, "I once followed him to a bar where he met the woman and they went in to talk. He hadn't told me he was going. I went back home and changed into a short top and skirt, like those hip-hop girls, I must have looked crazy . . . and I went back to the bar and walked in . . . Ruari must have said, 'Nigerian women are crazy!'" She said she is mostly upset with Ruari because "I have a certain lifestyle that I want to lead and he is not motivated the way that I am. He does not care. He has been so depressed . . . I want him to understand that there is nothing he can do for this woman." She said, "His family is always calling me. They want to know how I'm doing. They see that he has changed for the better since he got with me."

Jennifer had a twin sister who died. She said, "I want to take in her two children and will be seeing my lawyer about getting them over here. They are my twin sister's children. But, [the Department of Justice] can give you so much trouble."

A DAY WITH SUSAN

I called Susan around one o'clock and arranged to meet her at her flat around two. Susan, a Nigerian immigrant who had obtained Irish resident status after marrying an Irish man, lived in a new flat in the trendy new Docklands area, a shipping area on the north side of the River Liffey near the Custom House that had become a major redevelopment area with a growing financial district and contemporary housing. Susan's apartment complex had the feel of a "high-tech" planned community and was adjacent to two nearly finished apartment buildings making their way to the high-rise status of the others, as well as a pristine-looking Spar (a convenience store chain) that supplied groceries to the surrounding community. There was also a smaller Spar near a canal area right off the Liffey, where benches rested around the body of water, offering rest and relaxation amidst the various corporate buildings near the housing complex. The neighborhood makeup was a representative blend of what is the new Dublin: young urban professionals, Muslim IT workers, East Asian students, African businessmen, and artists. It had a very new feeling to it; so new that it would almost lack personality if it weren't part of such an innovative and fresh Dublin residential plan.

I called Susan on my mobile. She was in her car dropping her friend off at the Spar and told me to keep straight down the road and I would come to Rose House [not the actual name]. I went to the gate and was just about to buzz when I heard Susan beeping for me. I hopped in the car. She said her friend was still in the Spar getting some things for lunch. We rode into the car park under her building. It was mostly empty, probably due to the fact that it was the middle of the workday, as well as the less than full occupancy of the building. She said that she and her husband had been looking for a flat for some time. "It was such a hassle, coming down from Dundalk." They were glad to find the place. She said that Dundalk was dangerous because it is near the border and there was a lot of IRA activity, also racism. Her husband, John, is from Dublin and wanted to leave Dundalk.

We took an elevator up to their flat, a very contemporary space with a sliding glass door off of the lounge area leading out to the entrance courtyard. John was sitting on the couch writing. We were introduced and I sat down at the dining table while Susan did some things in the back. She had a head wrap on when we met up. When she returned she was wearing the wig she often dons, so I figured that was why she had left the room. I talked to John. He told me of his time living in New York and Palm Springs.

In the meantime, Susan's friend, Nia, returned with grocery bags and we were introduced. Nia went to the kitchen. I tried to strike up a conversation with her, moving away from my talk with John. She smiled a lot. I figured I was too direct. I told her about my research and asked if she was from Lagos. She said, "No," but was not forthcoming with where she was from. I casually asked if she liked it here (I meant Ireland). She said, "Yes, it's okay." I made it clear that I was talking about Ireland. She said, "Yes, it's okay." I said, "That's a switch. Most people I talk to say it could be better." She smiled. I asked her if she lived in the building. She said, "I live here with Susan." I would later find out that she and Susan met at the hostel in Dundalk. I was not sure what Nia's immigration status was or if she was still on the books as residing in Dundalk. But, her evasiveness was not surprising. At the time, she did not know me or what consequences would come from being forthcoming about her circumstances.

Susan returned to the kitchen area and got some wine out. She asked if I would like some milk. I declined the offer. Later she mentioned, "Everyone here drinks milk. They drink so much of it. In Africa we just drink water. I like water. Milk makes my stomach bad." Nia prepared the lunch and, for a second, I wondered if she was playing the role of "maid" in the household. But, Susan said, "Oh, Nia is so good to me. She is like a mommy. She cooks for me." The wine was the very sweet Lambrusco Bianco that is served at most African events and restaurants. John asked us, "You like that crap? It's horrible, too sweet."

Before leaving for a meeting, John said to me, "You'll probably still be here when I get back." He was used to Susan and her friends spending hours together. When lunch was ready, I told Susan that I wasn't very hungry. She insisted that I eat. She said, "You have to." I knew that she meant it would be a big offense if I did not eat something. Nia, who was not having the omelet and boiled potatoes that Susan and I were lunching on, sat on the couch eating rice and meat. "She likes heavy food," Susan said. As we ate, Susan told me various stories about her life. Nia relaxed on the couch and was occasionally included in the conversation. She listened, but was not very vocal. I made attempts to include her. She was shy around me at first, but began to feel more comfortable around me as the day progressed.

Susan met John at the hostel in Dundalk where she lived and he worked. When she came into the country in May 2000, she was temporarily placed in Dublin at the hostel on Gardiner Street in the north city center. She recollected:

> When I first came here, I was so sick. I thought coming to Europe would be great. You think it's going to be perfect. Then I get here and it's rainy and so cold compared to where I'm coming from. I was so sick. I went to this doctor. I was in the waiting room. You know they are very slow here.

It takes forever for the doctor to get to you. I fell asleep. When I woke up, the doctor was calling my name. I had written it on the list at the desk. He's saying, "Susan. Susan." I looked up. Oh, he was so short I said, "How can this man be a doctor?" I thought I was still sleeping. I said, "Jesus Christ." I think he heard me. He was used to it, I think. You know, he was so short. He had the face of a man, but he was this high. (She held her hand just over a meter off of the floor to illustrate his height.)

I asked Susan if the doctor was a "dwarf." She said, "Yes. But, at the time, I thought, 'What kind of country is this?'" She continued:

He was so helpful. He gave me money, said anything I need he would help me with. . . . We became the best of friends. I was attracted to him. It did not matter that he was small. But, we were good friends. . . . When they were moving me to Dundalk, I went to him to see if there was anything he could do. But, when I got to Dundalk, I started to see that it was okay there. They took us on trips, hiking and to the mountains, things like that. So, I just decided to stay there.

Susan said she used to spend a lot of time in her room at the hostel in Dundalk. She had a television to keep her company. John, while working at the hostel, used to ask her, "Why don't you get out more?" She said they would talk about her getting out more, bantering back and forth.

One time we were in a meeting at the hostel . . . Nia and I were in charge of cooking food for the Africans and there was a suggestion that others do it too because it was too much for us to do it all the time. So, anyway, these two Nigerians were arguing over it and John said, "Some of you Nigerian women are crazy, but I am going to marry a Nigerian woman." Everyone was looking around, saying, "Who? Who?" He said, "It's Susan." So from then on we were hanging around together. But, one day we were on the bus going somewhere and he was singing this song, it sounded like an African song. I said, "What was that song you were singing? Sing it again." He said, "I can't. I just made it up." I couldn't believe him, just making it up. Well, from that moment on, I really loved him . . . I said, "I really love this guy."

When we met, Susan and John had been married six months. She showed me the wedding album. His brother from New York who owns a pub, sister who played in a band that had just toured California, and parents were in attendance. John's father, according to Susan, is a very well-

known businessman. "You mention his name. Everybody knows ———."
Susan also became very close to the owners of the hostel in Dundalk.
"They were very helpful with the wedding." She wore a traditional European gown for the ceremony and, for the reception at a local pub, dressed in a traditional Nigerian gown with headpiece which she had sent to her from Nigeria.

After lunch, we sat on the couch to watch the wedding video and look at the photos. The wedding occurred on a sunny day in Dundalk. The professionally done video features the theme songs from the American television programs *Mission: Impossible* and *Happy Days*. In typical twenty-first-century Ireland style, mobiles are ringing during the ceremony. (Someone can be heard taking a call.) Susan is very teary, and John very nervous. She told me, "I could not stop crying. I was crying everywhere. My eyes were so red." There is the traditional cutting of the tiered white cake. The still photos, mostly taken by Nia, are standard wedding party shots. I told her she could be a professional. She laughed. Susan said she still hadn't sent pictures home to her family "but they were asking for them."

WANDA

Wanda is a resident from Nigeria. She and her Irish husband had been married for two years when we first met. She came over to Ireland seeking asylum and received permanent resident status after her marriage. She and her husband were preparing for their first child:

> Some African people were telling me that "Your children are no-place if you have them with a white man . . . because you will never take them home. They will not be Irish, but they will not be African either." I say that if I want I can take them home. But, I did not want to marry an African man . . . the African men here are all crap. . . . Also, I did not want the hassle. . . . With an Irish man, it is just you and your husband and your children. You have your life. . . . In Africa, you have to deal with the whole family, his family telling you how to behave in their home and your home . . . they set the rules . . . and if they don't like you . . . if they think you are taking their brother or son away from them, they will cast spells on you . . . they will break up the marriage and you won't know what happened to the couple. One minute they are in love and everything is fine and then they are bickering over little things and he is saying that she is trying to change him . . . or sometimes family may think you are spending too much of the husband's money. They will come right into your

house and look in a pot that is boiling and say, "Oh, you have this or you have that. I want some" . . . and they will take it . . . or they may say, "Oh, she is just spending all of my brother's money. Look at her." . . . And if the husband dies, they will kick you out in the street. . . . Oh no, I could not deal with that. Unh-Unh.

Wanda says she grew up in a polygamous family. Her mother left when she was ten. "It was all just too much for my mother." So, Wanda lived with the second wife, who was introduced into the family while Wanda's mother was still in the house.

My stepmother was so mean. She did not like my mother's children. One time she pushed my little sister and broke her arm. Her arm is still bent from it. I can still hear the little girl screaming. She went to live with my mother after that. . . . It was so hard being a little kid and not being able to do anything about the bad treatment. . . . When we were older, we did not even speak to my father. We lived in the same house and said few words.

She lived at home until coming to Ireland. She ran a business out of her home before emigrating. Wanda, still speaking of life back home in Nigeria and the freedom life in Ireland offers her, recollected talking to her grandmother about a sister-in-law:

This woman [sister-in-law] is the type to take care of her husband's every needs, bathing him, everything. . . . When you come to visit her, forty-five minutes later she has a big mean spread out for you. . . . She is amazing, she does things I could never do, but my grandmother was spreading rumors that she was a bad person. I said, "Grandmother, why do you say those things about that woman? She cooks, cleans. She works so hard. She does things that I could never do!" My grandmother said, "Oh, Wanda, you don't understand . . ." I said, "Grandmother, what is to understand? You cannot marry your son. This woman does everything for him." I said, "Grandmother, you are fucking crazy. Leave this woman alone." Well, my sister-in-law came to me later and thanked me. She said, "I don't understand what I have done wrong." I told her not to worry about it, just "marry your husband," I said, "Marry your husband." . . . Well, after that, the family introduced him to a second wife. They brought her around and now they see that she does not do anything and they see how good the other wife is and now they want to break it off. I said, "You introduced her into the family. You began a process and you can't go back on it. Let him marry her. Let him marry her. You get what you deserve." They say, "Oh, Wanda, you just say what's on your mind." I do.

LELA

Lela, a Nigerian immigrant seeking asylum, casually talks about people casting spells.

I was raised as a Christian and do not know how to cast spells. But, I believe it happens all the time. I want to open a restaurant. But, I do not want drinking in the place because I am a Christian. [I ask her about the Lambrusco she's drinking.] Wine is okay and people can bring wine. I just don't want the drunks in there. I want an Irish and African restaurant, where different kinds of people can come together and eat. Irish food and African food.

AN EVENING WITH SAMMY

Sammy rang me on his mobile at 7 PM, as planned, to meet up at a chosen destination. I chose Forum, the Nigerian-owned bar at the corner near my flat. When I arrived, he was not present. I sat at the bar, ordered a Guinness, and nodded at three gents seated at the end of the bar (two Africans and a European, reflecting the usual multiethnic mix at Forum). Sammy arrived shortly after. He sat next to me and I ordered a Guinness for him. It was my treat and the last of the night. He insisted on paying for the rest and I let him, despite an occasional light protest on my part. It was clearly a matter of honor and persisting would have offended him, as the overarching theme of the evening was the quest for self-reliance and the "doing for self" of the Igboman.

We moved to the back of the bar so that we could hear each other better. Much of the discussion centered on Sammy's quest for a wife. But, in the midst of his longing, he outlined several needs of the Igbo man and aspects of the social structure of Igbo life. In the case of marriage, he explained in detail why, despite his desire to marry an Igbo woman, he could never marry an Igbo woman who came to Ireland. I'll get to these points, but first I should mention that he stated that, of the Nigerian population in Ireland, the Igbo are very few and that if the Igbo had been the first Africans to come to Ireland in large numbers, rather than the Yoruba, the Irish would treat blacks differently. He believes that there is a particular quality inherent to the Igbo that the Yoruba do not possess. He explained that this could be understood through language. But, if one does not understand the language, he said one could get a bit of this understanding through close proximity to the Igbo. He believes that Igbo people "do not push as much as Yoruba people."

In the midst of this discussion, he mentioned the abundance of African women with babies in Ireland. He explained that this is for residency issues and said, "It is all too much. Having babies to stay in the country is too much." Near us was a table of young Yoruba women. Sammy said, "I could never approach them, because they would only think I want to marry them and have a baby to stay in Ireland. I could never achieve success by using a woman, but this is what some women may think."[5]

Returning to the qualities that an Igbo man looks for in a woman and the reasons Sammy cannot marry an Igbo woman who has migrated to Ireland, he explained:

> A woman must, first and foremost, make a man happy by caring about his problems. Igbo do not travel much and if an Igbo woman travels here, she would not feel the need to involve herself in her husband's problems because she would consider his problems his own, not hers . . . because he did not bring her here. She came here on her own. A lot of Nigerian women want to be like Irish women. They want to do what they want to do and they forget about the man who loves them.

Sammy moved to the next quality a woman must possess: humility. "A woman must be humble," he said. "She should ask her husband's permission to do certain things and if he says 'no,' she should obey. But, an Igbo woman who comes here on her own would feel she did not need to ask her husband, because he did not bring her to Ireland. A woman should be willing to be a wife." I asked Sammy what he meant by "be a wife." He said, "To be a wife she must make her man happy and be humble."

We talked for about three hours. He got additional pints. The atmosphere was hip and youthful. Sammy received a couple of calls on his mobile from a friend who was selling a car on the street outside the bar. "The insurance was not granted to him for the make of car he had because they said he was too young for a cheaper rate, so he's selling it." [Individuals under the age of twenty-five pay more for insurance.] Sammy said, "Sometimes people just buy a cheap car and don't get the insurance. When the *gardai* [police] pull them over, they just walk away from the car."

Before we left, a group celebrating a birthday came into the bar. Adding to the multicultural mix, they were Spanish and sang along to the Ibiza club mixes playing over the music system broadcasting British MTV in stereo. Sammy waited for me at the door while I spoke to one of the co-owners.

Next, we went over to Eternity [not the actual name], a store by day with an informal restaurant and bar in the back. Sammy said that when the owner's wife is around, there is food served. But, she was, he thought, away in Nigeria. We went in through the store and into the back area. I said "hello" to the men in the back. The place was not crowded. Sammy spoke Igbo with the men and told me the place was closed for the evening. We said "goodbye" and left. As we were walking down Parnell Street Sammy saw two friends coming out of a building, a Nigerian man and white Irish woman. Sammy and the man spoke in Igbo. Sammy said he wanted to stop by "this place" to see the friend who had been calling him (re: the car sale). We went into the building and up to the second floor. Sammy led me ahead and I walked in first. The apartment was a typical older Dublin studio with a small kitchen area with a miniature refrigerator, a bed, couch, and small bathroom off of the kitchen space. Everyone greeted me. A Nigerian named Shakur was on the couch watching Alan Parker's *Mississippi Burning,* the film about the FBI and the American civil rights era. Two white Irish women were sitting on the bed. I was introduced to all. Carl, the resident of the flat, was sitting with one of the women, his girlfriend. Terrance, who was selling the car, came in later and sat with the other Irish woman, his girlfriend. Carl offered me a drink. I said beer was fine. Sammy and I sat on a sinking couch next to Shakur. I was given a large can of beer that turned out to be cider.

Terrance asked me where I was from, then noted that he sounded like Irish people "because all they ever ask is 'Where are you from? Where are you from?'" Sammy, who often takes photographs at Igbo weddings and other events, had his camera with him. Pictures were taken of all of us. Carl had a state-of-the-art stereo system and American R&B and rap CDs. We all hung out in the flat until two in the morning.

Besides the fact that "hanging out" often leads to a trip to a local African establishment or a club, this was a very typical Dublin evening for young immigrants (and most of the immigrant population was in their twenties, which was no oddity in Dublin, a city with a large youth and young adult population) who have access to a flat and additional funds. African friends and members of one's ethnic group would often provide a space and help out those who are not in a good financial situation or are in need of housing (either as residents or as a respite from life in the B&B/accommodation center). Some individuals seeking asylum supplemented their state allowance with "off the books" work, others rotated funds amongst themselves, some had resident status and were legally able to work, and some received financial help from the homeland. For some individuals (male and female) courting an Irish partner not only offered companionship, but could lead to resident status as a result of marriage and/or parenthood.

GEORGE

George is a businessman, who traded electronics between Ghana and Nigeria before coming to Ireland. But, in Ireland, he worked in a factory, off the books.

> My mother is Ghanaian and my father is Nigerian. I'm a businessman. Most Igbo go into business. We like to work for ourselves. . . . I went through Istanbul and Brussels to get to Dublin. Because my mother is Ghanaian, I put Ghana on my asylum application. But, people here know that I am an Igboman regardless of what it says on my application. . . . You know, people come [to Ireland] for many reasons. People come to get away from witchcraft or the feeling that something is not right. Sometimes they hope to return home when the person that put bad luck on them leaves or dies.

While George discussed spells, I thought of an interview with Markie, an IT worker who is of Nigerian (Igbo) and Cape Verdean parentage, who said, "I don't believe in the Igbo witchcraft. It's just an excuse for something bad happening. It only has power over you if you believe that it does."

NICOLETTE

Nicolette is a Congolese immigrant. When we met, she was studying English at a refugee center run by a Christian organization. During our discussion, which consisted of a combination of my broken French and her broken English, she told me that she was concerned about the type of English she is learning. She said that she was sorry that she is learning English in Ireland because she does not want to have an Irish accent. Nicolette said, "The best English is America and London. . . . Also I do not want to speak like Nigerians. Their English, it does not sound good."

DAVIS AND I AT ETERNITY

I set up a meeting with Davis, a Nigerian immigrant who is seeking asylum, at a local hangout, Eternity [not the actual name], to discuss life in Dublin. Eternity, a Nigerian-owned store/barbershop/restaurant on Parnell Street, has an underground quality that makes it the alter-versions of the Nigerian-owned grocery shop, Tropical Store, and Jean's restaurant (Jean, a Congolese immigrant, ran a restaurant on Moore Street). While Jean had a late-night scene behind the half-closed gate that "those in the know" slipped under, Eternity seemed very underground and extra-legal. In fact, except for the front and middle sections, it was not licensed for food and alcoholic beverage sales. One had to walk a gauntlet to get to the backroom and, though I never experienced it, I suspected some potential customers got stopped before they made it to the fourth door. The first door was the one you entered from Parnell Street. Then you walked through a dusty foyer/short hallway and on your left was the door into the shop. You entered and shelves filled with hair products (oils, shampoos, relaxers, and weaves) blocked your vision. Voices could be heard coming from your left, but you couldn't see anyone; they were on the other side of the shelves dealing with customers. If you looked to your right, there were a few steps leading up to a windowed door into the barbershop area, which you could see into from the shop because it was behind a thin wall with large Plexiglas windows. Often, the barbershop door was open and you could see into the small space, consisting of barber chairs and several men, mostly Yoruba, talking amongst themselves. Mostly, the men in the barber shop ignored a woman who entered alone; usually out of respect (just in case you were the partner of one of the other men present) or, as one woman told me, "because they may not feel you're worth noticing."

There was a smell of marijuana in the barber area. The odor was coming from behind the fourth door, which was closed, but opened frequently as people went in and out. Behind the fourth door was a large room with a snooker table, tables and chairs, a small kitchen with an open serving window, and a booth toward the back with a mirror window. Davis told me, "[The booth is] where they smoke marijuana. . . . The owner does not like it if they smoke out here." Regardless, the smell of marijuana from the booth filled the room. The snooker table was right in front, nearly blocking the doorway. Men were crowded around playing, talking loudly, joking. Big plates of rice with meat and sauce on top were being served through the kitchen window. Customers got their own drinks out of the front shop or walked into the kitchen where there was a stack of drinks. The owner's wife, Nella, took the money and served the food. She also bussed tables and handled the general upkeep of the backroom. While I was there, a woman came in with a few men. She spoke to someone and left. The rest of the crowd, except for Nella and me, were men. There were approximately twenty African men sitting and standing around throughout the backroom, with others coming and going. Some men smoked in the mirrored booth, some showed up and sat down with plates of food, and others argued and joked around the snooker table.

Eternity is unofficially a men's club and, more specifically, a place for Nigerian men. Most are Yoruba, as the owner is Yoruba. Davis is Igbo and pointed out that there were a few other Igbo men there. He introduced me to his Igbo friend, Bob, who was wearing a big Philadelphia Flyers jersey and sipping a malt drink. Davis said that he does not like the food at Eternity because he does not like the way the Yoruba make the sauce. He said, "It is different from Igbo cooking because [the Yoruba] use more pepper and oil."

We were right across from the television, which had the *MTV Select Show* playing. The latest hits from Westlife, Britney Spears, and Jennifer Lopez (J-Lo) flickered from the screen and filled the room with music. Davis and I were near the mirrored booth and I noticed a sign remained on the mirrored window announcing a New Year's Eve party (New Year's Eve had been three months before). I pointed it out to Davis. He laughed. Davis told me he was about to hit his one-year anniversary in Ireland. He had come in April 2000. We talked about his life in Dublin.

> It's boring here because I can't work. I don't know when it's going to work out with my application [for asylum]. . . . I live in a hostel with about twenty others. They are from three to four in a room. There are five or six other Nigerians there and some from the Congo, Ghana, Cameroon, and South Africa. And some Romanians. . . . I'm in a small town. We go to the pub. People are friendly, but it is difficult to meet Irish girls. They are shy with blacks. . . . The Irish are not very exposed. Sometimes there are problems if the Irish guys think you're going to take their girlfriends. . . . But, some Irish guys are okay. We do not have problems. I have Irish friends.

Davis went to the front and got us some beers. They were large 500-ml bottles. I wanted to try the Nigerian beer, a lager called Gulder (a beer imported by Nigerian import/export agents in Dublin). He got a Guinness for himself.[6] Davis brought some glasses to our table and told me that he has a sister who is a quality control officer for Gulder. "She came to Ireland a few months back on a business trip to the Guinness offices." Another sister is an accountant in Lagos. "I have a younger brother who is in his last year of school and preparing for exams in Nigeria." Davis said he would like to own a "high fashion boutique." I remembered when I first met him, he was wearing a designer suit and I noticed that he had a keen sense of fashion. Weeks later it became evident that, while it was a nice suit, it was his only suit and he wore it to most events. He, like most asylum seekers, immigrants and students, had come to Ireland with very few possessions.

While we talked, Davis received a few calls on his mobile. A friend came over and listed some numbers for him. I asked if it was a betting game, as in "playing the numbers." He said with a laugh, "I don't gamble. I always lose." Earlier I had asked him if he won anything at snooker. He said, "When I bet, I always lose. So, I don't bet." (I would later find out from five other informants that a numbers/lottery game was being run out of the location, as well as some marijuana sales.)

We left Eternity and headed down Parnell Street. A friend in Canada rang Davis's mobile. He spoke in Igbo with a few words of English. "Dublin is Dublin. Same old same old . . . Nothing happens . . . Trying to get by . . ." Davis had told me earlier that he would like to move to Canada someday.

CLIFFORD

Clifford, a Nigerian asylum seeker who would like to take a computer training course, talked about his work experiences and the more controversial, albeit underground, aspect of seeking asylum. He said, "People are just coming here to work. Any Igbo would want to come here to make money so that they can return with a lot of money and start a business . . . usually import/export." He said that people will say, "'My father was killed, my mother was murdered'" but "it is all a lie. They want to make money and go back home." He said, "Yoruba people will stay. But, Igbo people are here to make a lot of money with a plan to return home. . . . People work here with foreign passports or marry someone so they can get papers." Regarding a recently married couple, he said, "You can make a lot of money in Germany. Michael [Nigerian husband of Elena, a German IT worker] did well here, but he needed the German passport. So, that's why he is with Elena."

Clifford then spoke about using a cousin's German passport to obtain employment in Ireland.

> I don't want a permanent job or to register with an agency because then they would have a picture and file on me, and if Immigration found I was working, I would be deported. So, I don't want any problems, until I get my papers . . . I take a job and work for a few weeks or months and if the employer says he wants to make me permanent, I don't go back to work.

I'm gone. If the employer tries to reach you for work again, you change the number or you just say it is a wrong number. If he keeps calling, you say, "Hey, I told you, there is no Harry here, it's a wrong number. You better check your number."

Clifford said that he got his driver's license in Waterford because it was easier to use fraudulent documents. "In a small town, they look at your papers and they don't know anything. It's easier." He then told me about a friend of his, Todd, who was working and putting money in a bank account:

> He had about 3000 pounds in his account. Every morning a group of Africans board a bus on Parnell to go to jobs in different factories. The *garda* control the bus [took over the bus] and ask for everyone's asylum identification. They got Todd's bank card and found out that he had 3000 in the bank, which he wasn't supposed to have. He's an asylum seeker and he got money in the bank, right? Then, they found out that he was registered with an agency. I told him it was not a good idea to register. The *garda* investigated him. They found out that he had fake papers. They were going to deport him. So, we sent money to a friend of mine in Canada for a ticket, so he could fly into Dublin. Then, Todd flew to Canada with [the friend's] passport and my friend returned home later with a Canadian ID.[7]

Clifford said that Todd might attempt to return to Dublin.

Clifford entered the country with a German passport. He went through Ghana and flew to the Ivory Coast, and then to Paris, where he made a connection to Dublin. "I paid money so they would not ask me questions when I left [Nigeria]. I thought I'd have problems in Paris if I was asked to speak German. But, I didn't have a problem. When I arrived here, I got rid of my German passport. Sometimes I work with a French passport."

Clifford continued, "I never dreamed of coming to Ireland. When I received the chance to do it, I asked people in my village and other villages if they'd ever heard of Dublin. They didn't know it. When I call home some people say 'Dublin? Where?' So, I just say London and they say, 'Oh, London. Okay.'"

Clifford said, "Dublin is the last stop in Europe." He waited a long time to come abroad. "In 1995, I tried to go and had no luck. I kept wondering when my time would come . . . but I tell people, 'delay is not denial.' . . . I do not rush things." He discussed his mother's evangelist having a vision:

The evangelist told my mother that he had a vision that I was going to get on a plane with a briefcase and then get off again and wave goodbye. At the time my mother did not know I was thinking of leaving. When she told me about her evangelist, I laughed and told her I was thinking of going . . . I was planning to go to Canada and on the way to the Canadian Embassy in Lagos, the bus I was traveling in had a head-on collision. People were killed and injured, but I did not have a mark on me. . . . From then on I knew a god existed.

He attends church in Dublin, but says he does not believe everything the preacher says "because I still go to parties and clubs."

Clifford talked about what he considers to be the difference between the Igbo and Yoruba:

The Yoruba cannot be trusted. In the 1966 war, the Yoruba betrayed the Igbo.[8] Yoruba will open up businesses here, like you see in Parnell [Street], but you would never see an Igboman doing that anywhere in the world. An Igbo man would make money and bring it back home. Many Yoruba left after the Biafran war and went to London and never returned. The Yoruba will set up a home and family and never go back, while the Igbo is always planning to go back. . . . I understand some Yoruba and I know when they're talking against me. At home and here, if a Yoruba wants to say something about you he will speak in Yoruba. . . . The Yoruba act superior and only when you have as much money as he does, will he be your friend. . . . Because the Igbo, we like to have a big house and car and impress each other, you know, invite you to stay in their home. Sometimes [the Yoruba] get jealous of you and will try to do things to get you in trouble or something. You cannot trust the Yoruba.

NICK

Nick, a resident from Nigeria, is a successful local businessman with enterprises serving immigrant and Irish communities. He is Yoruba and discussed his commitment to crossing national and ethnic lines within Dublin's African Diaspora community:

There are no major divisions among the Nigerians in Ireland. . . . In Lagos, we have a lot of diversity. But, with other nationalities, I do see a division. Angolans and Zairians keep amongst themselves. . . . The language barriers often separate the communities. Francophone Africans have it more difficult because of the language barrier and the French way of doing things is different from the English, and in Ireland it's more the English way. . . . Some Francophone people see me as more approachable and will invite me to parties. When I show up, they say, "Hey, he really came." You will not see another English-speaking person there. . . . At Nigerian parties you may see a South African, but you will not see a Zairian. . . . The groups need to reach out to each other more and network more. If an Angolan has great information, a Nigerian will not hear about it or it will take a long time for that information to get to him. . . . I would like to develop more events which bring the communities together to talk about problems or each other's experiences. We tried a football match between two nations last year, with Zaire versus Nigeria at Fairview (a local park). They had music. But, it rained, which spoiled the event.

A SAINT PATRICK'S DAY

I met Roland at Forum around half past eight. Roland, an accountant and entrepreneur, is an Irish resident who came from Nigeria to set up his import/export business in 1996 before the beginning of significant African migration to Ireland. He worked in the main accounting department of a well-known Irish chain of stores. "When I first came here, there were very few of us. I knew a few guys from back home. That's it. Now, it's very different and all these Irish guys think you're an asylum seeker. I tell them I work in an office. I came here to start a business, not be an asylum seeker. They don't believe me."

The atmosphere in Forum was rather mellow, considering it was St. Patrick's Day. The parade had been canceled due to Foot and Mouth Disease spreading throughout England, Northern Ireland, and the northern Republic. So, the usual amount of revelers was not spilling into the pubs. However, it was early, and a multicultural jazz band was set up in the back of the bar, preparing to play their first set at 10 PM. This was the first Saint Patrick's Day at Forum which, before it was bought and remodeled by two Nigerian entrepreneurs, had been a traditional-looking Irish pub. Instead of booths, wood paneling, and small windows, the place now had large windows, comfortable lounge chairs and couches, mood lighting, and a sleekly designed bar with contemporary stools. Over the past few years in Ireland, the multicultural spirit, as seen in Forum, had been reflected throughout the Saint Patrick's Day Parade; African dance and music have been included along with the traditional bagpipes and giant mums pushing prams. However, this would have to wait until May, when the parade finally occurred. The belated event would turn out to be a weekend-long celebration with a kick-off featuring a march of Dublin's high school students, who represented many spaces beyond Ireland, including African nations.

Roland and I had a drink and chatted with one of the co-owners of Forum. Roland said a friend of his wanted to know if we would like to come to his flat in Donnybrook (south of Dublin city center). Roland said he had brought his car, which he had purchased a few months before and used as a taxi to "occasionally pick up extra change." He said he mainly "bought the taxi plate as an investment." The plan was that we would hang out at his friend's place and when his friend's girlfriend arrived, we'd all go out to a pub.

While we were having our drinks, Roland slipped out to check on his car. It was parked in a yellow zone and he wanted to move it. When he came back, he told me, "A drunk woman in Parnell Street wanted a taxi. I said I was off duty. She yelled, 'You black bastard!' After she said that, I thought 'Now, I'm really not going to take you.'" He said that he got in the car and waved for her to come around to the other side, as if he were going to go on duty for her. Just before she could open the door, he put his foot on the gas pedal and drove off. The car was now parked on North Great George's Street, near my flat. He took the taxi sign off the top.[9]

We left Forum and drove to Donnybrook, where we met his friend, Marcus, a resident from Nigeria who had lived in Ireland for twenty years. Roland tapped on the basement window so that Marcus would come up to the parlor level of the apartment house and let us in. We walked through the hall toward a basement. A white Irish man was entering his flat. Marcus spoke to him. Roland and I said "hello" and followed Marcus to the dilapidated basement. The flat was a small studio—not quite a bedsit—with a low ceiling. There was a sink, stove, and refrigerator in the room. The bathroom was outside in the hall and only contained a toilet. The shower and bathtub were off of the upstairs hallway and shared by the building residents.

Roland and I sat on the couch. I noticed a picture of the Beatles circa 1965 (before the hair became genuinely long in their hippie phase). I asked Marcus if he was a fan. He said, "No, I use it to cover the fireplace." The fireplace was not functional and let in a draft if not covered. He also had posters of Bob Marley and Malcolm X on the corner walls near the window and a large poster of Tupac Shakur over his bed. Pamela Anderson's poster was behind the front door. Marcus had an extensive collection of videotapes (at least one hundred). "I love to tape documentaries. I like to keep up with politics." He had a top-of-the-line wide-screen television, which he connected to an equally state-of-the-art stereo system.

The technology was the center of the space, while everything else in the room read as poverty (e.g., small space, sunken couch, worn plumbing and utility fixtures).

Marcus was unemployed and having trouble securing a job. He came to Dublin to study marketing and then stayed on to pursue legal studies. At the time of our meeting, he was having difficulty finding work in the legal profession and had been depressed. He explained:

> Twenty years ago, it was so different. There was no money here. Everyone was the same. They treated you well. Twenty years ago, I wanted to spend the rest of my life here. . . . Now, they think you're an asylum seeker or a refugee. . . . It is a different Ireland . . . I feel like the farmers with the foot and mouth problems must feel. It is psychologically difficult. You have your sheep and everything is fine and then all of a sudden everything changes.

However, Marcus also said that "If Roland and I . . . if we had come now, we could have had an accounting firm. This guy drives a cab, because we can't get anything. We could have had a big firm. Right, Roland?" Roland nodded and said a soft, "Yes."[10]

Marcus's neighbor, Paul, the white Irish man we had seen when we entered the apartment house, stopped by the apartment. Paul is originally from Limerick, but he lived in London and Paris for six years. He had just come back and was working for *Iarnród Éireann* (Irish Rail). For a while, we all discussed a new book on the hidden aspects of government bureaucracy in Ireland. Then, while we watched a series of Tina Turner videos that Marcus had taped, Paul took out a sugar cube–sized amount of hash wrapped in cling film, warmed it with a lighter and began to roll it with tobacco. He and Marcus smoked. Roland passed on it. They offered me some. I passed, too. Next, we watched a political satire about a variety of Irish characters that go to New York's Saint Patrick's Day parade. Marcus was excited about the satire and knew each political reference. "That guy's supposed to be Gerry Adams!"

While we sat around, Marcus cooked a Nigerian dish of rice, chicken, and tomatoes. Paul and I passed on it. Marcus knew I was a vegetarian and offered me rice. But I had eaten already. Roland ate a big plate. I nursed a whiskey (Marcus kept an ample supply of Irish whiskey in his flat). After Marcus and Roland ate, Marcus rolled some more hash. Paul asked me if I liked Fela Kuti, the late Nigerian political music superstar. Paul is a big Fela fan and talked passionately about Fela's early music influences, including the jazz he liked in 1960s London. Marcus joined in on the discussion of the art, craft, and politics of Fela Kuti. He had every album, cassette tape, and CD and Paul came over frequently to partake of the collection. Fela's music is a powerful hybrid of jazz, African rhythms, big band–style orchestrated instrumentals, and a free jam style that brings a psychedelic Grateful Dead–like quality to it. As "Original Suffer Head" played, Roland gave me the standard English translation of the lyrics in Yoruba, Nigerian pidgin, and slang, some of which I already knew. Paul, though Irish, did not need the translation. He was well versed in things Fela.

Paul asked Marcus if he liked the hash. Marcus did. Roland said it looked lighter in color than usual. Paul said it was made from a lighter part of the plant and noted, "Years ago, you would know what kind of hash you were getting, especially Moroccan." Marcus said, "The good African hash does not come to Ireland. The African market mainly goes to the US." Paul said, "Some people cut the hash with cleaning fluid and other things." Roland interjected, "If you know that, you shouldn't be smoking it." This discussion turned to a current high-profile Irish drug/murder trial, the Gilligan case. John Gilligan was accused of drug trafficking and the murder of journalist Veronica Guerin. He was convicted on the drug counts, but the murder could not be proved. Marcus played a videotape about the Gilligan case that had been broadcast on RTÉ earlier in the week. There were shots of large amounts of hash and bundles of money. Marcus rewound the tape and paused on the shot of the money. While looking at the paused shot of rolls of Irish pounds, Marcus shouted, "Look at that! They wanted more! That is just greed. Just greed!"

We surfed through some television channels and settled on St. Patrick's Day sports coverage. Marcus, Roland, and Paul laughed about the shamrocks on the lapels of the commentators. Paul joked, "Marijuana has been legalized."

Paul packed up his fags and hash, finished his whiskey, and bid us goodnight around eleven. We made plans to head out to a club around half past eleven and Marcus rang his girlfriend to arrange our meeting, as she had to get a baby-sitter and was not able to come to his house. Marcus and his girlfriend, who is Irish, have a daughter. They live separately. We were talking about the New York Saint Patrick's Day parade and Marcus said, "I was watching the parade and a black guy said that he was Irish and that he may not look like it to you but he has Irish ancestors." Marcus continued, "Maybe someday, ten, twenty years from now, there will be blacks here saying 'I'm Irish.' Maybe my daughter will. But, she is really Nigerian."

Before we left, the discussion led to Eternity [not the actual name], the Nigerian-owned shop on Parnell Street. Marcus said that he and the owner of Eternity came to Ireland around the same time twenty years ago. "But, [the owner of Eternity] is only about business." Marcus complained that when he and Roland last went into the shop, the owner sold Roland a yam that was bad. Roland said it was bad, but believed that, in all fairness, the owner told him it was not good and only charged him 4 pounds because it was bad. Roland said, "I didn't mind. I just wanted to give this guy my business." Marcus said, "Well, this guy should not give you a discount on a bad yam. He should have given it to you for less than four pounds." Roland said, "Business is business. He's a nice guy. It was only four pounds. He said there was a rotten spot on it, so he was only going to charge me four pounds instead of six. I just wanted to give him my business." Marcus appeared to view it as a moral wrong. "We came here together. . . . He just wants to make money. . . . If it is rotten, you don't just sell it for four pounds." The yam discussion would have gone on longer. But it was time to leave.

The three of us got into Roland's car and headed toward Walkinstown, a County Dublin suburb about five miles southwest of the city center and reflective of the urban/suburban sprawl the Dublin region has become. We arrived at the Red Cow Inn and the adjoining club, Club Diva. Clubbers were hanging out in the car park and queuing up to go inside the venue. We got out of the car and a white Irish woman came toward us. She said, "Perfect timing." It was Miriam, Marcus's girlfriend. Marcus, Miriam, and Roland stood around looking hesitant about going into the club. I waited for a decision to be made. Marcus got back in the car, saying the crowd was too young. Roland said to me, "He thinks there may be some trouble if the crowd is young." Marcus explained, "When you go to a club, you want to mix with other people. If they are too young, there will be no conversation." Roland later said, "We could have a good time with each other at the club. . . . Marcus gets scared something is going to happen, that there will be trouble. He was beat a few times by some young ones and just doesn't want trouble. So he makes up an excuse."[11]

We left the club parking lot. Marcus got into Miriam's car and Roland and I followed them to another locale of Dublin sprawl, Tallaght; a town that had a negative reputation at the time because of the high crime rate on the west side. A few weeks before our visit, Dublin Bus had stopped running through several housing estates in the area after bus drivers were beaten.[12] Mostly Tallaght is typically suburban, with all of the townhouses looking the same. We pulled into the car park of a local Gaelic Athletic

Association (GAA) club.[13] As we walked toward the front door of the contemporarily designed club, I heard a Beatles medley playing. I looked toward an upstairs window, where the main activity was, and saw a guitarist strumming. Miriam said, almost apologetically, "There's a guitarist on now" and added, "But he'll be finished soon."

It was after midnight when we entered the first-floor lobby. We were introduced to Miriam's father, who was leaving, and headed upstairs to the Saint Patrick's Day party that was taking place in a large lodge-like space with high wooden beams. The open room was filled with club members of all ages; all Irish, all white. Teenagers hung out in corners with Bacardi Breezers and Smirnoff Ice drinks while their parents looked on, pints of Guinness and lagers in hand. It was an all family St. Patrick's Day gathering. We ordered pints of Guinness and followed Miriam through the crowd to a place where some friends of hers were sitting. A man gave me his seat. Miriam is no longer a member, but her family is, and people know her so she said there was no problem being admitted, as GAA membership would normally be required. It was unclear how much negotiation took place before we came in or whether any of it involved a concern about "race."

Miriam introduced us to her friends and then, in a mock pout, mentioned that they were getting ready for a holiday in Spain and she could not go. Marcus asked why she couldn't go. She turned to Marcus and, referring to their daughter, said, "Because I have a fourteen-month-old baby to take care of." I said, "Marcus, you can take care of the baby." Pretending he could not understand such a request, he responded, "I do not speak . . . I do not speak Gaelic." There was laughter. But, it was apparent that Marcus, even after twenty years away from Nigeria, preferred the more traditional role of Nigerian men (albeit other nationalities, as well) and maintained limited involvement with the day-to-day care of his small child. Miriam appeared exasperated, but not surprised by Marcus's response.

Roland, Marcus, and I—three black individuals—were an oddity in the GAA club. Tim, a friend of Miriam's family, got very close to me and asked, "Do you like the Guinness?" I said, "Who wouldn't?" He said, "That is no answer. I asked if you like the Guinness. Now, if I ask you 'Do you like Guinness?' what do you say?'" I said, "Yes." He said, "Right. You said, 'Who wouldn't?' That's bullshit." He seemed annoyed (and rather intoxicated). But he moved away. Next, he spoke to Roland, who had already told him he was from Nigeria. Tim asked if Roland was in school. Roland said he had finished school a long time ago. Tim asked him again, "Where are you from?" Roland said, "I told you I am from Nigeria." Tim said, "Is there a problem asking you twice?" Roland ignored the question. Tim asked, "Why did you come here from Nigeria?" Roland smiled and said, "That is a private matter."

A teenager who remembered Marcus from a prior visit to the club came over to us and said, "Hey, man. How are you doing?" He greeted Roland and me as well and offered a 1970s soul-style handshake with a thumbs-up. The Irish teenager's display was somewhat exaggerated, but it was apparent that he believed that it was the appropriate greeting for black individuals.

We stood for the Irish national anthem at the end of the evening. This was timely for me, because the night before I had heard a late-night radio program with a listener call-in about clubs deciding the tradition of playing the anthem at closing was outdated and that "kids today talk through the anthem." It was also mentioned, "If a bunch of British lads on a stag holiday don't stand, regardless of the reason, it can lead to a brawl with some Irish lads." So, there we stood. Marcus leaned a bit. Roland was slow to get up. I put my pint down. A few lads could be seen balancing full pints as they moved through the crowd to their table, completely disinterested in the anthem. *"Sinne Fianna Fáil A tá fé gheall ag Éirinn . . ."* [*Soldiers are we whose lives are pledged to Ireland . . .*]. At the anthem's end, Roland, Marcus, and I, along with most of the other GAA members, cheered and clapped.

Before leaving, a woman came up to us. She enthusiastically shook each of our hands and wished us a happy St. Patrick's Day. Assuming there would be a language barrier, she spoke slowly, taking care to make eye contact and enunciate. It became apparent that she was not only offering holiday wishes. She was welcoming us to the country.

NATHALIE

Nathalie is a Congolese immigrant. She was awaiting word on her asylum application.

> I go to English classes. I speak Lingala and French. I like the classes because I want to have a restaurant in Ireland. I'll make food from home and have Irish people and Africans eating in the restaurant. Maybe outside Dublin. It is difficult to start something here. But, I can do it.

MELVIN

Melvin, a second-level (high school) student from Nigeria, at age twenty is older than his classmates. His classmates, though, are unaware of this because he is small in stature and resembles someone younger than twenty. He and his sister came to Dublin from Nigeria. Melvin is preparing to take exams and study engineering at an Irish university. During the time of our discussion, second-level teachers were on strike and there were complaints that students in their final year would not be prepared to take exams for the leaving certificate (similar to the U.S. high school diploma) and university placement.

> I study a lot now, with exams coming. But, I am confident I will do well. Some students say they won't do well because of the strike, but those are the ones who don't study anyway, you know. I had some trouble with English. I'm good at science. So, the teacher is going to help me with English so that it doesn't affect my university plans. . . . When I'm not studying, I play computer games and call friends on the phone or I e-mail them. Sometimes I go to clubs with friends. I have some Irish friends from school. But clubs are expensive, so I stay home a lot. Sometimes my sister and I go to church.

KUNLE THE ARTIST[14]

I first met Kunle, a resident from Nigeria with a recently accepted asylum application, at the Anti-Racism Campaign (ARC) "Asylum Blues" fund-raiser gig. He was there to perform his poetry, inspired by his life as an immigrant in Ireland. I introduced myself and we talked for a long time. He is very vocal and "not afraid of anything," he said. He was angry about the "Lift the Iraqi Sanctions" movement being discussed at the event. Kunle, who is Yoruba, said, "The Muslims have wreaked havoc in my home country of Nigeria. Their belief that they are superior and no one can rise above them is the problem." He was referring to the Hausa. He stepped on the stage of the smoke-filled venue, sat on a chair, and performed his poetry for the crowd. The audience listened intently. A few folks talked during the presentation, as they were too intoxicated to acknowledge the silence around them and also too intoxicated to sit in silence.

We met for an interview in Rathgars (South Dublin) several days after the ARC gig. We had seen each other in passing earlier in the day on Moore Street. He was en route to a meeting with the leader of the Angolan Community Association to get information for a website he was developing. I was en route to a meeting with the Nigerian owners of a new internet business. We said we'd see each other later.

Later, I walked to the Harold Cross Road and, via mobile, Kunle gave me directions to an area not far from his home. "Pass the post office and you will see me. Okay? I see you now. Do you see the yellow sign? I am across from it." Kunle lives in a small studio. It was chilly inside, as there was not much heat. When we entered the hallway of the building, I smelled spices. The aroma was coming from his flat, where he was cooking a Nigerian stew. He later offered me some and I expressed surprise at his cooking a meal, as it was afternoon and we were merely meeting over tea. He said, "In Nigeria, it is common for people not to ask you to dinner and to surprise you with a meal when you arrive." We talked about food a while; vegetarianism, cooking styles, his gaining weight after eating too much pork in Ireland and having "to cut it out."

Kunle said he left Nigeria for two main reasons: (1) "I do not believe in Nigeria. It was artificially formed and is really several nations," and (2) "I am tired of the corruption." He explained:

There are pay-offs and evil everywhere in the world. So, I left for a "lesser evil." Ireland is a lesser evil. In Nigeria, I had to pay police at roadblocks. One Sunday, a day when there are usually no police blocks, while on a bus to Lagos, the bus was stopped and the driver paid the police. When we drove on, I stuck my head out the window and shouted to the police, "Thief! Thief!" Two kilometers down the road, the cops pulled us over. The people on the bus were frightened and pointed at me, "You started this! You!" It was one cop who took me off of the bus. The cop brought us back to the police blockade up the road. He says, "What did you say?" I said, "What did you hear?" I was slapped. Seven officers were standing around me. I was not afraid of them, I was just very annoyed after being slapped and I told one of the officers that he had no right to slap me and I said, "I have your badge number and I'm going to police headquarters when I arrive in Lagos." Well, the one in charge apologized and they placed me on the next bus. What bothered me most is that no one on the bus stood up for me. It was a whole busload of people against one cop. They could have killed him and said, "let's go." People don't stand together in Nigeria. They just want to avoid conflict and anyone who stands up for his rights is considered a troublemaker. I have friends who have to pay people off to get phone lines. At least in Ireland, when you want a phone, you sign a contract, put a deposit down, and your phone is on. I have a friend in Nigeria who was given a number but the line was not hooked up for months later. So, the process had begun, but no one was accountable. This is the problem all over Africa, pay-offs, corruption. I once went through Benin en route somewhere else and I had to queue up to pay an official to stamp my ECOWAS (Economic Community of West African States) passport. I said I wouldn't do it and the guy grabbed me by the throat . . . I was just so sick of it all.

Kunle is a graphic artist and taught art in secondary school in Nigeria. At the time of our discussion, he was working through the Community Employment (CE) scheme, in which he worked nineteen hours a week doing graphic design until he could secure a regular job.

Getting a job is difficult. The minute an employee sees a foreign name, forget it. . . . I tried to get into council housing and brought an investigator out to see where I was living. The investigator said that Africans were not being put in council housing because they wanted to prevent conflicts. This means they cannot police their own people or it was just a way of saying they did not want to give housing to blacks. Then why did they sign on the UN human rights convention if they are not willing to provide housing for refugees?

Kunle told me that he would like to develop a website as a means of educating Irish people about Africans. He used to go to schools with the Association of Refugees and Asylum Seekers in Ireland to tell people about life as an asylum seeker. He said he would like the site to serve as a bulletin board and means of connecting with various African artists, organizations, restaurants, and other social venues throughout Ireland.

A Later Meeting with Kunle

Kunle and I had been in some communication via e-mail over the holidays regarding software he needed from America. In the end, he was able to get it in Dublin. He also sent me a Christmas card from his website. I next saw him at a conference titled "Ireland: Pluralism or Prejudice?" in February at the Royal Dublin Hotel. He was handing out flyers for the website.

A week later, we met for dinner near the trendy Temple Bar area. Kunle seemed quite nervous in the restaurant. "I'm sometimes uncomfortable being out," he said. This I had witnessed with other African immigrants. The nervousness comes from a combination of being stared at because one is seen as not belonging in a particular space, the feeling that one is constantly being observed (as an oddity), and fearing there could be at least a verbally racist incident. We were in a very friendly space that

I frequented, but I understood that his concern would come in any public setting. I observed he was very relaxed at home and markedly uncomfortable in public spaces. He did not present as the same person who had once told me, "I'm not afraid of anything!"

After ordering, we began to talk about his website. He had some sections of the site that were incomplete with a series of "dummy" links. Kunle told me that he just did not have the time to maintain the site on his own and was looking for help from an Irish computer student. I asked him how many hits his site received per day. He said, "I will not tell you that." I explained that I was not judging him or the site, I just wanted to get a sense of how many individuals were visiting the site, particularly since he was considering including advertisements to help pay for the maintenance cost. He replied, "I have gotten positive responses from people, mainly Irish people." He went on to say that "Black people are not catching on, yet. I have gone around to businesses and organizations four or five times asking if they want to put information on the website and still no response." He said that he had made rounds, offering to include information about various organizations on his site (gratis) and the African groups have been slow to respond. Also, he said that trust was an issue.

> They think I'm a "fraudster." I wanted to put some information from a Congolese business on the site. The owner seemed interested. I gave him my name and when he found out I was Nigerian, he said, "I do not know what you will do with my name. You may try to get into my bank account." He wouldn't give me any more information. . . . This continues to be a problem. They think I'm going to cheat them because I'm Nigerian. Even the businesses I list on the website have not put my flyers in their windows. They say they will, but they haven't.

The site has an African community profile page in it, in which personal profiles are included. Kunle said he was having trouble getting people to participate. "They run away when I try to take a picture!"

Kunle told me that he was working on a free magazine that he planned to place in shops in the area. He said he believed "it will take the hard copy of the magazine to lead people to the website." The advertising package would include the printed copy and the zine. He said, "Initially, the site will just be a source of information. The other day, someone phoned me to find out where an African shop was located. I think the magazine will also serve as a type of 'golden pages.'"

I asked him what made his project different from *Metro Éireann*, the multicultural Irish paper started by two Nigerian journalists. Kunle became enraged. He said, "I will tell it to [the publishers'] face, I hate that paper. . . . They are too linked to NGOs that have state connections, so they will criticize something or say Ireland is racist in private, but not in the paper. . . . I say that Ireland is racist and I will say it in the magazine." He also said, "*Metro Éireann* focuses on all immigrant groups. I am only interested in Africans. Their need for advertising and money from certain groups hinders their ability to speak out about African issues."

We talked more about his life in Ireland. "I would never invite my family to come to Ireland. I do not come from a family of beggars. If they come here, they will be asylum seekers, refugees. . . ." I asked if they would visit on holiday. He said, "They would have no reason to come here on holiday. Maybe what I am saying is strange." I explained that very little was strange or shocking to me. He continued, "Growing up in Africa, people thought America and the West was paved with gold. People would come back with stories that said so. But I have seen Ireland and Irish people and now I know that is not true."

A COMMUNITY MADE, RATHER THAN THWARTED

The African Diaspora experience in Dublin undoubtedly reflects the immigrant desire to better oneself and find a place within Irish society, as exemplified by individuals like Nicolette and Nathalie, who were studying English, Melvin, working to complete a second-level degree at age twenty, and various entrepreneurial endeavors, such as the vision of an African and Irish restaurant considered by both Lela and Nathalie, and Jennifer's cleaning business that she started with her husband (". . . I have to work for myself. I can't work for other people.") Yet the experiences of African migrants can also be characterized by a process of maintaining cultural traditions and ethno-cultural identity in the space of Dublin, as seen at the Congolese wedding which featured popular dance music (i.e., rumba and soukous), culinary choices (e.g., fish in a peppery sauce with kwanga), and the groom anticipating the long-awaited arrival of the bride. In addition, the salience of cultural traditions and identities was evidenced in the Yoruba social scene at Eternity, the support of the Igbo at the Nigerian/German wedding reception—particularly as expressed by "chairman" Timothy ("If I die, they know what to do with me. They know that my body must be sent back to Igboland")—and as demonstrated by individuals such as George, of Ghanaian and Nigerian ancestry, who strongly identified as an "Igbo man."

Additionally, the process of community making occurred in spiritual arenas, as exemplified by Wanda (". . . I do not want drinking in the place because I am a Christian"), Melvin ("clubs are expensive, so I stay home a lot. Sometimes my sister and I go to church"), and Clifford, who describes his spiritual awakening after the realization of an evangelist's prophecy ("People were killed and injured, but I did not have a mark on me. . . . From then on I knew a god existed"). Though it is not in the purview of this project to present an extensive examination of the religious life of the community, it is important to note here that the significant extension of organized spiritual endeavors from the homeland became integral to creating a community with a potential permanence in Ireland (see Ugba 2009). In 2001, it was estimated that there were approximately forty African Christian churches of various—mostly evangelical—denominations in the Dublin area (M. Clifford 2001). The presence of the African churches was a new phenomenon in Ireland, but most had connections to denominations in African nations and other African Diaspora sites in Europe. Often the congregations met in informal settings or, in several cases, met periodically in already established Irish churches in the evenings, late nights, and/or with bimonthly regularity. Services also reflected the linguistic diversity of the African Diaspora community, with pastors presenting sermons in English, French, and regional African languages.

Whether developing a business, planning a cultural event, worshipping in a storefront, or asserting an identity long established in the homeland, the diverse group of African migrants engaged in a process of making an African Diaspora community in Dublin and, in effect, constructing black identity as integral to new renderings of Irish identity. Yet, it is a twenty-first-century African Diaspora community, one that must both acknowledge the mutual experience of continental Africanness and racialization as black while simultaneously living out the diversity of this experience and rejecting the fast reduction to a monolithic continental African or black identity as constructed by a retrogressive European or white gaze. Furthermore, the making of the African Diaspora community has inevitably involved new identity formations and familial relationships that incorporate the diversity of the global site of Dublin. This is particularly evidenced by the cases of out-marriage and interethnic partnerships among both African men and women who are marrying or partnering with white Irish or other European partners. Certainly, it is apparent that there are partnerships occurring for the strategic desire to gain legitimacy in the state, as exemplified by the Nigerian/German wedding about which Clifford commented, "Michael needed the German passport." However, out-marriage and interethnic relationships have also developed in less calculating contexts as a result of cross-cultural interaction leading to legitimate bonds. This is exemplified by the account of Jennifer, who described being jealous of her husband's friendship with his ex-girlfriend and the support of her in-laws ("His family is always calling me. They want to know how I'm doing. They see that he has changed for the better since he got with me"), the experiences of Susan, who described the evolution of her attraction to her partner while he was working in the hostel where she resided ("I really love this guy"), Marcus, the longtime resident who has a daughter with his white Irish girlfriend with whom he maintains a relationship outside of cohabitation, and also, in the previous chapter, the relatively stoic response of Jacob, an employed resident of Ireland originally from Angola, whose French girlfriend of two years had recently left Dublin ("We were friends and you never know what can happen. You don't know where life will take you").

Additionally, in some cases, out-marriage presents an escape from cultural traditions and the expectations of relationships in the African homeland. Wanda blatantly stated: "But, I did not want to marry an African man . . . the African men here are all crap. . . . Also, I did not want the hassle. . . . With an Irish man, it is just you and your husband and your children. You have your life. . . . In Africa, you have to deal with the whole family. . . . They set the rules." While Wanda asserts a desire for a different family relationship, Sammy sees an African woman's independence as problematic: "A lot of Nigerian women want to be like Irish women. They want to do what they want to do and they forget about the man who loves them." Wanda, who is Yoruba, would not be Sammy's first choice of a mate because he desires an Igbo woman and, relying on an erroneous yet prevailing representation, sees Yoruba women as liable to "think I want to marry them and have a baby to stay in Ireland." Yet, Sammy's disinterest in marrying an Igbo woman who has migrated to Ireland highlights a negative perception of women's mobility and the independence, or at least drive, that is inextricably linked to the decision to migrate. As he stated: "Igbo do not travel much and if an Igbo woman travels here, she would not feel the need to involve herself in her husband's problems because she would consider his problems his own, not hers . . . because he did not bring her here." Above all, Sammy sees the potential control of a woman as desirable, yet many migrant women are disinterested in maintaining that form of spousal relationship. Thus, Sammy's view of the woman who knows how "to be a wife" as one who "must make her man happy and be humble" starkly contrasts with that of the lived reality accounted in the previous chapter by Henrietta, a professional who must also contend with outside perceptions of her required role in her relationship with her husband, Peter, who is also a professional from Nigeria. She states that after her children were born, "People said, 'Oh, Peter is a horrible man, making his wife go back to work so soon.' You know how Africans are. . . . Peter and I are partners."

The process of community making, as seen in the previous chapter and this one, involves a constant negotiation of racism, whether it is because, as Davis noted, "the Irish are not very exposed," or as Kunle succinctly expressed it, "Ireland is racist." However, cultural and ethnic conflicts are not solely relegated to the black/white and African/Irish binaries. Significantly, cultural and ethnic conflicts emerge within the African Diaspora community and complicate the potential for a cohesive realization of a black community in its singularity. The diversity of the African Diaspora community and the cultural plurality of communities within it are exemplified through individuals such as Sammy, who blames the Yoruba for bad treatment of blacks in Ireland. Believing that the "Igbo do not push as much as Yoruba people," he contends that his ethnic group would have been more positively received in Ireland than the Yoruba, thus paving the way for better race relations. In another contentious example, Clifford, who harks back to Biafra in his discussion of the contemporary relationship between Igbo and Yoruba, asserted that "You cannot trust the Yoruba." Nicolette, a Congolese migrant who was studying English, notably places the Irish, along with Nigerians, at the bottom of her hierarchy of proper English speakers, stating, "I do not want to have an Irish accent" and "I do not want to speak like Nigerians. Their English, it does not sound good." Kunle, who attempts to cross ethnic and national lines with his website and magazine, finds his work thwarted by non-Nigerian Africans who think he is a "fraudster" and, therefore, has difficulty getting advertisers because, as he noted, "They think I'm going to cheat them because I'm Nigerian." Meanwhile, in an effort to address these intra-diasporic conflicts, the successful Nigerian businessman, Nick—who believed that that there "were no major divisions among Nigerians in Ireland" but observed more conflicts between Francophone and Anglophone communities—worked to cross ethnic lines through his presence at Francophone activities and by organizing cultural conflict resolution events, such as a football match between Congolese and Nigerian teams.

Earlier I addressed the loss of a prior socio-economic class status resulting from immigration, particularly for individuals seeking asylum. Also reflecting an inherent diversity, the African Diaspora community in Dublin emerged amidst a significant negotiation of class status among African migrants. As exemplified in the previous chapter, Henrietta, a Nigerian accountant for an IT multinational company, may appear anomalous to Irish individuals who expect her to be an asylum seeker, but she also experiences the presumption of a different class status (i.e., working class) among the African Diaspora community. This was evidenced by her Nigerian neighbor who assumed she worked in a factory and, as Henrietta exclaimed, "She thought I was lying when I told her where I worked and gave her my office number." Henrietta's work ethic is also at odds with some of her Nigerian neighbors, as she describes: "When I get up at five to take care of the children and go to work, they are asleep. When I come home, they are in front of the telly. What kind of life is that? I have daughters and I want them to see their mother working, making a life, not sitting around sleeping all day and watching telly." In the account of Michel, the son of a former Minister of State in Zaire (Democratic Republic of Congo), also examined in the previous chapter, he not only presents a cross-national critique of Anglophone Africans, noting that "Nigerians sometimes do not know you. They are not your friend. They say hello, but that is it," but also states that individuals from the Middle Congo (Republic of Congo)—as opposed to the Congo (DRC or former Zaire) where he is from—speak poor Lingala and are "not considered as worldly as those from the Congo." Nevertheless, for the pragmatic Jacob from Angola there are no colonial distinctions worth making. Regarding socializing with individuals from the Congo, he stated: "We speak French. We speak Lingala. We are the same people. We were separated because of French colonialism. But, we are the same people." However, Jacob defensively explained his reason for not socializing with Nigerians: "Look, you see. I like everybody. I do not hate anybody. I just don't know any Nigerians."

Amidst the various intra-diasporic national, ethnic, and cultural conflicts, African Diaspora community making also involves reconciling the reality that the migration to Ireland occurred because the homeland did not offer the security—economic, safety, or familial—needed to live a healthy life and optimize one's life chances. Hence, there are inevitable internal critiques of the community itself. For example, as evidenced in this chapter, many African migrants present a scathing interrogation of the sometimes duplicitous circumstances in which individuals have come into Ireland. As Clifford candidly expressed: "'My father was killed, my mother was murdered' . . . it is all a lie. They want to make money and go back home." Certainly, as discussed above, duplicity and deceit are often required when facing Irish immigration policies that render many claims of harm, need, or desire to better oneself outside of the criteria for asylum. Additionally, within this internal critique or self-interrogation, it is apparent that there are differential migration experiences, including legitimate asylum seekers, dubious applicants, migrants who—like Henrietta, Peter, and Roland—are working for multinational and local corporations, and the few individuals present before a substantial African Diaspora migration, such as Marcus, who recalls, "Twenty years ago, it was so different. There was no money here. Everyone was the same. They treated you well. Twenty years ago, I wanted to spend the rest of my life here. . . . Now, they think you're an asylum seeker or a refugee. . . . It is a different Ireland." His lament is also an interrogation of the common reduction of black presence to asylum status and the implicit problems that emerge when a population is overwhelmingly placed in a social group that is maligned—albeit wrongly—throughout popular and state-level discourse and policy.

Furthermore, the process of coming to terms with the reasons for African migration to Ireland also involves a substantial interrogation of the homeland. Thus, Kunle, who stated, "I do not believe in Nigeria," laments that the British colonial formation of the country is at odds with the ethnic groups within it and vociferously critiques the corruption in the state. To Kunle, Ireland is merely a "lesser evil." To expand on the notion of a "lesser evil," it is also evident that a mediation of witchcraft and spells that originated in the homeland remains salient in the context of Ireland. Wanda, amidst her critique of African men and family life in Nigeria, spoke of family members "casting spells" on in-laws they did not like. Lela, while envisioning a restaurant business and working through the contradictions inherent in her desire to adhere to alcohol-free values in an Irish society where drinking is a significant part of social interaction ("Wine is okay . . . I just don't want drunks in there") also discusses spells ("I was raised as a Christian and do not know how to cast spells. But, I believe it happens all the time"). In another example of this not-so-uncommon area of discussion,[15] George contends that "People come [to Ireland] to get away from witchcraft or the feeling that something is not right. Sometimes they hope to return home when the person that put bad luck on them leaves or dies." Further exemplifying the interrogation of the homeland, we see examples of violence in African nations trumping the impact of racism in Ireland, as noted in the previous chapter by Jacob from Angola ("There are problems. They are political. It is hard to talk about them. I don't like politics"), and also Terrence from Liberia ("Some people very close to me died back home. I've seen some very difficult things, you know").

Moreover, the critique of the homeland is accompanied by the realization that there will have to be an engagement with the Irish sociocultural landscape and, ultimately, the process of making a new life in

Ireland. This is apparent through the aforementioned business plans that would cater to African and Irish communities, the attempts at learning English and receiving an academic qualification in Ireland, inter-ethnic marriages and partnerships, and attempts to participate in social activities and venues, such as pubs or, as in the St. Patrick's Day account, GAA events. Yet, negotiating these experiences—even forging "integration"—inevitably involves a reconciling and interrogation of prior notions of Ireland and, more broadly, Europe, as well as one's perceived place within the West. In the previous chapter, Jacob commented, "If you are black in a white country, a European country, you are going to have some problems." Representing the end of the fantasy of the West, Kunle stated, "Growing up in Africa, people thought America and the West was paved with gold. . . . But I have seen Ireland and Irish people and now I know that is not true." Susan, whose comments on the weather become a metaphor for this contrast between fantasy and reality, noted, "I thought coming to Europe would be great. You think it's going to be perfect. Then I get here and it's rainy and so cold compared to where I'm coming from." However, we see that Clifford, who tells people in his Nigerian village that he is in London because it is more recognizable to them than Dublin, had no such illusions. Representing a challenge to the perception of hoards of Africans scheming for a much-coveted journey to the Emerald Isle, Clifford describes Dublin as the "last stop in Europe" and, quite frankly, states: "I never dreamed of coming to Ireland."

Ultimately, the accounts in this chapter and the previous chapter illustrate the complexity of the lived experiences of the African Diaspora in "retro-global" Dublin. It is apparent that even in the context of the major "retro" aspects of the society highlighted in this volume (retro-accommodation, retro-space, retro-documentation, and retro-inaugurals) combined with the inextricably linked Irish ethno-cultural biases and racism (manifest in immigration policy, physical attacks, verbal abuse, and public discrimination), the African Diaspora community maintains its diversity (national, ethnic, cultural, linguistic). Of course, inextricably linked to this diversity, some individuals continue to advance essentialist understandings of other African communities that predate the arrival in Ireland; thus perpetuating beliefs that are retrogressive in their own regard and reflect the salience of conflicts emerging from continental African national, cultural, and regional affiliations and representations. In effect, these intra-diasporic tensions prohibit the realization of a cohesive African Diaspora identity, exposing a diverse community that is a culturally pluralist entity only united in the response to the all-encompassing experience of social retrogression related to anti-black racism and xenophobia in Ireland. The circumstances examined in this chapter represent an instance of contemporary global African Diaspora communities asserting their diversity in spite of the challenge of retrogressive racialized constructions of black/white binary identities. As evidenced in the 2006 Census, it is apparent that African Diaspora communities are ensuring the inevitable transformation of the Irish national identity and the overall socio-cultural landscape of the nation.

We have seen Ireland experiencing the rapid growth of a new African Diaspora community amidst its first national foray into a significant position in the global economic arena. The Irish nation, from 2000 to 2001, is represented as a "social laboratory" in which to consider the intervention of global African Diaspora communities in the process of forging the realization of *actually* modern societies. As we will see in the three seemingly disparate African Diaspora communities of Dublin, New Orleans, and Paris, there is no turning back the push for interrogation, even when retrogression appears to trump progress.

PART 2.

THE GLITCHES OF MODERNITY

DUBLIN
The Olukunle Elukanlo Case

On March 14, 2005, a twenty-year-old Nigerian student, Olukunle Elu-kanlo, who had lived in Ireland since 2002, was deported to Nigeria. He was two months away from sitting for his Leaving Certificate examinations, the culmination of Irish second-level education. The circumstances of his deportation and mass support from his fellow students at Palmerstown Community School in Dublin, as well as the anti-racism community—particularly Residents Against Racism—led to a national outcry and debate. He was deported in the middle of the night along with thirty-four other Nigerians (Bray 2005). Elukanlo arrived in Ireland alone at the age of fifteen after his father was allegedly shot to death and his mother went missing in Lagos (V. Browne 2005; Gallagher et al. 2005). However, his asylum claims were deemed unfounded and he was scheduled for deportation on March 31, 2005. When Elukanlo went to the *Garda* (police) National Immigration Bureau to file an application for appeal on March 15, 2005, he was detained at Dublin's Cloverhill Prison and then brought to the Dublin Airport for deportation.

Elukanlo was widely reported as being deported in his "school uniform," which lent an air of youthful innocence to his person and ordeal after being left on his own in Lagos after his deportation. Meanwhile, the popular concern was echoed in the state-level debate. It became imperative that members of Parliament place pressure on the Minister for Justice, Equality and Law Reform to reverse the deportation order and return Elukanlo to Ireland. This is apparent in a statement Deputy Joe Costello directed at then Minister for Justice Michael McDowell during adjournment debates of the *Dáil Éireann* (House of Representatives) one week after the deportation of Elukanlo. Costello states:

I am raising an extremely important issue this evening. The deportation of a 19-year-old youth to Nigeria raises many other issues, such as the Government's immigration policy, which deserves to be debated in the House at an early opportunity. We witnessed last week the spectacle of men, women and children, who had been taken by the *Garda* while engaged in one area of activity in their lives, arriving at the airport to be deported. Those who were deported were in school uniforms or on their way to work, while others had been asked to turn up at the immigration bureau. They were taken to the airport after being given a brief period of time to collect some clothes. Mobile telephones were taken from those being deported in some cases, so that they could not contact friends, relatives or lawyers. A couple of people who were able to contact lawyers were not deported because they secured a review of the circumstances of their deportation. (*Dáil* 2005a)

The fact of being "in school uniforms or on their way to work" further underlines the precariousness of the status of individuals without the decisive right to remain in the country, as their sense of liberty or freedom is always lived as tenuous, a state of being that can be easily disrupted by a sudden state-sanctioned removal of their persons from the nation. Also, the confiscation of mobile phones runs deeper than the act of disconnecting individuals from justice for it also reflects the popular Irish perception that some migrants are "economic" and not eligible for asylum, as the contemporary migrant does not easily fit the representation of the malnourished "refugee" cut off from the modern world and its technologies.

To add further context, I'll briefly turn to a March 2002 statement made by Minister for State Mary Hanafin on behalf of Minister for Justice John O'Donoghue regarding a bilateral readmission agreement between Nigeria and Ireland, which highlights the contradictions inherent in the intention of the state and its subsequent actions regarding asylum applications and human rights directives. In response to concern that such an agreement with Nigeria would circumvent the dictates of the United Nations High Commissioner for Refugees (UNHCR), during her presentation of the readmission agreement to the *Oireachtas* (Parliament) Select Committee on Justice, Equality and Defense and Women's Rights, Hanafin states:

As the Minister did on many previous occasions, I emphasize the Government's continued commitment to meeting the State's obligations under the 1951 Geneva Convention and 1967 protocol on the status of refugees, the main international legal instruments aimed at the protection of refugees. As the committee will be aware, *in line with our obligations under the convention and protocol, we have a fair, transparent and independent process in place for dealing with asylum applications.* Considerable progress has been made in dealing with applications since the Minister established the Office of the Refugee Applications Commissioner and the Refugee Appeals Tribunal, and the allocation of significant additional resources to both the asylum and immigration processes. (Houses of *Oireachtas* 2002; emphasis mine)

The desire to process asylum applicants more expeditiously is undoubtedly related to the need to clear a backlog which reached a high of 11,437 in 2000, leaving asylum seekers in a legal limbo for which the state received much criticism (Irish Refugee Council 2005; INIS 2005). Yet, it was apparent that the state interest in freeing asylum applicants from an interstitial place was more weighted with the intention of removing them from the nation than regularizing their presence and, therefore, participation in the nation.

The readmission agreement was subsequently ratified by the Irish government in March 2002, which facilitated the rapid deportation of Nigerians with unfounded asylum applications, particularly as the accelerated or "fast-track" procedures implemented under the Immigration Act 2003 allowed for the opening of reception centers and the requirement of daily "sign-ins" for asylum applicants from designated "safe countries." However, most notably, Ireland had not designated Nigeria a "safe country," which it had done for other nations with which it held readmission agreements, such as Romania and Bulgaria. Also significant is that by the time of Elukanlo's case—and even as late as 2009—Nigeria had not ratified the readmission agreement; although Minister for Justice, Equality and Law Reform Michael McDowell noted in a related debate that "both sides are operating in the spirit of the agreement, particularly in the area of repatriation" (*Dáil Éireann* 2005b).

By 2005, even though asylum applications had been processed through the Office of the Refugee Applications Commissioner (ORAC) and Refugee Appeals Tribunal (RAT) since 2000, the actuality of transparency and fairness in the deportation process was still in question. Though quicker, it remained unclear how the process effectively worked, and the act of being taken away at the last minute with little option for recourse did not aptly represent fairness. This, above all, demonstrated that Ireland's drive to remove Nigerians—the largest African Diaspora population represented in the nation—trumped the concern with human rights violations in Nigeria. So, we see Ireland as reluctant to give Nigeria "safe country" status but not adverse to hastily deporting individuals back to an implicitly "unsafe" Nigeria, thus contradicting the avowed adherence to the 1951 Convention and 1967 Protocol that the state affirmed when deciding to ratify the readmission agreement in 2002 (see White 2009a).

In addition to the disavowal of human rights violations and the related potentiality of *refoulement* that the debate around Elukanlo's case brought to light, the state-level discourse on his case interestingly presents an example of one diaspora being used to support the maintenance of another; that is, attempting to curtail a reversal of diaspora and, by extension, acknowledge and facilitate the mutual pursuit of freedom. For example, in the aforementioned *Dáil* debate in March 2005, Deputy Costello pointed out the hypocrisy inherent in the deportation of Elukanlo and the other Nigerians around St. Patrick's Day: "Last week's deportations took place on the eve of St. Patrick's Day, when the Minister, Deputy McDowell, and some of his colleagues were out of the country commemorating the far-flung diaspora of Irish people who went abroad, legally and illegally, to find a better life and to escape persecution. It is a cruel irony that the deportations took place just as those celebrations were about to begin" (*Dáil* 2005a). Costello's statement acknowledges an Ireland and Irish Diaspora that through poverty, colonial subjugation, and anti-Irish racism had not yet fully benefited from the modern project and, like African Diaspora communities, was amidst the rougher edges of modernity. Costello's sentiments, which have also been voiced in various forms by others who consider the contradictions inherent in an Irish anti-immigration stance, juxtapose the earlier Ireland with the globally focused exportation of Irishness via St. Patrick's Day celebrations throughout its diaspora; global celebrations that require an acknowledgment of Irish out-migration without a consideration of the more difficult aspects of the historical—and contemporary—experience in the homeland and host land.

The irony which Costello considers in the context of Elukanlo's case also highlights the extent to which Ireland has succumbed to a new narrative, one that embraces whiteness along with its exclusionary baggage and its uneasy European identity; an uneasy Europeanness that, EU-related economic success notwithstanding, is still uncomfortable to the Irish, as seen in the initial pro-nationalist rejections of the Nice and Lisbon Treaties in 2001 and 2008 (see E. Harris 2008; H. McDonald 2009). Yet, Europhilia is more attractive than embracing a multiethnic/multiracial Ireland and the perceived loss that entails; paradoxically, a loss that is a result of EU membership. Of course, as this volume indicates and argues, contemporary European identities cannot be exclusively racialized as white. However, implicit in the conflict at the core of the black Irish and overall black European experience is that to numerous Irish individuals and, undoubtedly, to myriad continental Europeans and the larger global community, the European link with an exclusively white identity still erroneously persists. So, the reputation of an Ireland of 100,000 welcomes and its related experiences of philanthropic and humanitarian endeavors must be tempered in the grasping of modernity; again, we see that a distancing from the prickly past is inevitable, for such distancing is what "lived modernity" requires.

As Ireland continued to attest to compliance with the 1951 Geneva Convention and 1967 Protocol amidst deportation cases such as that of Elukanlo, arguments about the low number of individuals receiving humanitarian leave to remain—the only option after an unsuccessful asylum application—continued to be an area of contention; again leading to the suggestion that the review process was inefficient, if not marred. In the same *Dáil* debate about Elukanlo's case, Deputy Ciarán Cuffe stated: "While over 4,000 people have been recognized as refugees in Ireland over the last three years, the numbers given leave to remain are extremely low. Only 75 former asylum seekers were successful at this stage last year while the number of deported people was eight times greater. The bar has been set very high and the basis for refusing some especially strong cases is questionable. The total number of aged-out asylum seekers who have applied for leave to remain on humanitarian grounds but not on the basis of being an Irish-born child is relatively small, perhaps 500" (*Dáil* 2005a). To underscore his point Cuffe evoked the Irish Diaspora experience in a contemporary context: "In the 1990s, 48,000 U.S. visas were granted under the Morrison scheme and the *Taoiseach* [Prime Minister] was busy in Washington last week attempting to regularize the positions of thousands more Irish emigrants. A double standard appears to operate. I call on the Minister to allow the young man in question and others like him to return to Ireland to sit their leaving certificate examination" (*Dáil* 2005a).

Here I would like to take a moment to consider Cuffe's reference to the U.S. Family Unity and Employment Opportunity Immigration Act of 1990, sponsored by Connecticut Congressman Bruce A. Morrison which, *inter alia,* provided amnesty for Irish citizens without legal status in the United States. The Irish American lobby for the bill was so strong that it was often known as "The Irish Bill" (see Howe 1990). Notably, in December 2005, during the first meeting of the U.S.-based Irish Lobby for Immigration Reform—an organization formed to address the same immigration issues that Cuffe notes were of interest to the *Taoiseach*—an Irish immigrant highlighted the lack of mobility and opportunity that comes when one is illegally present in a state: "It's getting harder and harder . . . We can't get driver's licenses, we can't do anything, and people are going home. Do I tell them to hang on for a few months? They just can't take the pressure of being here anymore" (McGoldrick 2005).

The comparison between the U.S. Irish condition and the Ireland Nigerian condition is even more noteworthy when considering the larger problematic of contemporary global migration, border controls, and an entrenched nativism that excludes regardless of how one is racialized. However, the *extent* of one's exclusion and how one is perceived in the larger quotidian experience in a host land is often contingent on how one is racialized. So, also apparent here is the way in which U.S. discourse racializes migration specifically enough to exclude the Irish—considered white and easier to integrate—in the superficial construction and representation of migrant identities. This, of course, enables the Irish that are illegally in the state to stay unnoticed as well as to receive amnesty opportunities that are not readily extended to, say, migrants from Central America. So, the comparison ends where race and ethnicity begin but is still notable because it implicates the willingness of the Irish government to support illegality in the United States for the humanity of its diaspora while ratcheting up deportation operations for individuals of other diasporas that are illegally present in its own nation. Also significant is that, as indicated by the above testimony of the Irish migrant in the United States, if faced with too many difficulties there is always the looming choice of "going home" when one can no longer "take the pressure," though undoubtedly for numerous Nigerians in Ireland a return home is a much more perilous option.

Amidst the debate about Elukanlo's case, the oft-expressed concern that making an exception for one failed asylum seeker would lead to increased migration to Ireland was circumvented by using a paternalistic argument in line with the "black baby" charity and missionary tradition. This involved the representation of Elukanlo as a child in need of support and, more specifically, the orphaned schoolboy. Also, the ultimate measure of belonging to the community, the act of "integrating," so crucial to the Irish experience in its larger diaspora sites, was considered by officials who argued on Elukanlo's behalf. Both of these circumstances, "the exceptional orphan" and integration, are expressed in Deputy John Curran's statement:

I regard him as an orphan because his father is dead and the location of his mother and the rest of his family is unknown. Some media reports have suggested that they might be in the United States or the United Kingdom, but Olunkunle does not know where they are. Olunkunle has spent about half of his teenage years in Ireland. He has adapted well during that time, for example by integrating with the local community, studying for his leaving certificate and working in a part-time job. He is a popular student and his deportation has touched the lives of everyone here who knows him. I have received numerous phone calls from people from all walks of life wishing to register their disapproval of the manner in which Olunkunle was dealt with. Less than three months away from his leaving certificate, a student was deported at short notice. I understand that today Olunkunle roams somewhere in Lagos and faces a very uncertain future. I ask the Minister to reconsider his earlier-stated position. I ask him to recognize Olunkunle as an orphan. The State and the Department should have observed a duty of care to Olunkunle when deporting him, but he was deported instead without reference to what lay ahead for him in Nigeria. He came here as a young person without any family. While I accept that we require an immigration policy, the manner in which Olunkunle was deported failed to take into account what he would face.[1] (*Dáil* 2005a)

The act of minors or youths traversing the globe in search of better and sometimes life-saving opportunities is not a new phenomenon, but Curran's statement certainly highlights the ways in which contemporary knowledge networks (e.g., word of mouth complemented by landline telephones, mobile phones, and websites) paired with aero technology (i.e., flights to Europe) facilitate a vision of global access that would have been less conceivable in earlier periods. Elukanlo's migration to Ireland demonstrates the way in which globality can be envisioned and realized in our contemporary context—no longer exclusively the story of the Irish migrant appearing in London or Boston after a sea journey but now as much about a Nigerian teenager stepping off a plane into Dublin Airport. Of course, Elukanlo's deportation also demonstrates the ways in which contemporary technologies can be used to negate a progressive rendering of globality.

It is also significant, as Curran notes, that Elukanlo was nearing the point at which he could receive an important qualification that would have an impact on his future opportunities, the Leaving Certificate. We can assume that through migration Elukanlo had intended to better his life chances, hence enabling the positive freedom to move beyond Nigeria as a means of ensuring more substantive freedom. This is exemplified in further remarks by Deputy Costello which also implicate the role of education in the process of social and cultural integration:

> Many people are eligible for deportation as they prepare to sit the leaving certificate, or even the junior certificate, and are being deported on that basis. I am sure the Minister understands the significant benefits, in terms of their future, of giving such people the opportunity to acquire some qualification from the Irish education system. None of the humanitarian reasons for deciding not to deport a young person, including that person's friends and other roots in the community, has been taken into consideration. That is contrary to the spirit of the Geneva Convention and the international laws relating to children. If it is still part of this country's ethos to be Christian and humane, the least we should do is to allow young people who have come to Ireland in difficult circumstances to stay here until they have finished their schooling. The Minister should suspend any future deportations of this nature. He should provide for a separate assessment when he considers ordering the deportation of a young person on the grounds I have mentioned. In such an assessment, he should consider the degree to which the person has been integrated into Irish society through the education system. (*Dáil* 2005a)

Costello's appeal exemplifies the modern desire to adhere to international human rights laws and, interestingly, through a plea to Ireland's "ethos to be Christian and humane," draws on an older modern argument that was historically prevalent when considering slavery and subsequent anti-lynching campaigns in the United States. This last gesture also continues the problematic tradition of embedding Christianity in notions of human rights, democracy, and freedom. But, to touch again on the Irish in the United States, which is certainly the supporting backdrop of the argument for Elukanlo's return, there is little doubt that the integration which Costello considers—particularly when it operates as a close cousin to the flawed idea of "assimilation"—is more difficult for individuals who are racialized differently than the majority in power. However, through the Elukanlo case, we see a process at work in which individuals of a community begin to reconceptualize their criteria for inclusion, supplanting exclusively race-based criteria with other ways of being, mostly facilitated by the knowledge which comes from knowing an individual rather than an uninformed representation of a group. In effect, through Elukanlo, we see a community's desire to protect "its own" taking on a more globally inclusive and, therefore, *modern* understanding of who belongs.

The passion in the case and the emotional tale of the community that supported Elukanlo, many of whom were in the *Dáil* during the debate examined here, are reflected in the following statement by Deputy Joe Higgins, which I have excerpted at length here:

I first heard the name Olunkunle Eluhanla on Monday, 15 March[2] when I saw descending on Leinster House 60 leaving certificate students from Palmerstown community school who were upset, worried and angry that their friend had been snatched from their company without even having time to say goodbye. He was dumped, a term I use advisedly, in Lagos without identity papers, money, family, a place to go or someone on whom to fall back. These circumstances in themselves constitute callous negligence by the State. Lagos is an extremely precarious place for work-ing class and poor people generally and especially for a completely lost young man in the uniform of his school. We are fortunate today that we are not here to mourn Olunkunle as he was assaulted in an attack which could have been even worse. It beggars belief that a leaving certificate stu-dent two months away from his final exams should be deported. I salute the students of Palmerstown community school for their solidarity and loyalty to their friend. They have come in large numbers with their teach-ers to the Public Gallery hoping the Minister for Justice, Equality and Law Reform will exercise compassion. They stand tall in contrast to comments in some media outlets that Irish youth is generally self-centered, cynical and callous. If the Minister will not listen to compassion, though I hope he will, he should at least listen to the voices of people in the commu-nity who ask him to set aside the general policy and exercise the discre-tion he absolutely has to allow the young man in question to return. Sup-porters of Olunkunle are examining whether there are legal grounds to challenge his deportation. While they may go to the High Court, people power must be brought to bear on the Government to ensure he is al-lowed to continue his studies. The Minister must see the howling irony of this callous deportation in the context [of] the *Taoiseach*'s request to the President of the United States of America to allow thousands of undocu-mented Irish people to continue their American lives legally. I ask the Minister to end the agony of Olunkunle Eluhanla and the distress of his friends. I ask the Minister to allow Olunkunle to return to his studies and the bosom of the community which obviously loved him and took him to its heart. (*Dáil* 2005a)

So, in considering the embrace of Elukanlo by his school community, we see that the extent to which a community "love[s] [an asylum seeker] and [takes] him to its heart" is a significant popular, albeit not state-level, measure of whether an asylum applicant is worthy of staying in the community. However, we must consider that Elukanlo's presence as an "exceptional orphan" also portends that the seemingly progressive community embrace is actually retrogressive when the criteria for acceptance involve something akin to mascot status or a "black baby" identity.

Higgins's passionate concern for Elukanlo's safety and appeal to the Minister for Justice to "see the howling irony of this callous deportation" in the context of Irish migrants in the United States underline what may be the greater "howling irony" of modernity, that full globality (i.e., movement and flows of people) is limited by state-centric needs—formed by conceptions of race, ethnicity, and cultural identity—and not sufficiently conceptualized as happening within a global cosmopolitan space of interaction. Our technology and the conscious spaces that such technologies enable (e.g., the internet, and even "old-school" telephones) suggest that the lived fluidity of borders is possible, but our policy actions and the will of what Higgins refers to as "people power" have not yet emerged to facilitate such a process.

The Minister for Justice, Michael McDowell, in his response to the deputies in support of Elukanlo noted that "a deportation process must be central to the proper running of any immigration and asylum system" (*Dáil* 2005a). After stating that Ireland adhered to the UNHCR guidelines regarding the protection of unaccompanied minors that entered the State, he explained:

> In this case, Deputy Cuffe stated that the person in question came here at the age of 15, but that is factually incorrect. In February 2002 the person referred to by the Deputies arrived in Ireland seeking asylum. The date of birth given in the asylum application indicated that he was 17 years of age. On the basis of that date he was by no stretch of the imagination what newspapers have described as a schoolboy but was 20 years of age when he was deported. Moreover, he verbally indicated to the escorting *Garda* team that he was 21 years of age. I am constrained by law from making public the exact details of the asylum claim and will not deal here with the credibility or strength of the person's original claim. The important point to note is that his claim was assessed by the two independent bodies[3] that came to the same conclusion, that he was not entitled to refugee protection. (*Dáil* 2005a)

McDowell's statement reflects the difficulties faced by aged-out separated children suddenly thrown into the legal world of adult asylum status with limited support (see Mooten 2006). Most significantly, McDowell's contradiction of supporters' accounts served to disrupt the representation of Elukanlo as an innocent youth or orphan, emphasize his ineligibility for protection under the UN Convention on the Rights of the Child, invalidate the claims of his community supporters, bring his honesty into question and, overall, help justify the decision regarding his asylum application. During his response, McDowell also said:

> In October 2003 the person concerned was informed that he was found not to be a refugee and was informed of the three options then open to him, first, to leave the State before his case was considered for deportation, to consent to the making of a deportation order in respect of him or to make written representations, within 15 working days, to me as Minister for Justice, Equality and Law Reform setting out reasons he should not be deported, that is, why he should be allowed to remain temporarily in the State. Representations were made by this person, which included the fact that he was a student. The case was examined under section 3 of the Immigration Act 1999[4] and section 5 of the Refugee Act 1996, prohibition of *refoulement*, including consideration of all representations received on his behalf and a deportation order was signed for him on 21 January 2005. (*Dáil* 2005a)

Regarding Elukanlo's subsequent deportation, McDowell explained that a deportation order was sent to Elukanlo's home with a letter that "instructed him to report to the *Garda* national immigration bureau on 3 March 2005." He stated:

> This letter was copied to his solicitors. He did not do as requested and was classified as an evader. On 14 March 2005, coincidentally on the day a charter operation to Nigeria was taking place, he arrived at Burgh Quay [*Garda* National Immigration Bureau], accompanied by a friend who described himself as his uncle. The person was advised by the *Garda* to seek immediate legal advice. He was detained and placed in Cloverhill Prison. I wish to make it clear that the *Garda* offered to escort him to his home to collect his belongings, which he declined. Furthermore, the *Garda* informed me that he was not wearing clothes which could be described as a school uniform. He was removed on the charter flight to Nigeria, leaving Dublin at 11:40 PM that night. (*Dáil* 2005a)

The legitimacy of the process having been expressed and validated, along with the implied criminalization of Elukanlo via an "evader" identity,

McDowell went on to debunk the accounts stated in the media and by deputies that Elukanlo was jailed and later attacked upon returning to Lagos:

> I have seen claims that the person in question was successively mugged and assaulted in Nigeria on his return. It is important to note that the charter flight was preceded by a senior *Garda* advance party, consisting of a detective inspector and detective sergeant, which situated itself in Lagos a day prior to the charter and remained there for 12 hours after the charter returned. On the flight all adults, including the person who is the subject of this debate, were handed a letter by a member of the *Garda* team informing each of them, among other things, of the presence of the two officers in the advance party in Lagos and that, upon disembarkation, they could contact them through the Nigerian immigration authorities for necessary assistance. (*Dáil* 2005a)

The statement led Deputy Cuffe to respond, "The Minister is living in a dream world" and Deputy Higgins to exclaim, "He was taken to jail" (*Dáil* 2005a). In response, the minister simply stated, "The person concerned did not seek assistance" (*Dáil* 2005a) which lent support to the disavowal that *refoulement* was an issue and placed the onus of responsibility upon Elukanlo rather than the state.

Next, McDowell addressed the issue of education. The following exchange among Deputies Joan Burton, Higgins, and Cuffe occurred as McDowell responded to Deputy Costello's request that deportations of students be ceased:

> Mr. McDowell: In regard to the substance of this case, Deputy Costello urged that we would not deport ———.
> Ms. Burton: The Minister never examined the file.
> Mr. Cuffe: The Minister is living in a dream world.
> An Leas-Cheann Comhairle (Speaker of the House): Order, please.
> Mr. McDowell: ——— the school-going children of non-national parents who are facing deportation while they remain in full-time education, and not to deport the young people who come to Ireland as unaccompanied minors while they also remain in full-time education. I ask Deputies to consider what would be the consequences of such a policy. In effect, no person in any form of education and, by implication, none of their family members could ever be deported from the State.

Mr. Costello: That is ridiculous.

Mr. McDowell: Furthermore, Ireland would send out a message to the world that it is assuming an obligation to provide education to those who have been found not to be in need of international protection and have otherwise no right to be in the State. A further implication of allowing this person to stay is that, as a matter of policy, a person who has lost one parent and who is not living with the other parent ——

Ms. Burton: That is absolute rubbish.

Mr. McDowell: —— should be allowed to stay and be educated here. Again, this is not a rational proposition and such a policy would lead to a chaotic immigration system.

Mr. Cuffe: It is chaotic as it is now.

Mr. McDowell: The suggestion that has come from some sources that I should not deport a person because he or she is a good student, implying that students who are less academically gifted can be deported, is indefensible.

Mr. J. Higgins: No one said that. That is an outrageous distortion of the facts.

An Leas-Cheann Comhairle (Speaker of the House): Order, please.

Mr. McDowell: The same applies to athletic prowess and participation in church activities.

Ms. Burton: It has nothing to do with that.

Mr. J. Higgins: What does that have to do with this case?

Mr. McDowell: I cannot discriminate against those who are less gifted or on grounds of religious activity. (*Dáil* 2005a)

McDowell's comments reflected the fear of immigrant-specific exceptionalism, therefore underlining the message that the state was not going to bend to protests from the populace regarding individual cases. Also apparent is the employment of classic egalitarian principles in a case that involves little transfer of liberty, meant to gloss over the inequalities at the root of decisions regarding one's acceptance within the state. In an effort to further emphasize the limited impact of public opinion on his decisions, McDowell continued by stating: "Despite uninformed criticism of the Irish asylum determination system by a small but vocal minority of groups in our country, our asylum determination system compares with the best in the world in terms of fairness, decision making, determination structures and support services" (*Dáil* 2005a). This reinforcement of the position of Ireland in the global arena also represented an attempt at reducing policy critics to a "small vocal minority" and quelling the activities of groups such as Residents Against Racism (RAR), an organization that was instrumental in Elukanlo's support campaign. This was evidenced when the minister proceeded to remind the House of an instance in which RAR supported an asylum case that was determined "manifestly unfounded":

> Mr. McDowell: When the true facts emerge exposing the untruths we are deafened by the silence of these same groups. In particular, a group calling itself Residents Against Racism organized an extensive campaign in respect of a person who claimed she was facing a sentence of death in a Muslim Sharia court in Nigeria. Its campaign involved demonstrations attended by Members of this House and considerable media coverage. It subsequently transpired that the claims on foot of which that extensive campaign was mounted had no shred of truth. Deputy Costello should remember that.
> Ms. Burton: That has nothing to do with this case. (*Dáil* 2005a)

On March 24, 2005, two days after the debate examined here, Michael McDowell announced that he was revoking Elukanlo's deportation order and that he could return to complete his Leaving Certificate on a six-month temporary student visa. The Nigerian office of the International Organization for Migration was charged with arranging Elukanlo's return with the Irish Embassy in the capital, Abuja. In a statement to the *Seanad Éireann* (Irish Senate), in which he directly names "the individual in question" (notably defying the state policy of maintaining the anonymity of asylum applicants), McDowell announced:

> I want to take this opportunity to inform the House that I announced at a press conference in the Department this morning that, on careful consideration, I decided to revoke the deportation order made in the case of Olukunle Elukanlo. I respect the genuine sympathy and solidarity shown towards him by many concerned people. I have been reflecting on this overnight and, on consideration of all the circumstances of the case, I felt the deportation order could have been made in such a way as to enable him to sit his leaving certificate before leaving the country. (*Seanad Éireann* 2005)

The popular press echoed the Socialist Party News headline "McDowell forced to back down on Kunle deportation" (*Socialist Party News* 2005) in characterizing McDowell's change in position as what an *Irish Times* article described as "bow[ing] to mounting pressure" (Logue and Collins 2005) and an *Irish Independent* headline noted, "Just this once: McDowell in climbdown on boy's return" (Brady 2005). Notably, in addition to the Palmerstown Community School students, RAR, and political officials, other individuals and groups had expressed support for Elukanlo's return to Ireland, including the Teacher's Union of Ireland, Arch Bishop of Dublin Diarmuid Martin, as well as numerous local schools and blogs (see RTÉ 2005a).[5] However, despite the public discourse, McDowell expressed a motivation to the contrary and framed the decision as an error that was rectified fairly, rather than taking a decision based on an individual's ability to muster support:

> I want to express gratitude to all those who communicated with me on both sides of the issue. Strangely enough, I want this House to know that the majority of communications I received backed the stance I was taking. In case anyone believes I was overwhelmed by traffic in the other direction, that is not the case. Even now, I am receiving flak for changing my mind. I want to emphasize that it is not a question of the volume of representations on any issue, because when one makes a deportation order, it is a serious matter. One is moving someone from one country to another country, nearly always against that person's wishes. One is frequently ending a person's dream and uprooting either an individual or an entire family. With the exception of a minority of undesirable people, there is practically no deportation order which is not fraught with emotional consequences if one thinks long and hard enough about it. These are all difficult decisions. I must confess that many of them can put one into a spin as to which way one should go. However, in the end, one must make a decision. (*Seanad Éireann* 2005)

McDowell's comments regarding "ending a person's dream" highlight the precariousness of contemporary diaspora circumstances for individuals facing the possibility of a reversal of diaspora and an unwarranted return home. His statement, particularly when the difficulty of "which way one should go" is kept in mind, makes the transparency of the asylum review process questionable, the means of review seem arbitrary and capricious and, furthermore, indicates that a very thin line is being traversed between justifiable determinations and *refoulement*. McDowell continued:

> Normally speaking, having made the decision, I stand by it.
> It is important to point out that, on many occasions in the past, I have deported people for whom the trauma and so on would be much greater

than this young gentleman's circumstances warrant. Many of these people had no friends in the media, school or anywhere else to protest on their behalf. One must also be careful in their case. In the past, all of us have seen leaflets and very detailed campaigns where the facts have been quite different from the public's perception. However, because these people have sought refugee status in Ireland, one is not entitled to fling open the file to the public to prove the truth. The precedent is that one cannot simply disparage someone and reveal matters they told the Irish State on the assumption that they would not be thrown into the public domain in order to justify ministerial decisions. Some ministerial decisions may appear quite tough on occasions, but I ask the public to accept that they are made on the basis of careful consideration of all the issues. . . . I want to emphasize this aspect to the people involved. As a society, we do not put asylum seekers into detention centers or holding centers where they are cut off from the community. We invite them into our communities. Generally speaking, they are housed in hostels on streets in villages, cities and towns. We encourage them to participate in the education system. When this continues for a long time, a relationship and friendship builds up between asylum seekers and people in the community and human ties are formed. However, the fact that a person is a good student, or that he or she has athletic prowess, is a good activist in a local church or whatever or has lost one parent and does not know the whereabouts of the other, are not grounds on which I can run a proper policy. It would be utterly wrong to say that a dull student or one with learning difficulties was more suitable for deportation. It would also be wrong to say that somebody who had a disability and was not going to win any athletics prizes was suitable, or somebody who was a civilian member of a church but not interested in it. (*Seanad Éireann* 2005)

McDowell's argument exemplifies the utility of a newly styled "doublespeak" in which policies and acts that do not lead to the realization of modernity are framed as modern; whereas bureaucratic procedures may seem progressive and, therefore, modern, the intent (i.e., removing individuals via a racialized anti-global project) is retrogressive and, therefore, anti-modern. McDowell places Ireland in the role of protecting asylum applicants from the public display of said migrants' dubious representations. Hence, we are presented with a justification for the lack of transparency in the asylum process; a transparency that, in a more progressive context, would protect migrants from faulty evaluations. Additionally, the assertion that Ireland does not use "detention centers or holding centers" for asylum applicants represents a nod to Irish humanitarianism without a full acknowledgment of the asylum accommodation requirements, particularly when we consider that the reception centers were already housing "fast-track" or accelerated procedures applicants by the time of McDowell's statement. Also, five years earlier, there had even been discussion about using "flotels" after *Taoiseach* Bertie Ahern's state visit to Australia in 2000 (see McKenna and Black 2000).

Furthermore, regarding McDowell's comments on education, even though individuals awaiting a decision on an asylum application are encouraged "to participate in the education system," the effect of such philanthropy is significantly limited by the prohibition of employment and the difficulties inherent in subsisting on a direct provision personal allowance of €19.10 per week. To further exemplify the lived experience of asylum in Ireland, an Irish Refugee Council press release about a 2006 hunger strike by Afghan immigrants seeking asylum noted, "Children are growing up without ever having seen a parent go out to work or indeed cook a meal and adults are almost totally isolated from Irish society" (Irish Refugee Council 2006).

McDowell's discussion about a migrant's suitability for deportation, in addition to the use of the egalitarian argument noted above, also reflects the larger issue regarding who has the opportunity to migrate. Green card applicants and other employment applicants must have an expected income of €60,000 for the former and a minimum of €30,000 for the latter (Department of Jobs, Enterprise and Innovation 2011). There are also some limited exceptions for green card applicants in "strategically important occupations" (e.g., IT, healthcare, finance) expecting an income of €30,000–€59,999 (Department of Jobs, Enterprise and Innovation 2011). Hence, we see that, regardless of the type of migration, one's suitability to either remain in the state or be deported from the state has economic dimensions and, as the lived experiences of asylum applicants demonstrate, if another option were available refugee status would not be the first choice. The predominant distinctions between economic migration and refugee migration rest along fine lines drawn through entrenched acts of racialization, as criteria for economic access provide mechanisms for the inclusion of individuals recruited for employment and the exclusion of individuals who are not recruited and, therefore, forced to seek asylum. In other words, whites are positioned as legitimate economic migrants and blacks are positioned to be penalized for economic migration.

McDowell, once again stating Elukanlo's name, perhaps reflecting the near-"superstar" status of his campaign as well as acknowledging the passion of the students rallying behind the Nigerian student, also announced:

> Olukunle Elukanlo will now come back to Ireland and has welcomed my decision. With regard to the students in *Pobalscoil Isolde,* Palmerstown, I was taken aback when I heard somebody had proposed they should receive counseling, especially coming up to their leaving certificate. If they were going to spend their Easter holidays campaigning for Olukunle to return to Ireland I wondered what affect that would have on their leaving certificate results, whatever about Olukunle's. I therefore decided the sensible counseling and help that I could give was to bring him back and to take personal responsibility for admitting that my original decision was a mistake. (*Seanad Éireann* 2005)

Interestingly, we see that McDowell's decision to correct a "mistake" is neatly expressed as a course of action taken to prevent Palmerstown students from neglecting their studies and having to seek counseling or psychological therapy due to the Elukanlo case. The issues of human rights, the principle of non-*refoulement,* anti-immigration politics, and racism are kept out of the equation, safely preserving public policies that will perpetuate the very circumstances that led to Elukanlo's deportation or McDowell's original mistake. McDowell's actions illustrate the process of circumventing the engagement with those uncomfortable dimensions of the modern project that Elukanlo's case inevitably forces the state to consider. Hence, due to a "mistake," Elukanlo's case can be framed as a mere "glitch" in an otherwise perfect system, rife with the contradictions such pronouncements involve. So, Elukanlo's situation is singled out as a mistake even as McDowell's reference to other deportation decisions indicates—in the true spirit of the passive voice—other mistakes have been made.

Before returning to Ireland, Elukanlo issued a statement titled "My ordeal in Nigeria" at a press conference in Lagos on March 25, 2005, in which he explained the circumstances of his deportation and thanked his supporters. Through his comments we see the utility of contemporary global political linkages in the quest for social justice. He stated:

> I have called this conference to thank my friends and school mates in Palmerstown Community School in Dublin who have been protesting and picketing over my unjust deportation to Nigeria by Irish government on March 15, 2005. I also wish to use this medium to thank the Socialist Party members, especially Joe Higgins TD, for their solidarity and sup-

port since my unjust deportation. For instance, Joe had contacted members of Democratic Socialist Movement (DSM), an affiliate of Committee for A Workers International (CWI) in Nigeria to secure me an accommodation and oversee my upkeep as all these efforts have contributed immensely to force Irish government to review this injustice and consequently, recall me.[6] (Elukanlo 2005)

Elukanlo went on to speak in defense of his case, voicing his own experience rather than through the voices of protesters and state officials:

I had got a date, March 31, 2005 for my deportation to Nigeria and had to go to immigration center on March 15, 2005 to lodge an appeal. From there, I was arrested and detained at Cloverhill Prison in Dublin. In the night, I was taken to Airport in Dublin without allowing me see or speak to my lawyer. There was no accusation against me and I was not given any paper to sign.

Gentlemen of the Press, I, along with 25 other adults and 9 children were put on a charted flight to Lagos from where we were locked up at Alagbon Prison. I was lucky to bail myself out through the assistance of one of the inmates who sympathized with my condition. I left the prison and had nowhere to go. In the process of walking around, I ran into some gangsters who thought I had money on me. I was attacked and molested. After this, I flagged down an incoming vehicle. The man stopped and I explained my situation to him. He took me to his house. There was no electricity, my cloths were already torn and was starving with no medication for injuries I had sustained.

I am very happy to inform you that on Thursday, March 24, 2005, I have been recalled by Irish government. I have however called this conference to draw the attention of the public to the victims of similar injustice who are not privileged to be lucky like me. (Elukanlo 2005)

Elukanlo's ordeal presents a clear contradiction to the Minister for Justice's account. Even as Elukanlo's attack cannot be officially substantiated, the imprisonment at Alagbon Close Prison experienced by the Nigerians repatriated on March 14, 2005, and subsequently experienced by others deported that year, was reported beyond Ireland (see *Nigerian Guardian* 2005; Shadare 2005). Most importantly, the imprisonment of the deportees upon their arrival at Murtala Muhammad Airport indicates that concerns about safety were warranted and makes suspect the reliability of the Irish officials in Nigeria whom McDowell asserted were present to assist repatriated individuals. This again exposes the question of *refoulement* and supports the allegations that deportees were placed in very vulnerable positions.

In the spirit of the socialist organizers of the press conference, Elukanlo—via a consideration of contemporary globalization—presents commentary that brings into question the function of a modernity that continues to exclude the poor:

> We are made to believe that the world is a global village. But it seems this assertion is meant for the rich. The rich could move their capital and investment around the world. They could relocate to live anywhere around the world. But for the poor working people, it is another ball game entirely. How could I have justified my years of schooling in Dublin and only be deported when I am due to write my Leaving Certificate examination in June, 2005? Many people have been deported in this manner and could have likely committed suicide as they will not be allowed to take a pin. In most cases, they are not allowed to take their children along. This could be frustrating.
>
> I therefore use this medium to appeal to Irish government in particular and other governments in all the continents of the world to review their immigration policies to be more humane.
>
> Once again, I thank all my school mates in Dublin, the Irish Socialist Party and its sister organization in Nigeria, Democratic Socialist Movement (DSM) for their support and solidarity. Without these people, I would have been wasted.
>
> Thank you all. (Elukanlo 2005)

In addition to his critique of globalization, Elukanlo succinctly places the issue of freedom of mobility in the discussion, highlighting the means in which one's economic circumstances dictate the extent to which restrictions are placed on one's presence in a range of societies. He also refers to the separation from children due to deportation, which underlines his own former status as a "separated child" or "unaccompanied minor" as well as the overall inhumanity that he considers.

Upon his return Elukanlo was greeted at Dublin Airport by a crowd of approximately one hundred supporters and what one news commentator described as a "chaotic scene" and "pandemonium" in which he waved the tri-color Irish flag, thanked all of his supporters, and said, "I'm staying forever! I'm not going anywhere!" (RTÉ 2005b). Photographers flashed away as he rode off in a chartered van, waving to the crowd. Elukanlo would later go to the High Court to apply for leave to remain on humanitarian grounds, a case that involved the fact that his Irish girl-friend had given birth to their son.

Undoubtedly, the Elukanlo case allows us to see the ways in which deportations bring the current rendering of modernity into question. This further indicates that globality at its most progressive (i.e., modern) is antagonistic to border controls and related racialized determinations of social, political, and cultural belonging. Even as we review the high profile case of Elukanlo, it is also important to consider that thirty-four other Nigerians were deported with him the night of March 14, 2005, and, as Deputy Costello noted in the *Dáil,* only a "couple" of individuals were able to reach solicitors in time to stave off deportation. Quite notably, the mass countrywide roundup of Nigerian asylum applicants recalls more aggressive acts resulting in historical African Diaspora "un-freedoms" (e.g., the Transatlantic Slave Trade, slavery in the Americas, and related fugitive laws) with a few captives escaping merely to endure a precarious existence, signifying the inevitable link to earlier African Diaspora engagements with supposedly modern public policies.

Among those who were able to prevent deportation on the night of March 14, 2005, were a Dublin-based dancer who accessed a judicial review, and four youths, ages eight to seventeen, in Athlone, County Westmeath, who went into hiding to avoid the trip to Dublin Airport and subsequently Lagos. The circumstances around both cases, particularly the high-profile media coverage of the children in hiding, led to responses from community members and political officials that offer further insight into the significance of deportations in projects that counter modernity. Also significant is that both cases intersect with the public outcry and political discourse regarding Elukanlo's deportation and approved return.

On Tuesday, March 15, 2005, a co-host of the RTÉ radio program *Morning Ireland,* Áine Lawlor, introduced a segment on the would-be deported dancer, Azekiel, by somberly stating, "A chartered plane left Dublin Airport for Nigeria overnight filled with men, women and children who had been rounded up by the *gardai* for deportation" (*Morning Ireland* 2005). Azekiel, it was noted, had recently been seen on the popular "Late Late Show" with other asylum seekers who were learning Irish and was active in the Dublin arts community (*Morning Ireland* 2005). Since he preferred not to discuss his case while it was pending, his friend, John Scott, choreographer and artistic director of the Irish Modern Dance Theatre (IMDT), described Azekiel's circumstances in an interview recorded the evening of the deportations. Scott, who has conducted workshops and generated performances with the Center for the Care of Survivors of

Torture, discussed Azekiel's temporary reprieve and offered the following assessment: "You'd think that now that they're in Ireland that their torture is finished, that their . . . that the trauma is over. But, in fact they go through another form of torture waiting for their case to be approved. I just think that St. Patrick is very lucky he is not living in this day and age. If he was to arrive in Ireland this week he would probably be put back on that plane tonight that's going out with the Nigerians on it" (*Morning Ireland* 2005).

Again we see the mention of St. Patrick in the context of the Nigerian deportations. Certainly, the references reflect the irony of the aforementioned *Taoiseach* visit to the United States for St. Patrick's Day events and involvement with discussions around Irish migrants in the United States that week, as well as the fact that the deportations took place three days before the holiday celebration. However, Scott's comments also underscore the way in which these St. Patrick's Day references bring modernity into question, as such references draw on a fifth-century figure to isolate discrepancies in our twenty-first-century rendering of modern society. The suggestion that the Britain-born Patrick would not have become the patron saint of Ireland had he been subject to contemporary border controls brings into question the prohibitive impact of modern border and residential restrictions. Even as Scott's analogy naturally breaks down when we consider the contemporary EU as an entity, it is still important to bear in mind that St. Patrick, a central figure in the construction of global understandings of Irish cultural identity, was as much an outsider as Nigerian immigrants, not to mention initially enslaved in Ireland for six years before his escape from the country and subsequent return. The idea of an outsider coming into Ireland and making a very significant social and cultural contribution is also echoed in another statement by Scott. In his profile at the IMDT website he includes the following message to arts colleagues:

> I am greatly concerned that the arts community is generally unaware of the gross miscarriages of justice and human rights taking place on a daily basis under the current asylum process.
>
> There are people amongst us who can contribute greatly as performers, dancers, singers, actors and spectators who are existing here in Ireland but outside our general society.
>
> . . . This is not a political issue—it is a human issue, a life or death issue, an artistic issue. Our responsible engagement of this issue will enhance our own work and have a positive effect on our entire society. What

is now taking place will be the basis of much art—Books, Plays, Dances, Operas in the next ten years. If we artists do not quickly act it will be to our shame and History and the international community of our colleagues and our audiences and our children will judge us harshly. (http://www.irishmoderndancetheatre.com; capitalization as in original)

We see here that there is a sense of loss in the idea of individuals being turned away or repatriated that extends beyond the violation of the individual but also suggests a societal violation, one that prohibits the potential growth of all societies. This sense of loss, I argue, emerges out of the perception that modern societies should work toward collaborations that facilitate progress, which involves the crossing of borders, cultures, and identities. It is well known that St. Patrick's act of converting the Irish to Christianity involved combining his cultural perspective on Christianity with the local cultural expressions of spirituality as seen through pagan symbols and rituals. Even if we're compelled to offer a contemporary critique of St. Patrick's actions as subversive, what is significant here is that the cultural fusion that facilitated his actions represents a combination of the outsider and insider working together to create what would eventually be defined as the *insider* cultural expression; one that is still valued and relevant in Ireland today. We may wonder what new forms of culture will be seen as "essentially" Irish in the future and whether these new forms will be paired with notions of progress or retrogression.

Iyabo Nwanze and Elizabeth Odunsi, two women from Athlone, County Westmeath, each boarded the night flight to Lagos with a five-year-old son. However, their deportation received an extensive amount of national and international media coverage, including a *Time* magazine article (Lavery 2005), because the swift roundup resulted in Odunsi leaving behind an eight-year-old son and Nwanze leaving a seventeen-year-old daughter and two sons, ages fourteen and eleven, in Athlone. The four children went into hiding on March 14, 2005, and as late as 2007 only Odunsi's son, who had been hiding in Dublin, emerged via a clandestine return to Nigeria to be reunited with his mother. The remaining three youths were still considered "illegal" by the Department of Justice (*Drivetime* 2007; Power 2007). The circumstances of the four children in hiding—the "exceptional orphans"—combined with the way in which the sudden deportations were carried out by the *gardai*, led to a large response from community members and politicians. The children's only caretakers had been their mothers, so there was also national concern about their safety, even after it was eventually revealed that they were being protected by anonymous friends in the Nigerian community and, by 2007, were no longer listed as "missing persons" by *An Garda Síochána* (see Power 2007; Reilly 2007).

Numerous reports of that afternoon in Athlone noted aggressive behavior on the part of the *gardai* searching for the families, including the act of entering homes without invitation or search warrants, using "foul language," and creating what commentator Philip Boucher-Hayes aptly described as "quite a kerfuffle" (*Five Seven Live* 2005). Nwanze reported that *gardai* called her a "black monkey" and told her to "shut up, you African bitch" (Murphy 2005). During the *gardai* search for Nwanze's seventeen-year-old daughter at the Our Lady's Bower Secondary School, Deputy Principal Noel Casey said, "It was heavy handed. It was a police state" (*Nine News* 2005). In an interview with Boucher-Hayes, one Nigerian woman, Miriam, described the impact of the *gardai* search on the Nigerian children in the Athlone community:

> They were, you know, like frightened that. But it is because my children believe that, I think, people like that, you know, like they are White, they must be maybe police or something. Maybe they're taking us away.
>
> And they have been hearing from the background that they are taking some people away. And for two, three days my ten year old boy has not been himself. He kept asking me, "Mummy, are they going to take us to Nigeria without you?" . . . [He fears] that we are going to be split up, that maybe that is the system nowadays, splitting people up without their mother. . . . (*Five Seven Live* 2005)

Boucher-Hayes, echoing Miriam's concern, noted, "And that's the story that I have heard again and again today. . . . That there are many children here who feel that they are or are afraid that they're going to be split up from their parents and they're quite scared about it" (*Five Seven Live* 2005). The division of families further exemplifies earlier African Diaspora experiences of inequality and lack of liberty, a contemporary corollary to a historical loss of control over one's personal and familial destiny.

Nwanzi and Odunsi had been in Ireland since 2001 and, like Elukanlo, were often described as "well-liked" members of their community (Cusack 2006). Two days after their deportation, a photo even surfaced of the two women with *Taoiseach* Bertie Ahern in a smiley pose at a 2002 school event in Athlone (Morahan 2005; Murphy 2005), further demonstrating that Nwanze and Odunsi had become model members of the community. In addition to the photo, which was used in the campaign for the women's return, the measure of belonging, "integration," was often employed to reflect upon their Irish experience. For example, at the time of deportation the women were receiving computer training through the Vocational Opportunities Training Scheme for unemployed adults, where their teacher described them as "fully integrated" at the school (Murphy 2005), exemplifying the women's attempt to contribute to the community in which they lived even though they were not permitted to work. Three months after the deportation, RAR member Rosanna Flynn, during an acceptance of a World Refugee Day award, held up the photo and told the audience, "Now, things have moved on, or rather, I'm afraid things have moved back. We are now integrating people *for* deportation" (Flynn 2005, emphasis in transcript). Flynn's statement implicates the way in which integration is seen as progression or "mov[ing] on" as opposed to promoting the opposite, which represents "mov[ing] back" or retrogression. Two years later, Nwanze, speaking from Lagos in an August 2007 interview, provided an indication of the extent to which the two women had embraced Irish society as well as the presumption of a legal status meant to accompany such an embrace: "I feel so sad, and I feel cheated. It's an injustice, an inhumanity to man. We'd started integrating. We felt more like Irish citizens" (Reilly 2007). While the notion of integration does not explicitly deny cultural pluralism, it does suggest an act of becoming culturally Irish or at least contributing to Irish communities in a manner that meets the various criteria of Irishness. So, we see individuals of the African Diaspora meeting the criteria for acceptance in the modern Irish society but finding themselves excluded due to complex constructions of global political policies, human rights discourse, and the underlying desire for racially specific national identities. In other words, black migrants are engaged in a process of calling a bluff and revealing the truth behind it.

The outrage over the *gardai* actions, the separation of children from their parents, and the fear for the children's welfare combined with the Minister for Justice's reversal of the Elukanlo deportation led to the mobilization of local school staff, community members, and *Teachtaí Dála* (TDs or Deputies of the Dáil) in support of the reuniting of Nwanze and Odunsi with their children in Ireland. The desire of supporters is echoed in the following statement from Deputy Liz McManus: "The minister has got to say, 'Look, in this particular instance I will be compassionate.' All he has to do is extend the period of time that they can stay here. The two women should be returned to their children and be allowed to finish their education. It's not very long to go before their exams. But, to have a situation at the moment that pertains where children are literally on the run is not acceptable in modern Ireland" (*Nine News* 2005). McManus's determination of what "is not acceptable in modern Ireland" is what is at the root of all of the outrage around the deportations, whether in the case of the children, Azekiel, Elukanlo, or the others on the flight to Lagos. That is, such actions are not in line with predominant perceptions of how modernity is to be expressed. If the contemporary understanding of modernity would be hostile enough to have prevented the iconic St. Patrick from arriving in Ireland, then there is a problem in the rendering of modernity. McManus's statement clearly implies that *gardai* rushing through schools searching for students, the act of suddenly deporting people on late-night flights to Lagos without any recourse, and the overall state-level lack of compassion for the circumstances of these individuals reflect a less-than-modern society. But, of course, Ireland is not alone in its inability to realize modernity and, again, it is the African Diaspora which repeatedly calls would-be modern societies on their detrimental failures.

NEW ORLEANS
Race Meets Antediluvian Modernity

When Hurricane Katrina worked its way east of New Orleans on August 29, 2005, it facilitated a violent reminder, for the few who had forgotten, that the meting out of equality was too often racially specific in the United States and that it was not a settled deal. As the news photos and video of individuals of the African Diaspora, reflecting what was then 67 percent of the city's population of 500,000 (see Frey et al. 2007), were presented in global media, reactions and reporting represented a shock that the United States was somehow still getting equality, liberty, and democracy so very wrong (see Sullivan 2005). In Ireland, RTÉ Washington Correspondent Robert Shortt, reporting from New Orleans and reflecting on the more notable occurrences after two weeks of coverage, wrote: "Across the way from the Superdome, this perfectly modern highway looking over this beautiful city full of skyscrapers and on that highway were just huddled hundreds of people in the most miserable conditions just carrying piles of clothes in plastic bags, waiting to be airlifted in military helicopters. A bizarre sight in America in the twenty-first century" (RTÉ 2005c). To add to the sense that modernity was lost, he went on to note that the breakdown in communication technologies combined with the difficulty in finding food and water led another journalist to tell him, "It's like you're back in the Middle Ages" (RTÉ 2005c). Meanwhile, French reporting on New Orleans, a city which represents a French legacy of an earlier period of globalization, looked upon the United States as a space that could not live up to its notions of democracy. A *Le Monde* article titled "After Katrina, America interrogates the flaws of its model" observed that the "hurricane highlighted the weaknesses of the organization of American society" (Lesnes 2005). Meanwhile, in the United States, the urgency of the situation and the frustration at the slow federal response were reflected in repeat clips of New Orleans Mayor Ray Nagin exclaiming, "Now, get off your asses and let's do something. And let's fix the biggest goddamn crisis in the history of this country" (CNN 2005). Most significantly, questions of racism, echoed by others, were made explicit by hip-hop artist Kanye West stating "Bush doesn't care about black people" on MSNBC (see de Moraes 2005). Jesse Jackson, black activist and head of the Rainbow-Push Coalition, expressed similar concerns in a CNN interview with reporter Anderson Cooper:

> Cooper: Do you really believe race has been a determining factor in the rescue and recovery efforts going on and the response by the federal government?
>
> Jackson: It is at least a factor. Today I saw 5,000 African Americans on the I-10 causeway desperate, perishing, dehydrated, babies dying. It looked like Africans in the hull of a slave ship. It was so ugly and so obvious. Have we missed this catastrophe because of indifference and ineptitude or is it a combination of the both? And, certainly I think the issue of race as a factor will not go away from this equation.
>
> Cooper: So, you're saying if the majority of these people in the Astrodome or in the shelters were white you say the evacuation, what, would be done faster, would be done better?
>
> Jackson: We have an amazing tolerance for black pain and for too long after our slave ships landed in New Orleans, you know, we tolerated in the name of God slavery for 246 years (INAUDIBLE) for another 100 years. We have great tolerance for black suffering and black marginalization. And today those who are suffering the most, in fact, in New Orleans certainly are black people and I think what I think pains me today we got seven more busloads of people out of New Orleans. There were about 5,000 people. All of them were African American and no busses had been there until we got—they were sent to (INAUDIBLE). So, I said where are the busses? They said they're on the way. Across the street were 150 busses empty because they have no place to take them, so we have no place, no plan of rescue or relocation or relief for these people. Most are black and so the (INAUDIBLE) is self-evident. (CNN 2005)

Throughout this exchange, Jackson neatly equates the contemporary African Diaspora condition in New Orleans with a latent modern period, noting the resemblance of the New Orleans Convention Center to "the hull of a slave ship" (see Duke and Wiltz 2005). His comments locate the contemporary experience as another instance on a continuum dating back to "slave ships land[ing] in New Orleans" that facilitates a "great tolerance for black suffering and black marginalization." The tolerance to which Jackson refers is important to consider here because the perpetuation of "black suffering and black marginalization" is enabled by the inability of individuals to fully apprehend that the perceived anomaly of racism in a purportedly modern society is indicative of the society's failure at modernity itself. That is, the untenable can only be *tolerated* if it is perceived as somehow beside the point or, as noted earlier, a mere "glitch of modernity" and not a pandemic-like crisis that has an impact on the whole of society, locally and globally.

At a Congressional Black Caucus meeting a month after the hurricane, New York Congressman Charles Rangel compared President Bush's inaction in New Orleans with Theophilus Eugene "Bull" Connor's 1963 attempt to suppress civil rights activists (see Clyne 2005). Rangel referred to Bush as "our 'Bull' Connor," equating his response to the crisis as a more modern articulation of the violence and oppression that marked the black quest for civil rights, equality, and freedom—a reflection perhaps of the distinction Joel Kovel made in 1970 between "aversive" and "dominative" racism (Kovel 1984). Arguably, the actions of George W. Bush and Bull Connor would not pass the test of precise comparison; however, images of police dogs and armed officials in 2005 New Orleans seemed a contemporary visual corollary to those events in Birmingham, Alabama. The difference today is that there is no need to actively stand in the path of progress with hoses and dogs when oppression can be perpetuated and progression halted through the more passive modes of infrastructural, social, and economic neglect. Further underlining the dangers of limited access to the wealth that modernity presupposes, Rangel stated that "if you're black in this country, and you're poor in this country, it's not an inconvenience—it's a death sentence" (Clyne 2005).

Numerous news reports referred to individuals leaving New Orleans as "refugees," suggesting a foreign population on the move. It was as if, several hundred years after the Transatlantic Slave Trade, the African Diaspora of New Orleans was experiencing another forced migration (see Breed 2005; Frank 2005; Robison and O'Hare 2005), not a result of coercion but of the need to flee to safety. Of course, it was not possible to flee from racism.

The idea of New Orleans refugees also resonated with race-contingent notions of global poverty, as global discourse and the international face of "refugee" status are frequently racialized as black. As in Dublin, this racialization perpetuates the misrepresentations of contemporary refugees, in particular, the mistaken assumption that individuals seeking asylum cannot be well-educated and middle-class *and* black. However, New Orleans, a city in one of the wealthiest nations in the world, seemed to neatly contain the preferred representation of the "refugee" and, until criticism of this came to the fore, it was difficult to locate media that interrogated the use of the word. One notable report on the usage came from *Boston Globe* columnist Adrian Walker, who wrote about a call to his office:

> "I have relatives in New Orleans, on my wife's side," he said. "Don't compound that pain by calling my relatives 'refugees.' Don't call U.S. citizens who are African American, and get displaced, 'refugees.'" Former New Orleans mayor Marc Morial made a similar point yesterday on NBC's *Meet the Press*. In the midst of pleading for more aid for the city, he paused to dispute its citizens' newly described status. "These are not refugees. Let's stop calling them refugees. They are American citizens." By Friday, I had been hearing and reading the same term for several days. At first, it struck me as ironic: Refugee, after all, isn't a term Americans normally apply to other Americans. Homeless, yes, even displaced, but who ever heard of an American refugee in America? (A. Walker 2005)

But, for the most part, until more thoughtful reflection and analyses emerged (see Dyson 2006; Masquelier 2006), few did a "double take" at the idea of implying that citizens of the United States moving from one U.S. location to another could meet UN criteria for refugee status; criteria that, *inter alia,* involves persecution (which, if such an argument were advanced, could implicate more about New Orleans than I am addressing in this volume).

The inattentive reporting did not stop at the idea of African Americans declaring asylum in the United States. Such inattention amidst an African Diaspora crisis was best exemplified when CNN's Wolf Blitzer stated: "You simply get chills every time you see these poor individuals, as Jack Cafferty just pointed out, so tragically, so many of these people, almost all of them that we see, are *so poor and they are so black,* and this is going to raise lots of questions for people who are watching this story unfold" (Blitzer 2005; emphasis mine). It is conceivable that Blitzer made this comment—which was well circulated by shocked viewers via the internet—because he was distracted by the demands of hurried production and the need to avoid the dreaded "dead air." But, what was more shocking is not the poverty or the implications of what could have really been meant regarding the melanin content of individuals on a television monitor. What is most notable here is that people were left to suffer for so long without receiving help, making it clear that not only had modernity on social progress failed them, but modernity on technology and ingenuity had failed them, too.

A 2006 Knight Ridder study indicated that there were proportionately fewer blacks than whites who died in the hurricane (51% to 44% out of an overall population that was 61% black and 36% white) (see Young 2006). This is, of course, significant in that it appears to counter the "left to die" rhetoric that supports the obvious and rampant devaluing of black life witnessed in New Orleans. But, even if blacks did not disproportionately die, it is clear that black representation among the stranded, whether due to a lack of transportation out or the fact of their concentration in the most damaged areas, still implicates a society in which individuals of the African Diaspora could not access freedom of mobility because of poverty and geographic isolation (see Frey et al. 2007). There is a coincidence—in the full meaning of the word—that constructed the face of the Katrina disaster as a black face: a meeting of deeply rooted historical racisms and poverty. Whether considered a juxtaposition or an inextricable linkage, the experiences of racism and poverty are prevalent in the lives of the greater African Diaspora community in New Orleans. Pre-Katrina statistics indicate that the New Orleans black poverty rate was 34.9%, with 59,000 out of the 111,000 poor blacks below 50% of the poverty level (Sherman and Shapiro 2005), and the unemployment rate in 2004 was 20% higher than the national unemployment level for all blacks nationally (Holzer and Lerman 2006), which was at 10% in 2004 (W. Rodgers 2004).

What is also significant is that well beyond the devastating event, blacks were still experiencing a disproportionate negative impact. A 2007 Kaiser Family Foundation survey indicated a "big racial divide in experience and views" and noted, "Twice as many African Americans as whites in New Orleans (59% vs. 29%) reported that their lives are still 'very' or 'somewhat' disrupted" (Kaiser Family Foundation 2007). Another 2007 report from the Institute for Southern Studies indicated that "at least 40% of the city's residents have not returned, disproportionately African Americans" (Institute for Southern Studies 2007). The results of Patrick Sharkey's 2007 empirical examination of the impact of Katrina demonstrate that the elderly and blacks experienced the most extreme impact of the hurricane and that individuals in New Orleans' black communities— as implicated in the sites where bodies were located—experienced the worst of the hurricane (Sharkey 2007). In a 2008 empirical study, which also confirms Sharkey's assessment, economist Gregory Price poses the question: "Was there a departure from egalitarianism in the public provision of disaster rescue services during Hurricane Katrina in the City of New Orleans?" (Price 2008: 18). He determines that "our results suggest that there was a political economy of Race and Class—as being black and poor increased the probability of dying, both at the census tract and individual level—as a result of Hurricane Katrina" and that "black and poor may indeed face higher environmental risks, as we find that being black and poor during Hurricane Katrina in New Orleans increased the probability of being a natural disaster fatality" (Price 2008: 18–19).

In the end, the Katrina aftermath brought to the fore the dire circumstances faced by those meeting at the intersection of American race-based exclusion and poverty, even leading George W. Bush to finally accept an invitation to speak to the NAACP in 2006, where, most significant for our examination here, he stated, "I understand that racism still lingers in America" and noted that "[f]or nearly 200 years, our nation failed the test of extending the blessings of liberty to African-Americans. Slavery was legal for nearly 100 years, and discrimination legal in many places for nearly 100 years more" (Associated Press 2006).

As noted above, New Orleans has not seen a return of its African Diaspora community to reflect pre-Katrina numbers. However, there is still a black majority, coming in at 60.2% of the city's population in 2010 (U.S. Census 2010), up from 58% recorded in 2007 (Frey et al. 2007). The looming suggestion that the limited return of the African Diaspora communities will positively change the city implicates the extent to which racist assumptions prevailed in the pre-Katrina New Orleans, in spite of the ways in which the city often constructed itself as different from the rest of the United States in its approach to racial coexistence. Of course, the coexistence is a legacy of earlier notions of French assimilation tinged with French revolutionary understandings of egalitarianism. As Louisiana Congressman Richard Baker stated, "We finally cleaned up public housing in New Orleans. We couldn't do it, but God did" (Sasser 2006). Baker's statement, one which would be echoed in the context of Nicolas Sarkozy's similar desire to clean up the Paris suburbs in 2005, makes *La Nouvelle Orléans* seem more French than ever.

THE LOSS OF *LIBERTÉ, EGALITÉ,* AND THE AMERICAN DREAM

During the early post–Hurricane Katrina period, the historically rich idea of returning Louisiana to the French persisted in popular discourse. In late September 2005 a satirical news article began circulating across blogs and humor websites titled "President Bush sells Louisiana back to the French" in which George W. Bush, rather than face the financial after-math of Hurricane Katrina, sells Louisiana for "25 million dollars cash" to "a giddy Jacques Chirac" in a transaction described as "The Louisiana Refund." The fictitious article quotes Bush saying, "Jack understands full well that this one's a 'fixer upper.'. . . He and the French people are quite prepared to pump out all that water, and make Louisiana a decent place to live again. And they've got a lot of work to do. But Jack's assured me, if it's not right, they're going to fix it." During the first Mardi Gras after the hurricane, a parade presented by Krewe du Vieux included a float with the Eiffel Tower, a sign reading "Buy us back Chirac," and throws or giveaways of flyers with the same demand (Jensen 2006). As exemplified in the Krewe du Vieux parade, the 2006 Mardi Gras included numerous other float themes that referenced the response to the hurricane and its aftermath, including a preponderance of Federal Emergency Man-agement Agency (FEMA) jokes, which were still present on T-shirts in Bourbon Street shops as late as 2008 (e.g., "Got FEMA?"; "FEMA: Failure to Effectively Manage Anything"; "FEMA Evacuation Plan: Run Dumb-ass Run").

The implication of a "buy back," in line with the overwhelming per-ception of a poor FEMA effort, is that France could have managed the im-pact of Hurricane Katrina much better than the United States of America; each sentiment wittily reflecting the sense of abandonment by and in-competence of the U.S. federal government. While it is out of the purview of this project to present a comparison between emergency management expertise in France and the United States, I would argue that the root of the humorous discourse is much more of a social critique than one of infrastructural management. Thus, the underlying message—even with some of the commentary occurring after the 2005 uprisings in the Paris *banlieues*—also forces a consideration of whether the French would have been better on race in contemporary New Orleans.

As I will discuss below, lest we engage in ahistorical idealism, it is im-portant to consider that even if the French approach to race initially af-forded free blacks and enslaved blacks more mobility than the Americans permitted, one's place within the social hierarchy still remained consis-tent with how one was racialized. In other words, the extent of one's ex-perience of freedom in New Orleans was contingent on both labor status (i.e., enslaved, indentured, free laborer) and where one located oneself between the perceived poles of African and European ethnic identities. Most significantly, in spite of the humorous implications and obvious im-practicability of a return of Louisiana to France, the need to renegotiate an arrangement made during the beginning of the nineteenth-century march toward modernity (aka "manifest destiny" in the American context) sheds light on the historical interconnectedness of contemporary global communities resulting from a range of complex colonial and postcolonial projects, all facilitating the very Frenchness of this *American African Diaspora* site. Above all, we see a desire to revisit a moment in time that would have significantly altered the trajectory of the American experience, a paradoxical figurative quest for retrogression in an effort to facilitate progression.

Nouvelle Orleans was established as the capital of French Louisiana in 1718, thus continuing the process of displacing indigenous populations, implementing new societies via forced labor, and claiming yet another space for European interests and endeavors. In 1763, after the loss of the Seven Years War, Louis XV ceded Louisiana to Spain. In 1800, Louisiana was returned to France through the Secret Treaty of San Ildefonso. After the successful uprisings of the Haitian Revolution and the subsequent declaration of the Republic of Haiti under Jean-Jacques Dessalines (see Dubois 2005), Napoleon sold the Louisiana territory to the United States of America in the 1803 Louisiana Purchase. Throughout these global transactions and geopolitical agreements, New Orleans continued as a vibrant city, encompassing African, European, and indigenous American cultural forms and expressions. Due to its French penal colony beginnings and status as a designated destination for deported French citizens who were considered less than desirable, the city of Nouvelle Orleans was also formed and perceived as a site of temptation, incorrigibility, and generally all things external to conservative renderings of the ideal Roman Catholic and, upon American presence, ideal Protestant society (see Dawdy 2008). But undoubtedly it is this coexistence and sometimes merging of individuals of various cultural backgrounds and socio-economic strata amidst labor hierarchies, mercantilism, global capitalism, and geopolitical conflicts that make New Orleans historically and contemporarily a global city. The idea of a modern society that is organically formed through cultural exchange leading to new cultural forms and more inclusive identities is often articulated as a global ideal or the seemingly utopian trajectory of the modern project of globalization itself (see Hayden and El-Ojeili 2009). If New Orleans represented that possibility, it was flawed and thwarted by an overarching maintenance of white French and, later, white American supremacy amidst the equally valuable societal and cultural contributions of African Diaspora communities and individuals of African descent in the city.

In early Nouvelle Orleans, African Diaspora communities, which heartily infused the very identity of the French city, consisted of individuals in bondage representing diverse West African ethnic groups, including Ardra, Bambara, and Wolof, and a free black population including individuals arriving directly from Saint-Domingue and others from Saint-Domingue via Cuba. Free blacks, particularly individuals who had both European and African ethnic backgrounds and claimed a *gens de couleur libres* (free people of color) or Creole identity, created an educated French-speaking and French Creole–speaking population that represented a middle tier between an enslaved black population and white Creoles (descendants of French and, later, French and Spanish colonists), but also perpetuated and solidified the very Frenchness of New Orleans (see G. Hall 1995; Sublette 2008).

The means by which a unique culture emerged in New Orleans is often explained through the story of a harmoniously interethnic and interracial city forming as a result of the geographic limitations of a space wedged between the Mississippi River and swamp land and the resulting close-proximity living. However, amidst the exchange of ideas and cultures that traversed racialized identities, the critical distinction between communities becomes most notable via the U.S. intervention into this somewhat Spanish and very French city. This is apparent in the construction of life on the other side of Canal Street—across from the mostly Catholic French Quarter—with the advent of the predominantly Protestant American sector or Garden District. This distinction is most significant when we consider that the American imposition also involved perpetuating the preference for a limited interaction between whites and blacks. This was based on the white American aversion to blacks, which was significantly different from the French and Spanish approach to interethnic living and the lifestyle of enslaved individuals. Yet, as noted above, it is also important to consider that even if enslaved individuals had significant mobility in New Orleans and free blacks and whites shared communities, whites were well placed at the top of the social hierarchy even in pre-American New Orleans (see Ingersoll 1991; Hirsch and Logsdon 1992; Kein 2000).

Louisiana seceded from the union in 1861 and joined the Confederacy in the American Civil War. The overriding anti-Anglo-Saxon and anti-northern sentiments, the election of Republican Abraham Lincoln, and a desire to maintain a racial and labor status quo prevailed in the argument for secession, in spite of the presence of a strong community of free blacks and New Orleans' substantial non-slaveholding immigrant population without an attachment to the peculiar institution—including numerous Irish migrants by the mid-nineteenth century (Hearn 2005; Winters 1991). However, if we are to fully consider New Orleans as a site that represents the further retrenchment from the ideal modern or progressive project, the more significant impact of the city's engagement with a racist, counter-egalitarian system occurred after the Civil War. That is, it was not until the proximity between whites and blacks was tested vis-à-vis the quest of *gens de couleur* and blacks for political rights and equality under the Reconstruction-era laws that we see, via Jim Crow laws, a definitive line being drawn between white citizenship and the rights of individuals of African descent to full citizenship (Ingersoll 1991; Hirsch and Logsdon 1992; Kein 2000; Hogue 2006).

It is no small event that the seminal test of equality, racialization, and citizenship in the United States was brought forth through the New Orleans case of *Plessy v. Ferguson*. The 1896 case, in which the Supreme Court upheld racial segregation and, in effect, racism in the United States of America, was launched in a city that was relatively adept at the blurring of the artificially constructed understandings of racial difference and, had there been a progressive ruling, could have conceivably expedited a process that would have rendered the racialized outcome of Hurricane Katrina improbable. In a thoughtful 2007 documentary film by Stephen Ives titled *New Orleans,* which effectively captures articulations of the cultural uniqueness of the city, historian Rebecca J. Scott states the following during an interview about the *Plessy* decision: "When we think back on this moment, and the lost opportunity, it is extraordinarily poignant. I think part of what makes it so painful, is to realize that when they lost in 1896, it meant that the entire country lost an opportunity to really embody the new birth of freedom that the Civil War had been meant to create. And it opened up the space for something very different to be built. And once that edifice of white supremacy was built it would be impossible to dismantle by normal political means" (Ives 2007; also see Scott 2005). There is a melancholy tension between the New Orleans that could have represented a multiethnic beacon in a modern nineteenth-century America and that which became complicit as the principal arbiter of how race relations would continue to function throughout the United States two centuries later.

In the same documentary, the late sculptor John T. Scott, expressing what will be the last commentary in the film, states: "The promise of that city is the lesson that can be learned from that city. At its best, when the people are doing what they do naturally—blending a seamless culture—it has a oneness about it that very few places in the rest of this country have. New Orleans' promise is we can teach America how to be America. If anybody's listening" (Ives 2007). The multiethnic interactions that produced the specific New Orleans culture to which John

T. Scott refers in the documentary have persisted simultaneously with the stark social, economic, and related political conditions that facilitate oppressive racial hierarchies throughout the United States; another instance of a narrative of progression that masks a more invidious retrogressive reality. Yet, the idea that New Orleans could "teach America how to be America," as John T. Scott so importantly puts it, also signifies an "otherness" of the city, perhaps suggesting to us that the ways in which the city deviates from more mainstream historical and contemporary American racial projects create a perception of New Orleans as an anomalous American society as opposed to a true American society. This, of course, further exemplifies the ways in which notions of progress are limited by retrogression, in that New Orleans becomes the oddity in the representation of the American Dream rather than a representation of the norm.

The Frenchness of the city as antagonistic to American socio-cultural formations also contributes to an otherness of New Orleans, particularly dating back to a nineteenth-century black, French-speaking Creole population that, even before *Plessy*, forced an alternative narrative of black presence in the United States. Undoubtedly—again not to entrap ourselves in the idealization of the pre-American French colonial experience—racial tensions were well built into the French understanding of blackness itself. We need only consider that Napoleon sold Louisiana to the United States after the carnage of the Haitian Revolution, a revolution required because France did not apply its newfound egalitarian ideals—e.g., the 1789 Declaration of the Rights of Men—to the rights of blacks in Saint-Domingue. Nevertheless, the black elite in New Orleans, particularly those who arrived as part of the Saint-Domingue Diaspora or Haitian Diaspora, were not immune to the infectious quality of French culture (see G. Hall 1995; Kein 2000). What is significant here is that the French approach to racial interaction involved a very different engagement with individuals of the African Diaspora, one that generated among blacks a rightful sense of entitlement of civil rights in a purportedly just democratic society. Thus, the *Plessy* case, in addition to its progressive interrogation of racial norms and democratic citizenship, represented an African Diaspora community's assertion of its right to humanity and its attempt at forcing a nation to reach its democratic ideal and to respect the Constitution as an expression of that democracy. As Harvey Fireside notes in the preface to his volume on the case, "Only rarely in courses on constitutional law were students told that the Fourteenth Amendment was hijacked for the benefit of corporations, instead of securing the citizenship of former slaves" (Fireside 2005: xix). Quite clearly, when *Plessy* failed, America failed and, as seen through the events of Hurricane Katrina, continues to fail.

The introduction to Fireside's volume is written by the former mayor of New Orleans, Marc H. Morial, who served until 2002. Notably, Morial is a member of a prominent black Creole family and the son of New Orleans' first black mayor, Ernest N. Morial, exemplifying a racialized power structure still operational in a city that maintains a dominant black Creole presence among the representative African Diaspora population. Morial explains that he considers the *Plessy* case an impetus for "that great flood tide of humanity out of the rural South to the urban North" and powerfully asserts: "In the *Plessy* decision, White Racist America had demanded through its spokesmen, the U.S. Supreme Court, that African Americans *stay in their place*. Instead, in literally millions of ways, African Americans declared over and over again: I will be free. That was the greatest consequence of the *Plessy* decision itself, and, let it be said, the great legacy of Homer Adolph Plessy and the black Creoles of Louisiana" (Fireside 2005: xii; emphasis in original). Morial's comments on *Plessy* bring us back to the consideration of the quest for positive freedom and the expansion of resources that is part of realizing that freedom. Undoubtedly, the North was also inextricably linked to modern inequalities, but the northward migration involved the quest for democracy and, at the least, a slightly better semblance of freedom.

In spite of the complexity of the New Orleanian cultural identity that is still claimed across racial and ethnic lines, the legacy of Jim Crow and its *de jure* and *de facto* racial oppressions nonetheless facilitated a circumstance in which black populations were highly represented in the areas of New Orleans more prone to the negative impact of natural disaster. The far-from-expeditious reaction to the victims of Hurricane Katrina merely takes us back to *Plessy* and a government that did not value the human rights of African Americans.

NORA IN 2008—THREE YEARS REMOVED

Upon arriving on the tarmac at the Louis Armstrong New Orleans International Airport one sees a large welcoming sign: "New Orleans. Linking the Americas to the World." Due to its place in the lives of indigenous populations, subsequent transitions via colonialism, and its eventual location in the American state of Louisiana, the history of New Orleans is about the building of a global cross-cultural space. Even if New Orleans is not exactly what Sassen had in mind when considering global cities, undoubtedly the city's location on the U.S. Gulf Coast, the activity in the Port of New Orleans, and the Louisiana oil industry place New Orleans at the nexus of historical and contemporary global transactions that inform and perpetuate a global identity, economically and culturally. As the Port of New Orleans website enthusiastically notes: "With the Mississippi River moving about 500 million tons of cargo each year—including chemicals, coal, timber, iron, steel and more than half of the nation's grain exports, the Port of New Orleans is America's gateway to the global market" (www.portno.com).

What is key here is that the global narrative of New Orleans, with its framing of self as a modern entity linking the Americas—North, Central, and South—to the world, must also reconcile the looming reality that this contemporary space of global linkage is also the site of one of the more noted disasters and glaringly evident representations of social and racial oppression in the twenty-first century: Hurricane Katrina. The argument follows that in order for New Orleans to revive its modern self it must transcend the effects of Hurricane Katrina and begin anew. Of course, I am arguing here that the impact of Katrina is not at all removed from the modern condition; most problematically and sadly, it *is* the modern condition. The excitement of the "gateway to the global market" or being the city that "Link[s] the Americas to the World" is about constructing a modern global reputation and, even more, it is about survival. So, from the moment one enters the city, the narrative of survival and revival persists.

The inevitable reminders of the lived experience of Katrina are ubiquitous, including closed businesses, trailers on the front lawns of property under repair, tilted and sunken abandoned homes, plots with three cement steps leading up to an empty space where a house once stood, and the myriad stories told by the individuals who survived. In spite of the probability that—now a few years removed—many non–New Orleanians have stopped considering Hurricane Katrina, every day the impact of the hurricane is faced directly by the residents of New Orleans, as such a reality would be impossible to deny or ignore. So, along with the myriad other aspects of life in New Orleans, Hurricane Katrina and its aftermath are integrated with the lures of tourism. Pubs and bars are just as likely to be visited after a Hurricane Katrina bus tour as after a traditional walking tour of the ghosts of the French Quarter. This is immediately apparent upon entering the airport, where travelers are quickly reminded—in case they forgot—about the seriously catastrophic experience of Hurricane Katrina in this global city. Along a hallway to an airport restroom area there is a "Hurricane Katrina Timeline" dating from Monday, August 29, 2005, to Tuesday, September 13, 2005, that presents information on the use of Armstrong International during the period: "Storm Shelter, Evacuee Drop Zone, Air Evacuation Center, Relief Supply Depot . . . Hospice and Morgue . . . Military Base . . . Tent City . . . FEMA Trailer Park Site." A sign near the timeline reads: "The Louis Armstrong New Orleans International Airport would like to thank everyone who participated in the historic events surrounding Hurricane Katrina." The space of the airport becomes a primer on the aftermath of the "historic events" by offering a briefing on a city attempting to return to what it once had been: a place with a rich cultural identity embodied by New Orleanians and embraced by tourists. But, simultaneously, the global identity expressed in the welcome on the tarmac suggests that the development of a new version of the city is under way.

Undoubtedly, the problem of New Orleans is partially a geographic one: the city is below sea level and its inhabitants live in the bottom of what is often described as a geological "soup bowl" (see Fitzpatrick 2006). However, most significantly, the impact of Katrina upon residents also has much to do with New Orleans' role as a microcosm of the undemocratic and anti-modern American version of race-based social inequalities. The New Orleanians I interviewed in March 2008, as they witnessed and participated in the "comeback" of the city, frequently expressed a sense of loss or the removal of an intangible energy tantamount to a death. Even though many believed a revival of the city was inevitable, the overall sentiment of what one interviewee described as a city "on life support" persisted.

While racing along I-10 from the airport heading downtown, a Bosnian cab driver, Adem, who migrated to New Orleans in 2001, expressed to me a common post-Katrina sentiment: "This city has no soul. It has no soul. You know, like a person, when his soul is taken out, it is not the same anymore. The black people made this city. The black people started this city. The black people made this city what it was. The music. The food. The dancing. The people in the street. . . . Now you go to work, you get paid, you bank it, you go home. . . . Now it is like any other American city." Adem's comparison of New Orleans to "any other American city" explains the blandness or perhaps "the Starbucks factor" that has an impact on many towns and cities struggling to retain something unique within increasingly corporate spaces that—give or take a product or menu item—facilitate sameness. Yet, also implicit in the sameness and made explicit in Adem's comments is the evident loss of blackness. The post-Katrina reduction of the African American population is quite notable in a city that derives its self-definition predominantly from cultural expressions of African Diaspora communities. It is interesting that this observation came from an individual from Bosnia and Herzegovina, inasmuch as the policies and programs that have discouraged many African Americans from returning to New Orleans have been described as "ethnic cleansing" (Fausset 2009; Hassan 2006). While "ethnic cleansing," which encompasses genocide and rape, implicates a much greater violence than that which facilitates the removal of many African Americans from New Orleans, the discourse on removing specific populations from the city—as exemplified by Louisiana congressman Richard Baker's comment that "God" via Hurricane Katrina "cleaned up public housing in New Orleans"—has fueled the understanding that a group of people, primarily African Americans, is being targeted for permanent removal from the city. Of course, various dimensions of blackness and African Americanness, like Frenchness, continue to play integral roles in all that defines New Orleans. However, even as the positioning of African Diaspora communities within New Orleans has historically created the culture of the city, currently a repositioning of blacks away from the city and far-flung amidst what is described as the "Katrina Diaspora" is fostering a new definition of the city.

While the vision of the *new* New Orleans, as initially outlined in the controversial plan presented by the "Bring Back New Orleans" Commission and later in the March 2009 draft of the New Orleans Master Plan, takes into consideration the pre-Katrina social conditions experienced by many African Americans in the city—particularly in the areas of housing and community building—the focus on tackling criminality and blight also perpetuates the retrogressive equation of fewer blacks with a more idyllic city. So, the remedies for the problems of "old New Orleans" are considered through the racialized discourse and representations that placed many black New Orleanians in grave circumstances long before the first wind of Hurricane Katrina. The policies and programs that make a return prohibitive for many African Americans are not only a result of the violence of a hurricane's destruction but they are also rooted in the historical violence of racism in its geo-social form, which must be addressed if New Orleans is ever to be truly new.

RACIAL AND SOCIAL CONSTRUCTIONS OF THE "NEW" NEW ORLEANS

The attempt to build a new New Orleans amidst retrogressive racial and social formations implicates the relativism that accompanies a generation's experience of progressiveness, regardless of its real manifestation. This is particularly exemplified when we consider the impact of racism upon the development of the infrastructure of New Orleans and its layout during the late nineteenth-century to early twentieth-century period. As Craig E. Colten very adeptly observes in his volume *An Unnatural Metropolis,* "[a]lthough Progressive Era reforms sought a type of environmental determinism, improving people by improving their environment, the exclusion of southern blacks illustrates an obvious choice not to include this group. New Orleans offers a grand panorama of this paradoxical struggle" (Colten 2005: 79). Colten explains that the Sewage and Water Board was slow to make key infrastructural changes related to drainage and sewage in African American and low-income areas throughout the 1920s, but that by the 1930s the "drainage and sewage system eventually reached citywide distribution with little apparent race or class bias"; however, "[t]his does not mean the city achieved environmental equity, but it indicates that rational engineering was prevailing over racism in terms of public works" (Colten 2005: 106). Furthermore, Colten writes: "Jim Crow . . . emerged through overt real estate policies and neighborhood-based financing of urban amenities. Although the improved drainage system opened new areas of black residences, at the same time it contributed to segregation, reflecting established patterns of turning low-value land associated with environmental problems over to minority populations. The development of lakefront property also required expansion of the drainage system, and this improvement contributed to segregation in the higher-valued area restricted to whites" (Colten 2005: 106–107).

Ultimately, as Colten discusses, the impetus for developing the infrastructure in African American communities in spite of anti-black sentiments involved a practical scientific understanding that areas of the city were linked and that, quite certainly, a drainage or sewage problem could have an impact on the health and welfare of the entire city (Colten 2005). However, these earlier circumstances also exemplify another phase of the modern project in which technological achievement is more progressive than the social dimensions of the society. This is particularly poignant when we consider that the Progressive Era, running from the late nineteenth century into the WWI period, is characterized by reform projects geared toward remedying inequalities in housing and labor conditions, addressing child labor concerns, providing aid for new immigrant populations, paying nominal attention to the rights of white women, facilitating civic change through philanthropic endeavors, and, *inter alia,* rooting out social injustices through the journalism of the time. Nevertheless, amidst this seemingly progressive moment that represents a shining example of what modernity hath wrought, we see the continued neglect, oppression, and overall disregard of the citizenship and humanity of blacks in America. Above all, this is an indication that a progressive movement could never be fully so until it included African Americans not only because it was *strategically* necessary but because it was the moral and ethical means of realizing the progressive modernity that the movement wished to advance. The glaring reality of the flawed progressiveness of the past is inextricably linked to the housing and living conditions of the myriad African Americans standing on the roofs of their homes in August 2005; for as long as racism was paired with progressiveness, it could not be a progressive movement at all.

NEW ORLEANS HOUSING: A DISASTROUS TOUR

Katrina disaster tourism serves the multifaceted projects of eliciting charitable concern, facilitating the human desire to gaze at tragedy, setting the record straight, and reaping some financial benefit from what is, for the tourism industry, no less than the "elephant in the room." However, there is tension among these competing projects, which is effectively exemplified through the commentary offered by the guide of a "Gray Line Hurricane Katrina Tour." At the beginning of the tour, the guide, Terrence, an African American who described himself as "born and raised in New Orleans," explained, "This tour is not political. I'm just going to state the facts and you can see what you think." While the apolitical approach may likely reflect a corporate interest in having Gray Line employees avoid the potential of offending a paying customer, Terrence's comments also effectively represent the range of voices that have emerged from a variety of African Americans throughout the post-Katrina city; overall, expressing complex experiences that could never be reduced to pictures on a cable news network or monolithic articulations of the African American experience and blackness in New Orleans.

The tour bus cruised away from the French Quarter—against expectations, situated on high ground along the Mississippi River—inland toward the lower-level layers of sadness. As the tourists gawked, shook heads at disaster, and listened for an explanation via the microphone, Terrence took care to note that "Some people made a conscious decision to stay," particularly those who had survived the 1965 Hurricane Betsy. Later, he directed our attention to a house where he had seen a wide-screen TV and two SUVs under a carport after the hurricane, suggesting that the economic wherewithal implied a conscious decision to stay rather than become victims of Katrina. He also addressed the fact that Katrina had an impact on a range of socio-economic communities and discussed the middle-class African American communities, stating that the Ninth Ward also encompasses the middle-class New Orleans East community, which he noted has "two or three very rich people . . . one of them is Fats Domino." As one interviewee later told me, "Some folks moved up to New Orleans East from the Lower Ninth Ward. It was like George Jefferson, moving on up to the East Side."

In the effort to bring a larger and more balanced picture, the tour cruised along the barren streets of the leveled Lower Ninth Ward as well as journeyed through a viewing of Katrina's impact in the middle-class communities of the predominantly white area of Lakeview and the now racially mixed area of Gentilly, and highlighted the damage to the million-dollar homes of the wealthy African American community of Eastover. Yet, in spite of the attempt at a neutral or apolitical discussion, the tour guide was clearly unnerved by the timeline of government aid and support. While pointing out the water line on an abandoned home, a discoloration marking the period of time in which the house sat nearly roof-high in floodwater, Terrence said, "CNN arrived on Wednesday. But, it took the government until Monday to bring help. I still don't understand that."

The tour rode through Pontchartrain Park, a predominantly black middle-class subdivision in the Gentilly area built in 1954. The neighborhood was originally developed for African American World War II and Korean War veterans and professionals barred from moving into the neighboring "whites only" Gentilly Woods and Gentilly Terrace. Terrence pointed at the Pontchartrain Park houses and said, "You're not just looking at destroyed property. You're looking at dead American dreams." While driving by the devastated homes with FEMA trailers parked in the once-manicured front yards on Mirabeau Avenue in Gentilly, Terrence poignantly expressed what he felt the home owners were saying or thinking: "I'm a soldier. I came back from World War Two. I came back from Korea. That's my dream there." In reality, if the Mirabeau Avenue veterans that Terrence envisioned happened to be African American, reflecting the majority of the current population in the area, immediately after either war they would not have been able to cross the racial line into Gentilly Woods to buy homes on Mirabeau Avenue. The adjacent Pontchartrain Park would have been the community that welcomed them until the Fair Housing Act of 1968 and subsequent white flight from the area blurred the lines between black Pontchartrain Park and white Gentilly Woods. Nevertheless, irrespective of when the veterans initially moved in, the front lawn trailers with the generators humming indicated that their American dreams were not quite dead, but certainly on life support.

The devastated homes along the Hurricane Katrina tour were yet another footnote to the story of African Americans returning from war to fight for the Four Freedoms only to find that freedom was still not an option for them. If they wanted some semblance of the American Dream, it would not be in Gentilly Woods, for that was built for whites. However, their Pontchartrain Park homes were built by the same company that built Gentilly Woods and were similarly designed. An early brochure for "the Negro park" states: "It's Pontchartain Park. Your dream home in a dream neighborhood" (see Reese 2007). Many African Americans would eventually live in those Gentilly Woods homes from which they were barred, and, after Katrina hit, when the New Orleans Public Library posted an archival brochure with the "hope [that] these images will be of some use to the residents of Gentilly Woods as they begin to return and rebuild," African American residents were in a position to use the literature that would never have been available to them before to rebuild the very homes that were initially never to be inhabited by them at all (Louisiana Division/City Archives 2006). The 1950s-era Gentilly Homes, Inc., brochure is titled "Plan Book for Gentilly Woods" and, providing insight into the allocation of land in New Orleans, states: "Here on some of the highest choicest land in the city, they have designed a beautiful section of 1,423 two and three bedroom homes" (Louisiana Division/City Archives 2006). The "highest choicest land" would not be available to African Americans until whites moved on to even "high[er] choicest land." Ultimately, the irony of an American Dream that excludes on racial grounds is that it is therefore an anti-American Dream. The post-WWII culture of the society, with its baby boom and belief in a superior form of American modernity vis-à-vis a postwar economy and the construction of the iconic American suburb, was still marred by racism (see Kushner 2009), indicating that an American Dream with racist contingencies is, for some, no more than an American Nightmare.

Several of the people I interviewed—like the Gray Line tour guide—made an effort to insert a stronger class discourse into the circumstances of New Orleans, moving away from reducing the conflicts and outcomes to race alone. This was particularly exemplified in comments made by Anita, an African American artist who was selling her paintings as part of an arts collective in the French Market area. During our conversation, she stressed class distinctions among the African American community and emphasized the lack of governmental support over "racial conspiracy theories" as having the greater impact on the outcome of Katrina. "It's about government mismanagement," she said. "It's not about race. The problem is socio-economic." She, like Terrence and others interviewed, attempted to broaden the perception that the story of Katrina is exclusively linked to the "black poor face" of black New Orleans, noting the impact upon other communities—black and white—outside of the Lower Ninth Ward. Anita also highlighted the structural differences that facilitated more damage to Lower Ninth Ward property. In addition to the issue of the position of the Lower Ninth Ward against a poorly built flood wall, Anita noted, "The difference between the impacts of Katrina is also because the houses in St. Bernard Parish are mostly brick and the Lower Ninth Ward houses were mostly wood houses." She also expressed concern about the reduction of hardship to solely a black experience: "How do you tell someone [who is white] in Gentilly or St. Bernard Parish that they didn't get help because the government didn't want to help black people? They lost everything, too."

To extend Anita's thoughts on race and class, it should be noted that as late as 2008, during a walk through the predominantly white Garden District or a ride on the St. Charles Streetcar, it was evident that there were still repairs under way along the tree-lined streets of large classic houses and mansions. There is little doubt that Hurricane Katrina had an impact on individuals regardless of ethnicity, race, or, for that matter, class. However, at issue is the disproportionate presence of African Americans in the low-lying Lower Ninth Ward, an area protected by a weak levy and a poorly built floodgate. It is difficult to examine the racialization of space in New Orleans and the economic circumstances that prohibit the return of middle-class African Americans and not consider racism in New Orleans and, by extension, the United States. As revealed in a 2006 Brown University study titled "The Impact of Katrina: Race and Class in Storm-Damaged Neighborhoods," it is evident that "the odds of living in a damaged area were clearly much greater for blacks, renters, and poor people" (Logan 2006: 7). Furthermore, the report suggests that "if the future city were limited to the population previously living in zones undamaged by Katrina it would risk losing about 50% of its white residents but more than 80% of its black population," leading the report's author, John Logan, to note that "the continuing question about the hurricane is this: whose city will be rebuilt?" (Logan 2006: 16).

REBUILDING A DREAM

The issue of housing in New Orleans and its relation to the American Dream is important to consider here because the very idea of the dream embodies the American rendering of a modern democratic society and

the related freedom conceptually associated with "the land of opportunity." Through housing, we see how "raced" opportunity can be and, via
the experiences of the African Diaspora in New Orleans, how exclusive
the dream can be. During interviews in the Lower Ninth Ward, I was
told of instances in which individuals who were residing in homes that
had been unofficially passed down from deceased relatives before Katrina could not receive aid or compensation after Katrina because they
did not have documents to prove ownership of their homes. While such
circumstances obviously prohibit a return to a property and rebuilding,
individuals who are able to produce papers and qualify for assistance also
have had difficulty reconstructing their American Dreams. As a real estate lender who serves African American communities noted in a *Times-
Picayune* interview, "This is discrimination based on the pre-storm value
of a house. . . . Someone in Pontchartrain Park can't rebuild, but you take
the same property in Lakeview and you'd get a lot more money" (Hammer 2008). Though individuals in low-income communities, which are
predominantly African American, qualify for Road Home grants, the full
utilization of the grant does not facilitate return.

The difficulties are primarily a result of the Louisiana Recovery Authority (LRA) and the U.S. Department of Housing and Urban Development (HUD) classification of the grants as compensation based on the
lower amount of either one's pre-Katrina home value or replacement costs
at $130 per square foot for homes more than 51% damaged, with a cap
of total compensation at $150,000 (Hammer 2008). Aware of the poten-
tial problem that some individuals would have raising capital in spite of
receiving a Road Home grant, HUD also provided up to $50,000 in ad-
ditional compensation for families making less than 80% of the median
income. In a hypothetical comparison between a home in the predominantly white area of Lakeview and a home in the predominantly black
area, the Lower Ninth Ward, the following example by *Times-Picayune*
reporter David Hammer offers a useful indication of the way prior economic disparities in housing options and home value placed homeowners in predominantly black areas at a greater disadvantage in comparison
to homeowners in similarly damaged areas that are predominantly white:

A 1,500-square-foot house totaled by storm waters in Lakeview, for example, might have been worth $250,000 before Katrina. In the Lower 9th
Ward, a home of the same size may have been worth $70,000. But while
the Lakeview owner's grant would be calculated on the basis of a $195,000
replacement cost, the 9th Ward owner's would be based on the much
lower pre-storm property value.

If both homes had been covered by $40,000 in insurance, the Lakeview home would have qualified for the full $150,000 Road Home grant and the 9th Ward applicant would have been left with $30,000. The 9th Ward homeowner would have been fully compensated for the pre-storm value of the property, while the Lakeview resident would be short $60,000.

Both likely would need more money to rebuild, but the fully compensated 9th Ward homeowner would need more. Lower-income families can apply for loans to close the gap, but they typically face more difficulty qualifying. (Hammer 2008)

So, even if an owner is able to access the additional $50,000 because of income, the securing of a loan and subsequent mortgage payments would be the likely next steps. A June 2009 Greater New Orleans Community Data Center (GNOCDC) repopulation indicator that monitors "residential addresses actively receiving mail" and compares the data to 2005 pre-Katrina results to track the extent of return also corresponded with a slower return in areas with difficulty accessing the advantage of Road Home grants, areas which are primarily mapped as maintaining predominantly black pre-Katrina populations (GNOCDC and Brookings Institution 2009; also see Plyer 2010). The Road Home problem exemplifies a prohibitive aspect of returning, but also sheds light on the continued racial dimensions of economic disparities, further indicating that the pre-Katrina planning of the city is inextricably linked to racism and the racialization of neighborhoods amidst progressive representations of modernity.

In 2008, Wendell Pierce, an actor who grew up in the 1960s and 1970s era of Pontchartrain Park, formed a redevelopment group focused on utilizing Road Home buyout property to rebuild and revitalize Pontchartrain Park and Gentilly Woods, as both neighborhoods were experiencing a slow return due to the combination of the inability of prior residents to fully finance rebuilding and a senior citizen population physically unable to return to the city (WDSU 2008). Pierce and his partners in the Pontchartrain Park Community Development LLC have focused on developing sustainable or "green" housing for "working middle-class" families, which would work in tandem with the New Orleans Redevelopment Authority (NORA) plan to rebuild homes around the renowned Pontchartrain golf course and to construct a "town center" on the site of the ruins of the Gentilly Woods Mall (Bohrer 2008). Notably for our consideration here, Pierce described his commitment to revitalizing this former beacon of African American middle-class living as offering a new generation a chance "to buy into the American dream" (Bohrer 2008). The complexity of the American Dream is made even more apparent when we consider a May 2009 triumph for Pierce's father, Army Corporal Amos Pierce. Corporal Pierce, who served in Saipan during WWII, should have received medals but was told that there was no record of his unit's achievements (Capo 2009). Corporal Pierce, in a WWL news report, is described as feeling "bitterness for six decades, so angry he ignored a letter from the military about the medals" (Capo 2009). But upon inquiry by Wendell Pierce, local investigative reporter, Bill Capo, and Louisiana Senator Mary Landrieu, it was revealed that Corporal Pierce should have received six medals. During an Armed Forces Day ceremony in which Corporal Pierce was finally awarded the medals in May 2009, his other son, Ron Pierce, a West Point graduate and retired U.S. army major, poignantly stated, "He truly believed in the American dream, and he bought into it. And when he would tell us we could do anything, he wasn't just spouting words, he meant it" (Capo 2009). Wendell Pierce also stated: "It's a great honor to stand here today. . . . But it's not just for us. It is for all the men and women who couldn't live to see this honor, and receive the honors that they received, but still have love and faith for this great nation" (Capo 2009).

Wendell Pierce's commitment to the American Dream and his related investment in reviving Pontchartrain Park exemplify the paradox of the African Diaspora engagement with the modern condition. That is, his important philanthropic efforts represent another significant example of black communities—amidst an ideology that neglects to consider them—embracing a dream that is so egregiously unrealized outside of a small space or subdivision that merely holds its promise. This again exemplifies the larger project of calling into question a modern ideology that is flawed, and attempting to rectify it by advancing an ultimately more progressive reality.

RETURN POLICY

The crucial question of "Whose city will be rebuilt?" again came to the fore in January 2006 when the "Bring New Orleans Back" (BNOB) Commission, developed by Mayor Ray Nagin in conjunction with the Urban Planning Committee, released its "Action Plan for New Orleans: The New American City." The Action Plan aimed to revive New Orleans with a "city-wide framework for reconstruction" that involved plans focusing on "Flood and Stormwater Protection," "Transit and Transportation," "Parks and Open Space," and "Neighborhood Rebuilding" (BNOB 2006: 14). The exuberant report beckoned New Orleanians to "Imagine the Best City in the World" (BNOB 2006: 13). Yet, the racialized dimensions of "best" became quickly apparent as critics of the plan pondered one of the key recommendations, the one suggesting, "Do not issue building permits in heavily flooded/damaged areas," as well as requiring evidence that a substantial number of individuals were returning to rebuild in these areas before permits would be issued (BNOB 2006: 41, 52, 61). In effect, if there was not a considerable number of individuals returning within a period of four months, the city would buy the land for the advancement of other building plans. This meant that if families could not return quickly enough to prove a substantial presence, quite certainly some "American Dreams" were not going to be rebuilt.

The rebuilding criterion was eventually reviewed and rescinded, as those who could return to rebuild were permitted to do so regardless of their neighbor's commitment or ability to do the same. But, the issues raised by the criterion highlight the impact of race, class, and the intersection of the two at the core of rebuilding New Orleans. Regarding class, a *World Socialist* article described the BNOB plan as "remaking New Orleans for the wealthy," and reporter Kate Randall wrote: "The plan amounts to a calculated and cruel scheme to permanently depopulate low-income parts of New Orleans and build up more affluent residential areas, as well as the tourist districts. There can be little doubt that wealthy Washington insiders and cronies of local and state politicians will have the option at some point to buy up the vacant land at fire-sale prices and make an eventual killing in the real estate market" (Randall 2006). The racial dimension, as meted out by a higher percentage of blacks than whites living below the poverty level in New Orleans, also suggests that the class-based disparity in who returns, as noted in the Brown University study, meant that a significant number of blacks would not receive building permits or have the financial wherewithal to return. Furthermore, the Housing Authority of New Orleans (HANO) and HUD demolition of the city's housing projects in favor of mixed-income communities, while certainly an indication of the neoliberal decentralization of poverty, also raised doubt that new housing units would be affordable enough for the former residents of the housing projects (Hassan 2006). The pre-Katrina housing projects were all at least 90% African American (Logan 2006: 13). The effort to remove the older housing projects amidst few other options for potential returnees was described as "ethnic cleansing," again taking us back to the Bosnian cab driver watching the cultural and ethnic landscape of the city abruptly and strategically shift. The trajectory of "the New American City" was commonly articulated as an opportunity to rectify past problems, albeit through the displacement of individuals rather than structural and social changes that could facilitate a more progressive vision of the new city.

The working draft of the City Planning Commission's long-term New Orleans Master Plan was released for public review in March 2009. The plan, titled "New Orleans 2030: A master plan for the 21st century," incorporated several pre-Katrina plans into post-Katrina plans for the next twenty years and, notably, did not include the more controversial rebuilding permit plan as presented by the BNOB committee. However, even if the more explicit limitation on rebuilding was rejected, there was still concern by African American communities that the Master Plan did not clearly outline the extent to which the low-lying communities, largely populated by blacks, would be rebuilt or receive immediate city services, including schools and parks (Fausset 2009). The description of the Master Plan, developed through input from officials, community members, and expert advisers, states that it "will focus on integrating and balancing the many interests and perspectives of neighborhoods, organizations and more, while defining a 'roadmap' for the city's future" and, particularly pertinent for our consideration here, upon completion will "[g]uide the city to actively seek positive change and deflect negative change, rather than simply react after change has occurred" (Master Plan Draft 2009). The Neighborhood and Housing section of the Master Plan reflects the concern about the viability of post-Katrina neighborhoods as well as captures the exuberance of starting over and having a second chance at constructing the city. The goal articulated under "Neighborhoods" is to "[p]reserve and enhance the physical, economic, social and cultural character and diversity of existing residential neighborhoods" (Master Plan Draft 2009: 6.1). One particular housing goal in the working draft is to "[r]estore existing housing to improve the quality of life of all residents" with the following policy decisions to be made regarding this process:

- Eliminate blighted conditions in all neighborhoods.
- Facilitate reuse of abandoned, vacant, or tax-delinquent residential properties.
- Preserve and enhance existing housing within New Orleans neighborhoods.
(Master Plan Draft 2009: 6.1)

The issue of urban blight is where the impact of Road Home Grants on the African American community meets the NORA plan and potentially further entraps black communities in a position of exile. While the BNOB-proposed four-month period to determine whether some communities should be rebuilt was soon deemed politically inexpedient, numerous African Americans feared that the Road Home Grants problem combined with NORA efforts would facilitate the same result.

This conflict is apparent in the city's Master Plan draft, in spite of the fact that the problems incurred by African American communities are explicitly addressed in the plan. The Master Plan explains that NORA "has played the lead role in acquiring vacant properties and getting them back into private hands for redevelopment wherever possible. In addition to expropriating blighted property directly, NORA receives from the state those properties whose owners choose to use their Road Home grants not to rebuild in the city but to relocate elsewhere" (Master Plan Draft 2009: 6.26). The Master Plan also acknowledges "the [Road Home] program's implementation has not been smooth. Since the program did not cover damages exceeding pre-storm home value, over 80% of grant recipients did not receive sufficient funds to fully cover storm damage costs" and, citing a PolicyLink report, notes "an average funding gap of $55,000 [and that the] funding gap was highest in some of the hardest-hit, largely black neighborhoods—$69,200 in New Orleans East and $75,400 in the Lower 9th Ward" (Master Plan Draft 2009: 6.28; PolicyLink 2008).

A second housing goal is to "[c]reate quality housing in neighborhoods of choice to meet the diverse needs of New Orleanians," which would involve the following:

- Provide sufficient housing for households at all income levels and all stages of the life cycle.
- Maximize geographic choice in all neighborhoods for households of different income levels.
  (Master Plan Draft 2009: 6.2)

While a PolicyLink report shows that homes built for mixed-income and working families have been successful in some parts of the city, such as along the Tulane corridor, which included public housing pre-Katrina and homes built in former industrial spaces, St. Bernard Parish is described as a space where "mixed income doesn't work" (PolicyLink 2008: 22). Primarily, "mixed income doesn't work" because new plans were prohibitive of enough development to house families that formerly lived in the area. The report states: "Where St. Bernard's 963 deeply affordable homes stood pre-Katrina, 465 new homes will be rebuilt—with only 153 of them affordable to the families who used to live there. The other 810 families will be displaced. Local residents and housing advocates continue to call on HUD and the Housing Authority of New Orleans to develop a plan that replaces all the lost federally-assisted homes" (Policy-Link 2008: 22). Also, other planned sites under the HUD Low Income Housing Tax Credit scheme were facing a deadline to complete financing by the end of September 2008 and as late as July 2008, primarily due to demolition delays, only 10% of the 8,143 units were prepared for rental (PolicyLink 2008: 20). The stall in the construction of affordable rentals continued to have an impact on the extent to which the African Diaspora population could return and thrive in the city, particularly as market rentals were up from an average of $676 for a two-bedroom rental in 2005 to $978 in 2008 (PolicyLink 2008: 32).

The third housing goal in the Master Plan Draft is to "[d]evelop an effective housing delivery system that is responsive to the changing housing needs of current and future residents" involving the following policies to be implemented:

> • Use innovative best practices in housing development to ensure both the short-term and long-term availability of affordable units.
> • Build public and non-profit sector organizational capacity to safeguard neighborhood interests and promote equitable recovery.
> (Master Plan Draft 2009: 6.2)

The outcome of "safeguard[ing] neighborhood interests and [the] promot[ion of] equitable recovery" will inevitably turn on the racial dimensions of political power; again raising the question of "Whose city?" and, I might add, "What kind of city?"

The post-Katrina transition in the city's political power structure has been well under way, as seen in the 2007 election of the first white majority City Council in twenty-two years. As one article astutely notes, after Katrina "New Orleans became almost overnight a smaller, whiter city with a much reduced black majority" (Nossiter 2007). Also, notably, in 2010 New Orleanians—from black and white communities—elected Mitch Landrieu, the first white mayor since his father, Moon Landrieu, ended a mayoral term in 1978 (see Krupa and Donze 2010). Nevertheless, the notion of a city with a "smaller footprint" constructed on higher ground, predominantly populated by whites, and the loss of low-lying residential areas, predominantly populated by blacks, combines the economic practicality of investing in areas less vulnerable to natural disasters with the legacy of racism in housing. Unsurprisingly, the "smaller foot-print" idea led numerous African American New Orleanians to question whether "smaller may mean whiter" (Dao 2006). For the most part, the discourse and potential policies related to affordable housing opportunities do not explode or suggest an end to racially specific housing. So, it remains to be seen whether providing "neighborhoods of choice to meet the diverse needs of New Orleanians" facilitates more racially diverse neighborhoods or merely creates neo-constructions of "white flight" in which whites remain and a "black flight" occurs as a result of the legitimization of black expulsion through buyouts and neglect.

RACE, CLASS, AND REMOVAL

Considering that many proponents of the New Orleans city planning efforts are also black—and putting aside the reckless presumption of uni-lateral racism on the part of whites—it is doubtful that the planners of the new New Orleans are interested in decreasing all of the black population, but are perhaps more engaged in the problematic process of decreasing the number of poor and working-class blacks. Their efforts indicate an interest in creating a city in which middle-class African Americans have a greater statistical presence than poor and working-class African Americans, which is in line with the trajectory of the overall project of reconstructing the city as a "New American City." It is difficult not to see the New Orleans Master Plan, amidst its intention of "[e]nhanc[ing] the 'public realm'—sidewalks, streets, and public spaces for neighborhood use and safety" and the persistent insidiousness of racism, as anything more than a contemporary urban fantasy derivative of the middle-class sensibilities of the post-WWII period, a fantasy inextricably linked to the American Dream and all of the injustice that prohibits its realization. However, ultimately, by integrating poor and working-class individuals—who will be mostly African American—into middle-class communities, the planners operate under the assumption that "white flight" and African American "class flight" will not prevail.

The March 2009 draft of the Master Plan does not explicitly work toward the eradication of racial segregation in New Orleans. When "diversity" is mentioned, it is considered in its socio-economic class formation rather than that of ethnic and racial diversity. The Master Plan includes the efforts to "[p]reserve and enhance the physical, economic, social and cultural character and *diversity* of existing residential neighborhoods" (Master Plan Draft 2009: 6.1; emphasis mine) and, as noted above, "[c]reate quality housing in neighborhoods of choice to meet the *diverse* needs of New Orleanians" (Master Plan Draft 2009: 6.2; emphasis mine). By emphasizing "neighborhoods of choice" in the context of providing broader access to individuals of various financial means, the planners are not able to foreground the racialization of "choice" and the racially coded implications of "neighborhoods of choice" as antagonistic to a *really* new New Orleans. Thus, the housing goals can be read as maintaining the racial status quo and doing no more than reproducing the old racially specific areas with newly configured socio-economic diversity.

As the Master Plan demonstrates, in itself the project of creating socio-economic diversity is no easy endeavor because the unacknowledged—yet implicit—dimensions of race and racism easily come to the fore. The complexity of the intersection of race and class is exemplified in the case of the residents of Eastover, a wealthy, predominantly African American gated community in East New Orleans. In 2008 the Eastover residents and supportive politicians organized the Eastern New Orleans Neighborhood Advisory Council (ENONAC) to resist the construction of the mixed-income housing complex, Levy Gardens, across a small lake from the neighborhood golf course and mansions. The residents, who were concerned about a potential decrease in property values, successfully won a court-ordered end of the construction until, according to city zoning laws, a required public hearing and City Council vote regarding the building of a multi-family housing unit in the area could be held (Hammer 2009b). The civil court ruling turned on the fact that the developers had initially applied to build one hundred mixed-income single family units on the seven-acre plot of land and by 2008 had changed their plan to the building of twelve three-story apartment buildings with no single-family units (Hammer 2009a).

The case paradoxically placed black residents and black state senate, state house, and city council representatives of East New Orleans in opposition to white developers who were fighting the suit based on the Fair Housing Act and the implied discrimination against African Americans, who would be the most probable residents of Levy Gardens (Hammer 2009a). The intricacies of intra-ethnic class tensions and the perception that such tensions could not be infused with bigotry on the part of the Eastover residents are neatly represented in a comment by ENONAC chairperson Sylvia Scineaux-Richard: "We're not here to discriminate. I mean, who would know better about discrimination than minority and black people?" (Hammer 2009a). Scineaux-Richard and her colleagues, amidst the ongoing argument that there is a disproportionate amount of affordable housing already placed in East New Orleans, were clearly engaged in the project of reversing the pre-Katrina downfall of the area through a return to its more solidly middle-class beginnings (see Williams and Warner 2007; Eggler 2009). But, rather than consider the question of space and race, Scineaux-Richard further deflected the accusation of discrimination by asking, "Are we not hurting the poor by stockpiling them in buildings three stories high?" (Hammer 2009a). In spite of the avowed concern for "the poor," the underlying issue is that regardless of socio-economic status (i.e., even if you live in a mansion), in the socio-geographic hierarchy of New Orleans race still trumps all.

The geographic impact of negative racialization upon middle-class African Americans is further evidenced in a February 2009 guest column in the *Times-Picayune* by Louisiana State Senator of District 2 Ann Duplessis, who along with two other African American officials, State Representative Austin Badon and City Council member Cynthia Willard-Lewis, was instrumental in developing ENONAC and advancing the Levy Gardens suit. Duplessis begins the column by describing the Louisiana 1970s oil boom–era exodus to East New Orleans, noting "families moved in large numbers to the sparkling new subdivisions of eastern New Orleans. Churches, schools and commercial developments sprang up, making the new community an extremely attractive one" (Duplessis 2009). This idyllic moment of the American Dream, particularly characterized by middle-class African American movement into the area and the white flight that was already under way, ended with the oil bust of the 1980s and what Duplessis describes as a "proliferation of apartment complexes whose owners warehouse rent-subsidized tenants" (Duplessis 2009). Offering a counterargument to the Levy Gardens developers' charge of a fair housing violation, she writes: "My constituents firmly oppose the proliferation of rentals in the area, especially by developers who seek to profit from federally subsidized housing tax credits" (Duplessis 2009). While Duplessis strategically questions the motives of the developers, who would be receiving federal block grants and state tax incentives, her district also includes the Lower Ninth Ward and the adjacent district of Holy Cross; presumably including constituents who would be served by projects like Levy Gardens irrespective of the developers' overarching intent. As James Perry,[1] Executive Director of the Greater New Orleans Fair Housing Action Center (GNOFHAC), explained, "The role of community leaders has to be to show we're open for business and say, 'If you come here with your business, we have enough rental housing for your employees. . . . But for now, it's been that New Orleans East is open if you bring homeownership, and that says, 'Don't come here, don't come here, don't come here'" (Hammer 2009a). Perry's assessment also sheds further light on the overall middle-class articulation of how the new city should be formed; emphasizing home ownership and property rights rather than the race and class conditions at the core. Above all, the Eastover residents' fervent resistance highlights the intersection of race, space, and political power in New Orleans amidst the quest to revive a devastated city.

The realization of socio-economic diversity becomes even more of a challenge when it is conflated with racism emerging from the top of the socio-geographic hierarchy. This is seen in the case of St. Bernard Parish and its precise exemplification of the modern retreat to old ways amidst the discourse of the new. In September 2006, St. Bernard Parish, which a 2007 U.S. Census Report recorded as 88.5% white and 10.2% black (www .census.gov), implemented an ordinance requiring that single-family home owners could only rent to blood relatives. Recalling the grandfather clauses of the Jim Crow era, the "blood-relative ordinance" was challenged by the GNOFHAC on the grounds that it was discriminatory due to the parish's 93% home ownership by whites (Warren 2006). The parish repealed the act in November 2006 and settled the suit. In total, by 2008 the parish ended up paying $156,271.92 for damage claims amounting to $32,500 and attorneys fees and costs of $123,771.92 (GNOFHAC 2008a). In a GNOFHAC press release, James Perry stated: "We hope that the result of this lawsuit sends a strong message to local governments that choose to enact discriminatory zoning ordinances. GNOFHAC is dedicated to achieving the mission of ensuring equal housing opportunities for all members of our community. Governmental efforts to exclude protected class members, intentional or not, will be challenged" (GNOFHAC 2008a).

In September 2008, the St. Bernard Parish Council banned the distribution of permits for the construction of multi-family housing which in effect limited the return or possible relocation of poor and working-class individuals in the parish. The ban further insured that African Americans, as well as many Latinos once resident in the parish before Katrina, would no longer be present in the already majority white parish (Ratner 2008). In December 2008, the GNOFHAC filed a motion alleging that the "moratorium on multi-family housing violates the Consent Order [related to the "blood-relative ordinance"] which enjoins the Parish from violating the Fair Housing Act and other civil rights laws that prohibit race discrimination" (GNOFHAC 2008b). Emphasizing the dubious legality and overall social impact of the multi-family housing ban, GNOFHAC general counsel Lucia Backsher was quoted by *The Nation*: "Local governments have been creating legal barriers—legal, in the sense they created laws—to prevent people who are African-American from returning. And I'm saying that because we all know what we're talking about here. Affordable housing or multifamily housing is where African-Americans lived. And if you don't let that kind of housing back, you're not going to give people who are African-American or Latino an opportunity to live [here]" (Ratner 2008). In March 2009, the parish's multifamily housing moratorium was struck down. United States Federal Judge Ginger Berrigan ruled that the ban was discriminatory because "the type of housing restricted or forbidden is disproportionately utilized by African-Americans" and cited a racial impact study by Calvin Bradford that determined "African Americans are 85% more likely to live in buildings with more than five units than whites" and "are twice as likely as whites to live in rental housing" (Kirkham 2009).

The American Dream—paired as it was in its twentieth-century form with post-WWII notions of modernity and progress—was not only lost through the flooding of a home but even more in the very existence of an impoverished Lower Ninth Ward or the whites-only exclusivity of Gentilly Woods that produced a vibrant subdivision like Pontchartrain Park. These disparities—via home ownership and home value—directly correspond with the lack of opportunities to accumulate wealth that are crucial to surviving emergencies such as Katrina and their aftermath (see Conley 1999).

AN AFTERNOON IN THE LOWER NINTH WARD

The visual representations of the Ninth Ward appearing in various news media illustrated a neglect that was difficult to disconnect from the racial implications, even as the circumstances were clearly more complex than an assertion that "Bush doesn't care about black people" could fully explain. Hurricane Katrina exposed the fact that many African Americans are not accessing the American Dream and revealed that the United States is still not equipped to make any significant changes to this circumstance. For those who were able to distance themselves from these conditions, the horror had arrived through their living room televisions, car radios, Blackberrys, and laptops, the impact of Katrina being far too difficult to ignore. Here I would like to present field data from an afternoon spent in the Lower Ninth Ward two years and seven months after Hurricane Katrina, as it highlights the disparity, inaction, and loss that are coterminous with the revival of New Orleans. The circumstances still extant in the Lower Ninth Ward are both a revelation of the truth of the city—racial and socio-economic distinctions can have devastating effects—and that the new city is not yet extant. In this respect, the Lower Ninth Ward poses a problem for the revival narrative and represents the uncomfortable evidence that, due to race and class, there is a limited commitment to fully reviving the area.

I went on the excursion with my mother, Margaret White. We asked about buses to the Lower Ninth Ward at our French Quarter hotel front desk. I was told, "There aren't any buses to the Ninth Ward because there's nobody there." I asked about buses running toward the area. Again, "There are no buses. There's nobody there." I asked about taking a bus that went near the area and was told it would leave us five miles away. The desk clerk suggested we take a tour. We said we had done that but would maybe consider taking a taxi. We were told about "taxi tours" to the Ninth Ward, which we later arranged.

We took a taxi to the Lower Ninth Ward community. First, we met a woman, most likely in her late sixties, coming out of her home. The house was brick and in good shape. But houses on both sides of her were empty, damaged, and not habitable. The disparity highlighted the impact of having wooden homes versus the costlier brick homes. The woman was waiting for a ride but said she'd ask her husband, whom she described as "the man of the house," if he would be willing to speak to us. We waited on the sidewalk. She returned to tell us that her husband was busy with his son. We thanked her for asking and wished her well.

Next, we headed down the street to speak to a group of men in front of a house [the woman in the brick house suggested we speak to them, volunteering, "They may look rough but they're not bad. You can talk to them. They're like my grandchildren."] As we walked toward the men, a woman in her late twenties to early thirties walked up to us and asked for money. She introduced herself as Rayanna but was later referred to as Linda by her acquaintances. Rayanna was eating crushed ice out of a plastic sandwich bag and said, "I'm so hungry." She asked, "Are y'all looking to buy a house?" We explained that I was conducting research and had come to visit the neighborhood. "Do you have some money so I can get a hot dog?" My mother gave her the snack she had packed in her bag—Weight Watchers crackers—and a dollar. Rayanna told us that she has two children and her sister took them for a ride so that "they can just get away from here for a while. It's depressing here." She later said, "My kids are sleeping in my car and I'm sleeping in this house over here. I can't stay in my house because I haven't cleaned it out yet. They drive around to check to see if you've cleaned it out. If not, you can't live in it." She took me to the abandoned house where she was sleeping. "This is so embarrassing," she said. She took me to the house and introduced me to two men, John and Ronald, who were sitting on the porch. "I'm going to show her where I sleep," she told the men. The four-room house was gutted and a mattress with a blanket sat on a floor. "I haven't taken a bath in a week," Rayanna said. "I can't even put my kids in school because I need their birth certificates. I can't get new ones because I don't have ID. It's fucking crazy. Nobody is doing shit for us." I asked Rayanna where she went after Katrina. She said, "We went to Texas. I don't never want to go back there. That is the most racist place."

Next, I went into a gutted house across the street. The floor, perhaps once carpeted or tiled, was now reduced to musty boards covered with dust and plaster. Rickety wooden poles held up the roof where walls once stood. The space was vacant with no signs of mattresses or squatting residents. Yet, a large stuffed animal—a green and pink dragon with a big tooth—lay on the floor.

Later, we talked with John and Ronald, the two men on the porch of the house where Rayanna slept. A third man, Mitchell, joined them. John talked about the FEMA money being spent elsewhere: "That money is lining their pockets. Not ours." He pointed in the direction of a mostly leveled neighborhood with remnants of steps that led up to houses, a few tilted homes still filled with furniture and personal possessions, a few trailers and a church and said, "They want to build casinos here. They'll make this whole fucking place a big casino. They don't want us to come back. . . . They'll offer me three thousand dollars and I'll take it and I'll be gone." Then, referring to the Make It Right project developed by actor Brad Pitt, John said, "Brad Pitt is building all those houses just over there. It's fucking bullshit. He's in front of the cameras riding a bike on the grass. 'Look what I'm doing!' He's over there making a movie."[2]

We told the men about the French Quarter hotel clerk who said that there weren't any busses in the area. Another man in the street, Art, said, "There are busses. There's one that runs right down this street." Later in our conversation, Ronald suddenly said, "Look! Look! There go the bus! See." I turned to look and saw it moving down the street. "I just wanted you to see it for yourself," he said.

Mitchell commented on the aid available: "They give people 50,000 dollars [for a house]. What the fuck are you going to do with that? They give them $850 a month. By the time they replaced their clothes and bought food, that money was gone. . . . We can't get jobs. Even our own people won't give us a job. . . . Like if you have dreadlocks, that's a deal breaker." Regarding the job options and indicating class differences, Art added, "They'll say you look too niggerish."

Highlighting a common issue when trying to gain support for a home, Mitchell said, "People owned their homes but they inherited them so they didn't have no insurance, the houses been passed on to them so they lost everything." John added, "There were houses in the middle of the street."

All around were abandoned houses. The flood wall and levee sat behind the development with the newly fortified sections apparent. The area resembled a cinematic representation of a war zone or the aftermath of some nuclear disaster. Only a few people remained. However, as the Gray Line guide, Terrence, rhetorically noted during his tour, "Is this repair or just a Band-Aid? You decide."

*   *   *

The infrastructural problems and the erosion of the shipping channel, the Mississippi River Gulf Outlet, that facilitated the flooding of 80% of the city (see NASA 2005) and subsequent damage of Katrina are undoubtedly a result of governmental neglect and mismanagement, bringing into sharp relief an inability to rise to modern standards of engineering. However, the continued displacement of families and the lack of resolution regarding what led to the estimated $81.2-billion-dollar damage and approximately 1,400 direct fatalities (U.S. Department of Commerce 2006) continued to linger well into 2011. Indicative of this, in April 2009 a civil negligence suit, the first trial specifically addressing the impact of Hurricane Katrina, was brought against the Army Corps of Engineers by six survivors of Katrina hoping to receive some compensation (see Jonsson 2009a). In November 2009 a federal judge ruled that the Army Corps of Engineers is liable for damages and awarded $719,000 to the four plaintiffs from the Lower Ninth Ward and St. Bernard Parish, which significantly laid the foundation for additional litigation (Jonsson 2009b; C. Robertson 2009). Even though the ruling was undergoing an appeal by the Department of Justice as late as January 2011, the Army Corps of Engineers (Team New Orleans) reported receiving "more than 490,000 claim forms" (U.S. Army Corps of Engineers 2011). If the individuals I met in the Lower Ninth that afternoon in 2008 could not receive immediate relief, perhaps the 2009 suit would bring further attention to their needs and the disparities that enabled the devastating conditions in which they found themselves.

A HUMAN RIGHT: THE UN ON THE UNITED STATES, RACE, AND KATRINA

The United Nations Human Rights Council (UNHRC) Special Rapporteur on contemporary forms of racism, racial discrimination, xenophobia, and related intolerance, Doudou Diène, released a report in April

2009. His mission to the United States occurred from May 19, 2008, to June 6, 2008, a period in which he had "extensive meetings with state institutions, including the Supreme Court, civil society organizations active in the field of racism, minority communities and victims of racism" in Washington, D.C., New York, Chicago, Omaha, Los Angeles, New Orleans and the Louisiana and Mississippi Gulf Coast, Miami, and San Juan (Puerto Rico) (UNHRC 2009: 1). In the report, above all, New Orleans and the aftermath of Hurricane Katrina becomes a microcosm for the issue of racism in the United States and the key areas where attention needs to be paid if racism is ever to be eradicated. The Special Rapporteur notes "the disproportionately high impact of Katrina for African-Americans" and that due to the reduction in the African American population "[t]he ethnic makeup of the city also changed" (UNHRC 2009: 22). Diène reports that "The overlap between poverty and race in the United States creates structural problems that go far beyond patterns of income. Rather, it interacts with a number of mutually reinforcing factors, such as poor educational attainment, low-paying wages and inadequate housing, which create a vicious cycle of marginalization and exclusion of minorities" (UNHRC 2009: 25). Furthermore, regarding Katrina, the report states: "The consequences of the overlap of poverty and race were clearly seen in the aftermath of Hurricane Katrina. Minorities, as the poorest segments of the population, lived in more vulnerable neighborhoods and were more exposed to the effects of the storm. It is thus not unexpected that these groups suffered from disproportional displacement or loss of their homes. Katrina therefore illustrates the pernicious effects of socio-economic marginalization and shows the need for a robust and targeted governmental response to ensure that racial disparities are addressed" (UNHRC 2009: 26).

The Special Rapporteur points out "the need to go beyond a legal strategy that guarantees non-discrimination" and states: "While essential, the legal strategy is only the first stage in the fight against racism. A long-term strategy needs to address the root causes of the phenomenon, particularly in terms of intellectual constructs, prejudices and perceptions. To fight these manifestations, the only effective solution is to link the fight against racism to the deliberate politically conscious construction of a democratic, egalitarian and interactive multiculturalism" (UNHRC 2009: 26–27). The project of linking racism to democratic and egalitarian ideals is made explicit here in a way that suggests that heretofore it has not been linked in a "deliberate" manner but more as a means of suggesting a lived experience rather than making it lived in reality. Racism must be considered in the context of the larger project and articulation of democracy and egalitarian ideals for it to ever be resolved. As I have argued throughout this volume, racism negates equality.

Significantly, the UN report presents an importantly fresh way to consider the function of multiculturalism. That is, multicultural projects have a range of impacts (see Martin 1998; Matuštík 1998; Willet 1998). The idea of an "interactive multiculturalism," as presented in the report, immediately moves beyond the less deliberate one-sided act of multiculturalism which involves the designated "others" bringing their "unusual" culture—usually via music and food—to the normalized culture with little impact beyond the point of contact and consumption. Diène deflects the more superficial instance of multiculturalism by centering it in a "deliberate politically conscious construction" that is strategically imperative. He further states: "[T]his is the most important problem the United States needs to face. A key notion in this regard is the need to promote interaction among different communities as an important means to create tolerance and mutual understanding, strengthening the social networks that hold a society together. Racial or ethnic communities in the United States still experience very little interaction with each other: racially-delimited neighborhoods, schools and churches prevail. The promotion of more interaction among racial minorities is an essential step that needs to be taken to address the root causes of racism in the United States" (UNHRC 2009: 27).

In order to develop a shared understanding of community and culture, even amidst difference, there must be the desire for "interaction among different communities" that extends beyond the act of the "different" individuals meeting the normalized white majority. The report places an emphasis on interactions between differently racialized ethnic minority groups, as this is also part of the problem of solidarity and other understandings of pan-ethnic relations (e.g., divide and rule). Interestingly, New Orleans, in theory, should represent a space in which multiculturalism has led to a de-centering of "otherness" because differently racialized groups constructed an identity contingent on the cultural contributions of each racialized group. However, in the end, New Orleans failed at multiculturalism and its mission of democratic equality because racial inequalities were never sufficiently conceived as counter to modern egalitarianism.

Among the final recommendations made, the Special Rapporteur, citing Principle 28 of the UN Guiding Principles on Internal Displacement, suggests: "The Federal Government and the States of Louisiana, Alabama and Mississippi should increase its assistance to the persons displaced by Hurricane Katrina, particularly in the realm of housing. The principle that 'competent authorities have the primary duty and responsibility to establish conditions, as well as provide the means, which allow internally displaced persons to return voluntarily, in safety and with dignity, to their homes or places of habitual residence' should be respected" (UNHRC 2009: 29). The Principle 28 recommendation reflects the reports that due to poverty, financial hardship, and the demolition of public housing, the option of return was prohibitive for many evacuees, particularly African Americans. This is also significant if we consider that, even if the individuals who evacuated Katrina were erroneously and inadvertently perceived as falling under the jurisdiction of the UN High Commissioner for Refugees (UNHCR), clearly their experiences are well placed in the realm of the human rights concerns of the UN. As discussed earlier, it is the mere fact of their condition in the contemporary United States that seems to have provoked commentators to consider their experiences external to the United States—in a sense, otherworldly. Quite crudely, it appeared that, to many commentators, blacks in desperate need and dire trouble signified some other faraway jurisdiction removed from the racism, poverty, and the overall manifestation of inequalities in the United States which the UN Special Rapporteur clearly indicates.

PARIS
The Liberating Quality of Race

Built during the 1960s period of urbanization and a booming industrial French economy, the *banlieues* were meant to provide adequate housing to immigrants who had come to work in the now closed factories. Generations later, they represent less a place for opportunity and mobility and more a trap of exclusion and nihilism. The main event that provoked approximately two weeks of burning and civil unrest in the Paris *banlieues* occurred on October 27, 2005. Two teenagers, Zyed Benna and Bouna Traoré, of Malian and Tunisian ancestry, respectively, were fatally electrocuted while hiding in an electrical facility after being chased—along with other teenagers—by police in pursuit of their identity papers, a common practice officially purported to curtail crime but in actuality one which facilitates the criminalization of youth of color and perpetuates the mistaken assumption that they are not citizens (see Johnstone 2005). The youths were mostly of North and sub-Saharan African descent and, therefore, represented communities that are restricted from a full realization of citizenship and removed from the idealist notions of what French society offers. For our purposes here, it is notable that an African Diaspora community is again in a position to expose the predominant ideological narrative of a nation as false or at least duplicitous. What is also significant is that while race-based inequalities are articulated in terms of immigration and cultural difference in the politics of disavowal in Ireland and explicitly presented as racial in the United States vis-à-vis its history of *de jure* racial exclusion, in France the articulation of race is silenced via its subsumption in the greater project of egalitarian discourse and perceived assimilation. So, even as race seems on the surface to be the clear indicator or mark of exclusion, the racial discourse has hinged on the inability to become French. The narrative of nationality trumping race is still operational in France but, as seen through the uprisings, the narrative is a misrepresentation of the lived reality of residents of the *banlieues*. These circumstances place black French in the position of forcing the nation to consider the mythical dimensions of republicanism, egalitarianism, and, above all, liberty.

The French census does not include statistical data about race. However, it is estimated that a minimum of between 2.5 million and 5 million blacks live in the nation of 59 million (Tagliabue 2005; Bennhold 2006). The peculiar engagement with equality via the exnomination of race was notably made apparent in an Irish interview during the uprisings. In the spirit of the interconnectedness and fluidity of the gaze of liberty upon those who are not presently adhering to it, I will turn to an Irish discussion about Paris.

In a television interview during the Paris uprisings, *Radio Telefis Eireann* (RTÉ) commentator Mark Little asked *Union pour un Mouvement Populaire* or Union for a Popular Movement (UMP) MP Jacques Myard and Oxford University Professor of Islamic Studies Tariq Ramadan: "Given that [Myard] raise[s] the experiences of Britain and potentially Ireland, what lessons can we learn from what has happened in France over the past twelve days?" (RTÉ 2005d). Myard, who had inspired the question by saying, "of course in Ireland you don't have this problem because you don't have four million immigrants," responded by noting the importance of "authority in the suburbs" and "social programming" (RTÉ 2005d). Ramadan stated: "First we have to say that Islam is a European religion and Muslims are integrated and Islam is not the problem. It is not a question of immigration. It is a question of equal citizenship. It is a question of acting against all kinds of racism and xenophobia against the Arabs and the Muslims. It's a question of social justice" (RTÉ 2005d).

Earlier in the interview, commentator Little explained that "[i]t does seem to many here in Ireland that the compelling story line here is about a group long-neglected by France striking back at the society which has neglected them. Is that how it looks to you in Paris?" (RTÉ 2005d). Myard responded by describing a "parallel society" inhabited by individuals in the suburbs, faulting "criminal organizations" and stating: "It has nothing to do with religion or things like that. I refuse to admit it because in those groups you have . . . Muslims, black Africans but also genuine French, you know, Christians" (RTÉ 2005d). Little asks, "The Republican ideal in France has always been not to emphasize racial or religious difference but isn't it time . . . that the French society began to accept that there are differences and there are difficulties for those people in those suburbs?" (*RTÉ* 2005d). Myard responds, "The point is that we are French and those kids are Muslims and French and they should behave like French citizens" (*RTÉ* 2005d). Ramadan, outraged, would later put it plainly: "He is not considering them as genuine French citizens. That is the problem" (*RTÉ* 2005d).

What is interesting about the exchange is that Ireland appears to be the voice of reason in a messy French battle. It is as if Dublin, a newly global city, has wisdom to offer Paris. Yet, what is significant for our purposes here is that, Dublin, if anything, is not far removed from the potentiality of similar events to that of Paris, as Ireland—like France—is committed to a modern global project that is contingent on the very inequalities such a project professes to negate. So, we see that Dublin tells us much about Paris, as its new global status in the late twentieth to early twenty-first century merely pairs it with the racialized global trajectory of the nineteenth century. Even a prior colonial status and, I would argue, nearly (but not quite) postcolonial status, combined with a history of negative racialization could not prevent Ireland from creating circumstances in which whiteness is exalted and cultural difference contested and critiqued in the context of the national. It is a flawed and currently inescapable position.

An Irish radio program also attempted to ask the questions not fully explored in the French arena, as commentator Cathal MacCoille interviewed French Ambassador in Ireland Frédéric Grasset:

MacCoille: There's a huge difference between foreign papers and French papers. If you read the French newspapers you wouldn't have a clue what you're talking about. You wouldn't know who was involved in the rioting. Whereas every foreign correspondent on this program—and newspapers all over the world—was making it absolutely plain: This is about North Africans. This is about Muslims. This is about immigrants or the children of immigrants. And yet the people of France in their own media and the official response certainly in the first week or so has been to, I don't know, speak as though the problem was not what it is.

    Grasset: . . . I think it appears that at first glance, there is, there was such a shock in our . . . opinion that there is some, I would say, self-restraint perhaps in telling things as clearly as they are and . . . the question is very much political, as well, because you can't . . . imagine quite clearly and easily what could be the consequences and the political consequences of all these riots. . . . Perhaps it is a blessing in disguise that groups . . . ethnic groups or religious groups are not fingered, not shown because it could trigger some political consequences on the medium term and long run which could be appalling. (RTÉ 2005e)

The concern for political consequences runs deeper than a mere re-election opportunity but also highlights the investment in the current condition—give or take a few social alterations via public policy and programs—that maintains the ideology of assimilation and the perception that with some attention (i.e., to crime and educational programs) a group of individuals will somehow rise to their Frenchness. Yet, even as MP Myard seems to espouse programs for the *banlieues* that would eliminate criminal rings, there is an implicit understanding that the majority of individuals residing in the communities where the programs would be launched are not "genuine French." To be genuine is to be racialized as white, yet racialization is not to be discussed at all. So, additionally, we see that the exnomination of racialization moves the discourse about "difference" away from things racial and into the realm of the cultural, which implies a personal choice or *freedom* rather than a projected condition; however, it is doubtful that a monolithic cultural expression of Frenchness would even be appealing to most of those included in the category of "genuine French." It is the lack of inclusion in French society that allowed then French Interior Minister Nicolas Sarkozy to make his well-publicized threat of "hosing down" the "scum" ("*racaille*," which carries a much richer race-contingent meaning than English permits) (see Pulham 2005). The desire to cleanse the society of undesirable (and black) problems is, as I noted in the previous chapter, not far removed from the desire to reconstruct a New Orleans devoid of impoverished blacks by avoiding the replacement of the affordable housing units destroyed (or cleansed) by Hurricane Katrina.

FRENCH CITIZENSHIP, IMMIGRATION, AND IDENTITY

The Nationality Act of 1889 solidified the *jus soli* acquisition of French citizenship, which was formerly a combination of *jus soli* and *jus sanguinis*. Yet, as also evident in Ireland, in recent years the right of *jus soli* citizenship has become increasingly limited. Rather than having citizenship automatically conferred, children born to foreign nationals in France have the option to formally become French citizens if they declare citizenship at the age of thirteen (provided a claim is submitted by the parents and the applicant has resided in France since age eight), at age sixteen (if they have resided in France since age eight), or at age eighteen (if resident in France for a minimum of five years since age eleven) (French Civil Code 2006). While persons born to French nationals within and outside of France are automatically considered French, as per the July 24, 2006, immigration and integration law individuals born in former French colonies prior to independence (i.e., former colonial subjects), once eligible for citizenship without a requirement of residence in France, are now subject to the same policies as other foreign nationals (see Weil 1996; Landor 1997; Weil et al. 2010). Longtime residents of France can submit applications to be naturalized. However, as Patrick Weil noted back in 1996, "today 95% of French people have never been required to state their individual desire to have the nationality that they have been assigned, just as virtually all nationality is assigned in the world—automatically and without any possibility of choice" (Weil 1996: 81; also see Weil 2009). This is a ramification of the nation's historical assimilationist approach to immigration and national identity that, Weil contends, leads to a French identity crisis. He writes:

[T]his logic, which bases nationality more upon codes of sociability and citizenship than on individual desire, does not allow French national identity to be readily defined. The French system, which presents several means by which to receive French nationality, fails to respond to a question which each individual must ask himself: who am I? . . . The French Republic therefore responds to the requirement for a common identity, necessary for the unity of any human group and therefore any nation, with symbolic republic values: you are French because you adhere (that is to say sociologically you can adhere) to republican values; those same values which give French citizens the desire to live together. (Weil 1996: 81)

The adherence to republican values to which Weil refers is no doubt synonymous with the assimilationist contingencies rooted in the acquisition of the type of Frenchness once described by Fanon regarding French colonial subjects in Africa and the Caribbean; a dictate in which positive assimilationist myths mask the pejorative racialization of immigrants / colonial subjects and present an unspoken mandate to erase one's prior cultural signifiers (e.g., Muslim dress, Senegalese accent). As Fanon contended long ago in Black Skin, White Masks: "The colonized is elevated above his jungle status in proportion to his adoption of the mother country's cultural standards. He becomes whiter as he renounces his blackness, his jungle" (Fanon 1967: 18). We need only look at the continuing debate around anti-Muslim and anti-immigration sentiments in France, particularly in its twenty-first-century form beginning after the September 11, 2001, events in the United States, the success of the anti-immigration right-wing National Front leader Jean-Marie Le Pen in the first round of the 2002 French elections, and later the 2005 uprisings in the *banlieues* to see the unresolved state of the French national identity and the function of "racial" identification (Bremner 2002; Crumley 2002; Webster et al. 2002).

Unlike the situation in Ireland, the current period of globalization does not present the genesis or first experience of large-scale migration to France. The largest periods of migration to France began in the nineteenth century, when workers from nearby countries (primarily Belgium, Spain, and Portugal) arrived in the nation to fill positions during the industrial revolution. The next period of immigration occurred during and after World War I (including North Africans, Turks, and Russians fleeing the Bolsheviks). The third significant phase occurred after World War II, when the dearth of available European (i.e., racialized as white) labor led to an increase in recruitment from the North African, Caribbean, Southeast Asian, and Sub-Saharan African French colonies, as well as the newly independent nations (see Hargreaves 1987, 1995; Weil 1996; Cesarani 1996).

The French presumed that the labor migrants would work until they were no longer needed and eventually leave the nation. Yet, even the 1974 ban on immigration to France did not eliminate the presence of the immigrants who, according to the criteria of family unification and birth, were French citizens. Furthermore, the ban did not include European immigrants, asylum seekers, and what would be considered "desired" professionals. Hence, the French national identity based on liberalism and egalitarianism was bifurcated, resulting in an "us" (white French-speaking) and "them" (everyone else) dichotomy that was further problematized by religious differences and ethnic affiliations. Despite the perception that "racial" and ethnic backgrounds were not significant issues—provided one fully apprehended the language and other aspects of French culture—the issue of difference remained, as Frenchness continued to be linked to "whiteness." As Fanon noted regarding the French Antillean: "Subjectively, intellectually, the Antillean conducts himself like a white man. But, he is a Negro. That he will learn once he goes to Europe; and when he hears Negroes mentioned he will recognize that the word includes himself" (Fanon 1967: 148).

The idea that citizens are fully integrated into French society is theoretically in line with the values and ideals facilitating the construction of the French Republic, yet the overwhelming exception taken to those who are remotely different (i.e., accent, ethnicity, religion) places "ethnically different" members of the Republic outside of what is acceptably French. This is exemplified in the case of Muslim immigrants (primarily from North Africa and Sub-Saharan Africa). While the predominantly Catholic nation superficially appears open to those who are not Christian, meaning individuals can worship as long as they otherwise remain culturally (and linguistically) French, underlying this apparent inclusiveness is the legacy of war with the colonies of North Africa and a more recent increase in the concern that Muslims are a threat to the nation (see Webster et al. 2002; Keaton 2006). As Jim House explained back in 1996 in his essay "Muslim Communities in France":

> Traditional French nationalism, which is inward-looking, and based very much on French Catholic "identity," continues to be influential within the main vector of racism in France, the Front National. . . .
>
> Current Front National discourse is very much an unsteady amalgamation of the two "logics" of traditionalism and the *Nouvelle Droite* within the far right in France. Forced to go outside the purely nationalistic base as regards the construction of the European Community and the "threat" posed by immigration, the protection of "European Identity" (never defined and hence posited in simply oppositional terms which is where the immense stock of historical hostility to Islam comes in) means that the conflation of "ethnic" and "religious" belonging is then made into a stereotype. North Africans . . . are the particular targets of such racism where the religious "coefficient" is arguably higher now than 25 years ago. (House 1996: 223)

House's example of the vilified Muslim identity and the assumption that individuals from the Maghreb or of North African descent are Muslims has a corollary in Ireland (beyond that of the influence of Catholicism), as the nationality or ethnic background of "Nigerian" is conflated with the social status of "asylum seeker," thus constructing a representational entity that is considered a threat to Irish identity, security, and the overall stability of the nation. While the Irish, for historical, cultural, and geographical reasons, do not as readily embrace the amorphous European identity as do the French, the Irish state does turn to the EU to remedy the potential problem of immigration, as seen through the 1990 Dublin Convention I and, later, Dublin II, which stipulates that immigrants should be returned to the state in which they first enter the EU. This is particularly advantageous for immigration opponents in Ireland, as flights to the island nation usually make connections at British or European continental airports first. However, despite the Convention's apparent ability to deter immigration to the nation, it is not yet rigorously enforced by members of the European Union.

House notes that the earlier immigrants from Poland and Italy were viewed as easier to assimilate into French culture: "Now that the vast majority of primary immigrants from the Maghreb, Turkey, and West Africa have decided to settle in France, [the] assertion of 'inassimilability' is arguably a way of making their presence seem definitively provisional on a socio-cultural level, whereas until the early 1970s it was presented more in economic terms" (House 1996: 224).

House, writing nine years before the 2005 uprisings, goes on to explain that it is not that "the economic aspect of discriminatory discourse has disappeared," but "it now has to compete with the more dominant socio-cultural argument" (House 1996: 224). Even amidst the early twenty-first-century global economic crises, the "socio-cultural argument" to which House referred remains the salient force because the argument cannot effectively be made that individuals of color in France are migrants contributing to the economy and/or economic distress—though the presumption of immigrant status persists. The reality, as seen in 2005, is that individuals of color are mostly French citizens. Yet, through unemployment, limited educational opportunities, housing conditions, and limited political representation, they are barred from contributing to the twenty-first-century rendering of the French economy, polity, and national identity itself.

BEFORE THE FIRE NEXT TIME: HOUSING CONDITIONS AS RACIAL CONDITIONS

In the case of Dublin we see housing considered in the context of asylum-based residences and in New Orleans the impact of Hurricane Katrina highlights the legacy of *de jure* housing discrimination in the city. In Paris and environs the issue of housing becomes a focal point that represents the combination of socio-legal status and social neglect resulting from racism. Whereas in Dublin housing becomes linked to a precarious migration status and in New Orleans housing for blacks is race-contingent in spite of the assumption of citizenship, in the African Diaspora communities of Paris, social status—something that can either afford or delimit housing opportunities in all locations—intersects with racism to perpetuate the presumption of foreignness and immigrant status regardless of French citizenship. The ubiquity of this problematic is particularly exemplified by the fact that the 2005 uprisings in the Paris *banlieues* were preceded by other burnings: the fires in April and August of 2005 in three separate Paris apartment buildings primarily inhabited by families of African descent.

Twenty-four individuals of African descent—including at least ten children—perished in the April 15, 2005, fire at the Paris-Opéra Hotel in Paris's 9th Arrondissement, seventeen individuals of African descent died in an apartment fire in the 13th Arrondissement on August 25, 2005, and seven individuals of African descent died in an apartment fire in the 3rd Arrondissement on August 29, 2005 (Lerougetel 2005; Schofield 2005). The living spaces were among the one thousand run-down and abandoned buildings identified by Paris officials that contain an estimated thirteen thousand families, the majority being of African descent (Schofield 2005). The burned buildings—some places for informal or unofficial residence and others for official placement by the housing authority—were described as infested with "cockroaches and rats," containing dangerously rickety stairs, and having no electricity and running water (Schofield 2005). Residents included families originally from Cote d'Ivoire, Senegal, and Mali; some "*sans papiers*" (undocumented) and "awaiting regularization" and others French citizens (Schofield 2005). Notably, the Hotel Paris-Opéra, site of the April 15 fire, was a hotel for "budget tourists and . . . short-term accommodation for homeless families" (Samuel 2005).

Although it was widely noted that numerous individuals living in the dilapidated apartments were rent-paying workers who could not access social housing due to shortages throughout the country, the political reaction to the fires deflected socio-racial problems and leaned toward the criminalization of building residents, representing the families as illegal "squatters" and undocumented immigrants (Lerougetel 2005; Schofield 2005). Notably, then Interior Minister Nicolas Sarkozy made the well-quoted remark, "The difficulty is that a whole heap of people, some of whom are undocumented, are massing in Paris, and there are not the conditions to house them" (Ceaux 2005; Lerougetel 2005). But, with the high representation of individuals of African descent killed in the fires and those still living in similarly squalid conditions, the racial dimensions could not be easily ignored and housing rights groups and advocates for the *sans papiers* demanded that the social housing system be repaired and that such tragedies never occur again.[1]

In 2001, the Group for the Study and Struggle against Discrimination (GELD) reported that while families from the Maghreb have significant difficulty accessing social housing, Sub-Saharan African families had even more difficulty due to family size and a resistance to renting to African families (Simon et al. 2001). Furthermore, not far removed from the issue of "mixed-income housing" that would emerge in the context of post-Katrina New Orleans, the GELD report criticized the French housing authority's interest in creating mixed social housing without regard to the racial dimensions of the housing problem (Simon et al. 2001). Four years later, in 2005, the problem persisted as families of African descent dwelling in the apartment blocks where the fires occurred were described as living in conditions of "desperate overcrowding" (Schofield 2005). When asked in a 2007 interview whether the problems in France were more social than racial, Patrick Lozès of *Le Conseil Représentatif des Associations Noires* (CRAN) or the Representative Council of Black Organizations, harked back to the apartment fires and vehemently responded:

> No! As a concrete example: In 2005, homes were burned. The media spoke of *sans papiers,* immigrants . . . whereas there were people in these slums who worked for the Mayor of Paris, who could afford housing. They died, not because of lack of income but because they had black skin. For this reason, the door was closed to them for access to housing. The value of our struggle is its correlation with other battles that also call into question republican principles: freedom, equality, fraternity. The system of French integration is based on a wonderful idea: do not make a distinction between old foreigners and new citizens. Except that for Blacks and Beurs, it does not work. Even when they are officially citizens, we do not recognize them as such. (Yadan 2007a)

Then, firmly placing the circumstances faced by black France in the realm of civil rights lest there be any confusion, he continued: "When you're black in France, you do not have the same civil rights as others. And too often, we try to relativize discrimination. It is a kind of denial of reality" (Yadan 2007a).

Deflecting the "denial of reality," a GELD report discussed during the period of the apartment fires indicated that Africans had a 58% chance of accessing social housing as opposed to the 75% chance for other groups (Lerougetel 2005). As one teenager who lived near the burned buildings in the 13th Arrondisement told a reporter, "France has screwed up, it's a crime. Why is it always blocks where there are blacks that catch fire? . . . Why is it always blocks inhabited by Africans?" (Lerougetel 2005). A few months later, the uprisings in the *banlieues* would further underscore the racial dimensions of the social housing problem and force a new engagement with the teenager's query.

LIBERTÉ, EGALITÉ, AND *FRATERNITÉ* (TAKE TWO): *LE RECOMMENCEMENT* OR THE NEW BEGINNING

The events of November 2005 in Paris were followed by governmental initiatives aimed at repairing the buildings of the *banlieues,* unprecedented discourse on methods of affirmative action or "positive discrimination" to work toward parity in education and employment, the nation's first black newscaster, Harry Roselmack on TF1 in 2006, and, quite notably, in 2007 a *Canal Plus* television series titled "*Dans la peau d'un noir*" ("In the skin of a black man") in which—à la John Howard Griffin in 1959 and the American F/X network "reality" series "Black White" in 2006—a black French family and a white French family employed makeup to switch places, explicitly demonstrating that race does have an impact on one's negotiation of French society. Yet, amidst the development of a set of black "firsts" in France, what is particularly significant here is that after the uprisings, the African Diaspora of Paris organized to seek recognition on racial terms rather than merely considering the issue of full citizenship in the context of immigrant identities or as residents of "*les quartiers difficiles,*" which inadequately addressed the race-based discrimination experienced in "postcolonial" France. The uprisings expedited the process of exploding the myths and narratives of racial equality in Paris as well as the idealization of France within and beyond continental Africa as a destination which global racisms have somehow bypassed (see Dominic Thomas 2006).

It is here that I would like to examine the ways in which the organization *Le Conseil Représentatif des Associations Noires* (CRAN), formed on the twenty-sixth of November in 2005, undoubtedly as an urgent result of the Paris uprisings, poses key questions that have forced a new articulation of equality and freedom in France. One of the first acts of the organization was to commission a national survey on race. Results revealed that of the thirteen thousand blacks who participated in the survey, 61% had experienced "at least one racist incident in the past year" and one in ten respondents were "frequent targets of racism," experiencing "verbal aggression" and "difficulty finding housing or jobs" (CRAN 2007a; BBC 2007). In a *Christian Science Monitor* article—adequately reflecting the perception of French identity and its reality—Le CRAN president Patrick Lozès is quoted: "'To be black and proud—that's not being anti-French,'" says Mr. Lozès, whose vision challenges France's color-blind model of assimilation. "'It's simply the liberation of a people who don't see themselves reflected in their country's public life—in its theater, television, medicine, and universities—except in negative images'" (Sachs 2007). The "color-blind model of assimilation" to which the article refers represents the key challenge for Le CRAN, as French society must reconcile the fact that not seeing color merely facilitates the ability to not see the misrepresentation and lack of representation of groups of *color*.

Notably, in October 2006, the organization met with Edgar Chase III, an African American business professor and vice president for facilities at New Orleans' Dillard University, who was also in Paris for a fund-raising event in support of the devastated university.[2] During a lecture and meeting on the means of achieving racial equality in France, Chase advised CRAN members, "Maybe you do a protest march. . . . But you send a positive message: 'We're doing this because we love France and want it to be able to compete in the global economy'" (Sachs 2007). Chase's words underline the inextricable connection between the social dimensions of globalization (or modernity) and the neoliberal economic dimensions; in other words, there will be no "march toward modernity" if we can't agree to march with equal footing.

The CRAN addresses several concerns in its mission. The organization "aims at fighting against discriminations and anti-black racism, as well as to value both the wealth and the diversity of Afro-West-Indian cultures" (lecran.org). Regarding the question of black visibility or invisibility in France, the CRAN website states:

> In principle to have a dark skin in metropolitan France is not the best way to go unnoticed. The paradox is that as individuals, Black people in France are visible and yet as a social group remain invisible. As a social group it seems as if they were not supposed to exist: the French Republic doesn't officially recognize minorities, and doesn't record them as such. One could be satisfied with invisible populations, or at least see no problem with it, as long as social and specific difficulties concerning them be recorded, identified, recognized. However it is not the case. And instead of remaining a quiet and normal status, invisibility is wrong. (lecran.org)

Notably, communitarianism is addressed at the website, an issue that is frequently presented in France when ethnic groups attempt to address inequalities. CRAN states:

The CRAN works for equality of chances, for a better representation of diversity within France. But this dynamic implies a questioning of the well-
established hierarchy. And those who are bothered by these criticisms
are those who take refuge behind abstract universalism which hides (and
very poorly) a symbolic male, white, bourgeois, catholic order. As a result,
an easy self-defence is used by those who are ill-at-ease with diversity:
they denounce and identify those who fight for equality, that is, Blacks,
Arabs, Jews, homosexuals, etc. as communitarians. In reality, the CRAN
says Yes to "Universalism" and No to "Uniformalism" (lecran.org).

It is significant that, in the French context, the issue of communitarianism must be addressed and denied before discourse on race can effectively ensue. Undoubtedly, it is not the American-style communitarianism of Amitai Etzioni,[3] with which former U.S. president George W. Bush
was often associated (see Goeriger 2001), but speaks to a separatism that
is worrisome to those who mourn the loss of "color-blind" egalitarianism.
Regarding French communitarianism, Armando Salvatore has noted that
it "would be probably best rendered in English as 'communalism': a political orientation effecting a fundamental erosion of citizenship and of
its postulates of equality in favor of a closed community identity and its
scarcely transparent norms" (Salvatore 2007: 143). This notion has been
applied to Muslim communities in the wake of Islam-phobic discourse
and its related conflation with other racisms (see Ramadan 2006), so it is
important and strategic that CRAN not become lost in the debate. Hence,
the espousing of "universalism"—in spite of its problematic insistence on
perpetuating the mainstream—neatly removes CRAN from the arena of
the dreaded "communitarianism" that carries a connotative thrust suggesting that it embodies the opposite of freedom.

From its beginning, the members of the CRAN presented "[t]wo major
types of anti-discriminatory policies" which they consider "possible and
desirable":

> First, a sanction policy against discriminatory behavior. The penal
> code acknowledges and curbs race discriminations, but one must admit
> that the justice of our country remains little active in the application of
> anti-discriminatory laws. Not enough lawsuits succeed. Judges are not
> well trained and often seem too little motivated with investigations and
> decisions concerning discrimination cases.
>
> Secondly, a policy which intends to actively promote diversity. This policy
> is called "affirmative action" in the USA and "positive discrimination" in

France. No matter what terminology, it is about coming up with devices that help put an end to the lack of diversity within too many political, economical and social authorities. The nature of these devices must become the core subject of a great national debate. (lecran.org)

The anticipated "great national debate" that the CRAN hoped to inspire during its early days, as will be discussed later in this chapter, emerges in a very different context from that initially suggested by the organization. The debate occurs in the realm of national identity, but undoubtedly the questions pushed forward by the CRAN serve as an impetus for such a consideration. Most certainly, the act of debate over "positive discrimination" would seem more of a radical accomplishment than the actual policy itself. That is, President Nicolas Sarkozy, even during his two terms as Interior Minister—as far back as 2003—had already expressed support of such a policy (see Smolar 2003). Sarkozy's discursive support for positive discrimination continued after the uprisings, in spite of his "*racaille*" comment and related reputation, while his soon-to-be electoral opponent, Dominique de Villepin, maintained the traditional French republican line, as indicated in a late November 2005 report in which he stated on RTL radio: "We say that when there are inequalities, we put them right. But we must not fix them by renouncing our French model, a universal model under which each individual is respected for who he is, independent of color. . . . We must correct the inequalities and fix handicaps . . . but without taking into account ethnicity or religion— which is the nature of positive discrimination" (*International Herald Tribune* 2005).

Due to Sarkozy's long-standing commitment, and barring a popular perception of communitarianism, there was no clear indication that such a debate would unfold in as contentious a manner as it does in the U.S. context. However, such zealous support in 2007 could be ignored; particularly because such a plan could not be quickly bolstered with more black representation in the Parliament. A CRAN report released on June 4, 2007, revealed that only 19 out of 3,777 candidates for the 2007 election were black, further underlining the disproportionately low representation of blacks in positions of power in France (CRAN 2007b; also see *Le Nouvel Observateur* 2007a; Mackenzie 2007).

In 2006 CRAN's negotiation of a redefinition of the words "colonialism" and "colonizer" offers particular insight into the greater role of such an organization. CRAN, along with the Movement Against Racism and for Friendship among Peoples (MRAP), actively criticized the 2007 *Le Petit*

Robert dictionary's definitions of "colonialism" and "colonizer," which describe "colonization" as "valorization and exploitation of countries that have become colonies" and "to colonize" as "to occupy a country in order to value and exploit its wealth" (Karoui 2007); or, as other translations offer a fuller understanding of the meaning of "valorization," the *Le Petit Robert* "colonization" definition can also read as "exploitation, getting the best return out of countries that have become colonies" (Associated Press 2006). The issue was made even more significant in the context of the February 23, 2005, French law that included the controversial article 4, which stated: "University syllabuses must grant the place that it deserves to the history of France's presence overseas, particularly in North Africa. School courses must . . . recognize the positive role played by the French presence overseas, particularly in North Africa, and must accord the prominent position that they merit to the history and sacrifices of members of the French armed forces" (Liauzu 2005).

After protests from activists, organizations, and scholars, the article was removed from the law in January 2006 (see Aldrich 2006). However, the impact of such brazen legislation clearly remained. Regarding *Le Robert* on colonization, Lozès, in a France 3 television interview, emphatically stated: "It's not acceptable to continue to put out a message that colonization may have had a positive role" (AP 2006). Lozès went on to state, "Our role is not to be the thought police. We don't want to dictate what is said. . . . But we don't want dictionaries to continue to make this country believe that colonization had positive outcomes" (AP 2006).

After forty years in print—and nearly a year of pressure by CRAN and MRAP—the definition was augmented to reflect current understandings or, as the CRAN website noted, "Knowledge about colonization has greatly *progressed*" (lecran.org; emphasis mine). It was announced on September 3, 2007, that the 2008 edition would include a quotation from Aimé Césaire's 1955 *Discourse on Colonialism*, which states that "colonization = chosification" (Montvalon 2007; Césaire 2001). Césaire's equation, which succinctly links the act of colonizing with its devaluing and objectifying intent, represents a bold move away from the possible entrenchment of a fantastical version of the colonial experience. Upon the announcement of this inclusion, CRAN stated to the press: "It's not just a matter of a victory over *Le Robert Editions* but a victory for all of French society, which progressively accepts a revisiting of its past, without misgivings and guilt" (*Le Nouvel Observateur* 2007b). Again, we see the social dimensions of progress and, by extension, modernity, being forged in the context of an African Diaspora experience. Above all, CRAN exemplifies the act of

African Diaspora communities pushing a society toward a real notion of progress, one predicated on real equality and the disavowal of falsehoods that facilitate current inequalities.

In 2007 the CRAN also openly criticized the High Authority for the Fight against Discrimination and for Equality (HALDE) on their website. The HALDE is an administrative body that France developed in compliance with European Union directives requiring that member states contain authorities that address and investigate discrimination and equality concerns (see http://www.halde.fr/). The CRAN aggressively critiqued the HALDE as inefficient:

> We have to admit that the HALDE, born over a year ago, is surprisingly silent, and doesn't work hard on efficiently fighting against race discrimination. In fact it minimizes or even mixes it with other forms of discriminations. Here, the HALDE principles are not at stake but its members' inactivity is. It is fair to give time to any new institution to settle down. But the minority population impatience is growing and the HALDE is not responding to its expectations. Instead of opening up a debate over the use of anti-discrimination tools, the HALDE remains silent and plays for time, evading the issue. (lecran.org)

Of course, what is most significant here is that racial inequalities were being considered at all. The ineffectiveness of the HALDE is more a result of the difficulties in removing state-level barriers to identifying and prosecuting discriminatory acts. This inability to move past the "taboo" of racial identification and to more aggressively address racist acts is evidenced on the HALDE website. In regard to the question, "I am a victim of racism; can I lodge a complaint with the HALDE?" the site notes:

> Racism is a serious offense that is punishable by law. The HALDE has the power to take action if discrimination has occurred. For this to be deemed true, there must be a difference in treatment with respect to another person in gaining access to employment, housing, property, etc., on grounds prohibited by law. When racism occurs in the form of insults or violence, there is no difference in treatment in a field covered by law, for the victim is not prevented from accessing a job, accommodations, or property. Thus, there is no discrimination in the legal sense of the term. The HALDE thus has no power over such offences. (http://www.halde.fr/)

In a 2007 interview with Sarah Elzas on Radio France International (RFI), HALDE representative Nepheli Yatropoulos explains: "The first year,

2005, 1,400 complaints. The second year we had 4,000 complaints. This year we are going to go over 6,000. That's a huge number. We get to be better known—and I think this is an achievement that in two and a half years we really exist as an institution in France" (Elzas 2007). Patrick Lozès, also interviewed for the same segment, states: "There's about 16 million people in this country. And we have about 20 percent of black and Arabs in this country; half of this country are women. We have gender discrimination; we have many kinds of discrimination. And it's only 5,000 cases! I think it's a joke" (Elzas 2007).

The RFI program includes a follow-up interview with a twenty-nine-year-old black French woman originally from Martinique, Marie-Noelle de Chevigny, described as "trilingual with a master's degree in international marketing," who is having difficulty securing employment. She states: "First I sent my CVs without photo. I had two or three interviews per week. I put my photo on my CV and I received perhaps one interview in three months. I collect objections—like a cocktail of objections. I'm young, 28 years old, so people think that I will get pregnant later. I am from Martinique, I am a black people [sic]" (Elzas 2007). A year later and still unable to secure work, when asked if she considered filing a discrimination report with La HALDE, indicating the difficulty in constructing a well-documented case, she noted, "If I had the proof. I would do it, sure" (Elzas 2007).

However, the reports have continued to increase. By 2008, the HALDE reported a total of 7,788 cases, 10,545 in 2009, and 12,467 in 2010 (www .halde.fr). Yet, quite poignantly, at the end of the 2007 segment Lozès stated: "I'm not that confident that we can continue this way. Unfortunately, it can end in something violent. I really, really want to be wrong— because I love my country, but clearly it is a time bomb—it exploded 2 years ago, nothing has changed. It will explode again—and I am afraid that the explosion could be very big—and I don't want this country to go to this, so if we can avoid it, let's avoid it" (Elzas 2007).

PUTTING ON THE PRESSURE: LE CRAN, POLITICS, AND THE REINFORCEMENT OF FREEDOM

> *Au pays des Droits de l'Homme, certains naissent moins libres et égaux que les autres.* In the country of the Rights of Man, some are born less free and equal than others. *Et ces citoyens de seconde zone ont souvent la peau noire.* And these second class citizens often have black skin. *Voilà pourquoi nous avons décidé de fonder le CRAN (Conseil Représentatif des Associations Noires).* That is why we decided to found the CRAN (Representative Coun-

cil of Black Associations). . . . *Pour faire enfin entendre la voix des Noirs de France, et faire évoluer la société sur des questions essentielles: discrimination positive, statistiques de la diversité, colonisation.* . . . To finally hear the voices of the Blacks of France, and to make the society evolve on these essential issues: positive discrimination, diversity statistics, colonization. . . .

(lecran.org)

Le CRAN *(Conseil Représentatif des Associations Noires) a été fondé le 26 novembre 2005.* CRAN (Representative Council of Black Associations) was founded November 26, 2005. *Il regroupe 120 associations et fédérations d'associations, qui ont pour objectif la lutte contre les discriminations, ainsi que la mémoire de l'esclavage et de la colonisation.* It includes 120 associations and federations of associations, which aim to fight against discrimination, and for the remembrance of slavery and colonization.

(lecran.org)

The mission of the CRAN and the organizations it represents brings forth the story of a negatively racialized group of French people—in a nation that denies the act and impact of racialization—asserting a core belief in the Rights of Man (or Human Rights) espoused by French society. In this effort, they must telecast, broadcast, and webcast the historical and contemporary failure of France to realize the essential elements of its core belief system—"*Liberté, egalité,* and *fraternité.*" There was slavery through the nineteenth century, colonization into the twentieth century (and in perpetuity in the contemporary overseas departments and territories), and now, in the twenty-first century blacks in France still must navigate a society in which, as noted in the above quote from the CRAN website, they are "born less free and equal than others." The contemporary "wake-up call" of the 2005 uprisings served as a concise reminder that if equality and freedom are doled out in lesser proportions to some citizens, then—by definition—there is no equality and freedom at all.

The CRAN mission "*faire évoluer la société sur des questions essentielles: discrimination positive, statistiques de la diversité, colonisation . . .*" can be translated as "to make society change on these essential issues: positive discrimination, diversity statistics, colonization . . ."; but *évoluer* in its meaning "to evolve" (as I have translated the verb in the above paragraph) better describes the function of the CRAN. This act of evolving or evolution, neatly paired with progress, is perhaps more ideological than Darwinian, but certainly indicative of the notion of progressing toward something perceived as better. In some sense, CRAN is in the process of helping black France transcend what their late countryman, Jean-François Lyotard, considered "le differend," as they attempt to address a substantial harm in a society that has an ineffective means of articulating that harm. The ellipses in the above mission statement ("colonization . . .") suggests there will be more areas for evolving or progressing in the future. Yet, in the seemingly perpetual battle of race and rights, the organization's acronym tells all: "avoir du cran" can be translated as "having guts" or "moxie" or "spunk," all of which are required in the global struggle for social justice in which Le CRAN is engaged.

The role of Le CRAN to serve as a watchdog organization that represents African Diaspora communities and forces the realization of French republican values is well exemplified in its relationship with President Nicolas Sarkozy. Leading up to his 2007 election as president, CRAN posed key questions to Sarkozy regarding, among other areas, the implementation of social housing, statistics on ethnic populations in France, and the development of a Black Cultural Center. As mentioned earlier, the former minister of interior, known for his *"racaille"* comment, had already expressed the duality of his neoconservative/"liberal" UMP center-right identity by apparently being sympathetic to far-right political agendas through his rhetoric during the 2005 uprisings and simultaneously expressing an ideologically contradictive commitment to positive discrimination (which would clearly not elicit enthusiastic support from the far right). Presidential candidate Sarkozy's responses to the CRAN survey in 2007 suggested a progressive agenda that would address numerous concerns set out in the CRAN's mission. The survey yielded the following thirteen commitments from Sarkozy:

1) Fighting against discrimination.
2) Implementation of diversity statistics.
3) Employment opportunities.
4) Increase in access to social housing.
5) "Better living in the banlieues" [Sarkozy states that his plan to achieve "better living" involves: "build[ing] a society of respect and equal opportunities, . . . promoting the return of businesses, public services, including transportation" [and] "promot[ing] equality of opportunity through education"]
6) Better attention to the status of overseas territories, particularly in the area of inequalities in air transport pricing [state intervention to lower air fares in spite of the air transport oligopoly in the territories].
7) Cultural and political recognition of the Creole language.
8) Increased relations between France and former colonies, particularly in the area of development funding.

9) French immigration policy that does not reinforce insecurity, racism, and xenophobia.
10) Voting rights for non-EU residents.
11) Policy of memory regarding France and colonialism and a School and International Center of Black Culture in France.
12) Ensure that security measures do not stigmatize youth, blacks, Beurs.
13) Programs for youth, particularly in the areas of student housing and an autonomy agreement [creating a pre-majority status to enable access to more social services]. (CRAN 2009b)

Sarkozy's commitments that support the interests of the CRAN are particularly significant as they are a French candidate's response to the needs of an explicitly racialized group in the context of the group's local concerns (e.g., housing, employment, criminalization of youth, voting rights) and diasporic concerns (e.g., lower air transport pricing from Guadeloupe, Black Cultural Center, recognition of French Creole language). Importantly, we see the expression of a black French agenda that is framed in the larger context of realizing a French republican agenda. When the CRAN asked Sarkozy what he would do about discrimination, he responded:

Les discriminations fondées sur la couleur de peau sont inadmissibles dans une République qui a porté sur ses frontons les notions de "liberté, égalité et fraternité." Discrimination based on skin color is unacceptable in a republic that has carried as its pediments the notions of "liberty, equality and fraternity." *Il faut transformer les égalités virtuelles en égalités réelles et ne plus se limiter à des principes comme le font, à certains égards, les défenseurs de notre modèle traditionnel d'intégration.* We must transform the virtual equality into true equality and not be limited to principles as are, in some respects, the defenders of our traditional model of integration. *C'est pour cela que je suis favorable à une discrimination positive à la française, celle qui nous permet à la fois de ne pas renier nos principes républicains (ne la fondant sur une base territoriale) et de prendre le taureau par les cornes (en promouvant des modèles positifs et méritants).* That is why I support positive discrimination for the French, so we can both not deny our republican principles (on a territorial basis) and take the bull by the horns (in promoting positive and deserving role models). (CRAN 2009b)

Though Sarkozy's comments on discrimination to the CRAN were presented nearly verbatim in other contexts,[4] they represent an articulation of the way French republican values in the twenty-first century can be linked to policy that will remedy the impact of race-based discrimination. Yet, quite clearly, this involves admitting that the "traditional model of integration" is not functioning. This tension between the old approach to inequality and something new on the horizon is undoubtedly tangled up in the interpretation of Article 1 of the French Constitution ("ensure the equality of all citizens before the law, without distinction of origin, race or religion"), the investment of some sectors of the populace—"the defenders"—in the belief in an extant egalitarianism (and, by extension, assimilation), and the strident ideological commitment of traditional antiracism groups to constructing policy that perpetuates the myth of an irrelevance of race for fear of somehow willing racism into being by addressing the key components of its form (e.g., ethnicity and race). These complex circumstances—emerging from both the French political left and right—are what the CRAN must traverse; a feat that could prove much more difficult than actually confronting the egregious racism and discriminatory goals of extreme right groups such as the National Front.

Sarkozy on Diversity: Rachida Dati and Rama Yade

After his election, President Sarkozy went on to tackle the issue of diversity in the governmental realm by appointing Rachida Dati as Minister for Justice, making her the highest-ranking official of Maghreb descent in French history, and Rama Yade, a woman of Senegalese descent (and daughter of Djibril Yade, personal secretary for the late Senegalese President Léopold Senghor), as Secretary of State for Human Rights. The appointments of two individuals of African descent overtly underscored the representation of Sarkozy as the head of state that would usher in the social and political transitions long neglected and expressed as desperately needed in the 2005 uprisings. However, the experiences of Dati and Yade, as played out in the media, political, and public discourse, reflect earlier forms of French racial paternalism and the traditional masking of a French power structure that remains white amidst a presumption of ethno-racial equality.

Also in 2007, Fadela Amara, daughter of Algerian immigrants, was appointed Junior Minister for Urban Affairs to head Sarkozy's recovery plans for the *banlieues* (see Lichfield 2008a). While Amara, along with Rama Yade and Rachida Dati, completes the trio of individuals of African descent who are a part of what is often described as Sarkozy's "Rainbow cabinet," her presence speaks more to ideological diversity (see Chrisafis 2009b). The appointment of Amara, a member of the Socialist party, a feminist, an activist with social housing roots and a long commitment to bettering life in the *banlieues,* could immediately exemplify Sarkozy's commitment to enacting change in the suburbs, potentially offer redemption for his 2005 *"racaille"* comment (of which Amara had been strongly critical), and show a commitment to transcending explicitly partisan problem-solving. Thus, Amara's ideological commitments to the left were more significant than her actual ethnicity, yet her experience of being North African in France and her life in social housing are integral to her position as "minister of the *banlieues*" (Lichfield 2008a). I will consider the significance of Rachida Dati and Rama Yade in this volume because even though the uprisings clearly led to Amara's appointment and it was not immediately expected that a vocal leftist would be willing to join the UMP government, her appointment is not only politically expedient but represents a practical choice due to her history of activism in the areas of immigrant rights and the *banlieues* (see McNicoll 2008). However, Dati and Yade, even though they were both UMP members by the time of their appointments and worked within traditional political arenas, were not necessarily the more intuitive appointments in their specific areas of experience.[5] Significantly, their appointments provide an even clearer indication of Sarkozy's post-uprising engagement with the issues of diversity and representation that were brought to the fore by the 2005 uprisings.

Soon after her appointment, Rachida Dati was widely criticized by ministers serving under her as being inexperienced and poor at management, which resulted in advisory and staff member resignations (see Simons 2007; Lichfield 2008b). Nevertheless, she remained in line with Sarkozy's conservative agenda and moved through substantial justice reform in the areas of criminal prosecution, sentencing, and immigration policy, even as she faced the opprobrium of judicial officials and lawyers (see Samuel 2009a; Cue 2008). Then, her controversial support of the issuing of an annulment to a Maghreb couple because the husband claimed that his wife misrepresented herself as a virgin before marriage led to further concern from progressive groups that would have otherwise supported the conservative Dati (see Lichfield 2008b). Finally, when the unmarried Dati became pregnant in 2008, the discourse focused on the unknown father and her immediate return to work five days after a caesarian section in January 2009. The abrupt postnatal return led to accusations that Sarkozy had "bullied" her into returning early by suddenly announcing major reform in the French justice system that would require her immediate attention (Lichfield 2009c; Chrisafis 2009a). Also, Dati's swift return elicited critical concern about the potential impact on maternity rights in the nation (see Beardsley 2009; Lichfield 2009c). By the end of January 2009, Sarkozy reportedly forced Dati to pursue a more anonymous position as a Minister of the European Union and to resign as Minister for Justice (Lichfield 2008b).

Meanwhile, as Dati endured the waves of discontent in her high-ranking cabinet position, Secretary of State for Human Rights Rama Yade was criticized by Sarkozy for expressing disapproval of Libyan statesman Muammar al-Gaddafi's visit to Paris in 2007. Yade, forcing Sarkozy to defend his commitment to human rights, stated: "Colonel Gaddafi must understand that our country is not a doormat on which a leader, terrorist or not, can come and wipe the blood of his crimes off his feet. France should not receive this kiss of death" (Bremner 2007).

As in the case of Dati, Sarkozy also reportedly encouraged Yade to "leave quietly" and take a position with the EUP, but Yade—who was still very popular among the French public—refused to do so (Samuel 2009a). It is also significant that due to her pointed criticism of racism and hypocrisy on the left, Yade did not receive considerable support from the Socialist Party amidst her internal UMP battles with Sarkozy (see AFP 2008). Finally, when Sarkozy orchestrated a reorganization of government in June 2009, the Minister of Human Rights position was eliminated and Yade was reappointed as Secretary of State for Sport, which was widely perceived as a punitive demotion (see Lichfield 2009a). In October 2009, she lost more favor with Sarkozy when she criticized his seemingly nepotistic attempt to appoint his twenty-three-year-old son, Jean Sarkozy, to head the government agency that manages the Paris financial and business district of La Défense (see Lichfield 2009a). Echoing the growing sentiments that she should leave her position, in late 2009 the London *Telegraph* reported that the French Junior Minister for Family Affairs Nadine Morano advised Yade, "If you don't agree with government policies, you should shut your gob or resign" (Samuel 2009b).

In both cases we see Sarkozy attempting to reconstruct France in a way that echoes its republican ideological commitments, albeit through a nod to only two "ethnic" individuals. Also significant is that even though the appointment of women may be perceived as a push toward gender equity, it played out more as a venue for a paternalistic or "bullying" role for Sarkozy as he worked to determine the trajectory of their careers when they asserted individualism and did not acquiesce to meet the political role that he wanted their presence to represent. The implication that two women of North African and Sub-Saharan African descent were to present a fast remedy to deeply entrenched racial—and gender—inequalities was exemplified early on, when in 2007, Sarkozy stated that "Rachida Dati has an obligation to succeed, because her presence is a message addressed to all the children of France" (Tossa 2007). The assessment of Dati's story and role is well presented in an article at the feminist website Muslimah Media Watch, that notes:

> As usual, no one's asking many questions about why all of these expectations are riding on only one person (or why, as president, Sarkozy isn't also being held accountable for the fact that there are still so few people of color represented within his cabinet). In this context, the fact that Dati has not always been especially popular with those working with her—who claim that she was unqualified to begin with, that she has pushed through new legislation with little consultation, and that she has caused many people working under her to resign—is seen not only as a result of her own personal failure (as opposed to also a result of pressures from Sarkozy) but also as a betrayal of all of those whose dreams she supposedly carried. (Muslimah Media Watch 2009)

The Muslimah Media Watch critique highlights the glaring lack of diversity within Sarkozy's government. Yet, it is also significant to consider that Dati is representative of a "bootstraps" or "rags to riches" success, with a Moroccan father who worked as a bricklayer and an Algerian mother who is often described as "illiterate" (see Simons 2007). In addition to the implicit socio-economic mobility, it must be considered that Dati is perceived as creating her own success in spite of key elements of French society that would be more inclined to prohibit her success (i.e., racism and xenophobia). If Dati created her personal success then, as noted by the Muslimah Media Watch, her downfall is constructed "as a result of her own personal failure" (Muslimah Media Watch 2009). Whether a personal success or failure, in both cases we see Dati positioned to represent the possibilities within a French system that requires the exnomination of race and, implicitly, racism, while simultaneously lauding the noteworthiness of her success "in spite of" the thing that shall not be named. Thus, at the state level, there is no direct consideration of how it is that in an egalitarian and free society, Dati—in the twenty-first century—could be the highest ranking individual of North African decent in French history. Furthermore, in not addressing the true problematic—racism in France—the sense of her "personal failure" incapacitates the consideration that the white French society which she professionally inhabits is not isolated from the very circumstances that make her success *noteworthy* in the first place.

By naming Dati and Yade to their positions and then removing them on terms that mask the potential narrative that makes racism explicit (i.e.,

Dati resigned to join the EU Parliament and Yade's position no longer exists, but she obtained another position in the government), Sarkozy neatly removed himself from the perception of racist activity and the reality that racism is operational within his own government. In this respect, Sarkozy managed to effectively perpetuate the more insidious discrimination and bias that characterizes racism in France.

A Matter of Accountability: Le CRAN and the Sarkomètre

In spite of the perception of the failure of those who did not rise to Sarkozy's vision, amidst his less-than-successful attempts at advancing a more inclusive France, the CRAN continued monitoring Sarkozy's progress and failures. In November 2009, the CRAN, in partnership with the feminist organization Mix-Cité, released "*Le Sarkomètre de la parité et de la diversité*" or "The Gender Parity and Diversity Sarkometer," a midterm report meant to check Sarkozy's progress in key areas to which he promised attention during his 2007 campaign. The Sarkomètre, described as inspired by the American "Obamater" used to examine the first-year progress of U.S. President Barack Obama, featured a Pinocchio-like caricature of Sarkozy's profile with the length of the nose indicating progress (short nose) or a lack of progress (long nose) in keeping his promises. The Diversity Sarkomètre specifically measured the progress of Sarkozy's promises that were expressed in the aforementioned CRAN questionnaire in 2007. Overall, Sarkozy's work in the area of "diversity" was not deemed successful, as CRAN's Louis-Georges Tin[6] explained:

Unfortunately, the picture is not positive. In 2007, Nicolas Sarkozy responded to the CRAN questionnaire. He had made commitments in 13 areas on the fight against discrimination, memory issues [colonialism and slavery], suburbs, etc. In total, 38% of promises were not kept at all, 62% with little progress, 0% of achievements were sufficiently advanced, 0% of promises fully kept. Worse yet, we found that in many areas, departments were not even aware of the commitments of the President! For example, Nicolas Sarkozy had supported the idea of a grand center of black culture, modeled on the Arab World Institute. When we contacted the various departments concerned, they did not know anything about it. Where are we today? Stalled! (CRAN 2009b)

All but five promises were described as "achieving little progress." The five remaining promises—regarding social housing, Creole, the relationship with former colonies, voting rights for non-EU citizens, and, as discussed by Tin, the Black Cultural Center—showed a long nose and were described as *"promesse pas tenue du tout"* ("promise not kept at all"). The CRAN expressed some positivity about the progress of the issue of diversity statistics, though it was noted that the UMP was "dragging their feet" on the issue and the Socialist Party was "hampering" the process (CRAN 2009b). Furthermore, as I examine in the next section, the CRAN had already conducted a survey in April of 2009 that showed "2 out of 3 French" people support diversity statistics, which offered the organization some hope in this regard (CRAN 2009b). More immediately, during the time the Sarkomètre was released, a committee was investigating the viability of gathering data on ethnicity in France and, simultaneously, a debate on national identity was being launched.

THE FREEDOM TO BE COUNTED: STATISTICS ON THE LEFT, RIGHT, AND NOWHERE

Nicolas Sarkozy expressed a commitment to ethnic statistics because, as he stated in the CRAN questionnaire in 2007, they would offer "a way of understanding the reality of discrimination" (CRAN 2009b). The commitment was exemplified in December 2008 when he appointed Algerian-born Yazid Sabeg as "Commissioner on Diversity and Equal Opportunity." In March 2009, Sabeg commissioned the Committee for the Measurement and Evaluation of Diversity and Discrimination (COMEDD), chaired by François Héran, formerly of the National Institute of Demographic Studies, to study the implementation of statistics and, overall, the viability of changing French law. In particular, the 1978 Data Protection Law prohibited the collection of data on ethnic or religious origin in accordance with Article 1 of the French Constitution ("ensure the equality of all citizens before the law, without distinction of origin, race or religion"). The debate over whether compiling ethnic data would be allowing a "distinction" of individuals and whether ethnicity statistics or what the CRAN prefers to call "diversity statistics" would be necessary in the effort to combat racism and discrimination is addressed by Le CRAN:

> In countries where they were introduced, diversity statistics help us to know precisely who was discriminated against, to positively address these situations. Currently, we have no tool of this kind in France.
> The CRAN hope that all discriminations are measured to **improve the plight of all minorities,** not just that of blacks in France. To call for di-

versity statistics, is to carry out a universal and Republican struggle. (CRAN 2009a; bold in original French)

In their steadfast pitch for "diversity statistics," we see the CRAN's challenge to race-based discrimination positioned as integral to French republican values. Also very significant is that the CRAN articulates their efforts in a "universal" context which, in one respect, removes them from the French discourse and "stigma" of communitarianism and, in another regard, allows them to simultaneously engage in an inter-diasporic and global conversation about world racisms.

The 2005 uprisings brought forth a new framing of equality discourse in France that works toward the realization of French ideals through an interrogation of prior approaches to anti-racism. Le CRAN is at the center of this new approach. This is exemplified in the divergent reactions and approaches to the collection of data on ethnicity. While Le CRAN advocates "diversity statistics" with the understanding that a clear indication of which ethno-racial groups are experiencing the brunt of discrimination in areas such as employment, housing, education, and the criminal justice system will be beneficial in countering discrimination in France, the more traditional or longer-established French anti-racism groups, such as SOS Racisme, LICRA (International League against Racism and Anti-Semitism), LDH–France (Human Rights League—France), and MRAP (Movement Against Racism and for Friendship among Peoples), have opposed ethnicity statistics. The complexity of this conflict among groups that, in theory, are working toward the same goal of ending discrimination and racism is indicative of the difficulties in reconciling an unwavering commitment to equality amidst a pervasively *unrealized* equality. While Le CRAN expressed a commitment to having data in order to clearly locate discrimination and its specific impact upon groups, SOS Racisme's position, among other opponents of ethnicity statistics, is rooted in the ideology that the singling out of ethnic groups is tantamount to identifying difference for invidious intent, as historically experienced during the Nazi occupation of France in World War II (see Shirbon 2009).

In March 2009, the French opinion research institute, CSA (Conseil-Sondages-Analyses), SOS Racisme, and the Union of Jewish Students of France (UEJF) conducted a poll and released the report titled "The Ineffectiveness of Ethnic Statistics in the Fight against Racism, Anti-Semitism and Discriminations," which concluded that 55% of French found such data "ineffective" (CSA 2009a). The SOS Racisme and UEJF commissioned study posed the question: "Do you consider the implementation of ethnic statistics in the general census of the population very effective, some-what effective, not effective or not at all effective in fighting against racism, antisemitism and discrimination?" (CSA 2009a).

Patrick Lozès responded to the study in his blog at *Le Nouvel Observateur,* writing, "I can only protest against the intellectual dishonesty in asking an incomprehensible question that confuses and mixes concepts, and drawing misleading conclusions" (Lozès 2009a). Explicating his concern that the question implicitly required respondents to provide an assessment of something that had yet to be attempted in France, Lozès went on to deconstruct the survey: "The term 'ethnic statistics' is reprehensible because it is not a matter of counting ethnicities, but [a matter of] the principles of our Republic itself (liberty, equality, fraternity), it is a question of putting them into practice. Ethnicities do not exist in our Republic, so they do not exist there [in the survey]. Recall that racism and antisemitism are hostile ideologies while discriminations are concrete actions that can be committed unintentionally and even by people devoid of any feeling of hostility" (Lozès 2009a). He then questioned the interpretation of "ineffective," noting that "[b]y definition, the statistics of diversity cannot be 'effective' against discrimination!" and stating that public policy fights discrimination rather than the "tools of measurement" of discrimination (Lozès 2009a). Further suggesting that SOS Racisme is not in line with new approaches to anti-racism, Lozès wrote: "It has been asserted for a long time, without empirical evidence, that statistics can only lead to communitarianism. While their implementation is sought by people who long for justice and equality, today SOS Racisme is taking another pathway" (Lozès 2009a).

The SOS Racisme poll was conducted via telephone calls on March 4 and March 5 of 2009 to 1,050 individuals age eighteen and over. The survey reflected a cross section of respondents and, outside of the variations addressed below, regardless of political leanings (i.e., far-left to right), age, region, and career, a higher percentage responded that ethnic statistics were "ineffective" (CSA 2009a).

The noticeable distinctions in the survey occurred within the groups that had a higher percentage of individuals responding "effective." For example, 51% of respondents in the educational category "without diplomas or primary school educated" thought the statistics would be "effective," 36% considered them "ineffective," and 13% did not answer the question (CSA 2009a). By contrast, 22% of respondents with over two years of higher education stated "effective," with 74% indicating "ineffective," and 4% not responding (CSA 2009a). Also, the higher percentage of respondents possessing vocational (high school) diplomas, baccalaureate (or high school–level) diplomas, and a baccalaureate plus two years of higher education noted "ineffective" in the range of 58%, 62%, and 68%, respectively (CSA 2009a). Thus, the results indicate that the higher one's level of educational qualification, the more likely one was to indicate that ethnicity statistics would be ineffective.

Furthermore, while individuals representing a range of occupations—including artisans, middle management, accredited professionals, administrative and service employees—considered ethnicity statistics "ineffective," the individuals in the *ouvrier* category (worker, laborer, blue-collar worker, etc.) leaned in the other direction with 47% noting "effective" and 46% "ineffective," with 7% not responding. Individuals in the unemployed category more decisively deemed the statistics "effective" with a representation of 53%, 46% determining "ineffective," and 1% not responding.

Additionally, though the report indicates that it is too small of a sample to be conclusive, 58% of individuals in the category "housewives" responded "effective," with 34% determining "not effective," and 8% not responding. While "housewives" are not defined as part of the paid labor force, it cannot be determined whether those identifying as such would also classify themselves as unemployed, which would also further suggest support for ethnicity statistics among the unemployed.

While one concern around the study, as expressed by Lozès, involved the validity of querying individuals about the effectiveness of a method that has not yet been tried, the poll is also problematic because it cannot be determined whether any individuals surveyed would directly benefit from anti-discrimination policies resulting from a clearer statistical representation of those who bear the brunt of discrimination and racism. In other words, were any blacks and Beurs in the survey pool? If so, considering that such a question implicitly could not be a part of the survey, how would we know? The three groups that had a higher percentage of "effective" responses offer some indication that individuals who are likely to be experiencing discrimination in education and employment were surveyed. The three groups that responded "effective" fit into the categories of "no diploma," "blue-collar workers," and "unemployed," which suggests limited opportunities and, paired with their interest in ethnicity statistics, could support the presumption that these groups contained a significant representation of blacks and Beurs. Also useful to consider, though still in the realm of heightened speculation that a lack of statistics requires, is that the "unemployed" (again, more inclined to support ethnicity statistics) had the lowest percentage of non-respondents of all categories in the survey (1%), which further suggests that they were very decisive about the potential beneficial impact of ethnicity statistics upon their communities.

Also noteworthy, the North was the only region that had a higher percentage supporting ethnicity statistics, with 55% indicating "effective," 41% "ineffective," and a 4% non-response. This could also be related to the unemployment of the respondents as, even before the global economic crises intensified in 2009, a 2004 Eurostat report indicated that Nord-Pas-de-Calais had "the second-highest unemployment rates of all the regions in metropolitan France," which included a large unemployed youth population. The Eurostat report, noting that residents of the province had the "lowest gross disposable income," also revealed that "the inhabitants of Nord-Pas-de-Calais are the least well off of all in the regions of the metropolitan" (Eurostat 2004). The region was a traditional site of immigration, with a textile industry and now moribund steel industry and coal mines. In March 2009 the national rate of unemployment was at 8.7%, whereas the rate in the Nord-Pas-de-Calais region was at 12.2% (EURES 2010). While the North is clearly a site of social concern, the SOS Racisme study exemplifies the intractable nature of avoiding ethnicity data, as the social concerns in the North and elsewhere continue to mask and, therefore, neglect ethno-racial concerns even in the attempt to remedy problems related to racism.

Less than a month after the SOS Racisme survey was released, between April 1 and April 23, 2009, Le CRAN commissioned the CSA to conduct a telephone survey. The pool of respondents encompassed a representative national sample of 1,006 individuals from a cross section (sex, age, profession) stratified by region and agglomeration community, and a second group of 493 self-identified "visible minorities" representing a sample of a cross section (sex, age, profession) stratified by region and agglomeration community. Noting the trailblazing fact of the CRAN survey, Lozès announced, "For the first time in France, we have taken the plunge and asked our citizens about feelings of belonging" (Lozès 2009b). The report, titled "The French, Visible Minorities and Discrimination," addresses five key areas:

1) The perception about inquiries to measure diversity.
2) Personal experiences of discrimination.
3) The perceived development of discrimination in France.
4) The perceived usefulness of a racism observatory.

5) Visible minorities and the creation of businesses. (CSA 2009b)

The first section of the report contains two key questions that serve as both a counter-survey and an answer to the SOS Racisme study. The first question asked:

> If a statistical survey was conducted about the feeling of belonging of the French to measure their diversity and better know discrimination, would you be strongly favorable, somewhat favorable, somewhat unfavorable or not favorable at all? (CSA 2009b)

The results showed a majority favorable response with 63% of the representative sample of the French populace and 69% of individuals in the "visible minorities" sample responding either "strongly favorable" or "somewhat favorable" to "feeling of belonging/diversity" statistics (CSA 2009b).

The second question, inclusive of a safeguard for data protection and supervision by the CNIL (National Commission of Information and Liberties), asked:

> If a statistical survey was conducted about the feeling of belonging of the French to measure their diversity and better know discrimination, and if the responses were self-declared, on a voluntary basis, anonymous, without retaining files and controlled by the CNIL, would you be strongly favorable, somewhat favorable, somewhat unfavorable or not favorable at all? (CSA 2009b)

The results indicated an even higher favorable response to the second question, with 65% of the representative French sample and 74% of the "visible minorities" sample responding either "strongly favorable" or "somewhat favorable" to the "feeling of belonging/diversity" statistics (CSA 2009b). Overall, younger respondents were more favorable, which suggests some combination of a significant concern about or an experience with the impact of discrimination, a generational shift in the engagement with French-style republicanism, and, at the least, an unsurprising willingness of younger individuals to try new approaches. In the representative French sample, 75% of individuals under age thirty were favorable, 71% of respondents between thirty and forty-nine years old were favorable, and 55% of individuals older than fifty noted favorable; 84%, 73%, and 60% in the age groups, respectively, responded favorably in the "visible minorities" sample (CSA 2009b).

Gender did not vary the results significantly, with an 8-point difference (61% men and 69% women were favorable) in the representative French sample and in the "visible minorities" sample, a 3-point difference (73% men and 76% women were favorable) (CSA 2009b). The more favorable percentage among women in both sets could find some resonance in the experience of gender discrimination that is not specifically addressed in the question, but could be implicit for those who experience such discrimination or the duality of racial and gender discrimination. Also, Le CRAN has linked its race-based struggle to struggles against gender discrimination, particularly in its partnership with Mix-Cité, a Joint Movement for Gender Equality, in the aforementioned *Le Sarkomètre de la parité et de la diversité* (The Gender Parity and Diversity Sarkomètre) (CRAN 2009b).

Notably, the representative French populace responses reflect higher "favorable" percentages from the Left (e.g., 67% from the *Parti Socialiste* or Socialist Party, 78% from *Les Verts* or the Green Party) and 75% from the centrist Mouvement Démocratique. Also, a majority of respondents on the right responded "favorable," with a 60% favorable response from the *Union pour un Mouvement Populaire* (UMP) respondents. The far-right respondents were represented by a statistically inconclusive pool of respondents with members of the Front National and its equally extremist offspring, Bruno Mégret's *Mouvement National Républicain,* resulting in a 31% favorable response (58% unfavorable). In the case of the extreme right—the only majority "unfavorable" group—because of pool size and without a corresponding follow-up question, it may not be possible to determine whether the "unfavorable" response was because the statistics are viewed as anti-Republican or if respondents did not favor the potentiality of successfully addressing discrimination.

The CRAN survey provides the more complex questions for consideration that the organization found lacking in the survey commissioned by SOS Racisme, as well as the evidence of discriminatory conditions needed to justify the missions posed in the above two questions (i.e., "measure diversity and better know discrimination"). The CRAN survey asked the sample of "visible minorities" whether they had experienced particular circumstances due to the "color of their skin." The areas of consideration included education studies, public services, housing, friends and loved ones, access to leisure activities, physical violence, damage of goods or vandalism, securing employment, and police. Fifty-nine percent of respondents indicated that they had experienced at least one of these circumstances due to the "color of their skin." This is particularly important, as it not only provides evidence of a social problem but specifically addresses the intersection of this social problem with the very real issue of race or not being "white" in France. Implicit in the European notion of "visible minorities" is that certain minorities are visible because they are not white; that is, they stand in sharp relief. To express these circumstances—police harassment, discrimination in housing, physical violence, etc.—in racially specific terms is problematic in France. However, Le CRAN is able to circumvent the paradox of asking about race *without* asking about race by engaging a self-identifying pool in the context of "*couleur de votre peau*" which, of course, is a proxy for race.

Also significant is that the survey directly asked "visible minorities" about the post-uprisings state of discrimination in France:

> Would you say that over the past five years, discrimination with regard to "visible minorities" in France has increased, diminished, has not changed? (CSA 2009b)

Seventy-nine percent of the respondents did not believe that discrimination had declined within the past five years, with 34% of that percentage indicating an increase in discrimination and 45% answering that it remained the same.

The final queries of the CRAN survey reveal that 49% of the "visible minorities" polled either have created their own business (13%), are in the process of creating their own business (10%), or plan to do so in the future (26%), suggesting a need for ethnicity-specific support and debunking any presumption of willful idleness (41% of those with businesses, working on a business, or planning to do so in the future were described as "*inactif*" or "not working"). Additionally, 71% of "visible minorities" supported the launching of a Racism Observatory, which would later be considered in 2010 in the aforementioned Héran report on ethnic statistics.

When the survey was released on April 28, 2009, Lozès, blogging about the highlights of the results, wrote: "We show the feelings of minorities on the progress around discrimination since the riots of 2005. . . . Are we risking further riots?" (Lozès 2009b). The next day, April 29, 2009, SOS Racisme issued a press release titled "*Survey CRAN: Diversion Continue!*" ("CRAN Survey: The Distraction Continues!"), arguing that it is not necessary to collect "sensitive data on the entire population" to assess diversity and that doing so would represent "great dangers" (SOS Racisme 2009). The SOS Racisme press release offered the example of assessing diversity at work by looking at individual areas, determining the levels of representation in those areas, and then conducting a comparison rather than surveying all employees (SOS Racisme 2009). They argued, "If the [CRAN survey] question had been posed in these terms, the answers given by the respondents would no doubt be very different" (SOS Racisme 2009). Regarding the issue of data protection and privacy, the press release notes that "Mr. Lozès claims that no files will be created," yet because a "proper measurement occurs over time" Le CRAN would have to "create files for comparison and use the data collected" (SOS Racisme 2009). SOS Racisme, deflecting the criticism of its March 2009 survey, describes the CRAN survey as "intellectually dishonest" because individuals polled about their "feeling of belonging" would default to "statistically exploitable classes" as the data on "the 'feeling of belonging' collected during the investigation turns into an ethnic category when results are aggregated" (SOS Racisme 2009).

The press release also highlights the tension inherent in the divergent engagements with anti-racism experienced by Le CRAN and SOS Racisme, particularly in the continued assertion that Le CRAN is creating a distraction rather than a substantive change. Regarding the CRAN survey data indicating youth support of statistics: "The survey also tends to believe that the majority of young people favor the establishment of ethnic statistics while results from a vague question merely demonstrate that young people are more aware than others of the problems of discrimination. The ongoing work of grassroots associations, which provide legal hotlines and advance knowledge of the law, explains that reality"[7] (SOS Racisme 2009).

Finally, SOS Racisme states that the focus on ethnic statistics by Le CRAN and the Yabeg commission (eventually Héran's report), "distracts from real issues and does in no way advance the fight against discrimination" (SOS Racisme 2009). Even if the question was reworded and if Lozès had articulated that comparative examinations were an implicit part of the function of having the data, it is not clear that the populace is as fearful of the data collection as SOS Racisme presumes in their assumption of "very different" responses. While the youth factor, as I also indicated above, may result from their experience with discrimination, it does not appear relevant whether it is reported to "grassroots associations" because such associations and grassroots legal hotlines are still operating in an environment in which state-level investigations into circumstances about race are hobbled by the inability to significantly address the systemic and institutional function of racism in French society.

On the day of the release of the CRAN survey results, Lozès was quoted in a *Le Monde* article stating that, regarding the issue of diversity and discrimination, "the survey concludes the debate. . . . It is now time to act"

(Van Eeckhout 2009). The debate would continue through the COMEDD investigation and the National Identity debate, examined in the next section. Yet, the desire to underline the end of the question of whether there was race-based discrimination in France, whether individuals were experiencing it, and whether there was a commitment to utilizing statistics that document the ethno-racial landscape was less an end to debate itself and more reflective of a desire to move French discourse on racism in a new direction. It was an expression of the plea for progress in its most dire form. As Patrick Lozès noted in response to the March 2009 sos Racisme study: "It is time that the players in this debate show more seriousness on this issue that concerns the experiences of millions of people. These people want the discrimination that plagues their daily lives revealed so that it can finally be tackled" (Lozès 2009a).

The COMEDD report was released by Héran on February 5, 2010, and upheld the ban on ethnic classifications and census queries regarding ethnic background but recommended the inclusion of a question about parental ancestry—nationality or birthplace of parents—as a means of gathering quantitative data on individuals with a recent immigrant background (Van Eeckhout 2010). Patrick Lozès described the report as ending "one phase" and beginning "a scientific and political phase," acknowledged the constraints of "the current legislative framework," and emphasized that "legislation is still needed" (Gérard 2010). Lozès, pressing for the commitments brought forth in the post-uprising political climate and still unrealized by the 2009 Sarkomètre, also stressed that Sarkozy must "keep his campaign promise and implement tools to measure diversity" (Gérard 2010). Additionally, the COMEDD report recommended that the HALDE have a discrimination observatory (Gérard 2010). When asked whether this could "serve as a body to monitor discrimination," Lozès pragmatically responded: "*Je salue cette proposition, mais ce n'est qu'une proposition.* I welcome this proposal but it is only a proposal. *Il faut attendre son application.* We must await its implementation. *Nous en sommes toujours à une étape de diagnostic, nous n'en sommes pas encore à l'action.* We are still in a stage of diagnosis, we are not yet in action. *Alors nous disons 'oui' à cet observatoire, dans la mesure où il améliorera la connaissance de la diversité.* So we say 'yes' to the observatory, since it will improve the understanding of diversity" (Gérard 2010).

The CRAN reaction to the Héran report appears weary of promises, which is not surprising in a society that five years after significant uprisings around racial inequality could merely consider an additional observatory —monitoring "discrimination" rather than explicitly "racism"—as a mode of tackling the mammoth problem. Also significant is that a highly problematic national identity debate—rife with questions of racism, anti-Muslim discourse, and anti-immigrant rhetoric—was drawing to a close during the time of the COMEDD findings.

THE GREAT DEBATE: REVIVING AND REVISING
THE FRENCH NATIONAL IDENTITY

While the ethnic statistics consideration was well under way, in November 2009 Nicolas Sarkozy charged Eric Besson, Minister for Immigration, Integration, National Identity and Development Partnership, with the task of launching a debate on national identity. Before considering this lofty debate, it is important to note that Besson's governmental position was created by Sarkozy when elected in 2007. The competing missions of the ministry, aptly described by a France 24 host as "explosive" (Owen 2010), are fervently justified by the state: "For twenty years, plans have been made to gather in one structure various aspects of immigration policy, which had so far been split up between the ministries of Interior, Foreign Affairs, Social Affairs and Justice. . . . With the aim of being both firm and human, we pursue four objectives: controlling migration flows, favoring integration, promoting the French identity and encouraging development partnership" (Ministry for Immigration, http://www.immigration.gouv.fr/).

The negotiation required when "being both firm and human" already indicates two diametrically opposed conditions. That is, implicit in this combination of ministries is the contradictory question as to whether one can be both firm on immigration and constructions of national identity while still seeing the humanity of others. Furthermore, which individuals become "the others"? This, of course, exemplifies the contradictions at the root of the modern mission within a nation that could both assert the Rights of Man and simultaneously have slaves and colonial subjects. In their contemporary rendering, the contradictions inherent in the questions of race, identity, and nationalism in France were the impetus for the fires in the Paris suburbs of 2005. So, any consideration of the Ministry for Immigration, Integration, National Identity and Development Partnership working to "promote the French identity" requires the question: What exactly is being promoted? The contradictions inherent in French renderings of its national identity, combined with transitions in areas of French culture, are at the core of the "Who are we?" question that is the implicit center of the French national identity debate. It is no coincidence that such a query is indicative of the questions that remained unanswered and unresolved four years after the 2005 uprisings.

The *"Grand débat sur l'identité nationale"* was launched on November 2, 2009, and featured an extensive website (including commentary from state and popular figures, response areas, video, and chat rooms) along with a series of town hall public meetings meant to get at the question: "Pour vous, qu'est-ce qu'être français?" (For you, what does it mean to be French?). There were forty thousand responses in the first month and, notably, within that period 15% were removed by the site moderator due to racist content (Gros de Larquier 2009). The comments[8] posted on the website offer a picture of the terrain which Le CRAN and—overall—black France must navigate as they locate themselves as integral to the French national identity rather than a peripheral consideration.

Numerous posts at the website consider the paradox of having a debate and its overall usefulness, as expressed by one respondent who, presenting an unattributed quote from philosopher Emmanuel Levinas, states: "To question identity is to already have lost it!" (polak, November 30, 2009). Another respondent noted, "Being French is to find the debate on National Identity ridiculous and shameful!" (Bokkal, December 2, 2009). There were also several responses that addressed cultural components such as singing *La Marseillaise,* the French national anthem, speaking French, and, as one post noted, "a tradition of a good red with cheese and a baguette" (Rachy, November 30, 2009). However, within the seventy-eight pages surveyed for this volume,[9] a substantial amount of responses addressed core French republican values, as exemplified in these three responses:

> Being French is to love one's country with its history and core values: freedom, equality and fraternity (Bibo, November 28, 2009).
> Being French is to be respectful of the democratic values of our country, defending the symbols: Freedom, Equality, Fraternity (Quentin, December 1, 2009).
> To be French is to be free (Albert, December 1, 2009).

The issue of freedom is important in the articulation of black freedom, but even as espoused in the context of how one considers one's Frenchness, such contributions to the debate were not equipped to interrogate the ways in which many French individuals are "not free" and whether if one is not free then, implicitly, one is not French at all.

One post from a French individual, who notes, "I was born in Africa, I'm Black," discusses showing his identity card that indicates that he is French and states, "I will be satisfied when my French compatriots are convinced that I'm French!" (Somal, November 27, 2009). His comment yet again reflects the racist assumption that blackness makes one's Frenchness suspect. This unrealizable Frenchness was echoed by respondents "of color" who were Muslim and other individuals with ancestry in various locations, including Morocco, Senegal, and Vietnam. Additionally, there were responses that directly addressed racism as counter to republican values. For example, one respondent noted, "[F]or me to be French . . . is within the law of the republic: liberty, equality, fraternity. There is no place for racism. Long live the republic. *Vive la France*" (Alex11, November 30, 2009). Another stated, "France is a country with all skin colors and religions" (Nathan, December 1, 2009). In addition to positioning racism and secularism as counter to French values, the national identity considerations also included respondents who addressed the French historical legacy in the context of contemporary obligations. This was particularly exemplified by a respondent who questioned whether to be French was to "enjoy" the "annuity built on slavery, colonialism and imperialism" and "to benefit from unequal exchange, the plundering of resources and the destruction of the environment of ¾ of the World" (Christian MASSON, November 28, 2009).

As reflected in the more crucial concerns about racism in the debate—online and offline—there were interpretations of French identity that were explicitly anti-Muslim and anti-immigration. One respondent lauded the 2009 Swiss ban on minarets and stated, "For me to be French is also defending historical values, our country is not a land of Islam and should not become one" (Lopez, November 30, 2009), and another noted, "France and our national identity is a cathedral in central Paris and not a mosque" (14Granada92, December 1, 2009). Such rhetoric led one respondent to complain that "The debate on national identity is being appropriated by extremists in our country" and that the discussion forums had become spaces for French "Muslim confessions" (serval, November 30, 2009). Another respondent wrote: "I note that the question, 'For you, what does it mean to be French?' here has turned into 'What immigration policy should France adopt?' Indeed, even if the charter of moderation provides that 'any racial or xenophobic attack or insinuation, based on beliefs or lack thereof, ethnicity, gender or sexual orientation' should be discounted in this discussion area, many reactions easily fall into this" (Gaelle, November 30, 2009).

Amidst the growing anti-Muslim and anti-immigrant discourse that became extensively associated with the "Great Debate" there were calls for the realization of the national identity in relation to the nation's human rights roots. One post noted, "WHAT BEING FRENCH is . . . The Dec-

laration on the Rights of Man and of the Citizen of 1789 and Article 1"
(Marie, December 1, 2009), and another wrote, "Being French is to be
proud to be part of a system that may be imperfect but which has always tended toward greater justice" (Aurelien, December 1, 2009). In
another example, notably linked to contemporary notions of progress,
an entry is posted by "Blaise Diagne," who describes himself as "name-
sake" of his "great uncle," the twentieth-century French parliamentarian
of Senegal. He writes that France is more than "land, flag, national anthem" but the first project of "men and women who built the course of
history" toward "social progress and the happiness of their descendants"
and that the "project is embodied in its values" of "Liberty, Equality [and]
Fraternity" (Blaise Diagne, November 30, 2009). In a second post, continuing his statement, Diagne writes of informing his children that their
great uncle passed a law allowing for the participation of Senegalese soldiers for France in World War II (as well as French citizenship of Senegalese) and that his own father was "French Senegalese" and fought for
France during World War II. He writes of "rais[ing] the profile of France
throughout the world" through "one's daily actions" and ends by noting
that "France shines on the world, because it consists of the world, from
Papeete to Fort de France, through Brasac-les-Mines" (Blaise Diagne—
continued, November 30, 2009). Diagne's response locates French identity as contingent on the contributions of individuals who are not racialized as white, therefore constructing a globally successful France
"shin[ing] on the world" because it does not locate itself in the global
narrative of whiteness but can articulate a more inclusive identity. His
comments rest on historical fact (e.g., the Blaise Diagne of the Parliament
and the black war effort for France), but also suggest that the work France
does toward raising its global profile will have to begin in the hexagon
itself.

Numerous responses reflected a conflict within France emerging from
the commitment to French equality amidst an exclusionary narrative and
narrow assumptions about the way Frenchness is embraced and contested. These conflicts and contradictions at the core of the French identity narrative are particularly exemplified in the following post:

French identity is to respect France and French laws,
To respect public services, police, gendarmerie, firefighters, teachers, etc.
Not booing the Marseillaise
Not burning cars if they don't like the police
Not wearing a veil covering her face because it is not part of one [single]
   French tradition

Not to be racist against blacks or against whites
Those who do not respect this do not deserve to live in France which has
   always been a land of welcome for anyone wishing to keep these principles! (SIMON, December 1, 2009)

This post suggests that in the process of "respect[ing]" French laws there
is little room for contesting French laws outside of positioning oneself as
disrespectful. Therefore, to challenge the police or gendarmerie for profiling and interrogating the Frenchness of individuals of color could be
perceived as disrespectful and, as outlined in this post, not French. The
reference to the 2005 uprisings ("Not burning cars . . .") makes this conflict explicit. But, furthermore, the belief that "wearing a veil" is outside
of French tradition indicates one of the ways in which something deemed
as other than French could be legally abolished. At the time of the debate, considerations were under way to write a burqa ban into law. So,
following the logic of this response, if such a law existed and a Muslim
woman challenged it, she would be perceived as not French because of
the very act of trying to have the "veil"—something already considered
outside of "French tradition"—included in the narrative of French identity. That is, by default, she risks not being seen as French because she
does not sufficiently "respect" the French law.

The respondent considers the booing of the Marseillaise, an act that
has occurred several times in the realm of football (soccer), as outside of
French identity. This is another example of the disabling of the ability to
protest French racism by placing the very act of protest—when engaged
to counter racism—as external to Frenchness. When Beurs and blacks
"boo the Marseillaise" ("*siffler la Marseillaise*") at matches with North
African teams, the seemingly disrespectful act is a strong method of expressing discontent with a greater French society that enjoys a mostly
black and Beur national team but has little respect for the blacks and
Beurs that are not on the team (see Crumley 2008).

Also significant is that the respondent places racist behavior outside
of the purview of Frenchness. Yet, tellingly, the notion that to be racist is not to be French is contradicted by his exclusion of the "veil" from
Frenchness. The exclusion of the veil results from the act of privileging
one racialized understanding of French identity over another (i.e., racism). Again, the prospect of a legal ban rooted in the assumption of "un-
French" behavior underscores the way in which racism becomes embedded in law. Furthermore, many French people engage in activities that
may not be considered traditionally French. Though not as relevant to
one's personal life as the wearing of a burqa, we must wonder why an un-

traditional visit to a Paris McDonalds is not included in the list of disqualifiers for French identity.

Additionally, by stating that the act of "burning cars" is not in line with French identity the respondent circumvents any assessment of the 2005 uprisings as a resistance to institutional racism which, following the logic of his post, would only show that numerous police officers and politicians are no longer able to claim their French identity (i.e., racism is not French). Finally, expressing an identity that is traditionally associated with Ireland, France is positioned here as "always a place of welcome" provided one obeys the rules. Again, we see the narrative of a benevolent welcoming French society of assimilation and republican values juxtaposed against individuals who are not willing to follow the rules; yet the act of welcoming or fulfilling the principles of the republic is never upheld and no one is held accountable for their absence.

In the end "*Le Grand débat sur l'identité nationale*" was overwhelmingly represented as unsuccessful, as any potentially thoughtful considerations were overshadowed by explicit racist, anti-Muslim, and anti-immigrant rhetoric and the overriding question of the political timing of the debate before elections in the nation. While a CSA Institute poll in early November 2009 initially indicated that 60% of individuals polled supported the debate when it was launched, a month into the debate a CSA poll showed that 50% percent of French wanted to either suspend or cancel the debate (see Vernet 2009; France 24 2009). The greater public opinion characterized the debate as an election-related scheme, particularly geared toward courting right-wing support for UMP candidates in upcoming elections; this was seen as being even more the case as the debate began to focus on immigration and Islam (Vernet 2009). The predominant public sentiment was further underscored as the campaign to ban the wearing of the burqa and niqab—a measure supported by Prime Minister François Fillon and President Sarkozy—continued throughout the "*Grand Débat*" (see Bidar 2010). However, the state framed the debate as an all-inclusive national mission. Fillon stated in a speech outlining the significance of the debate, "You know, I've never been one of those who thinks that the time for nations is over. Our nation is our protection and it is our springboard," and asserted: "It is a debate that is neither right nor left. France is our common good, and everyone has a duty to consider the best way to better love and better serve our country. To reject this debate and stigmatize the idea that our people can have a singular identity, is to leave the way open for extremists, including their success which is based precisely on the alleged weakness of our national consciousness" (Fillon 2009). In the same speech, Fillon passionately contends, "Here and there, it was argued that this debate was dangerous and it would revive suspicions. But the danger is precisely not to debate!" (Fillon 2009). Meanwhile, Besson, echoing the commitment to the national debate, noted that "Debate doesn't boost extremism, taboos do" (Samuel 2010).

Sarkozy challenged opponents of the debate: "Those who do not want this debate are afraid of it. . . . Behind the differences, oppositions, contradictions, there is the profound unity of our culture. . . . Our identity is both singular and plural. . . . It is in thought, language, lifestyle [and] landscape" (*Libération* 2009).

As Besson, Fillon, and Sarkozy placed the problematic aspects of the debate—racism and xenophobia—in the realm of extremists, it was still impossible for them to extract their narrative of transcending "taboos" to get at the "profound unity" from their own considerations of burqa bans and conservative UMP immigration discourse. Throughout the debate, the racist and anti-immigrant implications were more salient for the general populace. As Makhete Cissé, a black Muslim who is a computer engineer and vice president of the committee supervising the building of a "Great Mosque" in the diverse city of Marseille, explained in a France 24 segment: "I have attended several debates. Eighty percent of the time the subject is Islam. It feels like Islam is the real core of this debate. It is indeed a good question but it isn't presented properly so the real question is quite simply how to integrate Islam in Europe and in western culture. That's the real debate. You can tell because nobody talks about civic problems or fundamental republican values" (Andre 2010).

The debate reached its end point on February 8, 2010, as an anticlimax, culminating with a list of suggestions and the appointment of an advisory group of parliament members, intellectuals, and scholars to continue to consult with Eric Besson on the issue of national identity. Fillon, upon announcing the new measures, described the debate as a "vital debate, essentially," praised Besson's leadership, and admitted that there had been "some slippage" (referring to xenophobic, anti-Islam, and racist discourse) but that "the national identity debate has met with popular success" with 340 town hall meetings nationwide, as well as 58,000 entries and 750,000 visitors on the website (see Dyèvre 2010; *Le Post* 2010). Fillon announced the implementation of several measures meant to encourage the experience of national identity, which included: (1) Flying the French flag in schools, (2) Hanging the 1789 Declaration of Rights in classrooms, (3) Starting in 2010, a "young citizen book" would be given to all students from elementary through college (high school) for stronger civics lessons, (4) Though not emphasized, providing the opportunity for the *Marseillaise* to be sung in French schools, and (5) Greater emphasis on French language acquisition for new migrants and newly naturalized citizens (see *Le Post* 2010; BBC 2010; France 24 2010). Fillon explained, "The emphasis will be put on the respect for the values of the Republic . . . notably the principle of equality between men and women . . . and the level of knowledge of the French language" (BBC 2010).

Around the launch of the national identity debate, the Irish and French shared an encounter that led John Lichfield, Paris correspondent of the *Irish Independent* and *Independent* (London), to consider the essence of French identity. He wrote about his septuagenarian Paris neighbor who had no interest in watching the World Cup qualifier match between Ireland and France because he felt that the national team was "not really French," which Lichfield surmised was due to "too many non-white faces in the line-up (seven out of eleven)" (Lichfield 2009b). Lichfield discusses French identity through the case of Thierry Henry, a French footballer whose father is from Guadeloupe and mother is from Martinique. Henry infamously led France to beat Ireland in the World Cup qualifier on November 18, 2009, through a dribble that should have been penalized (he touched the ball with his hand rather than his foot). Lichfield, considering that Henry "celebrated madly and then told the referee that it was a foul, when it was too late to change the outcome," writes:

> Seen from abroad, rightly or wrongly, the French are viewed as a nation that likes to ignore rules (from nuclear tests to priority for pedestrians) and, at the same time, maintain a rather high-flown opinion of themselves.
>
> They want to be the nation of human rights but to mumble under their breath about black French footballers not being French. They want . . . to be a champion of the Third World but to be mildly racist. They want the French West Indies to be French but not the French West Indians, like Henry's parents. They want to have it both ways.
>
> There are many other, wonderful things about the French, just as there are other wonderful things to say about Henry. But on the evidence of the last few days, whatever my neighbor might say, Henry's national identity could only be French. (Lichfield 2009b)

Lichfield's observations—through the microcosm of sport—expose core contradictions in the contemporary rendering of the French modern project. Yet, furthermore, the case of France's win over Ireland is much more telling than the story of world sport alone, as it brings forth a key question of global justice: How does justice occur if injustice is not successfully challenged? Notably, after the France-Ireland incident the then Irish Minister for Justice Dermot Ahern petitioned the International Federation of Association Football (FIFA) for a re-match and stated: "They probably won't grant it as we are minnows in world football but let's put them on the spot. . . . It's the least we owe the thousands of devastated young fans around the country. Otherwise, if that result remains, it reinforces the view that if you cheat, you will win" (*Irish Independent* 2009).

Ahern's inquiries, along with then Irish Prime Minister Brian Cowen's announcement that he would discuss the issue with a reluctant Sarkozy at an EU meeting, led the United States press to describe Ireland's quest as a desire for "soccer justice" (*NBC Sports* 2009). France moved forward to the World Cup in South Africa. Even if the concern about the message "if you cheat, you will win" did not register, the incident is only indicative of the many silences and conditions that remain unchallenged on the social and political world playing field.

FORGING PROGRESS AND THWARTING RETROGRESSION IN THE REPUBLIC

The literature, press releases, interviews, websites, and other media coverage of the efforts to better the lives of blacks in France represent an ongoing mission to move France forward. Individuals such as Rama Yade, Patrick Lozès, and Pap N'Diaye, who sits on the CRAN Science Council, each bring forth a body of literature and ideas meant to express the diverse experiences of African Diaspora communities in France, realize the equality and freedom of the rhetorical national narrative, and actively expose the areas in which the narrative continues to fall short. When asked why she wrote her book *Noirs de France,* Yade stated: "Following the fire in the building on Vincent Auriol Boulevard in Paris, I did not like how the residents of that building were presented in the media: it was as if they were newly arrived migrants from Roissy [airport] while these people were French. . . . I said to myself: 'What if this disaster had not only highlighted the flaws in housing policy, but those of the integration of people of African origin in our country?'" (Yadan 2007b). She added, "We should get used to the idea that one can be black and French" (Yadan 2007b). The process of France "get[ting] used to the idea" also involves the hurdle of transcending the overwhelming presumption that France already *had* gotten used to it. In this effort, as seen with the Sarkomètre, the debate over ethnicity statistics and Rama Yade's own experiences in the UMP government, the individuals and organizations that work to augment the profile of black France must persistently check the commitment to their concerns of both the ideological and political right and left. Yade made this clear: "The political elite want to retain power for themselves. In fact, if you're not a 50-year-old white man, you have little chance of access to important political positions. From this point of view, I believe that French society is more advanced than the leaders on this issue" (Yadan 2007b).

The idea that French society is "more advanced than the leaders" in the problematizing of whiteness as a contingent qualification for political power underscores the link between race and notions of progress. In Yade's assessment, we see some members of the society ("French society") challenging race-contingent (and age-contingent) political power and representing an "advanced" populace that rejects white privilege in government. Those who maintain the status quo are then not "advanc[ing]" or progressing, which firmly places them in the realm of the retrogressive, as they curtail the nation's advancement or progress.

Pap N'Diaye, who serves on the Science Council of Le CRAN, is a scholar at the *École des hautes études en sciences sociales* (EHESS) and author of *La Condition Noire: Essai sur une minorité française*. He ponders both explicit and subtle racism in his work (see N'Diaye 2007). In a France 24 interview, when asked if he had experienced discrimination in France, he explained:

Well, I don't have a very serious experience of discrimination. I've never been turned down by an employer when applying for a job, for example. I'm on faculty in a university and I've never experienced the weight of discrimination and racism the way a black worker, for example, or black employee would experience it. However, being black in France means also experiences . . . an experience of small discriminations, very small things, small remarks often characterized by a form of paternalism. For example, I have an ID, a faculty ID and my faculty ID is often checked at the library as if this ID was false. So it's little . . . little things, nothing serious but very subtle ways to demonstrate that you are considered and looked down (upon) by other people. (Sanke 2008)

Though his own experiences of discrimination may not be as invidious as for individuals trapped in a Paris hotel or the *banlieues,* N'Diaye's comments provide a further indication that France has yet to realize the potential of the modern project or notions of progress. Particularly interesting is that N'Diaye offers an example of the United States as more adept at challenging discrimination and racism than France. This, of course, becomes another example of the required revision of the old myth of French egalitarianism that was more easily pedaled before the 2005 uprisings. When asked by host Andrea Sanke, "Where would you like to see a greater black presence?" N'Diaye responded:

> One of the crucial steps is political life. When you compare the American political life to French politics the contrast is so obvious. In French politics we have hardly any black politicians, a handful from overseas departments and that's about it—one minister. And the necessity of diversity in politics is absolutely obvious to me because the lack of minority politicians has effects on French society. Often blacks are seen as workers, employees, people who cannot do much in schools. It is also true among business leaders. There are hardly any minorities among their ranks so there is still a long way to go when comparing the French situation to that of Britain or the United States. It is obvious that France is way, *way* behind, years behind in fact. (Sanke 2008; emphasis in audio)

Patrick Lozès also considers the United States in the equation of progress on race, as he explained in an *Evene* interview shortly after the publication of his book *Nous, Les Noirs de France* (Lozès 2007):

> All acts of discrimination are not necessarily racist. Combating racism amounts to fighting against falling rain and it can take a great deal of time, while the fight against discrimination can quickly equip people with an umbrella. In the U.S., they do not fight against racism, but legally they are armed against discrimination. In France, we tried to fight against racism and it is clear today that simply screaming that races do not exist is not enough. Since then we have not developed a real public policy to fight against discrimination. That is the originality of our struggle, to do what has not yet been done. (Yadan 2007a)

The case of black France further underlines the sentiment that progress can be measured in terms of a society's engagement with "race" and "racism" as well as the impact of difference upon that society. In other words, in theory and quite obviously, "social progress" does not involve working toward a more racist society, but involves the act of moving away from the realization of such a society.

I indicated in part 1 of this volume that during the early period of conducting research on the African Diaspora communities of Ireland, when I would leave and return to Dublin from the United States or England, it was like traveling back in time to a space of more egregious racism (see White 2002a). The fact of blackness was such an anomaly that heads would turn on the street upon seeing a person of African descent. Progress is contingent on the idea of transcending not only years (i.e., moving forward in time, as we can only do), but shedding the cultural and racialized experiences that are seen as dysfunctional remnants of the past. This engagement with progress occurs across time and space, reminding us that we continue to rethink progress and what is socially acceptable in the realms of life, culture, nationalism, and global engagement. This is particularly evident when we consider that in post-2005 France, individuals such as Lozès and N'Diaye look toward the United States to locate a more progressive challenge to race-based discrimination and systemic racism. Yet, for many black Americans in the early to mid twentieth century, France was a space of refuge from the racism and discrimination of the United States. In this respect, we are witnessing a significant shift in the extent to which racism is deemed tolerable in the twenty-first century. That is, even as James Baldwin offered some significant critiques of French racism in the mid twentieth century, France was still upheld as a better option than the American Jim Crow south.[10] This, of course, highlights the reality that it was never the case that the white French were not racist or that they were *extraordinarily* inclusive, but that their engagement with blacks was *less intolerable* than *de jure* and *de facto* racism in the United States at the time. Today, the limited opportunities for blacks in France echo the very thing that was abhorrent to twentieth-century blacks in the United States.

The shift in the American articulation of French egalitarianism following the 2005 uprisings is neatly exemplified in a blog produced for the very purpose of dispelling the myth of French "*egalité, liberté, fraternité.*" In 2007, an African American video blogger began "RottenFrance," a series in which she discussed racism in France. Maintaining her anonymity,[11] she states: "I won't give you my name but I will tell you that I am an American who has been residing in France for the past four years" (RottenFrance 2007b). In one of her early posts "RF" tells her audience that she will be "talk[ing] about specific things that . . . concern Americans who are interested in what's going on in Europe" and expresses a sincere disappointment that France is not in actuality living up to its republican values: "France is a terribly terribly racist country. Now, I, for one, deeply loved France. I was a Francophile. I studied France. I took degrees in the language. I studied the history. And I studied the culture. So what does that mean? That means that someone who is terribly pro-

France and is well disposed to indulge every possible favorable thought finally has to come to the realization that France is a terribly . . . terribly racist country with a lot of injustice going on and I want to make you aware of it" (RottenFrance 2007b). "RF" makes explicit the historical and temporal disjuncture one experiences when predominant understandings of social progress are contradicted by retrogressive actions. In another earlier posting, she says:

> First of all, when you come to France . . . when you first come to France you're going to get the impression that you have stepped back in time. France operates with the same values and behavior patterns as we used to have in the 1950s. What that means is that it's a joke to be black and so people laugh at black people and you'll see images of black people in magazines and on television and in comic books and drawn up in different places with giant red lips and black black skin and giant white googly eyes. They think that's funny. We as Americans, we've moved beyond that. We think that's vulgar to laugh at the way a human being is. . . . French people, in the extreme difference of Americans, think that being black is something that you laugh at. Whereas we have discarded images such as Aunt Jemima and Uncle Tom and we no longer have black skinned mammies and so forth, whites here in France still do that, making jokes about being black, saying things like "Oh, do you see things all black?" (RottenFrance 2007b)

The acceptability of racist caricatures and juvenile race-based humor are abhorrent to "RF" but her comments also reflect the more pervasive frustration that comes with "going back in time" or retrogressing to an earlier engagement with racial difference instead of finally "mov[ing] beyond this" or progressing (RottenFrance 2007b). As exemplified in the case of New Orleans, the United States is not immune to retrogression, and in various blog segments "RF" does acknowledge U.S. racism. However, her posts particularly work to reconstruct France as a nation that is not yet up to pace in the world of social progress and the manifestation of the *real* modern society. Her genuine dismay that France is a country "with the same values and behavior patterns as we used to have in the 1950s" further indicates that if twenty-first-century France resembles mid-twentieth-century America, then 1950s France only seemed socially better on the race issue to 1950s African Americans because it was *relatively* better at the time. This also suggests that because there was no *de jure* racism in France, the social movements that led to the dismantling of segregated systems in the United States and the discursive shifts that were paired with these movements did not occur in France. Therefore, until recently, the French did not work toward cultivating the sensitivity to or willful curtailing of the offensive and racist discourse that "RF" condemns in her blog.[12]

In another post, further exemplifying the social trajectory of progress, "RF" interrogates France through the question of modernity and media representation:

> First of all, I'd like to say with no equivocation this country is shockingly racist. *Shockingly, shockingly* racist. Even though there are all the accoutrements of a modern society you'll find people living just as we lived in 1950, where one is deeply gratified when you see a black face on television for the first time. . . . From early on in [U.S.] history we've had black participation in all parts of our media. . . . Here . . . there is really very little participation, just as it was back in the 1950s [U.S.]. Only, 1950 is 57 years ago. So, we have to wonder why France is still living in 1950 where black people have no representation in television. (RottenFrance 2007a; emphasis in audio)

Most notably, the references to the United States in "RottenFrance" indicate that even after Hurricane Katrina, an egregious example of the persistence of racism in the United States that was covered throughout France, the United States is still positioned in the French black rights movement as representative of what France has yet to achieve or reach on the continuum of progress. The use of the United States as a barometer of social progress was exemplified in the aforementioned France 24 interview in which Pap N'Diaye considered black representation in politics and the business sector, explaining that France is "way, *way* behind, years behind in fact" (Sanke 2008; emphasis in audio). In another example, reflecting the limited opportunities for blacks in France in areas of professional employment, in the 2007 RFI radio interview mentioned earlier in this chapter, Marie-Noelle de Chevigny, a black French woman described as "trilingual with a master's degree in International Marketing" who had been looking for a job for two years in France, discussed her plans to secure employment in the United States: "I spent two weeks in the United States—I was very impressed, because people don't care about the fact that I'm black—they just want to know what we can do for them. So, when you have to go to an interview—you are not afraid. You are not thinking that they will be surprised because I am black or whatever. . . . I think that I have to try something because in France I did everything I could. I have to think about myself, because I am 29 and I have to work, you know" (Elzas 2007).

The comments from Chevigny highlight a major shift in perception resulting from the exposure of the social and racial reality of France. That is, it is no longer unimaginable that the United States could be a guide for France in the fight against racism. Significantly, such reversals or revelations are a necessary means of moving into a realm of actual social progress and, implicitly, modernity. Whether in the case of the fantasy of a welcoming Irish society coexisting with mass deportations or the illusions of equality in both the United States and France, the exposure of the reality facilitates dialogues and considerations that work toward addressing the overriding issue: global racisms limit potentially modern societies.

AULNAY-SOUS-BOIS: A SPACE OF EXPOSURE

The Paris suburb of Aulnay-sous-Bois was a key site of the 2005 events that led to the national introspection, public policy considerations, and community organization discussed throughout this chapter. In addition to the community of Clichy-sous-Bois, where teenagers Zyed Benna and Bouna Traoré met an untimely death, the social housing of Aulnay-sous-Bois served as a focal point for the 2005 uprisings, particularly as global media reported the burning of a Renault dealership in the area. In the United States, CBS News reported:

> In the tough northeastern suburb of Aulnay-sous-Bois, youth gangs set fire to a Renault car dealership and burned at least a dozen cars, a supermarket, and a local gymnasium. (CBS/AP 2005a)

CBS News, as did several other networks reporting the Associated Press coverage, explained:

> The rioting has grown into a broader challenge for the French state. It has laid bare discontent simmering in suburbs where African and Muslim immigrants and their French-born children are trapped by poverty, unemployment, discrimination, crime, and poor education and housing. (CBS/AP 2005b)

In Ireland, an RTÉ News report (using Reuters coverage) on the tenth night of the uprisings succinctly captured the community frustration about the uprisings, the racism that elicited the violent response, and the continuous criminalization of *banlieues* residents:

> In Aulnay-sous-Bois, a rundown Parisian suburb of 80,000 inhabitants, several thousand residents marched past burnt-out vehicles behind a "No To Violence, Yes To Dialogue" banner. This afternoon, the French interior minister Nicolas Sarkozy warned rioters of stiff jail sentences for arson. (RTÉ 2005f)

Aulnay-sous-Bois is one of the many sites that are problematically and euphemistically represented as the *"quartiers sensibles"* (sensitive areas), facilitating what Sylvie Tissot and Franck Poupeau have described as the "spatialization of social problems" (Tissot and Poupeau 2005; also see Tissot 2007) and echoing the concerns of Patrick Lozès that the social context masks the racial roots of the condition through a "denial of reality" (Yadan 2007a). However, a tour of a site such as Aulnay-sous-Bois forces one to experience the neat intersection of race, space, and, at the risk of being too obvious, the social conditions that place races in spaces. That is, the post-2005 attention to ameliorating the *"quartiers difficiles"* (difficult areas)—to use another state-level and popular euphemism—addresses a quality-of-life issue without the full realization of how one's quality of life is "raced" in Paris and its suburbs. This circumstance finds its corollary in the city plans of New Orleans, as programs are under way that replicate earlier socio-racial geographic conditions—only with nicer homes. The key difference in New Orleans is that racial discourse remains at the core of resistance, and commentary on the post-Katrina housing condition is paired with race statistics to support or deflect claims of inequality; even when "mixed income" and "prior ownership clauses" work to mask the racial underpinnings, race comes to the fore. In the Paris suburbs, without quantitative data on ethnicities that disproportionately experience the impact of life in the *banlieues,* the concern with race can only emerge from groups such as Le CRAN, as the means of addressing problems in the *banlieues* can otherwise only occur through available social data that exclude race (e.g., employment and income statistics). So, while Le CRAN and other advocates battle for ethnic statistics or diversity statistics and conduct surveys on "visible minorities," the state-level attention to all things racial through the lens of the social—and, by extension, immigration and integration—has hobbled the effort to make an effective impact on the problem of racism and discrimination. This, of course, can only forecast and necessitate more uprisings because, quite simply, a refurbished unit in social housing does not explain why an individual of African descent cannot secure employment, educational opportunities, or other appropriate housing. With this in mind, I will turn to my field notes on a visit to the Paris suburb of Aulnay-sous-Bois.

A Journey to Aulnay-sous-Bois—August 2006

During the uprisings of 2005, I was in Germany, about 40 kilometers outside of Frankfurt, at the first Black European Studies conference. The events in the Paris suburbs became the backdrop of the conference, as we watched reports at the end of the day's proceedings. There was an awareness that Germany would not necessarily be isolated from the events—nor was it to be expected in a country with its own troubling engagement with "visible minorities." On Monday, November 7, 2005, when five cars were burned by "arsonists" in the Moabit district of Berlin and also a car dealership in Bremen was burned, the events were described by German police as an imitation inspired by the events in the Paris suburbs (see Peters 2005). In August 2006, I was in Berlin and had the opportunity to see the Moabit district. Though the area did not carry the remnants of the burnings in the way that I will describe in the case of Aulnay-sous-Bois, undoubtedly the peripheralization of Moabit's predominantly Turkish community and their continuous grappling with the social conditions that would inspire what was described as a "copycat" act was evident. I recalled a few days earlier when, within an hour of arriving in Berlin, a German taxi driver proceeded to tell me about the Turkish community who "don't want to work" and "don't want to speak German" and "don't mix with Germans." All this he expressed without regard to the citizenship restrictions that have hindered the level of "integration" he perhaps envisioned. However, as the case of France exemplifies, a policy of integration and assimilation does not eradicate the peripheralization of those deemed "other" by the majority populace.

In August 2006, I also took a closer look at a Paris *banlieue*. My partner on the journey, Ian Fleet, and I (carrying our younger son, seven months in utero) traveled from Montmartre in the 18th Arrondissement of Paris on the Metro to connect to the RER (Réseau Express Régional) for a Charles de Gaulle Airport–bound train. After approximately forty-five minutes of commuting on the RER, we arrived at Aulnay-sous-Bois station. We left the station with the hope of walking to the site that was—along with Clichy-sous-Bois—a major place of activity during the uprisings just nine months before. Instead, we found ourselves walking through the town of Aulnay-sous-Bois which, in the environs of the train station, resembled a quaint village with the expected range of shops and cafés. The towering vision of the social housing of the Paris suburbs, so prominent in the United States, Ireland, and other global media, was nowhere in sight. Our journey to the euphemistically named *"quartiers sensibles"* would require an additional journey by bus.

We stopped by the Dumont Library to inquire about the events of 2005 and to obtain directions. A helpful librarian wrote down bus directions and told us that it was "mostly quiet" in the town during the uprisings though transport had been stopped. She gave us directions to the bus that would take us to the social housing areas in the northern part of town, as well as a map featuring five *"Bibliothèques d'Aulnay-sous-Bois,"* which gave us a sense of the area. We eyed #4 on the map, a library that we would see later when we walked through *les cités* (housing projects). We then literally and figuratively headed to the other side of the tracks (RER tracks) in order to catch the 617 Bougainville / Le Marché bus to the northern area of this suburb that featured so prominently in the 2005 events. After a twenty-minute bus ride and traversing the contrast of middle-class homes that sit on the edges and around the perimeter of the buildings of the *"quartiers sensibles,"* our commute from Paris ended upon our arrival in the less-than-quaint social housing of Aulnay-sous-Bois.

Not yet a year after the uprisings, outside of one of the many architecturally dull towers—cement with peeling paint the color of rust marked the style—sat a wheel-less burnt-out car on a cement block, resembling a preserved artifact of 2005. We followed a sign to a *Centre Social* or community center and went inside to inquire about life nearly a year after the uprisings. One of the employees of the Center gave us a tour of the premises, which was a space to support educational programs, early childhood needs, cultural events, and a range of opportunities for social interaction. We looked around a while and saw a few adults and children involved in activities—drawing, crafts, playing—in different rooms off of a narrow hallway. The schedule of leisure activities posted in the small lobby of the Center announced gymnastics, sewing classes, cooking programs, family outing opportunities, and French and English classes occurring throughout the various *quartiers* or apartment building areas. We were given a copy of *Oxygène,* the then monthly magazine of the town of Aulnay-sous-Bois, which featured a draft of the future of the *quartiers,* involving the refurbishing of apartments as well as the gradual demolition of the towers to be replaced by smaller-scale housing that would "profoundly and forever transform the quarter to make it more pleasant to live in for its residents" (*Oxygène* 2006:13).

Outside of the community center, the renovation scheme was merely in its early stages as the area behind the center was blocked by barriers and a large hole where construction machinery signaled a transformation under way. A representative in the community center explained that the hole would eventually become the "family garden" sketched in the diagram of the future form of the *quartiers*. There were no playgrounds in sight, but just outside the *Centre Social,* a young girl of Sub-Saharan African descent, around eight years old, played tennis against the wall of a towering building next to the center. Two boys with a bicycle, both of them also of African descent, joined her for play by the wall and next to a tilting fence that barred entry into the muddy construction area. We greeted each other and they continued to play as we moved on, continuing our tour of Aulnay-sous-Bois.

There were large billboards posted around the complex announcing the *Programme de Rénovation Urbaine,* forecasting a better life for residents. As one sign announcing the renovations of the Brise and Zephyr quarters read: "*Amélioration du cadre de vie*" ("Improving the living environment"). Next, we walked along a pathway past a sports café and toward a long three-story-high, mostly gray cement building with letters across the top noting the *Centre Commercial* in red and the *Forum Galion* in blue. The large and looming stretch of building served as both a shopping mall and residence, with apartments on the upper floors and in an adjacent tower. The *Centre Commercial* and *Forum Galion* apartment structure and integrated shopping precisely represents its place in the past and present. The buildings reflect a social housing plan reminiscent of the 1960s and 1970s era in which they were built. Part utilitarian and suggesting a once "modern" project that enticed new migrants to the opportunities of the time with their contemporary amenities and the lure of jobs, the buildings were now looking moribund, dull, lightless, and representative of joblessness and the lack of opportunities in the hexagon.

A stroll through the *Centre Commercial* revealed many permanently closed shops. Among the open shops in the sparsely lit mall were a black hair product and wig shop, internet and telephone café, two *halal* butchers, and a bakery. When we left the shopping mall and walked through a courtyard where an occasional market occurs, we came upon #4 on our map of local libraries that we were given by the librarian in town, the *Bibliothèque Municipale Annexe*—Elsa Triolet; notably named after the Russian-born writer who was active in the French Resistance during the Nazi occupation. Triolet had now become a name on a municipal library amidst a new form of resistance. In sharp contrast to the renovated Dumont Library in town, the *Bibliothèque Elsa Triolet* was a small one-story building that did not deviate from the predominant architectural style of the quarter at the time. In retrospect, it is also noteworthy to see Triolet in this context, as her efforts to ward off an invidious racialized ideology were as much about holding France true to its egalitarian commitments as the outcry and outrage of 2005 were to those who were involved. The context and historical moment may be different but the principles—*egalité, liberté,* and *fraternité*—have been theoretically maintained along with the post–World War II reinforcement of Article 1 of the French Constitution (. . . France shall be an indivisible, secular, democratic and social Republic. It shall ensure the equality of all citizens before the law, without distinction of origin, race or religion. It shall respect all beliefs . . .).

Beyond the desolate mall and library, in front of another residential tower, a group of men, women, and children—mostly of Sub-Saharan African descent—had several grills set up. They prepared and grilled corn on the cob to sell to passersby, neighbors, and people waiting at a nearby bus stop; representing entrepreneurial endeavors, taking control of one's financial destiny, and creating a marginally better income in a place with few employment options and limited prospects.

Planning Anew and Renewing the Old

The Aulnay-sous-Bois urban renewal plan—under the auspices of *Programme de Rénovation Urbaine* (PRU) (Urban Renewal Program) with *Groupe Logement Français* (French Housing Group) was set for a period from 2005 to 2011. The PRU brochure outlines the timeline and scope of the renovations to the following *quartiers:* Zéphyr (2005–2006), Brise (2005–2006), Alizés (2006–2007), Étangs Est (2004–2006), Merisier (2005–2006), Aquilon (2005–2006), Galion (2006–2009), Vent D'Autan (2005–2008), and Étangs Ouest (2006–2010) (PRU 2005).

The PRU brochure features a photo of Gérard Gaudron, then mayor of Aulnay-sous-Bois, and Éric Madelrieux, then Gérance Regional Director of *Groupe Logement Français,* the housing management group, smiling and examining papers that resemble a planning document, and announces the plans for the various quarters of Aulnay-sous-Bois social housing. Deflecting the potential concern about a lack of community input, the renovation ideas are explicitly presented in the brochure as a response to clearly defined needs determined through interactions with *quartiers* community members. For example, resident "David D." is quoted, "*Dans les tours, il y a trop de monde. Tout se degrade*" ("In the towers, there are too many people here. Everything is deteriorating"). The PRU responds: "*Aujourd'hui, les tours ne correspondent plus au mode de*

vie et aux attentes des locataires. Elles sont difficiles à entretenir" ("Today,
the towers no longer correspond with the way of life and expectations of
the tenants. They are difficult to maintain") and explains that they will
demolish twelve of the fourteen towers and replace them with smaller
residences (PRU 2005: 1). In another example, accompanied by a photo
of a colorful contemporary playground, resident Nathalie N. is quoted:
"Il manque des squares pour les enfants, avec des bancs pour les mamans"
("There's a lack of squares for children, with benches for the mums").
The PRU responds: *"Dans le quartier des Étangs et sur des terrains de la
RN2 par exemple, le PRU va permettre de créer des aires de jeux pour les
enfants avec des bancs."* ("In the Étangs quarter and in the fields by the
RN2, for example, the PRU is making it possible to create play areas for
children with benches") (PRU 2005: 1).

Across the various *quartiers* the PRU envisions the completion of private green spaces with flowers, opening new roads, improving parking
areas, extending walkways, and reinforcing lighting in public areas. The
RN2 (National Route 2)—which features the aforementioned green area
in the middle—is envisaged as undergoing a "transformation into a grand
boulevard" with nearby shops and public services and a business area
that will create jobs (PRU 2005: 2). Also, a picture of the proposed new
Galion residential buildings next to the *Centre Commercial* shows a series
of four-story brightly colored peach and white buildings surrounded by
trees, bushes, and flowers. There are also balconies outside of individual
units on the top three floors and patios on first-floor units. According
to the PRU brochure, the new Galion would take form upon the "renovation and transformation" of the building, the demolition of the west
terrace area, renovation of apartments—including new bathrooms and
windows—and the demolition of the towers that border the RN2 (PRU
2005: 2).

The Aulnay-sous-Bois urban renewal project, costing €263 million
(PRU 2005: 2), addresses the structural deficiencies implicated in the social
housing problem but does not necessarily address the race- and ethnicity-
based problems that facilitate black and Beur representation in the suburbs. This was further exemplified in May 2009 upon the demolition
of the Renault Garage, the Aulnay-sous-Bois location that drew global
media attention when the dealership and several cars were burned during the 2005 uprisings. An article in the now weekly *Oxygène* magazine
stated: "The last symbol of the riots of 2005 is set to disappear. Tuesday,
the diggers begin clearing the site" (*Oxygène Hebdo* 2009: 3). The short
article, which featured pictures of workers preparing the diggers and a
small group of residents and politicians gathered for a symbolic cere-

mony, stated that it would take fifteen days to clear the site and begin a "project that integrates with the economic development of the town" (*Oxygène Hebdo* 2009). While the photos depict an optimistic crowd, some smiling and clapping, the presumption that a building alone can signify the "last symbol of the riots of 2005" again privileges the structural dimensions of an ethnic and racial problem. Quite certainly, a new building on the Renault Garage site—even one that is set to be the premises of "commercial activity and offices and allow for the creation of jobs" (*Oxygène Hebdo* 2009)—does not address the racial and ethnic dimensions of the significant social problems that set the dealership afire in the first place.

CONCLUSION
Toward a Modern Future

The preceding chapters have considered instances of social retrogression amidst seeming progression in the overarching context of global societies that are perceived as modern. To foreground these instances, I have considered Dublin in the conceptual framework of a "retro-global society," which I define as *a formerly lesser-developed, new global society that retains pervasive and highly conspicuous social elements or constructs that are more indicative of earlier periods of globalization.* I have particularly considered these "retro" circumstances in relation to notions of equality and freedom that are expressed through the republican and democratic values represented as integral to modernity.

The 2005 events in Dublin, New Orleans, and Paris brought forth questions about the ways in which contemporary African Diaspora communities are truly free and how freedom or a lack of freedom resonates with contemporary assumptions about modernity. Moving beyond technological advancement as progress, I have also considered the way in which contemporary understandings of modernity, when conflated with current dimensions of globalization, involve basic levels of material consumption that can serve as signs of progress, such as the opportunities to achieve employment, to travel freely, to have decent housing, and to not be impoverished in a wealthy world. I have also argued that if these signs of progress are all part of our twenty-first-century understanding of freedom, then there are still African Diaspora communities—and numerous other communities beyond this study—that are not free. So, this leads us to consider the social dimensions of modernity and the way—via those events perceived as anomalous or mere "glitches"—societies are forced to account for the intimate relationship modernity has with inequality. These inequalities, as they continue to emerge in a range of circumstances (e.g., deportation, migration, poor housing, natural disasters) will not be easily transcended through the mere espousal of technological advancement, ratcheting up global monitoring institutions or, most ineffectively, repeating the litany of textbook definitions of democracy and freedom. The circumstances evidenced by the experiences of African Diaspora communities indicate that what is most needed in Dublin, New Orleans, Paris, and numerous other sites, for that matter, is a commitment to substantive changes that radically and actively extricate contemporary policies from the rooted racism and inequality inherent in modernity at its inception.

The persistence of retrogressive elements in societies is exemplified by the way that the "retro" conditions and events discussed in the case of Dublin in 2000 and 2001 in part 1 of this volume become further problematic in 2005 Dublin and resonate with the events in 2005 New Orleans and Paris examined in part 2. While "retro-housing" found its expression in the dispersion of asylum seekers—a predominantly black population—from Dublin to restrictive living conditions in accommodation centers throughout the nation, in New Orleans black communities were subjected to race-based inequalities in home ownership and minimal advantages from loan support due to pre-Katrina home values that corresponded with the prevailing ethno-racial hierarchy, and in Paris black communities were subjected to discrimination in social housing and the general housing market as well as the substandard living conditions seen in the apartment fires of 2005. As "retro-spatiality" was manifest in the minoritization of black communities through the concentration of African Diaspora entrepreneurship and social opportunities in the Parnell Street and seemingly tenuous Moore Street areas of the Dublin north city center, in New Orleans the legacy of the *de jure* and *de facto* spatial segregation of black communities resulted in the substantial location of African American–owned property and rentals in low-lying areas that were more prone to hurricane-related destruction; and in Paris the significant location of African Diaspora communities in social housing outside of central Paris in the *banlieues* facilitated a structural manifestation of the already extant social exclusion and isolation experienced by black and Beur communities of France. "Retro-documentation," which is exemplified through the asylum identification card and related profiling of blacks due to the presumption of a questionable status in Dublin, also becomes relevant in the case of New Orleans because the loss of documentation due to Hurricane Katrina prohibited the return of African

Americans to previous houses or land, thus enabling the purposeful exclusion and/or removal of individuals, which is undoubtedly the desired result of most profiling. In Paris, the patrolling for undocumented individuals or *sans papiers* has criminalized African Diaspora communities as well as reflected the presumption that blacks and Beurs are not legally in the nation and, implicitly, could not be French; actions that were implicated in the deaths of Zyed Benna and Bouna Traoré and the subsequent 2005 uprisings. Finally, while the inaugurals or "firsts" in Dublin, such as the first anti-racism protest by African immigrants, the launch of an African webzine, and the development of the Black Actors Workshop, reflect a nation with a substantial black population for the first time, post-Katrina New Orleans, a city already known for its black presence and numerous black "firsts," experienced "firsts" that were ironically more retrogressive than inaugural events. In 2007, the electorate of New Orleans selected its first predominantly white city council in twenty-two years and, in 2010, elected its first white mayor in thirty-two years, both circumstances indicating that the struggle toward black representational power in a city once defined by its black residents but not led by them was now being reversed in the twenty-first century. Meanwhile, in Paris and the French nation, the post-uprising years would find journalist Harry Roselmack as the first black national news presenter in 2006, Rachida Dati and Rama Yade highly positioned in the Sarkozy government in 2007, and Le CRAN, a first in its own right, pushing forth the nation's first extensive query about racial belonging in 2009. Also, whether in Dublin, New Orleans, or Paris, we see a comparable desire for black communities to be represented not only through media, but acknowledged through hard statistical data (i.e., the 2006 Census in Ireland, the importance of accurate numerical data indicating African Americans returning to post-Katrina New Orleans, and the advocacy for ethnicity or diversity statistics in France). Overall, each location is characterized by the overriding sentiment in both popular and state-level discourse that the circumstances experienced by individuals of the African Diaspora—whether deportations, poor housing, racism in employment, or racist popular representations—are anachronistic and should not be a part of the narrative of twenty-first-century modern societies.

In the sense that there are diaspora spaces (Brah 1996), transnational spaces (see P. Jackson et al. 2004; Vertovec 1999, 2001; Pries 2001; Smith and Guarnizo 1998), and spaces of media or mediascapes (Appadurai 1997) brought forth in this project, there is also an underlying documentation of discursive spaces throughout this book. When considering "discursive spaces" I find Juana Rodriguez's conceptual understanding very useful. In her examination of identity in the discursive spaces of activism, law, and cyberspace in the context of "Queer *Latinidad*," Rodriguez explains: "Discursive spaces exist as sites of knowledge production. The clinic, the prison, the classroom construct fields of knowledge and have historically existed to define subjects. Discursive spaces need not be institutional, however; the chatroom, the bar, the street corner, the computer screen also serve to define subjects and construct knowledge practices. These spaces have their own linguistic codes and reading practices, as they engage in hiding and revealing their own internal contradictions. Objects, art, texts, buildings, maps can also create knowledge, change history, refigure language" (Rodriguez 2003: 5–6). Later in the text, Rodriguez notes: "Discursive spaces are not autonomous; they are permeable and heteroglossic. They seep into one another, contaminating and enriching ideas and disciplines. There is a continual movement as individuals, texts and ideas migrate across spaces, informing and transforming knowledge production" (Rodriguez 2003: 35).

Whether participating in a march down O'Connell Street to protest the beating of a Nigerian youth, producing a magazine to counter racist representations of blacks, or conducting a food strike in an asylum accommodation center that belies Irish humanitarianism, whether forcing the adherence to fair housing laws, using a Hurricane Katrina tour to clarify the television representations of African Americans during the disaster or revitalizing a historical black neighborhood in New Orleans with the "American Dream" in mind, whether demanding better social housing in the Paris *banlieues*, calling for a new definition of "colonization" in *Le Petit Robert* or advocating for black rights in the context of French republican values, there is a conversation occurring, from various perspectives and in multifocal and multivocal ways. The African Diaspora communities examined in this book are amidst discursive spaces that are, as described by Rodriguez, "creat[ing] knowledge, chang[ing] history, and refigur[ing] language" (Rodriguez 2003: 5–6). The idea that discursive spaces are "not autonomous" but rather "permeable and heteroglossic" and that there is "migrat[ion] across spaces" certainly implicates the utility of the technological dimensions of modernity, but, also, quite significantly represents the potential for revising predominant understandings of modernity. Additionally, the "internal contradictions," as Rodriguez points out, may be characteristic of discursive spaces, yet—and I am extending this to my own consideration of discursive interrogations of modernity—such spaces also indicate the potential for transcending, reconciling, or challenging *inherent* contradictions. Through the conditions of individuals of the African Diaspora in this book, we have seen the construction of a discursive space in which a convergence of individuals, social and ethnic groups, non-governmental organizations, state-level actors and policy makers across three cities in three nations engage in a reflexive dialogue that draws on historical and contemporary circumstances to address key events and global concerns. Most significantly, the inhabitants of this discursive space are engaged in the monitoring of social retrogressions that flagrantly and egregiously prohibit the lived reality of modernity, as seen in the outrage (and, for many, shock and incredulity) in 2005 after the countrywide roundup and deportation of Nigerians from Dublin airport, upon the sight of stranded African Americans floating through communities devastated by Hurricane Katrina, and during the incendiary nights of black and Beur resistance in the uprisings in the Paris *banlieues*.

AN ONGOING CONVERSATION

I will briefly present one final example of the inner workings of the discursive space that is formed as a result of contemporary events, intertwined histories, notions of progress, and the African Diaspora in Dublin, New Orleans, and Paris. The January 12, 2010, earthquake in Haiti, an event occurring from natural disaster yet made more disastrous by a legacy of inequalities, further exemplifies the quest for *real* modernity that is precipitated and forged by African Diaspora communities. After the devastating earthquake, the black French organization, Le CRAN, continued its commitment to addressing concerns that reflect the connected histories of blacks in France, the French overseas departments, and former colonies. The history of Haiti's 90-million-gold-franc debt to France after independence in 1804, which was not paid in full until 1947 and is undoubtedly implicated in the poverty within Haiti, was addressed on February 17, 2010, when Nicolas Sarkozy became the first French head of state to visit Haiti in its entire national history (see Leparmentier 2010). Sarkozy pledged €326 million for aid through 2012, which included €40 million that had already been committed to pre-earthquake Haiti for aid, and Haitian debt cancellation of €56 million. Described by a *World Socialist* reporter as displaying "a mixture of cynicism and imperialist arrogance," Sarkozy stated to Prime Minister Réne Préval: "If I may say so, Mr. President, please do not rebuild the way it was before" (Lantier 2010). While Le CRAN "welcomed the gesture" of canceling Haiti's debt, as seen with the *Sarkomètre* in the previous chapter, the organization also desired to ensure that Sarkozy met his promise of better relations and support for former French colonies. Thus, the question of reparations for Haiti remained an important concern. Le CRAN described a "double debt" to Haiti and posted the following on the organization's website, excerpted here:

> After the proclamation by the General-in-Chief Jean-Jacques Dessalines of the Republic of Haiti on 1 January 1804, in 1825 it was imposed upon Haiti by a royal order to pay France 150 million gold francs to "compensate the old settlers"!
>
> The amount of this "freedom" debt was reduced to 90 million francs in 1838. This amount represents about six years of budget revenue for the state of Haiti.
>
> The CRAN has said that this shameful debt has significantly affected the budget of Haiti, which has had to resort to numerous and expensive loans from banks, including French ones, to honor this "ransom." Haiti has also been forced to levy heavy taxes on the Haitian people.
>
> **The debt paid for its independence has been one of the causes of economic and social backwardness in Haiti. It has limited the development of this country.**
>
> **The CRAN asks Nicolas Sarkozy to return the debt and repeal the treaty of February 18, 1838.** (CRAN 2010; bold in original French)

It is important to consider the gravity of Sarkozy being the first French head of state to visit since that successful battle for human rights known as the Haitian Revolution, a revolution inspired by the very republican values that were not to be applied to black individuals. The monetary contribution from France may reflect global expectations that wealthier nations would provide substantial assistance, but Sarkozy's presence particularly acknowledges the long, ideologically contradictory and problematic history between the two nations. This troublesome history is brought forth by the CRAN's reference to a purchase of "freedom" and the desire for reparations. The CRAN's comment explicitly engages the question of progress and freedom by linking Haiti's purchase of freedom to "economic and social backwardness" and a "limited . . . development." This suggests that the opposite circumstances, increased development and those tenets of modernity known as "economic and social progress," were flawed by the particularly paradoxical inability of France (in spite of the "Rights of Man") to accept the freedom of people of African descent as a given without simultaneously considering their value as human property.

Notably, even one year after the comments were posted at the CRAN website, there was only a lone comment about the organization's demands. On February 21, 2010, "Denis" queried: "Why always the return to the distant past!! It's not a question of the money! France and Germany can even get along, while the last world war isn't even as far away! Let's move forward!" (CRAN 2010). Denis's post, of course, assumes that the "distant past" is not connected to the present and that progress or "moving forward" could be achieved through an agreement to forget. Yet, it also presents a poignant example of how predominant notions of modernity are able to persist amidst stark social inequalities. While Sarkozy did not agree to reparations, his presentation of funds, debt cancellation, and historical visit reflect the inability to forget, particularly because African Diaspora communities trapped in an earthquake, black French in Paris, and a larger global community could not forget France's history and its obligations.

The remembering and recalling was particularly evidenced in the United States, home of the city of New Orleans in which numerous descendants of those early Haitians reside. In an effort to explain the extent of the root causes of the devastation in Haiti, the U.S. news media provided a continuous stream of history lessons—some informed and others problematically uninformed—to a very interested popular audience. On the uninformed side, U.S. evangelist Pat Robertson offered an egregiously retrogressive analysis of Haitian freedom as a result of swearing "a pact to the devil" [sic] and further stated, "They said, we will serve you if you'll get us free from the French. True story. And so, the devil said, okay it's a deal" (Media Matters 2010). However, the informative lessons considered slavery in the French colonies, the Haitian Revolution, and moved on to the Louisiana Purchase (see CNN 2010; CBS 2010; NPR 2010), which provided a smooth segue into further considerations of New Orleans and the inequalities exposed by Hurricane Katrina.

The earthquake in Haiti also placed former president George W. Bush in a position that left observers wondering if he was attempting to amend his ignominious legacy related to the slow response to Hurricane Katrina (see Kennedy 2010). Upon a request from President Barack Obama, Bush joined former president Bill Clinton to create the Clinton Bush Haiti Relief Fund (Baker 2010). When asked during an interview on the U.S. program *Meet the Press* about critics of Obama's response to the Haitian crisis, Bush stated, "I don't know what they're talking about. I've been briefed by the president about the response. And as I said in my opening comment, I appreciate the president's quick response to this disaster" (NBC 2010).

Meanwhile, in Ireland, a week after the earthquake, during statements about support for Haiti in the *Dáil Éireann* TD Billy Timmins queried about the possibility of accepting Haitian refugees in the nation and stated, "[W]e should consider taking refugees from Haiti. God knows, we have enough empty residences throughout the country that could house people" (*Dáil Éireann* 2010). While Timmins's assertion that Ireland has "enough empty residences" for Haitians may have been sincere, it notably belied the narrative of deluge-like influx that has accompanied anti-immigration—particularly anti-African immigration—rhetoric in the nation. His query also begged the question as to whether Ireland would open doors to more black migrants and, if so, would they better fit the representation of "black babies" than, say, middle-class Nigerian migrants. Irish Independent columnist Kevin Myers, discussing the "showbiz" or celebrity response to Haiti, responded to Timmins's comments: "Actually, a good idea, since the numbers sort of match. We have over 300,000 empty houses, and according to one of those splendid government analysts in Port-au-Prince, the capital has 609,000—not 600,000, or 610,000, but 609,000—homeless people. We can clearly house the lot, two per house (nuclear families not being one of Haiti's strong points). Moreover, our cultural diversity would be enormously enriched with the arrival of over half a million voodoo worshippers" (Myers 2010).

The racist representation of Haitians notwithstanding, the comments of Myers—whose oeuvre notably includes a 2008 column titled "Africa is giving nothing to anyone—apart from AIDS" (Myers 2008)—actually bring forth the political question as to whether any Irish politician, regardless of party affiliation, would consider accepting Haitian refugees amidst an abysmal economy and an ongoing overzealous attempt to remove potential Nigerian refugees from the nation. So, in spite of Myers's consideration of the Haitian family unit or the "voodoo worshippers"— more racist cheekiness in the context of Irish "cultural diversity" (see chapter 4)—the question does represent another instance of the rhetorical maintenance of Ireland's humanitarian reputation while simultaneously keeping black individuals at a distance (see White 2009a). Thus, in March 2010 the Department of Foreign Affairs announced that Ireland would offer €13 million to Haiti over a three-year period and include emergency funding and €1 million to assist with debt cancellation (Department of Foreign Affairs 2010). However, even as the second anniversary of the earthquake neared, the arrival of Haitian refugees was not yet imminent.

In this book, through the cases of Dublin, New Orleans, and Paris, we have seen that African Diaspora communities in the twenty-first century—in all of their diversity and in spite of prevalent ideologies of freedom and equality—still must contend with the race-based discrimination, misrepresentation of black identities, and anti-black social inequalities that were embedded in notions of modernity over two centuries ago. Whether a consideration of Nigerian migrants in the context of the Irish Diaspora during a debate in the *Dáil Éireann,* the development of policies and plans to imagine a post-Katrina New Orleans as a "New American city," or the launching of a national debate on French identity, in each site examined in this book African Diaspora communities have forced poignant and potent state-level discourse, policy, and reflections on the way in which societies would proceed or *progress* in the twenty-first century.

Modernity has contingencies. Therefore, it will not be realized until there is a significantly impactful recognition that, *inter alia:* (1) Nigerian migration to Ireland is not disconnected from earlier nineteenth-century British colonialism in Africa and Ireland and that addressing migration through spatial restrictions and deportations can only afford the Irish an opportunity to replicate the oppressions they experienced in previous centuries, (2) the fact of African Americans living and dying in the Lower Ninth Ward during Hurricane Katrina is not disconnected from the segregated housing and race-based power structure that disproportionately placed blacks in detrimental conditions in spite of their impact on the character and culture of the city, and (3) the racism and discrimination experienced by contemporary black France is not disconnected from earlier acts of French colonialism and the negative racialization of blackness in spite of the rhetorical myth of assimilation.

This book suggests that there is a conversation under way that involves the *progression* toward a truly modern future. However, in the meantime, individuals of the African Diaspora—and myriad other communities—will continue to endure the deficiencies of "retro-global" societies and the "modernity" these societies presumptuously embrace.

NOTES

1. Schäfer states that globalization involves "agents and factors that increase the *geographical range* of things" (Schäfer 2007; paragraph 14; emphasis in original).

1. DECOLONIZATION, RACISM, AND THE RETRO-GLOBAL SOCIETY

1. Hart argues that black individuals were not necessarily a novelty in Ireland, particularly Dublin (Hart 2002: 19). However, the estimated population of eighteenth-century Ireland ranged from approximately two million in the first half of the century to approximately four million by the end of the century (e.g., see Cormac Ó Gráda et al., "Eighteenth-century Irish population: New perspectives from old sources," *Journal of Economic History* 41.3 [September 1981]: 601–628 [624]). Thus, I would argue that even Hart's less conservative estimate of three thousand blacks throughout the eighteenth century represents a small black presence in the nation and makes it more likely that *most* individuals in eighteenth-century Ireland—particularly outside of Dublin—would have considered a sighting of a black person a very rare occurrence.

2. For more on Douglass's experiences in Ireland, see Patricia Ferreira, "'All But a Black Skin and Wooly Hair': Frederick Douglass's Witness of the Irish Famine," *American Studies International* 37 (June 1999), 69–83. Also see her compelling examination of the Dublin edition of *Narrative of the Life of Frederick Douglass* as representative of the ways in which Douglass's experiences in Ireland significantly contributed to his liberation and political voice, in Patricia J. Ferreira, "Frederick Douglass in Ireland: The Dublin Edition of His Narrative," *New Hibernia Review* 5.1 (*Earrach/ Spring* 2001), 53–67.

3. For more on Daniel O'Connell and the abolition movement, see Bruce Nelson, "'Come Out of Such a Land, You Irishmen': Daniel O'Connell, American Slavery, and the Making of the 'Irish Race'," *Éire-Ireland* 42.1 and 42.2 (*Earrach/Samhradh* /Spring/ Summer 2007), 58–81. Also see the archival website, *The Liberator Files,* maintained by the Boston African American National Historic Site. Among the online collection are *Liberator* articles, commentary, and speeches related to Daniel O'Connell

and his Irish American critics, http://www.theliberatorfiles.com/category/oconnell-daniel/.

4. For more on the impetus for Allen's expatriate status—his interracial marriage with Mary King Allen—and their subsequent life in Ireland and, eventually, England, see Sarah Elbert's edited volume of Allen's 1853 *The American Prejudice Against Color* and 1860 essay *A Short Personal Narrative,* in Sarah Elbert, *The American Prejudice Against Color* (Boston: Northeastern University Press, 2002).

5. Gregory Stephens, in his insightful consideration of "multiracial public spheres," describes Frederick Douglass as "a sex symbol and model of intellectual growth" to "women of all colors" (see Gregory Stephens, *On Racial Frontiers: The New Culture of Frederick Douglass, Ralph Ellison, and Bob Marley* [Cambridge: Cambridge University Press, 2000], 2).

6. The discourse on the construction and impact of the "Celtic Tiger" economy ranges from ebullient expressions of a "new Ireland" (e.g., see Foster 2008) to more sobering explications, particularly regarding the facilitation of U.S. foreign investment through low tax rates and other incentives rather than a corporate multinational commitment to Ireland and Irish workers. For this latter analysis, see Colin Coulter's introductory essay to Coulter and Steve Coleman's edited volume *The End of Irish History?* (Coulter and Coleman 2003). Regarding globalization, immigration, racism, and identity, also see Steve Loyal's essay, "Welcome to the Celtic Tiger: Racism, Immigration and the State" (Loyal 2003) and G. Honor Fagan's "Globalised Ireland, or, Contemporary Transformations of National Identity?" (Fagan 2003) in the Coulter and Coleman volume.

7. Patrick Hayden and Chamsy El-Ojeili, in the introduction to their edited volume *Globalization and Utopia: Critical Essays,* present an interesting discussion about the demise of utopian discourse among scholars and theorists by the late twentieth century, mostly due to its association with "fanciful, unrealistic dreaming" and rhetorical use in the bolstering of totalitarian regimes (Hayden and El-Ojeili 2009: 3). In the twenty-first century Hayden and El-Ojeili see "an implicit and sometimes explicit rejuvenation of utopianism" (emerging in the writings of Pierre Bourdieu, Russell Jacoby, Immanuel Wallerstein, and others) particularly resulting from the end of discourse on "happy globalization" (Hayden and El-Ojeili 2009: 8).

8. For a compelling examination and interrogation of the impact of globalization on world peace, particularly regarding violent conflicts outside of Western countries, see Perry, *Falling Off the Edge: Globalization, World Peace, and Other Lies.*

9. The debate regarding British colonialism and Ireland continues. For a multidisciplinary examination of the various remaining questions around nineteenth-century Ireland's status as a British colony, see the essays in McDonough, *Was Ireland a Colony?*

2. STATUS, NUMBERS, AND THE "RETRO" REVEALED

1. 1) Individuals with work permits. (Employer demonstrated that the worker is needed and an Irish national or other EU national was unavailable to fill the space.)

2) Individuals with work visas and work authorizations. (Applications made to the Irish Embassy in the country of origin to be eligible for available positions in areas where there were worker shortages; usually highly skilled labor, including medical fields, information technologies, construction engineering.)

3) Individuals with business permissions. (Individuals were required to invest at least IR£300,000.)

4) Individuals with student visas. (Individuals with valid passport and registration in a course of study.)

5) Individuals on tourist visas. (Application made through the Irish Embassy in country of residence, usually approved for one month. Some nations, such as the United States, do not require a visa; tourists receive an entry for three months and then may apply for an extension at the *Garda* National Immigration Bureau. Tourists from the following African nations do not require a tourist visa: Botswana, Lesotho, Malawi, Seychelles, South Africa, Swaziland, and up until 2010, Mauritius.)

6) Convention refugees. (Those granted refugee status under the 1951 Geneva Convention and 1954 UN Convention Regarding Stateless Persons.)

7) Program refugees. (UNHCR Refugee Resettlement Quota Program; Individuals invited by the Irish government at the request of the UNHCR due to a humanitarian crisis.) Ireland increased its quota from 40 to 200 individuals in 2005, which led to a slight increase in potential program refugees from African nations, e.g., 10 refugees from African nations in 2000 (6 from Rwanda, 3 Sudan, and 1 Liberia) and 84 African refugees, all from the Democratic Republic of the Congo via Tanzania, in 2009. Between 2000 and 2009 there were a total of 290 program refugees from African nations out of a total of 929 program refugees accepted by Ireland (Office of the Minister of State for Integration).

8) Asylum Seekers. (Persons applying for refugee status under the 1951 Geneva Convention.)

9) Naturalized Irish Citizen. (Before 2005, individuals could apply after at least five years of residence within a nine-year period; after 2005, as a result of the Irish Nationality and Citizenship Act 2004, one "must have had a period of one (1) year's continuous reckonable residence in the State immediately before the date of the application and, during the eight (8) years preceding that, have had a total reckonable residence (excluding the asylum-seeking and student visa periods) in the State amounting to four years" [INIS].)

10) Post-nuptial Citizen. (During the period examined in this section, one had to be married to an Irish citizen for at least three years to declare status. After the Irish Nationality and Citizenship Act 2004, it became required that "You have had immediately before the date of the

application a period of one year's continuous residence in the island of Ireland, and . . . have had, during the 4 years immediately preceding that period, a total residence in the island of Ireland amounting to 2 years" [INIS].)

11) Leave to Remain. (Granted by the Minister of Justice, Equality, and Law Reform for study, employment, business, or because one is a dependent of an Irish or EEA citizen; individuals who do not meet the convention and program refugee requirements, but are permitted to remain by the Minister of Justice, Equality, and Law Reform on humanitarian grounds.)

12) Leave to Remain, based on parentage of Irish Citizen. (Before the Irish Nationality and Citizenship Act 2004, parents of Irish citizens were permitted to remain in the country, as Irish citizenship was based on a *jus soli* policy. The Act stipulates, "A person born in the island of Ireland, since 1 January 2005, shall not be entitled to be an Irish citizen unless a parent of that person has, during the four years immediately preceding the person's birth, been resident in the island of Ireland for a period of not less than three years or period the aggregate of which is not less than three years" [Irish Nationality and Citizenship Act 2004 (INIS)]. While there are cases in which an individual has parented a child who is eligible for citizenship [e.g., an Irish parent] and a parent may receive leave to remain on these grounds, the circumstance does not automatically confer such a status or halt a deportation.)

13) Persons awaiting approval for leave to remain. (Included in this group are individuals with failed asylum applications, rejected residence permits, and revoked immigration and residency status; if approval is not granted, individuals will be deported.)

14) Complementary Protection. (Persons protected under the European Convention of Human Rights 1950, the International Covenant on Civil and Political Rights 1966, and the Convention Against Torture 1984; such subsidiary protections are often the last-chance option to challenge a deportation order.)

The list is compiled from data available in 2010 at the Department of Enterprise, Trade and Innovation (formerly Employment) (DETE), Irish Naturalisation and Immigration Service (INIS), Department of Justice, Equality, and Law Reform, Department of Foreign Affairs and Office of the Minister of State for Integration. Additionally, Tanya Ward's comprehensive report prepared in 2001 provides very useful data on the earlier immigration period (Ward 2001).

2. A 2001 Irish Center for Migration Studies (ICMS) report includes data on "Non-EU Countries with at least 300 Work Permit Holders in Ireland" in 2000. Of the 18 nations with "at least 300," South Africa was the only African nation (Mac Éinrí 2001). Immigration into Ireland: Trends, Policy Responses. Outlook Report. http://migration.ucc.ie/irelandfirstreport.htm. Accessed May 2, 2010.)

3. Upon conversion to the Euro, the penalty became €634.87 and/or one month in jail.

4. In 2001 the Department of Justice did not maintain data on the number of non-European Economic Area (EEA) students. The limited data available were mostly general tallies. Data now provided to the Central Statistics Office (CSO) by the Department of Education and Skills (DES) offers some retrospective information: in 2000 and 2001, there were 304 and 415, respectively, African students enrolled in third-level education. However, there is no specific breakdown of African nations of origin (DES 2000–2008). Further implicating the lack of comprehensive data on non-EEA students, in January 2010 the Department of Justice released origin data on non-EEA students from 2006–2008 compiled through data at the Garda National Immigration Bureau, which keep data on students in courses for longer than ninety days, and the Irish Naturalisation and Immigration Service (INIS) (established in 2005), which manages student visa requests. Sheila Power, the Director of the Irish Council for International Students (ICOS), stated, "These are very useful statistics and a much better indicator of the real picture of non-EEA students in Ireland compared to the data on general release. As part of its internationalisation strategy and as a matter of good public information policy, the Government, through INIS, should be encouraged to release visa and non-EEA student registration statistics on a regular basis" (ICOS 2010).

5. In May 2010 at Trinity College Dublin, the first conference was held for students of African descent throughout the nation in an effort to form the African Student Association of Ireland (ASAI) (see the ASAI website: http://asaireland.wordpress.com/).

6. The Traveller Community also petitioned for an ethnicity query on the census to support the group's quest for recognition as an "ethnic minority" by the state. They have received support for ethnic minority status from the Equality Authority, UN Human Rights Council, Amnesty International, and the now defunct NCCRI. See the Irish Traveller Movement (ITM) website: http://www.itmtrav.ie/; also see Fiona 2009 (accessed May 6, 2010); also see Gartland 2009.

7. For more extensive examinations of the evolution of ethnicity statistics in the Irish Census, see King-O'Riain 2007. Also see Cadogan 2008.

8. Also notable for the calculation of individuals racialized as "Black" in Ireland is that it cannot be determined from the data whether individuals who identified as "mixed background" are including a "Black background" in the "mix." In the ethnic or cultural group category, "other including mixed background," 2,231 individuals indicated an African nationality, which included 504 individuals noting South African, 130 noting Nigerian, and 1,597 "other African nationality." Also notable, in the "Total Irish" nationality category 12,934 individuals indicated an ethnic or cultural group as "Other including mixed background" (Irish Census 2006b). Since respondents could only choose one identification box, it is conceivable that some individuals who are racialized as black but assert a "mixed" ethnic or cultural identity are included in the "Other including mixed background" category.

9. The early use of "Africans and Afro-Caribbeans" reflects a lack of data on the profile of African Diaspora communities. While there were Caribbean nationals

in Ireland at the time, later data would reveal that the new black population predominantly consisted of recent migrants from continental Africa. The use of "Afro-Caribbean" suggests that, devoid of any prior research on the community in Ireland, a British ethnic minority model was used.

10. By February 2006, the Equality Authority announced that discrimination in housing on racial grounds was "widespread" throughout Ireland and that the office was investigating ten discriminatory landlord cases (see Walsh 2006).

11. A revised version of the text was posted on the RIA website in 2011, which notably does not include the harsher phrasing (e.g., "until you are deported") but still explains the same policy. See the RIA website http://www.ria.gov.ie/en/RIA/Pages/Reception_Dispersal_Accommodation for the 2011 version and, for the text originally posted on the RIA website prior to 2011, http://www.politics.ie/forum/current-affairs/37474-nigerian-woman-high-court-67.html; http://www.politics.ie/forum/current-affairs/7023-afghan-protestors-removed-st-patricks-cathedral-20.html; or http://www.africadublin.com/id7.html.

12. In January 2002 the Irish currency conversion to the Euro occurred. Some remarks, comments, and accounts in this volume predate the conversion, so Irish Pounds are used or mentioned. Upon conversion, the direct provision personal allowance became €19.10 per adult and €9.60 per child per week.

13. *The Irish Times* reported that Okenla "admitted serving as a special assistant and private secretary to Nigeria's chief security officer during the unpopular regime of former Nigerian president Sani Abacha," had "amassed significant wealth in [Nigeria]," and he had stated that his "role was to submit the names of the then president's opponents to Strike Force, a group of select soldiers with a record of brutality, who eliminated opponents by killing them" (*Irish Times* 2006).

14. Ireland began collecting biometric data (fingerprints) in March 2010 for visa applications. Exemplifying the nation's aggressive monitoring of Nigerian migration to the nation, the Irish Naturalization and Immigration Service (INIS), responding to the FAQ "Who needs to provide fingerprints?" states that "Collection of biometric data will commence in Nigeria . . . and is likely to be rolled out in other locations at a later date" (INIS 2010).

3. MEDIA REPRESENTATION AND BLACK PRESENCE

1. I have referred to this artist only by the pseudonym "Kunle" to maintain his anonymity when discussing sensitive issues.

2. The series also featured a story line with a Kurdish refugee played by Paul Tylak, an Irish actor and comedian of Irish and Sri Lankan descent.

3. "Fair City" is the only English-language soap opera produced in Ireland. It premiered in 1989 and, as of 2006, is also the nation's longest-running soap opera.

4. I received the opportunity to audition for the part while conducting fieldwork in the new Black Actors Workshop in Dublin. Initially, the character was supposed to be a British woman named Mahogany. I auditioned as British, but when I got the part and they realized I was American, the director thought it would be interesting

to have an American character. They mentioned a back story of an Irish father and an American upbringing, though it was never made explicit in the scripts. It is interesting that at that time the only black character that could be envisioned was British or American, rather than born or at least raised in Ireland. By the time the series went into production, Mahogany's name had changed from an ode to Diana Ross to an ode to a tennis player, "Venus" (it is possible that the skin tone appellation was deemed too insensitive, though I was not privy to that conversation). Several people in Dublin's African Diaspora community, upon seeing me on the cover of a popular television magazine, expressed pride at, as one person put it, "seeing a black woman on the cover." Although I do not think that being the "first" on an evening soap opera in the role of what an Irish edition of *The Mirror* headlined "'Venus Mantrap': Sex mad beauty in Fair City love triangle" (Friel 2001) necessarily helped the cause of African Diaspora communities in Ireland, it did afford me several opportunities to conduct interviews in which I spoke out about racism in the nation. Also, as a researcher, it provided a very useful opportunity to observe significant spaces of Irish cultural production from the inside.

5. Jackie Healy-Rae is a member of the *Dáil Éireann* (Irish Parliament) representing South Kerry. He was well known for his anti-asylum-seeker rhetoric. In 2000, when asylum seekers were first being dispersed amidst his constituents in Killarney, he infamously stated, "I am firmly in favor of helping refugees who are genuine. And I am not racist. But I am warning you in six months' time you will be writing about civil rumpus in this country" (Lucey 2000a).

6. In 2010 the digital radio station, RTÉ Pulse, launched The Speakerboxx, a two-hour show billed as "Ireland's first nationwide Hip Hop and R'n'B show" (http://www.rte.ie/digitalradio/pulse). The hosts are DJ Mo-K (Mo Keating), a white Irish DJ from Dublin, and DJ Tando (Tando Mat), a black Zimbabwean DJ who notes on his Bebo page that he is from "Dublin, Ireland/Harare, Zim." Reflecting an Ireland ten years removed from the wonder of the 2001 *Slate* article, DJ Tando's promo on his Facebook page mentions that he is "expanding his fan base considerably with his independently promoted South African nights attracting a huge African following playing the best in afro house" (DJ Tando 2010).

7. In September 2000 Dublin Bus driver Gerry O'Grady became the first person to be convicted under the Incitement to Hatred Act 1989. RTÉ reported that O'Grady was accused of telling a Gambian passenger, Matthew John, "that he could not eat on [the bus], that we do not eat on buses in this country and to go back to where he came from" and using "the term 'nig-nog'" (RTÉ 2000). The ruling was overturned in April 2001 because it was determined that, while offensive, O'Grady's comments did not meet the criteria of the Act (see RTÉ 2001).

4. RACISM, IMMIGRANT STATUS, AND BLACK LIFE

1. For more on this Anglo-Irish architectural tension, see Kevin Corrigan Kearns's 1983 study on the preservation of Georgian Dublin, which considers the inherent con-

flicts in the Irish quest to preserve the architectural remnants of British subjectivity and Protestant rule (Kearns 1983).

2. As late as 2009, there was still significant resistance to this plan, with groups such as the Save Moore Street Committee and the Georgian Society of Ireland expressing concern about the impact of the development plans on historical buildings—including sections of the National Monument Buildings on Moore Street that were integral to the 1916 Easter Rising—and how it would "detract from [O'Connell Street's] 18th Century urban form" (O. Kelly 2009). Meanwhile, proponents, such as the Moore Street Traders Committee, "welcome[d] the proposed development" because of the "prolonged dereliction" of the area (O. Kelly 2009).

3. It was very common at anti-racism and multicultural-focused meetings in Ireland to have speakers from the immigrant communities discuss their circumstances. While it put a "face" on the discussion, it also objectified the individuals and elicited a degree of sympathy (and spectacle) external to the politics at hand.

4. Nigerian immigrants to Ireland during the time were mostly Yoruba and Igbo with a few Hausa/Fulani (though Hausa/Fulani, due to a predominantly elite status in Nigeria, had little reason to emigrate at the time). Only wealthier Itsekiris, like Sadya, would have the money to leave.

5. For a detailed examination of the conflicts in the oil-rich yet impoverished Niger Delta during the period in which Sadya left the region for Ireland, see Ukeje 2001.

6. Asylum applications deemed "manifestly unfounded" are, as defined by the UNHCR, "not related to the criteria for the granting of refugee status laid down in the 1951 United Nations Convention relating to the Status of Refugees nor to any other criteria justifying the granting of asylum." These criteria also apply to fraudulent applications (United Nations High Commissioner for Refugees 1983). The 1951 Convention and 1967 Protocol stipulate that "a refugee is someone who has left his or her country of origin owing to a well-founded fear of being persecuted for reasons of race, religion, nationality, membership of a particular social group or political opinion and is unable or owing to such fear is unwilling to avail himself or herself of the protection of that country, or to return there, for fear of persecution" (UNHCR 2010).

7. These considerations were a prelude to a Readmission Agreement with the Nigerian government signed by Minister for Justice John O'Donoghue in August 2001. The Readmission Agreement, never ratified by Nigeria but enforced all the same, provides accelerated procedures or "fast tracking" (including weekly check-ins with the *gardai*) for Nigerian asylum applicants and expedites deportations of Nigerians (see White 2009b). Substantial violent conflict has persisted among the Itsekiri, Ijaw, and Urhobo, as well as other ethnic groups in the region. In 2009 an Amnesty International report stated: "The oil industry in the Niger Delta of Nigeria has brought impoverishment, conflict, human rights abuses and despair to the majority of the people in the oil-producing areas" (Amnesty International 2009).

8. Kwanga preparation is a laborious process, which involves a minimum of three days of soaking the cassava, the pounding of cassava into paste, folding the paste into banana leaves, and between four and eight hours of steaming.

9. June had been concealing the abuse even when she moved through the African Diaspora and anti-racism communities with a veneer of positivity. While my own fieldwork did not reveal rampant domestic abuse among African Diaspora communities in Ireland, June's experience highlighted the way in which the intersection of domestic violence and a precarious status in the state intensified the victimization and powerlessness already experienced by many migrant women that I interviewed. For an informative examination of the impact of domestic violence for migrants in Ireland as well as the available resources and approaches for challenging abuse, see Paula Fagan 2008.

10. This was a common sentiment expressed to me by members of the African Diaspora in Ireland, indicating the reflexive relationship among African and African Diaspora communities in the Irish, American, and continental African contexts.

11. Max was not merely being evasive. Some immigrants had been living in Dublin awaiting word on asylum for nearly a year, so intimate relationships developed. His response echoed the complicated negotiations some immigrants were making to balance the desire for a partner and the practical need of gaining residence status, thus preventing a return to perilous conditions in the homeland.

12. There was a backlog of approximately 12,000 asylum applications around the time of Max's application interview in June 2000, which led Minister for Justice O'Donoghue to increase the processing staff from 170 to 540 employees in July 2000 (Brady 2000a). By comparison, there were a total of four (4) asylum staff members in 1997 (Brady 2000a).

13. The communitywide experience of racism does not erase the fact that black women were perceived as less threatening than black men, particularly in the context of dating. For example, during numerous interviews—in spite of the growing prevalence of interethnic/racial relationships during the period—African men spoke of being challenged by white Irish men when attempting to talk to a white Irish woman at a pub or club. However, I also observed that white Irish men would feel free to speak to African women and, due to racial power dynamics in the nation (i.e., asylum seekers were fearful of harming their application status), could do so without retaliation from African men. The lack of a challenge from African men did not necessarily indicate consent or acceptance, but more often reflected a power differential.

5. A COMMUNITY IN THE MAKING

1. By 2009 there would be a contentious debate about who would be the king or "eze" of Igbo in Ireland. Though there were two designated choices—which was the reason for debate—Timothy was not one of them. See Reilly 2009.

2. Edward was eligible to apply for a Residence Card on the grounds that his spouse, Nora, is an employed EU citizen.

3. It is not unusual to see American or European pop cultural casual clothing worn at dressier or fashionable events, primarily because (1) immigrants have brought limited clothing to Dublin and (2) in the homeland, as well as in Ireland, there is a certain cultural cache in wearing American clothing, particularly with logos or no-

ticeably foreign designs. (This is seen in the Irish community, as well. New York Yankees caps were popular during my tenure in the nation.)

4. In a prior interview, Luambo revealed to me that his father held a prominent position in Laurent Kabila's government. Luambo's father, fearing for the safety of his family, thought it would be best if they left the DRC. Laurent Kabila was assassinated in January 2001.

5. At the time of this study, there were no available statistics regarding the percentage of immigrant women having newborns versus permanent residents and Irish citizens. It was common to observe African women who were pregnant or had infants and there was anecdotal evidence, as well as information I gained through interviews, to suggest that some women (and men, for that matter) were choosing pregnancy/parenthood as a means of staying in Ireland because the parents of children born in Ireland (considered citizens by birth) received "leave to remain." However, reflecting racist assumptions more than fact, it was never evidenced that African women were overwhelmingly choosing pregnancy to secure their status in the nation (see Lentin 2003). This was prior to the 2004 referendum that ended *jus soli* citizenship rights in the nation. Those nearly mythical individuals who did choose pregnancy for immigration purposes were accused of engaging in a corrupt and manipulative act, but more they highlighted the desperate need of migrants to remain in the state and an immigration system that was increasingly difficult to penetrate if one was racialized as black.

6. Nigerians often said they preferred the Guinness in Nigeria because it is stronger than what they get in Ireland. There is a large Guinness campaign in Nigeria and it is a well-known product. I asked Guinness workers in Ireland if there was taste customization of Guinness in Nigeria and was told there is not. Even if it does not have a higher alcohol content, it appears that nostalgia and the connection to the homeland is what makes it such a popular drink among the Nigerian community of Dublin that they import a traditional Irish tap beer in a 500-ml bottle from Nigeria. The taste and packaging serve as a reminder of home.

7. An identification card was sufficient and his passport was not necessary for his return. This was before September 11, 2001.

8. Clifford was referring to the 1966 coup in which Igbo in the north were massacred by the primarily Hausa elite, the subsequent civil war, and creation of the Igbo nation of Biafra which existed throughout the conflict from 1967 to 1970. Yoruba, among other ethnic groups, were enlisted to fight on the Nigerian side against Biafra. For an interesting cultural theory analysis of the ethnic and geopolitical conflict, see Nancy Spalding 2000.

9. In Dublin during the course of any day, it was common for individuals of African descent to experience some form of ethnicity-based or "race"-related conflict; sometimes subtle, other times more overt. The majority of immigrants I interviewed expressed the sentiment that in Ireland one never knew when the next epithet or potentially violent moment would occur, but the possibility was always in mind. All of the African immigrants I interviewed had experienced some type of ethnicity-based/racial bias or prejudice during their time in Ireland. In Roland's taxi incident, he had

the rare opportunity to exercise power in his response to a racist incident, which was not the case for many immigrants.

10. Marcus's comment reflected his belief that there were more opportunities for financial success in "Celtic Tiger" Ireland than when he had first arrived in the 1980s but, due to his current lack of resources or depleted resources, he was no longer in a position to take advantage of the opportunities now before him.

11. Age may have been a concern, as Roland and Marcus were on the older end of the immigrant population (both were in their early forties). Yet, Roland tended to interact and socialize in younger settings (and with younger immigrants), while Marcus was more fearful of the possible repercussions of being among large groups of other Africans (because it would draw attention), young white Irish, and white Irish groups he did not know.

12. See Ni Cheallaigh 2001.

13. The GAA, which was formed in the late nineteenth century during British rule, shortly before the development of the Irish language movement, was at the root of the Irish Renaissance and is at the core of what is considered contemporary Irish identity, with its Catholic roots, national interests, and promotion of traditional Irish sports. An Irishness that is implicitly "white" has been a key component of this identity and, though there have been players of African and Irish parentage in the amateur and professional ranks of the GAA, anti-black (and anti-Protestant) racism has been prevalent at GAA events. In recent years, racism in the GAA has been addressed by groups like SARI (Sport Against Racism in Ireland) and the GAA's strategic plan on integration (see F. Kelly 2008; GAA 2009).

14. Sections of Kunle's interview and related accounts included here, as well as an examination of his website development, were presented in my paper "No Strings Attached: IT and the African Diaspora in Ireland" at the conference *AfroGeeks: From Technophobia to Technophilia,* sponsored by the Center for Black Studies at the University of California at Santa Barbara in May 2004.

15. For more on this growing—not to mention intriguing—area of consideration regarding supernatural harm and witchcraft in relation to human rights and asylum policies, see Jill Schnoebelen.2009.

6. DUBLIN

1. In numerous cases, Olukunle Elukanlo's name is misspelled in the public records and media reports either due to mispronunciation, misinformation, or typographical error. In lieu of the use of "[*sic*]," I have kept the misspellings in the excerpts presented in this volume.

2. The date of Olukunle Elukanlo's deportation was the night of Monday, March 14, 2005. It is often stated as Tuesday March 15, 2005, perhaps because it occurred near midnight on the fourteenth. I have left all incorrect dates and days as originally stated in the excerpts included here.

3. The minister is referring to the Office of the Refugee Applications Commissioner (ORAC), where asylum seekers lodge their first application for refugee status, and the Refugee Appeals Tribunal (RAT), the government office that handles appeals

of applications that are not recommended by the ORAC. An unsuccessful appeal results in deportation or individuals can seek review at the high court level in an effort to receive leave to remain on humanitarian grounds.

4. The part of Immigration Act 1999, section 3, which pertains to deportation orders, that applies to Elukanlo's case is defined in subsection 2(f) as: "a person whose application for asylum has been refused by the Minister" (Immigration Act 1999).

5. See, for example, http://www.wicklowhills.blogspot.com; http://www.sluggerotoole.com; http://saoirse32.blogsome.com/; http://www.briangreene.com.

6. The statement is presented here as it was written for the Lagos press conference and subsequently posted online. Any typographical and grammatical errors in Elukanlo's text remain here as in the original.

7. NEW ORLEANS

1. James Perry would later run unsuccessful campaigns for mayor of New Orleans in February 2010 and for a seat in the state House of Representatives in May 2010.

2. The Make It Right project was founded in 2007 by Brad Pitt. The mission is "to build 150 affordable, green storm resistant homes for families living in the Lower Ninth Ward when the storm hit" (see http://www.makeitrightnola.org/).

8. PARIS

1. For more on the struggle and activism around the April and August 2005 fires and regarding inadequate housing for "*sans papiers*" and French citizens, see the websites of the Paris-based organizations *Droit au Logement* (DAL) (http://www.droitaulogement.org/ [accessed March 15, 2010]) and *Droits Devant* (http://www.droitsdevant.org/ [accessed March 15, 2010]). Both organizations have done extensive work in the fight for housing rights in France and have successfully mobilized communities around the issues of migration, housing, and citizenship.

2. For brief commentary on the fund-raiser (a luncheon, "Surviving Katrina—the Aftermath," that occurred on October 5, 2006), see the now inactive Parler Paris website ("Paris from Dusk to Dawn," October 9, 2006). The site can be accessed via Google cache at http://www.parlerparis.com/issues/pparis9-10-06.html (snapshot taken June 26, 2011). Dillard, a historically black university, had not reopened all of its buildings—some of which featured the sign "Please pardon us while we rebuild our campus"—when I visited the campus in the spring of 2008. However, students were on campus again after attending classes at a local Hilton Hotel, the library had recently reopened after a post-flood renovation, and students were in the theater department preparing for a spring production of the musical *Raisin*.

3. For an extensive range of subjects and texts to which Etzioni applies a communitarian analysis, see his website, http://www.amitaietzioni.org.

4. An April 2007 letter from presidential candidate Sarkozy to the *Réseau de Citoyen des Associations Franco-Berbères* (CFB) addresses specific cultural and linguistic concerns of the Berbers and includes the "Discrimination . . . is unacceptable"

paragraph but excludes "based on skin color" (see http://www.cbf.fr/ [accessed November 10, 2009]).

5. Rachida Dati studied at *École nationale de la magistrature* (ENM). She had never held public office before her appointment as Minister for Justice. Before this appointment, her related experience included working as an advisor to then Interior Minister Sarkozy on a delinquency bill and later serving as his spokesperson during his 2007 campaign. Rama Yade is a graduate of *Institut d'études politiques* (IEP) of Paris. Her prior experience included working as an administrator in the Senate, director of communications at the parliamentary television station, *Public Sénat,* and, in public office, serving as National Secretary of Francophonie in 2006 before her 2007 appointment as Secretary of State for Human Rights. Notably, Yade was thirty years old when appointed in 2007 which, along with the racial variable, led to accusations of inexperience (European Parliament http://www.europarl.europa.eu/; Portail du gouvernement http://www.gouvernement.fr/ [accessed April 12, 2010]).

6. Louis-Georges Tin is also active in the fight for LGBT rights and against homophobia. See his edited volume *The Dictionary of Homophobia: A Global History of Gay & Lesbian Experience* (Vancouver, B.C.: Arsenal Pulp Press, 2008).

7. Notably, the SOS Racisme survey also included some data on the response of individuals aged fifteen to seventeen in its results, but because of the sample size determined the pool was too small for it to provide any conclusive analysis. The SOS Racisme survey showed that of individuals ages fifteen to seventeen, 44% noted "effective," 44% "ineffective," and 12% did not respond. On the other end of the age range, of individuals seventy-five and over, 46% noted "effective," 42% "ineffective," and 12% did not respond (CSA 2009a).

8. I have included the names given and date posted on the public website. The site requests that one enters "*votre nom/pseudo*" (your name/nickname). So, for the most part, names are pseudonyms, e-mail names, blog aliases, first names only, and full names that are not substantiated or verified on the site and, in some cases, clearly meant to reflect the respondent's content or offer a cheeky nod to a historical figure (e.g., Albert Camus). Surprisingly, three months after its launch, there were only ten posts from "anonyme."

9. I reviewed a sample of seventy-eight response pages as a means of determining key themes that would suggest the experiences reflected in the over forty thousand respondents to the national identity debate online query. My examination was not for the purpose of compiling quantitative data, but to obtain a range of qualitative data in order to further contextualize the experiences and significance of black France amidst a French national identity debate. The responses included here are translations from French into English. Posts were frequently written in a conversational and informal style. In some cases, I have altered the punctuation for clarity.

10. See James Baldwin, *Notes of a Native Son* (Boston: Beacon Press, 1955); also see James Baldwin, *Nobody Knows My Name* (New York: Vintage Books, 1993).

11. "RF" appears on camera but does not give her name. Her desire to remain anonymous is understandable considering that she has been the subject of chat on

white supremacist websites, such as Stormfront. See the Stormfront thread titled "Migrant warns fellow Africans away from 'misery' Europe," http://www.stormfront.org/forum.

12. Undoubtedly, the twentieth-century Négritude movement—à la Aimé Césaire, Léopold Senghor, and Léon Damas—rearticulated the meaning of blackness. However, the movement could not necessarily shift the French racist engagement with black representation. Thus, "RF" must contend with 1950s-era humor in twenty-first-century France and black France must rewrite the narrative of black identity that goes beyond Fanon's "Look, a Negro!" moment. The 2007 short mockumentary *La Solution* offers a satirical take on the critical concerns of black France about contemporary representations of black identity. The film notably begins with a quote from Enlightenment thinker Charles de Secondat, Baron de Montesquieu, who in support of the French institution of slavery, notoriously noted: "*On ne peut s'imaginer que Dieu, qui est un être sage, ait mis une âme bonne dans un corps tou noir*" (I can't believe that God, who is wise, has put a good soul in a black body"). *La Solution* was produced by Alsott Prod and written by Timour G and Bilham; available at http://www.youtube.com/.

REFERENCES

Abedin, Mahan. 2011. "Tunisia: Islamist leader returns from exile—an interview with Rashid Al-Ghannoushi." *Le Monde Diplomatique.* January 31. http://mondediplo .com/ (accessed March 10, 2011).

Adas, Michael. 1990. *Machines as the Measure of Men: Science, Technology, and Ideologies of Western Dominance.* Ithaca, N.Y.: Cornell University Press.

Afoloyan, J. 2001. "Publisher's Letter." *Heritage,* March–April 2001: 7.

AFP. 2008. "Rama Yade crée la polémique en accusant la gauche de racisme." *Agence France-Presse.* February 20. http://www.afp.com/ (accessed November 20, 2009).

Albrow, Martin. 1997. *The Global Age: State and Society beyond Modernity.* Stanford, Calif.: Stanford University Press.

Aldrich, Robert. 2006. "Colonial past, post-colonial present: History wars French style." *History Australia* 3.1: 14.1–14.10.

Amnesty International. 2009. "Oil industry has brought poverty and pollution to Niger Delta." *Amnesty International.* June 30. http://www.amnesty.org/ (accessed April 4, 2010).

Anderson, Nicola. 2001. "Gardai probe into 'White Forever' website." *Irish Independent.* August 25. http://www.independent.ie/ (accessed March 11, 2010).

Andre, James. 2010. "National identity: Who is really French?" France 24. Hosted by Genie Godula. January 22. http://www.france24.com/ (accessed February 5, 2010).

Anny-Nzekwue, Peter. 2008. "Africa, Stereotypes and Redemptive Power of Bisi Adigun and Roddy Doyle's *The Playboy of the Western World.*" *Dublin Quarterly.* January and February. http://www.dublinquarterly.com (accessed April 25, 2010).

———. 2009. "Bloody Battle of Mulduhhart." *Xclusive.* http://www.xclusive.ie/ (accessed April 2, 2010).

Appadurai, Arjun. 1997. *Modernity at Large: Cultural Dimensions of Globalization.* Minneapolis: University of Minnesota Press.

Associated Press (AP). 2006. "Bush invokes civil rights in NAACP speech." July 20. http://www.msnbc.msn.com (accessed August 30, 2007).

Baker, Peter. 2010. "He Doesn't Miss Limelight, but Bush Is Back in It." *New York Times.* January 17. http://www.nytimes.com/ (accessed January 20, 2010).

Balzano, Wanda. 1996. "Irishness—Feminist and Post-colonial." In Iain Chambers and Lidia Curti, eds., *The Post-colonial Question: Common Skies, Divided Horizons.* 92–98. London: Routledge.

Barber, Benjamin. 1995. *Jihad vs. McWorld: How Globalism and Tribalism are Reshaping the World.* New York: Crown.

Baudrillard, Jean. 1994. *The Illusion of the End.* Oxford: Polity Press.

BBC. 2002a."Asylum seekers given 'smart' ID cards." *BBC News.* January 31. http://news.bbc.co.uk/ (accessed February 10, 2010).

———. 2002b. "Move towards compulsory ID cards." *BBC News.* February 5. http://news.bbc.co.uk/ (accessed February 10, 2010).

———. 2007. "First French racism poll released." January 31. http://www.bbc.co.uk/ (accessed August 15, 2007).

———. 2010. "France unveils national identity plans." *BBC News.* February 9. http://news.bbc.co.uk/ (accessed February 12, 2010).

Beardsley, Eleanor. 2009. "Minister Sparks Maternity Leave Debate in France." NPR. January 19. http://www.npr.org/ (accessed January 27, 2009).

Beck, Ulrich. 1992. *Risk Society: Towards a New Modernity.* Thousand Oaks, Calif.: Sage.

Beck, Ulrich, Anthony Giddens, and Scott Lash. 1994. *Reflexive Modernity.* Cambridge: Polity Press.

Beck, Ulrich, Wolfgang Bonss, and Christoph Lau. 2003. "The Theory of Reflexive Modernization: Problematic, Hypothesis and Research Programme." *Theory, Culture & Society* 20.2: 1–33.

Beddoe, John. 1885. *The Races of Britain: A Contribution to the Anthropology of Western Europe.* Bristol: J. W. Arrowsmith.

Bennhold, Katrin. 2006. "Black anchor fills top spot on French TV—Europe—International Herald Tribune." *New York Times.* August 2. http://www.nytimes.com/ (accessed July 27, 2007).

Bensel, Richard Franklin. 2000. *The Political Economy of American Industrialization, 1877–1900.* Cambridge: Cambridge University Press.

Berlin, Isaiah. 2002. *Liberty: Incorporating Four Essays on Liberty.* Henry Hardy, ed. New York: Oxford University Press.

Bernstein, Iver. 1990. *The New York City Draft Riots.* New York: Oxford University Press.

Bidar, Abdennour. 2010. "La burqa, symptôme d'un malaise." January 23. *Le Monde.* http://www.lemonde.fr/opinions/ (accessed February 1, 2010).

Billig, Michael. 2001. "Humour and Hatred: The Racist Jokes of the Ku Klux Klan." *Discourse & Society* 12:3: 267–289.

Blitzer, Wolf. 2005. *The Situation Room with Wolf Blitzer.* CNN Transcripts. September 1. http://www.cnn.com/ (accessed August 25, 2007).

BNOB. 2006. "Action Plan for New Orleans: The New American City." January 11.

Report. Bring New Orleans Back Commission and Urban Planning Committee. http://www.bringneworleansback.org/ (accessed June 25, 2009).

Bohrer, Becky. 2008. "'Wire' star leads redevelopment of Gentilly." August 9. Associated Press (accessed June 30, 2009).

Brady, Tom. 2000a. "Staff trebled in bid to cut down refugee backlog." *Irish Independent.* July 6. http://www.independent.ie/ (accessed April 3, 2010).

———. 2000b. "Shortage of housing for asylum seekers has reached crisis levels." *Irish Independent.* November 25. http://www.independent.ie/ (accessed April 21, 2010).

———. 2000c. "New deal to curb asylum seekers' scam." May 11. *Irish Independent.* http://www.irishindependent.ie/ (accessed March 22, 2011).

———. 2000d. "Crackdown on crime gangs trafficking in bogus refugees." July 18. *Irish Independent.* http://www.irishindependent.ie/ (accessed March 22, 2011).

———. 2005. "Just this once: McDowell in climbdown on boy's return." *Irish Independent.* March 25. http://www.independent.ie/ (accessed September 6, 2007).

Brah, Avtar. 1996. *Cartographies of Diaspora.* London: Routledge.

Bray, Allison. 2001. "STATE's pounds 9M TO KICK OUT BOGUS REFUGEES; Minister to make deal with Nigeria." *Irish Mirror.* August 13. http://www.freelibrary.com/ (accessed March 22, 2011).

———. 2005. "Nigerian Olunkunle wins visa clearance to return." *Irish Independent.* March 28. http://www.independent.ie/ (accessed August 30, 2007).

Braziel, Jana Evans, and Anita Mannur, eds. 2003. *Theorizing Diaspora: A Reader.* Hoboken, N.J.: Wiley-Blackwell.

Breed, Allen G. 2005. "As last refugees escape, New Orleans turns to its thousands of dead." Associated Press. September 4. http://www.fostersonline/ (accessed July 10, 2007).

Breen, Claire. 2008. "The Policy of Direct Provision in Ireland: A Violation of Asylum Seekers' Right to an Adequate Standard of Housing." *International Journal of Refugee Law* 20.4: 611–636.

Bremner, Charles. 2002. "Left out in the Cold after Worst Defeat in Decades." *Sunday Times.* June 17. http://Sunday-times.co.uk (accessed June 19, 2002).

———. 2007. "Human rights minister brands Muammar Gaddafi's visit to France a 'kiss of death.'" *Times of London.* December 11. http://www.timesonline.co.uk/ (accessed January 10, 2009).

Brockliss, Laurence, and David Eastwood, eds. 1997. *A Union of Multiple Identities: The British Isles c. 1750–1850.* Manchester: Manchester University Press.

Brown, Jacqueline Nassy. 2005. *Dropping Anchor, Setting Sail: Geographies of Race in Black Liverpool.* Princeton, N.J.: Princeton University Press.

Browne, M. 2001. "Something Happened on the Way to the Forum." *Metro Éireann.* March 2001: 11.

Browne, Vincent. 2005. "Hard to understand McDowell's mindset." *Sunday Business Post.* March 27. http://www.thepost.ie/ (accessed September 1, 2007).

Butler, Kim D. 2001. "Defining diaspora, refining a discourse." *Diaspora: A Journal of Transnational Studies* 10.2: 189–219.

Cadogan, Marian. 2008. "Fixity and Whiteness in the Ethnicity Question of Irish Census 2006." *Translocations* 3.1: 50–68.

Capo, Bill. 2009. "Action Report: Actor's father, a WWII vet, finally receives medals." WWL. May 26. http://www.wwltv.com/actionreport/stories/ (accessed June 30, 2009).

Casey, Sinead, and Michael O'Connell. 2000. "Pain and Prejudice: Assessing the Experience of Racism in Ireland." In Malcolm MacLachlan and Michael O'Connell, eds., *Cultivating Pluralism: Psychological, Social and Cultural Perspectives on a Changing Ireland*. Dublin: Oak Tree Press.

CBS. 2010. "Haiti's History: Revolution, Subjugation." *CBS Sunday Morning*. January 17. http://www.cbs.com/ (accessed January 20, 2010).

CBS/AP. 2005a. "France Riots Spill into 8th Day." *CBS News* and *Associated Press*. November 3. http://www.cbsnews.com/ (accessed August 29, 2011).

———. 2005b. "Arsons Hit Troubled Paris Suburbs." *CBS News* and *Associated Press*. November 4. http://www.cbsnews.com/ (accessed August 29, 2011).

Ceaux, Pascal. 2005. "Un incendie dans un immeuble parisien a fait 17 morts." *Le Monde*. August 27. http://www.lemonde.fr/ (accessed January 20, 2010).

Central Statistics Office. 1994. *Annual Population and Migration Estimates, 1987–1994*. Dublin: Central Statistics Office.

———. 1997a. *Annual Population and Migration Estimates, 1997*. Dublin: Central Statistics Office.

———. 1997b. *Census 1996 Principal Demographic Results*. Dublin: Stationery Office.

Césaire, Aimé. 2001. *Discourse on Colonialism*. New York: Monthly Review Press.

Cesarani, David. 1996. "The Changing Character of Citizenship and Nationality in Britain." In David Cesarani and Mary Fulbrook, eds., *Citizenship, Nationality and Migration in Europe*. 57–73. New York: Routledge.

Chrisafis, Angelique. 2009a. "French justice chief Dati 'plans' to quit." January 23. http://www.guardian.co.uk/ (accessed February 10, 2010).

———. 2009b. "Frédéric Mitterrand adds colour to Nicolas Sarkozy rainbow cabinet." *Guardian*. June 23. http://www.guardian.co.uk/ (accessed January 12, 2010).

Clarke, Kamari Maxine, and Deborah A. Thomas, eds. 2006. *Globalization and Race: Transformations in the Cultural Production of Blackness*. Durham, N.C.: Duke University Press.

Clifford, Michael. 2001. "Praising the Lord in Stonybatter." *Sunday Tribune*. February 11, p. 11.

Clyne, Meghan. 2005. "President Bush Is 'Our Bull Connor,' Harlem's Rep. Charles Rangel Claims." September 23. *New York Sun*. http://www.nysun.com/article/20495 (accessed August 22, 2011).

CNN. 2005. *Anderson Cooper 360 Degrees*. CNN Transcripts. September 2. http://www.cnn.com (accessed July 30, 2007).

———. 2010. "Earthquake in Haiti." *The Situation Room*. January 12. CNN. http://www.cnn.com/ (accessed January 20, 2010).

Cohen, Robin. 1997. *Global Diasporas: An Introduction*. London: University College London Press.

Colaiaco, James A. 2007. *Frederick Douglass and the Fourth of July*. New York: Palgrave Macmillan.

Colten, Craig E. 2005. *An Unnatural Metropolis: Wresting New Orleans from Nature*. Baton Rouge: Louisiana State University Press.

Conley, Dalton. 1999. *Being Black, Living in the Red: Race, Wealth, and Social Policy in America*. Berkeley: University of California Press.

Cook, Adrian. 1974. *The Armies of the Streets*. Lexington: University Press of Kentucky.

Cooper, Frederick, and Ann L. Stoler, eds. 1997. *Tensions of Empire: Colonial Cultures in a Bourgeois World*. Berkeley: University of California Press.

Coser, Rose L. 1991. *In Defense of Modernity: Role Complexity and Individual Autonomy*. Palo Alto, Calif.: Stanford University Press.

Coulter, Colin, and Steve Coleman, eds. 2003. *The End of Irish History? Critical Approaches to the Celtic Tiger*. Manchester: Manchester University Press.

CRAN. 2007a. "Le 1er baromètre des populations noires de France." Le CRAN website. June 22. http://lecran.org/ (accessed August 26, 2011).

———. 2007b. "Candidats Noirs et Legislatives : Les statistiques de la diversité." Le CRAN website. June 4. http://www.lecran.org/ (accessed August 30, 2007).

———. 2009a. "FAQ sur les statiques de la diversité." Le CRAN website. June 21. http://lecran.org/ (accessed January 23, 2010).

———. 2009b. "Le Sarkomètre de la parité et de la diversité." Le CRAN website. November 5. http://lecran.org/ (accessed January 23, 2010).

———. 2010. "Le CRAN demande à Nicolas Sarkozy de rembourser la double dette de la France envers Haïti." Le CRAN website. February 18. http://lecran.org/ (accessed February 20, 2010).

Crowley, Helen. 2000. "Women and the Domestic Sphere." In Stuart Hall et al., *Modernity: An Introduction to Modern Societies*. 343–360. Oxford: Blackwell.

Crumley, Bruce. 2002. "Why France Lurched to the Right." *Time*. April 22. http://www.time.com (accessed July 2, 2002).

———. 2008. "Booing the Marseillaise: A French Soccer Scandal." *Time*. October 15. http://www.time.com/ (accessed December 22, 2009).

CSA. 2009a. "L'efficacité des statistiques ethniques dans la lutte contre le racisme, l'antisemitisme et les discriminations." Survey Commissioned by SOS Racisme. March 5. http://www.csa-fr.com/ (accessed January 20, 2010).

———. 2009b. "Les Français, Les Minorités Visibles et Les Discriminations." Survey Commissioned by Le CRAN. April 28. http://www.csa-fr.com/ (accessed January 20, 2010).

Cue, Eduardo. 2008. "The Storm around France's First Muslim Cabinet Minister Rachida Dati." *US News and World Report*. December 24. http://www.usnews.com/news/ (accessed November 20, 2009).

Cullen, Paul. 1997. "Influx of Asylum-Seekers Causes Concern." *Irish Times*. February 26. http://www.ireland.com (accessed October 21, 2000).

Curtis, Lewis P. 1968. *Anglo-Saxons and Celts: A Study of Anti-Irish Prejudice in Victorian England*. New York: New York University Press.

———. 1996. *Apes and Angels: The Irishman in Victorian Caricature.* Washington, D.C.: Smithsonian Institution Press.

Cusack, Adrian. 2006. "Gone but certainly not forgotten." *Metro Éireann.* August 21. http://www.metroeirrean.ie/ (accessed July 9, 2008).

Dáil Éireann. 2005a. Adjournment Debate. "Deportation orders," volume 599, March 22. http://historical-debates.oireachtas.ie/ (accessed July 24, 2007).

———. 2005b. "International agreements," volume 608, October 20. http://historical-debates.oireachtas.ie/ (accessed July 24, 2007).

———. 2010. "Haiti Earthquake Statements." January 21. http://debates.oireachtas.ie/ (accessed March 30, 2010).

Dao, James. 2006. "In New Orleans, Smaller May Mean Whiter." *New York Times.* January 22. http://www.nytimes.com/ (accessed June 26, 2009).

Davey, Monica. 2011. "Democrats Missing, Wisconsin Vote on Cuts Is Delayed." *New York Times.* February 17. http://www.nytimes.com/ (accessed March 11, 2011).

Dawdy, Shannon Lee. 2008. *Building the Devil's Empire: French Colonial New Orleans.* Chicago: University of Chicago Press.

Dear Daughter. 1996. Directed by Louis Lentin. Dublin: Crescendo Concepts.

DeFaoite, Dara. 2007. "Town elects first black mayor." *Irish Independent.* June 29. http://www.independent.ie/ (accessed April 2, 2009).

Department of Enterprise, Trade and Employment (DETE). 1994. *Work Permit Statistics.* Dublin: Department of Enterprise, Trade and Employment.

———. 1995. *Work Permit Statistics.* Dublin: Department of Enterprise, Trade and Employment.

———. 1996. *Work Permit Statistics.* Dublin: Department of Enterprise, Trade and Employment.

Department of Foreign Affairs. 2010. "Minister of State for Overseas Development Peter Power pledges €13 million to Haiti's recovery." Press Release. Department of Foreign Affairs (Ireland). March 30. http://www.foreignaffairs.gov.ie/ (accessed May 10, 2010).

Department of Jobs, Enterprise and Innovation. 2011. Guides to Employment Permits Schemes. http://www.djei.ie/labour/workpermits/guidelines.htm (accessed August 21, 2011).

Department of Justice, Equality and Law Reform. 2001. "O'Donoghue Signs Readmission Agreement with Nigerian Government in Abuja." Departmental Press Release. August 30, 2001. http://www.justice.ie (accessed April 10, 2002).

Department of Justice, Immigration and Citizenship Division. 1994. *Annual Return of Registered Aliens for the Year 1994.* Dublin: Garda Síochána.

———. 1995. *Annual Return of Registered Aliens for the Year 1995.* Dublin: Garda Síochána.

———. 1996. *Annual Return of Registered Aliens for the Year 1996.* Dublin: Garda Síochána.

DES. 2000–2008. Domiciliary Origin of Students Enrolled in Full-time Third Level Institutions. http://www.cso.ie/ (accessed May 2, 2010).

Dinu, Marin. 2007. "Modernity after Modernity." *Theoretical and Applied Economics* 8.513: 53–60.

Dirlik, Arif. 2000. "Reconfiguring Modernity: From Modernization to Globalization." December. Paper presented at the "Entangled Modernities" conference, House of World Cultures, Berlin. Rome: Society for International Development. Available at http://www.prdatta.com/Documents/DBA/Globalisation/Articles/Modernity %20to%20Globalisation.pdf/ (accessed August 31, 2011).

DJ Tando. 2010. Personal Information. Facebook. http://www.facebook.com/djtando/ (accessed May 5, 2010).

Dobbins, Tony. 2001. *Implications of new EU equality directives in Ireland.* Report. European Industrial Relations Observatory. http://www.eurofound.europa.eu/eiro/ (accessed January 17, 2010).

Donohoe, Miriam. 1999. "O'Donoghue may introduce smart card for asylum-seekers." *Irish Times.* October 10. http://www.irishtimes.com/ (accessed November 10, 2009).

Dolan, Pamela. 2000. "Fury over Racist Attack." *Mirror* (London). April 26. http://www.highbeam.com/ (accessed May 10, 2010).

Douglass, Frederick. 1852. Speech given before the Rochester Anti-Slavery Sewing Society, Corinthian Hall, Rochester, N.Y., July 5. Pamphlet published by Lee, Mann and Co. (Rochester, N.Y.). Available at the University of Rochester Frederick Douglass Project, http://www.lib.rochester.edu (accessed August 12, 2011).

———. 1999. "Letter to William Lloyd Garrison, January 1, 1846." In Philip S. Foner, ed., *Frederick Douglass: Selected Speeches and Writings.* 17–20. Chicago: Lawrence Hill Books.

Doyle, Roddy. 2000. "Spuds" in *Guess Who's Coming for the Dinner* (chapter 5). *Metro Éireann.* October, p. 7.

Drivetime. 2007. "Documentary on six children deported." RTE Radio One. December 14. http://www.rte.ie/radio1/drivetime/ (accessed July 24, 2008).

Dubois, Laurent. 2005. *Avengers of the New World: The Story of the Haitian Revolution.* Cambridge, Mass.: Belknap Press.

Duke, Lynne, and Teresa Wiltz. 2005. "A Nation's Castaways." *Washington Post.* September 4. http://www.washingtonpost.com/ (accessed August 30, 2007).

Duncan, Dawn. 2002. "A Flexible Foundation: Constructing a Postcolonial Dialogue." In D. T. Goldberg and A. Quayson, eds., *Relocating Postcolonialism.* 320–333. Oxford: Blackwell.

Duplessis, Ann. 2009. "City's east stakes out its vision." *Times-Picayune.* February 4. http://www.nola.com/ (accessed July 7, 2009).

Dworkin, Ronald. 2002. *Sovereign Virtue: The Theory and Practice of Equality.* Cambridge, Mass.: Harvard University Press.

Dyèvre, Dephine. 2010. "Fillon enterre l'identité nationale avec des mesurettes." *L'Express.* February 8. http://www.lexpress.fr/ (accessed February 20, 2010).

Dyson, Michael E. 2006. *Come Hell or High Water: Hurricane Katrina and the Color of Disaster.* New York: Basic Civitas Books.

Edwards, Brent Hayes. 2003. *The Practice of Diaspora: Literature, Translation, and the Rise of Black Internationalism*. Cambridge, Mass.: Harvard University Press.

Eggler, Bruce. 2009. "Affordable housing plan draws opponents from gated Lake Carmel in east New Orleans." March 25. http://www.nola.com/ (accessed July 14, 2009).

Eisenstadt, Shmuel N. 2000. "Multiple Modernities." *Daedalus* (Winter) 129.1: 1–29.

Elukanlo, Olukunle. 2005. "My ordeal in Nigeria." *Socialist Party News*. March 28. http://www.socialistparty.net/ (accessed September 6, 2007).

Elzas, Sarah. 2007. "Equal Opportunities." Radio France International (RFI) (English Service). Transcript. Aired December 27. http://www.toucanradio.org/ (accessed January 10, 2010).

EURES. 2010. "Labor market information—Nord-Pas-de-Calais." European Employment Services (EURES). Employment Portal. http://ec.europa.eu/eures/ (accessed March 24, 2010).

Eurostat. 2004. "Portrait of the Regions—France—Nord-Pas-de-Calais-Employment." Eurostat Report. http://circa.europa.eu/irc/dsis/regportraits/info/data/fr3_emp.htm (accessed September 1, 2011).

Fagan, G. Honor. 2003. "Globalised Ireland, or, Contemporary Transformations of National Identity?" In Colin Coulter and Steve Coleman, eds., *The End of Irish History? Critical Approaches to the Celtic Tiger*. 110–121. Manchester: Manchester University Press.

Fagan, Paula. 2008. "Migrant Women and Domestic Violence in Ireland: The Experience of Domestic Violence Service Providers." Paper. Dublin: University College Dublin. http://www.ucd.ie/werrc/Paulafaganresearch.pdf/ (accessed April 28, 2010).

Fanon, Frantz. 1967. *Black Skins, White Masks*. New York: Grove.

Fausset, Richard. 2009. "New Orleans rebuilds, but along the same lines?" *Los Angeles Times*. May 31. http://www.latimes.com/ (accessed June 24, 2009).

Featherstone, Mike, ed. 1990. *Global Culture*. London: Sage.

Fillon, François. 2009. "Débat sur l'identité nationale." Speech presented on December 4. *Portail du Gouvernement*. http://www.gouvernement.fr/premier-ministre/ (accessed February 2, 2010).

Fireside, Harvey. 2005. *Separate and Unequal: Homer Plessy and the Supreme Court Decision that Legalized Racism*. New York: Carroll & Graf.

Fitzpatrick, Tim. 2006. "New Orleans, Hurricane Katrina, and the Oil Industry." EnvironmentalChemistry.com. June 30. http://environmentalchemistry.com/ (accessed June 19, 2009).

Five Seven Live. 2005. "Philip Boucher-Hayes talks to members of the Nigerian community in Athlone, Co. Westmeath." March 25. http://www.rte.ie/ (accessed July 8, 2008).

FLAC. 2009. *One Size Doesn't Fit All—a legal analysis of Direct Provision, 10 years on*. Executive Summary of Report, Free Legal Advice Centers (FLAC). November. Dublin: Free Legal Advice Centers. http://www.flac.ie/ (accessed April 19, 2010).

Flynn, Rosanna. 2005. Speech given at Ireland's UNHCR World Refugee Day Awards. June 16. http://www.indymedia.ie/ (accessed July 11, 2008).

Foner, Eric. 1999. *The Story of American Freedom.* New York: W. W. Norton & Company.

Foster, R. F. 2008. *Luck and the Irish: A Brief History of Change from 1970.* New York: Oxford University Press.

France 24. 2009. "Poll shows most French back 'National identity' debate." November 2. http://www.france24.com/ (accessed January 20, 2010).

———. 2010. "PM Fillon wraps up divisive debate on 'national identity.'" France 24. February 8. http://www.france24.com/ (accessed February 10, 2010).

Frank, Thomas. 2005. "Astrodome to become new home for storm refugees." *USA Today.* August 31. http://www.usatoday.com/ (accessed July 10, 2007).

French Civil Code. 2006. "Of French Nationality," *Book 1: Of Persons.* April 4, 2006. Articles 17–33.2. Available at Legifrance, http://www.legifrance.gouv.fr/home.jsp and http://195.83.177.9/upl/pdf/code_22.pdf (accessed August 26, 2011).

Freud, Sigmund. 1989. *Jokes and Their Relation to the Unconscious.* New York: W. W. Norton & Company.

Frey, William H., Audrey Singer, and David Park. 2007. "Resettling New Orleans: The First Full Picture from the Census." Brookings Institution. September. http://www.brookings.edu/ (accessed September 14, 2007).

Fricker, Karen. 2007. "The Playboy of the Western World." *Variety.* October. http://www.variety.com/review (accessed April 20, 2010).

Friedman, Jonathan. 1995. "Global System, Globalization and the Parameters of Modernity." In M. Featherstone, S. Lash, and R. Robertson, eds., *Global Modernities.* 69–90. London: Sage.

Friedman, Thomas. 1999. *The Lexus and the Olive Tree.* New York: Farrar Straus Giroux.

Friel, Jenny. 2001. "'Venus Mantrap': Sex mad beauty in Fair City love triangle." *Mirror* (London). May 10. http://www.highbeam.com/ (accessed April 20, 2010).

Fukuyama, Francis. 1989. "The End of History?" *The National Interest* 16 (Summer): 3–18.

———. 2006. *The End of History and the Last Man.* New York: The Free Press.

GAA. 2009. Inclusion and Integration Strategy 2009–2015. Report. Gaelic Athletic Association. http://www.gaa.ie (accessed September 13, 2009).

Gallagher, Padraic, Anthony Wilkie, and Des Hackett. 2005. "Hope, Friendship and Hardwork won the day." *Teachers Union of Ireland News* 27.4: 16.

Gartland, Fiona. 2009. "A question of ethnic identity." March 3. *Irish Times.* http://www.irishtimes.com/ (accessed May 6, 2010).

Gérard, Mathilde. 2010. "Discriminations: 'Une loi est nécessaire.'" *Le Monde.* February 5 (accessed February 6, 2010).

Giddens, Anthony. 1990. *The Consequences of Modernity.* Stanford, Calif.: Stanford University Press.

Gilroy, Paul. 1993. *The Black Atlantic: Modernity and Double Consciousness.* Cambridge, Mass.: Harvard University Press.

GNOCDC and Brookings Institution. 2009. "Population Recover." August. *New Orleans Index,* 18. Report. Greater New Orleans Community Data Center and Brookings Institution Metropolitan Policy Program. http://www.brookings.edu/~/media/

Files/rc/reports/2007/08neworleansindex/200908_Katrina_Index.pdf (accessed August 30, 2011).

GNOFHAC. 2008a. "St. Bernard Parish to Pay an Additional $123,771.92 in Settlement of Blood Relative Rental Ordinance Lawsuit." July 2. News Release. GNOFHAC. http://www.gnofairhousing.org/ (accessed July 6, 2009).

———. 2008b. "Fair Housing Center Seeks Repeal of St. Bernard Parish Multi-Family Moratorium." GNOFHAC. December 18. News Release. GNOFHAC. http://www .gnofairhousing.org/ (accessed July 13, 2009).

Goeriger, Conrad F. 2001. "A Wider Bush Plan for Religious 'Communitarianism.'" *American Atheist.* August 1. http://www.americanatheist.org/ (accessed September 1, 2007).

Green, Charles. 1997. "Conclusion: Beyond the 21st Century." In Charles Green, ed., *Globalization and Survival in the Black Diaspora: The New Urban Challenge.* 379–386. Albany: State University of New York Press.

Grennan, Sinead. 2000. "Villages 'Cannot Veto Immigrant Influx.'" *Sunday Independent.* May 7. http://www.independent.ie (accessed August 2, 2001).

Gros de Larquier, Ségolène. 2009. "Sur la Toile, le dèbat sur l'identité nationale bat son plein." *Le Point.* December 2. http://www.lepoint.fr/ (accessed February 1, 2010).

Habermas, Jürgen. 2002. "Modernity: An Incomplete Project," trans. Seyla Ben-Habib. In Hal Foster, ed., *The Anti-Aesthetic: Essays on Postmodern Culture.* 3–15. New York: New Press.

Hall, Gwendolyn Midlo. 1995. *Africans in Colonial Louisiana: The Development of Afro-Creole Culture in the Eighteenth Century.* Baton Rouge: Louisiana State University Press.

Hammer, David. 2008. "Did Road Home treat all neighborhoods fairly?" *Times-Picayune.* May 27. http://www.nola.com/ (accessed June 24, 2009).

———. 2009a. "Apartment plans for east N.O. opposed; Foes of complex near East-over recruit legislators to their side." *Times-Picayune.* January 23. http://www.nola .com/ (accessed July 7, 2009).

———. 2009b. "Judge halts construction of controversial Levy Gardens apartments in eastern New Orleans." *Times-Picayune.* February 10. http://www.nola.com/ (accessed July 7, 2009).

Hannerz, Ulf. 1996. *Transnational Connections: Culture, People, Places.* London: Routledge.

Hargreaves, Alec G. 1987. *Immigration in Post-War France: A Documentary Anthology.* London: Routledge.

———. 1995. *Immigration, "Race" and Ethnicity in Contemporary France.* London: Routledge.

Harris, Eoghan. 2008. "Going from messing Eire to Mise Eire." August 3. *Irish Independent.* http://www.independent.ie/ (accessed December 5, 2009).

Harris, Joseph E. 1996. "The Dynamics of the Global African Diaspora." In Joseph E. Harris, Alusine Jalloh, and Stephen E. Maizlish, eds, *The African Diaspora.* 7 21. College Station: Texas A&M University Press.

Hart, William A. 2002. "Africans in Eighteenth-Century Ireland." *Irish Historical Studies* 33:129 (May): 19–32.

Harvey, David. 1989. *The Condition of Postmodernity: An Enquiry into the Origins of Cultural Change.* Oxford: Blackwell.

Hassan, Ghali. 2006. "'Ethnic Cleansing' in New Orleans." *Global Research.* Center for Research on Globalization. June 25. http://www.globalresearch.ca/ (accessed June 25, 2009).

Hayden, Patrick, and Chamsy El-Ojeili, eds. 2009. *Globalization and Utopia: Critical Essays.* New York: Palgrave Macmillan.

Headrick, Daniel. 1988. *The Tentacles of Progress: Technology Transfer in the Age of Imperialism, 1850–1940.* New York: Oxford University Press.

Healy, Tim. 2004. "Nigerian jailed for failure to produce ID papers." *Irish Independent.* October 15. http://www.independent.ie/ (accessed April 22, 2010).

Hearn, Chester G. 2005. *The Capture of New Orleans, 1862.* Baton Rouge: Louisiana State University Press.

Held, David, and Anthony McGrew. 2007. *Globalization/Anti-Globalization: Beyond the Great Divide.* Cambridge, UK: Polity Press.

Held, David, Anthony McGrew, David Goldblatt, and Jonathan Perraton. 1999. *Global Transformations: Politics, Economics, and Culture.* Palo Alto, Calif.: Stanford University Press.

Hennessy, Mark. 2001. "O'Connell Says Era of Celtic Tiger Over." *Irish Times.* November 8. http://www.ireland.com (accessed January 25, 2002).

Herbert, Bob. 1997. "Days of Terror: 1863 Draft Riots in New York City." *New York Times.* October 19, section 4: 15.

Hesse, Barnor, ed. 2000. *Un/Settled Multiculturalisms: Diasporas, Entanglements, "Transruptions."* London: Zed Books.

Hickman, Mary J., et al. 2005. "The limitations of whiteness and the boundaries of Englishness." *Ethnicities* 5:2 (June): 160–182.

Hirsch, Arnold R., and Joseph Logsdon, eds. 1992. *Creole New Orleans: Race and Americanization.* Baton Rouge: Louisiana State University Press.

Hogue, James Keith. 2006. *Uncivil War: Five New Orleans Street Battles and the Rise and Fall of Radical Reconstruction.* Baton Rouge: Louisiana State University Press.

Holt, Thomas C. 1999. "Slavery and Freedom in the Atlantic World: Reflections on the Diasporan Framework." In Darlene Clark Hine and Jacqueline McLeod, eds., *Crossing Boundaries: Comparative History of Black People in Diaspora.* 33–44. Bloomington: Indiana University Press.

Holzer, Harry J., and Robert I. Lerman. 2006. "Employment Issues and Challenges in Post-Katrina New Orleans." Urban Institute. February. http://www.urban.org/afterkatrina/ (accessed August 30, 2007).

House, James. 1998. "Muslim Communities in France." In Gerd Nonneman, Tim Niblock, and Bogdan Szajkowski, eds., *Muslim Communities in the New Europe.* 219–240. London: Ithaca Press.

Houses of *Oireachtas.* 2002. Select Committee on Justice, Equality, Defense and

Women's Rights. "Bilateral Agreements: Motion." March 27. http://www.irlgov.ie/ committees-02/c-justice/020327/Page1.htm (accessed July 23, 2007).

Howe, Marvine. 1990. "Irish-Americans Praise New Immigration Bill." *New York Times.* October 7. http://www.nytimes.com/ (accessed July 1, 2008).

Hughes, Louis. 1897. *The Autobiography of Louis Hughes, Thirty Years a Slave: From Bondage to Freedom, the Institution of Slavery as Seen on the Plantation and in the Home of the Planter.* University of North Carolina at Chapel Hill Libraries Documenting of the South. http://docsouth.unc.edu (accessed March 28, 2001).

Huntington, Samuel P. 1996. *The Clash of Civilizations and the Remaking of World Order.* New York: Simon and Schuster.

ICMS. 2001. "Refugee Information Service Factsheet 1." *Irish Center for Migration Studies.* December. http://mig82.ucc.ie/ris/ris.htm (accessed May 2, 2010).

ICOS. 2010. "New data improves picture of non-EEA students in Ireland." Februrary 1. Media Release. Irish Council for International Students. http://www.icosirl.ie/ (accessed May 2, 2010).

Ignatiev, Noel. 1995. *How the Irish Became White.* London: Routledge.

Ingersoll, Thomas N. 1991. "Free Blacks in a Slave Society: New Orleans, 1718–1812." *The William and Mary Quarterly* 48.2: 173–200.

INIS. 2005. "Statement by the Minister regarding the Real Facts about the Asylum and Deportation Systems." Irish Naturalization and Immigration Service. June 7. http://www.inis.com (accessed July 1, 2008).

———. 2010. "Who needs to provide fingerprints?" Biometric Data Information. Irish Naturalization and Immigration Service. http://www.inis.gov.ie/ (accessed May 5, 2010).

Inkeles, Alex. 1960. "Industrial Man: The Relation of Status to Experience, Perception, and Value." *American Journal of Sociology* 66.1: 1–30.

Inkeles, Alex, and David H. Smith. 1974. *Becoming Modern: Individual Change in Six Developing Countries.* Cambridge, Mass.: Harvard University Press.

Institute for Southern Studies. 2007. "The bottom has fallen out." *Blueprint for Gulf Renewal: The Katrina Crisis and a Community Agenda for Action.* August/September. http://www.iss.org/ (accessed August 15, 2007).

International Herald Tribune. 2005. "Sarkozy and Villepin draw battle lines over 'positive discrimination.'" November 25. http://www.iht.com/ (accessed August 15, 2007).

Irish Census. 2006a. "Usual residence, migration, birthplaces and nationalities." Volume 4. Central Statistics Office. http://www.cso.ie/census/ (accessed July 16, 2007).

———. 2006b. "Ethnic or Cultural Background (Including the Irish Traveller Community)." Volume 5. Central Statistics Office. http://www.cso.ie/census/ (accessed January 12, 2009).

———. 2006c. "Census 2006 New Questions." Central Statistics Office. http://www .cso.ie/census/ (accessed January 12, 2009).

Irish Examiner. 2000. "Comedian." *Irish Examiner.* November 10, 2000. http://www .examiner.ie (accessed November 15, 2000).

Irish Independent. 2000. "Fake identity papers seized in asylum raid." September 19. http://www.irishindependent.ie/ (accessed March 22, 2011).

——. 2001. "Attitudes to Immigrants Should Be Open and Inclusive." *Irish Independent.* February 5. http://www.independent.ie (accessed February 6, 2001).

——. 2009. "Ahern calls for replay after handball win." November 19. *Irish Independent.* http://www.independent.ie/ (accessed December 1, 2009).

Irish Refugee Council (IRC). 2001. "Direct Provision and Dispersal—18 Months On." October. http://www.irishrefugeecouncil.ie/ (accessed February 5, 2010).

——. 2005. "Two years in Limbo—enough is enough!" Irish Refugee Council. January 18. http://www.irishrefugeecouncil.ie/policy01/ (accessed July 1, 2008).

——. 2006. "Post-Afghan hunger strike reflections on Ireland's asylum system." May 24. http://www.irishrefugeecouncil.ie/ (accessed July 20, 2006).

Irish Times. 1998. "Prison Picketed in Deportation Protest." *Irish Times.* December 16, 1998. http://www.ireland.com (accessed March 16, 2001).

——. 2000. "Judge tells asylum-seekers not to resort to crime." *Irish Times.* August 8. http://www.irishtimes.com/ (accessed March 22, 2011).

——. 2006. "Deported Nigerian man fails with legal challenge." *Irish Times.* July 14. http://www.irishtimes.com/ (accessed May 6, 2010).

Ives, Stephen. 2007. "New Orleans." *The American Experience.* PBS. http://www.pbs .org/wgbh/amex/neworleans/index.html (accessed May 20, 2009).

Jackson, Joe. 2000. "Samantha Mumba." *Hot Press* 24.20 (October 25): 18–22, 85.

Jackson, Peter, Philip Crang, and Claire Dwyer, eds. 2004. *Transnational Spaces.* New York: Routledge.

Jameson, Fredric. 1991. *Postmodernism, or The Cultural Logic of Late Capitalism.* Durham, N.C.: Duke University Press.

Jensen, Lynne. 2006. "Krewe du Vieux is satirical appetizer." *Times-Picayune.* February 11. http://www.nola.com/mardigras/ (accessed June 2, 2009).

Johnstone, Diana. 2005. "Paris Is Burning, Rage in the Banlieue." *Counterpunch.* November 9. http://www.counterpunch.com/ (accessed August 30, 2007).

Jonsson, Patrik. 2009a. "'First real trial' about Katrina under way." *Christian Science Monitor.* April 20. http://www.csmonitor.com/ (accessed June 2, 2009).

——. 2009b. "Army Corps liable for Katrina damage, US court finds." *Christian Science Monitor.* November 19. http://www.csmonitor.com/ (accessed August 24, 2011).

Kaiser Family Foundation. 2007. "Major House-to-House Survey Finds New Orleans Residents Hit Hard." Kaiser Family Foundation. May 10. http://www.kff.org/ (accessed July 27, 2007).

Kant, Immanuel. 1991. "Perpetual Peace: A Philosophical Sketch." In H. Reiss, ed., *Kant: Political Writings.* 93–130. Cambridge, UK: Cambridge University Press.

——. 1999. *Practical Philosophy.* Cambridge, UK: Cambridge University Press.

Karoui, Hichem. 2007. "The French Paradox: Assessing Social and Political Landscape Changes in France." Media Monitors Network. May 15. http://www.mediamonitors .net/ (accessed August 30, 2007).

Kearns, David. 1983. *Georgian Dublin: Ireland's Imperiled Architectural Heritage.* Newton Abbot, Devon, UK: David and Charles.

Keaton, Trica D. 2006. *Muslim Girls and the Other France: Race, Identity Politics, and Social Exclusion.* Bloomington: Indiana University Press.

Kein, Sybil. 2000. *Creole: The History and Legacy of Louisiana's Free People of Color.* Baton Rouge: Louisiana State University Press.

Kelly, Fiach. 2008. "Race taunts won't put me off GAA, says young player." *Irish Independent.* July 25. http://www.independent.ie/ (accessed August 30, 2009).

Kelly, Olivia. 2009. "Carlton cinema site development 'could undermine character of O'Connell Street.'" *Irish Times.* April 21. http://www.irishtimes.com/ (accessed April 2, 2010).

Kennedy, Dan. 2010. "Obama's Haiti is not Bush's Katrina." *Guardian.* January 14. http://www.guardian.co.uk/ (accessed January 20, 2010).

Keogh, Dermot. 1998. *Jews in Twentieth-Century Ireland: Refugees, Anti-Semitism, and the Holocaust.* Cork: Cork University Press.

Kerr, C., J. Dunlop, F. Harbison, and C. Myers. 1962. *Industrialism and Industrial Man: The Problems of Labour and Management in Economic Growth.* London: Heinemann.

Kiely, Ray. 1998. *Industrialization and Development: An Introduction.* London: Routledge.

King-O'Riain, Rebecca Chiyoko. 2007. "Counting on the 'Celtic Tiger': Adding ethnic census categories in the Republic of Ireland." *Ethnicities* 7.4: 516–542.

Kirkham, Chris. 2009. "Federal judge rules against St. Bernard Parish in multi-family housing lawsuit." *Times-Picayune.* March 26. http://www.nola.com/ (accessed July 6, 2009).

Kovel, Joel. 1984. *White Racism: A Psychohistory.* New York: Columbia University Press.

Krupa, Michelle, and Frank Donze. 2010. "Landrieu Landside." *Times-Picayune.* February 7. http://www.nola.com/ (accessed February 8, 2010).

Kushner, David. 2009. *Levittown: Two Families, One Tycoon, and the Fight for Civil Rights in America's Legendary Suburb.* New York: Walker & Company.

Laguerre, Michel S. 1998. *Diasporic Citizenship: Haitian Americans in Transnational America.* New York: St. Martin's Press.

———. 1999. *Minoritized Space: An Inquiry on the Order of Things.* Berkeley: University of California Institutional Governmental Studies Press.

———. 2000. *The Global Ethnopolis.* London: Palgrave Macmillan.

Landor, Jeremy. 1997. "North African Workers in France: Processes of Integration and Exclusion." *Contemporary Politics* 3:4: 381–400.

Lane, Damien. 2001. "Asylum Babies Scandal; Exclusive: 5,000 Nigerian women abuse legal loophole and give birth in Republic to get permanent residency." *Irish Mirror.* November 28. http://www.freelibrary.com/ (accessed March 22, 2011).

Lantier, Alex. 2010. "Mass protests greet Sarkozy visit to Haiti." February 19. World Socialist. http://www.wsws.org/articles/2010/feb2010/hait-f19.shtml (accessed August 6, 2011).

Lavery, Brian. 2005. "Bring Them Back." *Time.* June 12. http://www.time.com/ (accessed July 15, 2008).

Lebow, Richard Ned. 1976. *White Britain and Black Ireland: The Influence of Stereotypes on Colonial Policy.* Philadelphia: Institute for the Study of Human Issues.

Le Nouvel Observateur. 2007a. "Peu de Noirs aux législatives, déplore le Cran." *Le Nouvel Observateur.* June 4. http://tempsreel.nouvelobs.com/ (accessed August 26, 2011).

———. 2007b. "Une citation d'Aimé Césaire pour définir la colonization." *Le Nouvel Observateur.* September 3. http://tempsreel.nouvelobs.com/ (accessed August 27, 2011).

Lentin, Ronit, ed. 1998. "Constitutionally Excluded: Citizenship and (Some) Irish Women." In N. Yuval-Davis and P. Werbner, eds., *Women, Citizenship and Difference.* 130–144. London: Zed Books.

———, ed. 1999. *The Expanding Nation: Towards a Multi-Ethnic Ireland.* Dublin: Ethnic and Racial Studies, Department of Sociology, Trinity College Dublin.

———, ed. 2000. *Emerging Irish Identities.* Dublin: Ethnic and Racial Studies Program, Department of Sociology, Trinity College Dublin.

———. 2003. "Pregnant silence: (En)gendering Ireland's asylum space." *Patterns of Prejudice* 37.3: 301–322.

Lentin, Ronit, and Robbie McVeigh. 2006. *After Optimism? Ireland, Racism and Globalisation.* Dublin: Metro Éireann Publications.

Leparmentier, Arnaud. 2010. "Visite historique de quatre heures de Sarkozy en Haiti." February 17. *Le Monde.* http://www.lemonde.fr/ (accessed February 18, 2010).

Le Post. 2010. "Fillon et le débat sur l'identité nationale: 'Il y a eu quelques dérapages, mais . . .'" *Le Post.* February 8. http://www.lepost.fr/ (accessed February 10, 2010).

Lerner, Daniel. 1958. *The Passing of Traditional Society: Modernizing the Middle East.* Glencoe, Ill.: Free Press.

Lerougetel, Antoine. 2005. "Paris: 48 African immigrants die in apartment block fires." September 1. World Socialist. http://www.wsws.org/ (accessed February 2, 2010).

Lesnes, Corine. 2005. "Après Katrina, l'Amérique s'interroge sur les failles de son modèle." *Le Monde.* September 8. http://www.lemonde.fr/ (accessed August 30, 2007).

Liauzu, Claude. 2005. "At war with France's past." *Le Monde Diplomatique.* June. http://mondediplo.com (accessed August 10, 2007).

Libération. 2009. "Sarkozy: le débat sur l'identité nationale 'est un débat noble.'" *Libération.* November 11. http://www.liberation.fr/ (accessed February 2, 2010).

Liberator. 1859. Coverage of speech given by Sarah Parker Remond to the Dublin Ladies' Anti-Slavery Association. March 11. Available at the University of Detroit Mercy Black Abolitionist Archive, doc. no. 20365(a). http://research.udmercy.edu/ (accessed November 12, 2010).

Libyan Republic Interim Transnational Council. 2011. "Council's Statement." Libyan Republic Interim Transnational Council website. Posted March 2011. http://ntclibya.org/english/ (accessed March 11, 2011).

Lichfield, John. 2008a. "Sarkozy 'Marshall plan' for poor suburbs falls short." *Independent.* February 9. http://www.independent.co.uk/ (accessed January 12, 2010).

———. 2008b. "Rise of Rachida Dati: The minister, the 'virgin bride' and the row that's dividing a nation." *Independent.* June 4. http://www.independent.co.uk/ (accessed January 21, 2010).

———. 2009a. "Sarkozy sidelines young black cabinet minister." *Independent.* June 24. http://www.independent.co.uk/ (accessed January 21, 2010).

———. 2009b. "France's crisis of national identity." *Irish Independent.* November 25. http://www.independent.ie/ (accessed January 20, 2010).

———. 2009c. "Workplace bullying blamed for Dati's return to work." *Independent.* January 11. http://www.independent.co.uk/ (accessed January 21, 2010).

Lloyd, David. 2003. "After History: Historicism and Irish Postcolonial Studies." In Clare Carroll and Patricia King, eds., *Ireland and Postcolonial Theory.* 46–62. Notre Dame, Ind.: University of Notre Dame Press.

Logan, John R. 2006. "The Impact of Katrina: Race and Class in Storm-Damaged Neighborhoods." Report. Available from http://www.s4.brown.edu/Katrina/report .pdf (accessed June 24, 2009).

Logue, Patrick, and John Collins. 2005. "McDowell lets Nigerian student return for exams." *Irish Times.* March 24. http://www.ireland.com/ (accessed September 1, 2007).

Louisiana Division/City Archives. 2006. *Plan Book for Gentilly Woods.* Gentilly Homes, Inc. July 2006. Louisiana Division/City Archives "Images of the Month." New Orleans Public Library. http://nutrias.org/~nopl/monthly/july2006/ (accessed June 30, 2009).

Loyal, Steve. 2003. "Welcome to the Celtic Tiger: Racism, Immigration and the State." In Colin Coulter and Steve Coleman, eds., *The End of Irish History? Critical Approaches to the Celtic Tiger.* 74–94. Manchester: Manchester University Press.

Lozès, Patrick. 2007. *Nous, Les Noirs de France.* Paris: Editions Danger Public.

———. 2009a. "Un sondage bidon sur 'l'inefficacité' supposée des statistiques de la diversité." *Le Nouvel Observateur.* March 15. http://patricklozes.blogs.nouvelobs. com (accessed November 12, 2009).

———. 2009b. "Combien de français favorables aux statistiques selon le ressenti d'appartenance?" *Le Nouvel Observateur.* April 28. http://patricklozes.blogs.nouvelobs .com (accessed January 24, 2010).

Lucey, Anne. 2000a. "TD warns coalition on threat of growing civil unrest." *Irish Independent.* May 2. http://www.independent.ie/ (accessed April 20, 2010).

———. 2000b. "Attitudes to Blacks Criticized." *Irish Times.* November 13. http://www .ireland.com (accessed November 15, 2000).

———. 2006. "Angry refugees go on hunger strike." *Irish Independent.* September 8. http://www.independent.ie/ (accessed January 12, 2010).

Lynott, Philomena. 1996. *My Boy: The Phil Lynott Story.* London: Virgin Books.

Lyotard, Jean-Francois. 1985. *The Post-Modern Condition.* Minneapolis: University of Minnesota Press.

Mac an Ghaill, Máirtín. 2000. "The Irish in Britain: The invisibility of ethnicity and anti-Irish racism." *Journal of Ethnic and Migration Studies* 26:1 (January): 137–147.

Mac Éinrí, Piaras. 2001. Immigration into Ireland: Trends, Policy Responses. Outlook Report. http://migration.ucc.ie/irelandfirstreport.htm (accessed May 2, 2010).

Mackenzie, James. 2007. "French parliament set to remain heavily white-group." *Reuters.* June 4. http://uk.reuters.com/ (accessed August 26, 2011).

Mander, Jerry, and Edward Goldsmith. 1996. *The Case against the Global Economy*. San Francisco: Sierra Club Books.

Marlowe, Lara. 2011. "Senators' absence stalls anti-union vote in Wisconsin." *Irish Times*. February 19 (accessed March 11, 2011).

Martin, Bill. 1998. "Multiculturalism: Consumerist or Transformational?" In Cynthia Willett, ed., *Theorizing Multiculturalism: A Guide to the Current Debate*. 121–150. Malden, Mass.: Blackwell.

Masquelier, Adeline. 2006. "Why Katrina's Victims Aren't Refugees: Musings on a 'Dirty' Word." *American Anthropologist* 108.4: 735–743.

Master Plan Draft. 2009. "New Orleans 2030: A master plan for the 21st century." March 20. Working Draft. New Orleans City Planning Commission. http://nolamasterplan.com/ (accessed June 25, 2009).

Matuštík, Martin J. Beck. 1998. "Ludic, Corporate, and Imperial Multiculturalism: Impostors of Democracy and Cartographers of the New World." In Cynthia Willett, ed., *Theorizing Multiculturalism: A Guide to the Current Debate*. 100–118. Malden, Mass.: Blackwell.

McCague, James. 1968. *The Second Rebellion: The Story of the New York City Draft Riots of 1863*. New York: Dial Press.

McClelland, David C. 1961. *The Achieving Society*. New York: Free Press.

McDonald, Henry. 2009. "Ireland votes yes to Lisbon treaty." October 3. *Guardian*. http://www.guardian.co.uk/ (accessed December 5, 2009).

McDonough, Terrence, ed. 2005. *Was Ireland a Colony? Economics, Politics and Culture in Nineteenth-Century Ireland*. Dublin: Irish Academic Press.

McGoldrick, Debbie. 2005. "Huge Support Greets New Lobby Group." *The Irish Voice*. December 14. http://www.irishvoice.com/ (accessed July 1, 2008).

McGrath, Paul. 2006. *Back from the Brink*. London: Century.

McKenna, Gene, and Fergus Black. 2000. "Refugee 'detention' hint sparks protest." *Irish Independent*. March 14. http://www.independent.ie/ (accessed September 6, 2007).

McManus, John. 2001. "The Tiger: Asleep or Extinct?" *Irish Times*. November 10. http://www.ireland.com (accessed November 11, 2001).

McNicoll, Tracy. 2008. "Fadela Amara: Madame Marshall Plan." *Newsweek*. March 1. http://www.newsweek.com/ (accessed January 12, 2009).

McVeigh, Robbie. 1992. "The Specificity of Irish Racism." *Race and Class* 33.4 (April): 31–45.

———. 1998. "'There's No Racism Because There's No Black People Here': Racism and Anti-Racism in Northern Ireland." In Paul Hainsworth, ed., *Divided Society: Ethnic Minorities and Racism in Northern Ireland*. 11–32. London: Pluto Press.

Media Matters. 2010. "Robertson's 'true story.'" Originally broadcast on *The 700 Club*. Christian Broadcasting Network. January 13. Posted at Media Matters. http://www.mediamatters.org/ (accessed January 20, 2010).

Memery, Clodagh. 2001. "The Housing System and the Celtic Tiger: The State Response to a Housing Crisis of Affordability and Access." *European Journal of Housing Policy* 1.1: 79–104.

Metro Éireann. 2007. "RTÉ: ethnic minorities 'not programmed out.'" *Metro Éireann.* January 11. http://www.metroeireann.com/ (accessed April 20, 2010).

Meylan, Greg. 2001. "Housing Crisis Could Undermine Society—Threshold." *Irish Times.* March 31. http://www.ireland.com (accessed August 2, 2001).

Midgley, Clare. 1995. *Women against Slavery: The British Campaigns, 1780–1870.* London: Routledge.

Mono. 2001. Episode 5. First broadcast May 2 by RTÉ. Produced by Colm O'Callaghan.

Monshengwo, Kensika. 2000. "Irish Identity?" In Ronit Lentin, ed., *Emerging Irish Identities.* 76–78. Dublin: Publication of the Ethnic and Racial Studies Program, Department of Sociology, Trinity College Dublin.

Montvalon, Jean-Baptiste de. 2007. "Le 'Petit Robert' ajoute une citation de Césaire à sa définition de la colonization." *Le Monde.* September 4. http://www.lemonde .fr/ (accessed September 10, 2007).

Moore, Kevin. 2002. "Rise in female workforce hits census." *Irish Independent.* April 28. http://www.independent.ie/ (accessed May 2, 2010).

Mooten, Nalinie. 2006. *Making Separated Children Visible: The Need for a Child-Centered Approach.* Dublin: Irish Refugee Council. http://www.irishrefugeecouncil .ie/ (accessed July 17, 2008).

Moraes, Lisa de. 2005. "Kanye West's Torrent of Criticism, Live on NBC." *Washington Post.* September 3. http://www.washingtonpost.com/ (accessed August 30, 2007).

Morahan, Jim. 2005. "Gardaí called to Nigerian embassy after passport fiasco." *Irish Examiner.* March 17. http://archives.tcm.ie/irishexaminer/ (accessed July 11, 2008).

Morning Ireland. 2005. "Emma McNamara speaks to John Scott, Director of the Irish Modern Dance Theatre, about his friend and dancer, Azekiel, who faces deportation." March 15. http://www.rte.ie/ (accessed July 8, 2008).

Murphy, Colin. 2005. "The women Bertie befriended are deported." Village—Politics, Media and Current Affairs in Ireland. March 19. http://www.village.ie/ (accessed July 15, 2008).

Muslimah Media Watch. 2009. "Rachida Dati's Rise and Fall." Article by blogger, Krista. February 5. http://muslimahmediawatch.org/2009/02/rachida-datis-rise-and-fall/ (accessed September 1, 2011).

Myers, Kevin. 2008. "Africa is giving nothing to anyone—apart from AIDS." *Irish Independent.* July 10. http://www.independent.ie/ (accessed March 30, 2010).

———. 2010. "Disasters—where would showbiz be without them?" January 26. *Irish Independent.* http://www.independent.ie/opinion/ (accessed March 30, 2010).

NASA. 2005. "Flooding in New Orleans: Image of the Day." August 30. National Aeronautics and Space Administration. http://earthobservatory.nasa.gov/ (accessed June 2, 2009).

NBC. 2010. George Bush interview with David Gregory. *Meet the Press.* January 17. MSNBC. http://www.msnbc.com/ (accessed January 20, 2010).

NBC Sports. 2009. "'Oui were robbed': Ireland wants soccer justice." November 19. NBC Sports. http://nbcsports.msnbc.com/ (accessed December 1, 2009).

NCCRI. 2002. Report of Incidents Related to Racism, October 2001 to April 2002. Report. NCCRI. http://www.nccri.ie/ (accessed December 1, 2009).

———. 2003. "Submission to the Draft Public Service Broadcasting Charter for RTE." Submission. National Consultative Committee on Racism and Interculturalism. August. http://www.nccri.ie/ (accessed May 2, 2010).

NCCRI and Equality Authority Ireland. 2003. *Case Study: Media Coverage of Refugee and Asylum Seekers in Ireland*. Dublin: NCCRI and Equality Authority Ireland.

N'Diaye, Pap. 2007. *La Condition Noire: Essai sur une minorité française*. Paris: Calmann-Lévy.

Nelson, Bruce. 2007. "'Come Out of Such a Land, You Irishmen': Daniel O'Connell, American Slavery, and the Making of the 'Irish Race.'" *Éire-Ireland*. 42.1 and 42.2 (Earrach/Samhradh/Spring/Summer): 58–81.

Ni Cheallaigh, Gillian. 2001. "Talks on Tallaght bus violence break down." *Irish Times*. April 4. http://www.irishtimes.com/ (accessed April 2, 2010).

Nigerian Guardian. 2005. "35 Nigerians repatriated from Ireland." *Nigerian Guardian*. March 17. http://nm.onlinenigeria.com/ (accessed July 23, 2008).

Nine News. 2005. "Ciaran Mullooly, Midlands Correspondent, reports as six Nigerian children remain in hiding." March 25. http://www.rte.ie/ (accessed July 8, 2008).

Nossiter, Adam. 2007. "Whites Take a Majority on New Orleans's Council." *New York Times*. November 20. http://www.nytimes.com/ (accessed June 25, 2009).

NPR. 2010. "A Look at Haiti's Political History." *All Things Considered*. January 18. http://www.npr.org/ (accessed January 20, 2010).

Nussbaum, Martha C. 1999. *Sex and Social Justice*. New York: Oxford University Press.

Nussbaum, Martha, and Amartya Sen. 1993. *The Quality of Life*. New York: Oxford University Press.

O'Brien, Jason. 2006. "Church leaders in plea to Afghan strikers." *Irish Independent*. May 19. http://www.irishindependent.ie/ (accessed January 12, 2010).

Onyejelem, Chinedu. 2009. "Nigerians to face off in Dublin 15." *Metro Éireann*. January 22. http://metroeireann.com/ (accessed February 5, 2009).

ORAC. 2001–2003. *Office of the Refugee Applications Commissioner Annual Reports*. http://www.orac.ie/ (accessed September 11, 2011).

———. 2002. *Office of the Refugee Applications Commissioner Annual Report*. Statistics. http://www.orac.ie/ (accessed April 19, 2010).

———. 2009. *Office of the Refugee Applications Commissioner Monthly Report*. December. http://www.orac.ie/ (accessed April 19, 2010).

Owen, Mark. 2010. "France 24, The Debate: French Identity. Where next?" France 24. February 8. http://www.france24.com/ (accessed February 9, 2010).

Oxygène. 2006. "Dossier: Programme de rénovation urbaine." *Oxygène* 244 (July/August): 10–13.

Oxygène Hebdo. 2009. "Ancien Garage Renault: Les Pelleteuses sont entrées en action." May 6. http://oxygenehebdo.fr/ (accessed February 2, 2010).

Pathak, Avijit. 2006. *Modernity, globalization and identity: towards a reflexive quest*. Delhi: Aakar Books.

Perry, Alex. 2009. *Falling Off the Edge: Globalization, World Peace and Other Lies*. New York: Macmillan.

Peters, Friederike. 2005. "Berlin Car Fires May Be Inspired by French Rioters, Police Say." *Bloomberg News.* November 7. http://www.bloomberg.com (accessed February 1, 2010).

Piot, Charles. 1999. *Remotely Global: Village Modernity in West Africa.* Chicago: University of Chicago Press.

Plyer, Allison. 2010. "Neighborhood Recovery Rates." Greater New Orleans Community Data Center. July. Available at http://www.neworleansindustrial.com/admin/newsfiles/GNOCDC_NeighborhoodRecoveryJune2010.pdf (accessed August 24, 2011).

PolicyLink. 2008. *A Long Way Home: The State of Housing Recovery in Louisiana 2008.* PolicyLink Report. August. http://www.policylink.com/ (accessed June 26, 2009).

Power, Ann-Marie. 2007. "Missing in Athlone." Documentary on One. RTE Radio 1, December 16. http://www.rte.ie/ (accessed July 8, 2008).

Power, Con. 2007. "The multi-cultural retail face of Moore Street." *Irish Independent.* May 2. http://www.independent.ie/ (accessed April 18, 2010).

Price, Gregory. 2008. "Hurricane Katrina: Was There a Political Economy of Death?" *Social Science Research Network.* September 16. http://ssrn.com/ (accessed June 2, 2009).

Pries, Ludger, ed. 2001. *New Transnational Social Spaces: International Migration and Transnational Companies in the Early Twenty-First Century.* London: Routledge.

PRU. 2005. *Aulnay-Sous-Bois, Programme de Rénovation Urbaine 2005–2011.* Brochure. http://www.aulnaysousbois.com/ (accessed January 20, 2010).

Pulham, Sheila. 2005. "Inflammatory Language." *Guardian Unlimited,* news blog, November 8. http://blogs.guardian.co.uk/ (accessed August 30, 2007).

Putterford, Mark. 2002. *Phil Lynott: The Rocker.* London: Omnibus.

Quarles, Benjamin. 1991. *Black Abolitionists.* Cambridge, Mass.: Da Capo Press.

Ramadan, Tariq. 2006. "Social Fracture in France." *Islamica Magazine,* Winter 2006. http://www.islamicamagazine.com/ (accessed September 5, 2007).

Randall, Kate. 2006. "City residents denounce 'Bring New Orleans Back' rebuilding plan." *World Socialist.* January 14. http://www.wsws.org/ (accessed June 25, 2009).

RAR. 2000. "Diary on Irish Racism." April 21. Residents Against Racism. http://struggle.ws/rar/diary97to2000.html (accessed September 1, 2011).

RAR Report. 2000. *RAR Report: Newsletter of Residents Against Racism* (Summer). http://struggle.ws/rar/ekundayo_case.html (accessed September 11, 2011).

Ratner, Lizzy. 2008. "New Orleans Redraws Its Color Line." *The Nation.* September 15. http://www.thenation.com/ (accessed July 6, 2009).

Rawls, John. 1999. *Theory of Justice.* Cambridge: MIT Press.

Redmond, Declan. 2001. "Policy Review Social Housing in Ireland: Under New Management?" *European Journal of Housing Policy* 1.2: 291–306.

Reese, Carol McMichael. 2007. "History of Pontchartrain Park." Slideshow. October. Pontchartrain Park Community Development Corporation. Available at http://www.pontchartrainparkcdc.org/community/history/slideshow/ (accessed August 23, 2011).

Reid, John P. 1987. *The Concept of Liberty in the Age of the American Revolution*. Chicago: University of Chicago Press.

Reilly, Catherine. 2007. "Nigerian boy back with mum." *Metro Éireann*. August 23. http://www.metroeirrean.ie/ (accessed July 9, 2008).

———. 2009. "Igbo 'king' hits out at critics." September 10. *Metro Éireann*. http://www.metroeireann.com/ (accessed September 14, 2009).

Remond, Charles Lenox. 1841. Speech given before a meeting of the Hibernian Anti-Slavery Society, November 19, published in *The Liberator*. Available at the University of Detroit Mercy Black Abolitionist Archive, doc. no. 06378. http://research.udmercy.edu/ (accessed November 12, 2010).

RIA. 2010. *Reception and Integration Agency—Monthly Statistics*. Report. Reception and Integration Agency. January. http://www.ria.gov.ie/ (accessed April 19, 2010).

Roberston, Campbell. 2009. "Ruling on Katrina Flooding Favors Homeowners." *New York Times*. November 18. http://www.nytimes.com/ (accessed August 24, 2011).

Robertson, Roland. 1983. "Interpreting Globality." In *World Realities and International Studies Today*. 7–20. Glenside: Pennsylvania Council on International Education.

———. 1992. *Globalization: Social Theory and Global Culture*. Thousand Oaks, Calif.: Sage.

Robison, Clay, and Peggy O'Hare. 2005. "23,000 Superdome refugees boarding buses for Astrodome." *Houston Chronicle,* August 31. http://www.chron.com/ (accessed July 10, 2007).

Rodgers, Nini. 1997. "Equiano in Belfast: A Study of the Anti-slavery Ethos in a Northern Town." *Slavery and Abolition* 18.2: 73–89.

———. 2007. *Ireland, Slavery and Anti-Slavery, 1612–1865*. London: Palgrave Macmillan.

Rodgers, William M., III 2004. "The African-American Experience in the Recent Recession and Job Loss Recovery." Center for American Progress, January 14. http://www.americanprogress.org/ (accessed August 30, 2007).

Rodriguez, Juana. 2003. *Queer Latinidad: Identity Practices, Discursive Spaces*. New York: NYU Press.

RottenFrance. 2007a. "My Life in France, Introduction, Part 2." August 20. YouTube. http://www.youtube.com/user/rottenfrance/ (accessed January 22, 2010).

———. 2007b. "Racism in France—Part One." August 21. YouTube. http://www.youtube.com/user/rottenfrance/ (accessed January 22, 2010).

RTÉ. 2000. "Dublin bus driver convicted under Incitement to Hatred Act." *RTÉ 9.00 News*. September 22. http://www.rte.ie/news/ (accessed April 21, 2010).

———. 2001. "Bus driver has incitement to hatred conviction quashed." *RTÉ 9.00 News*. March 12. http://www.rte.ie/news/ (accessed April 21, 2010).

———. 2005a. "TUI joins call for return of Nigerian student." *RTÉ News*. March 23. http://www.rte.ie/ (accessed September 1, 2007).

———. 2005b. "Deported Nigerian student back in Ireland." *Six One News*. April 1. http://www.rte.ie/ (accessed September 1, 2007).

———. 2005c. "Robert Shortt, Washington Correspondent, and Paul Cunningham reflect on what they have seen of Hurricane Katrina's devastation and its aftermath." *Morning Ireland.* Sept. 9. http://www.rte.ie/ (accessed September 1, 2007).

———. 2005d. "French government in bid to quell Paris riots." *Prime Time.* November 8. http://www.rte.ie/ (accessed August 30, 2007).

———. 2005e. "France suffers worst night of rioting to date." *Morning Ireland.* November 7. Interview with French Ambassador Frédéric Grasset. http://www.rte.ie/ (accessed September 1, 2007).

———. 2005f. "Tenth night of violence in French cities." November 5. http://www.rte.ie/ (accessed September 1, 2007).

Sachs, Susan. 2007. "Blacks in France: We Have a Dream, Too." *Christian Science Monitor.* January 14. http://www.csmonitor.com (accessed August 30, 2007).

Sadiki, Larbi. 2011. "The Egypt-Tunisia freedom council." *Al Jazeera.* February 27. http://english.aljazeera.net/ (accessed March 11, 2011).

Said, Edward W. 1978. *Orientalism.* New York: Pantheon.

Salvatore, Armando. 2007. "Authority in Question: Secularity, Republicanism and 'Communitarianism' in the Emerging Euro-Islamic Public Sphere." *Theory, Culture & Society* 24.2: 135–160.

Samuel, Henry. 2005. "20 die as fire sweeps through Paris hotel." April 16. *Telegraph.* http://www.telegraph.co.uk/ (accessed February 1, 2010).

———. 2009a. "President Nicolas Sarkozy to push Rama Yade out of government." *Telegraph.* January 28. http://www.telegraph.co.uk/ (accessed November 20, 2009).

———. 2009b. "Rama Yade told to 'shut your gob or quit' French government." November 4. *Telegraph.* http://www.telegraph.co.uk/ (accessed January 21, 2010).

———. 2010. "French minister defends national identity debate." *Telegraph.* January 4. http://www.telegraph.co.uk/ (accessed February 2, 2010).

Sanke, Andrea (2008) "'The Interview on France 24'—episode: Considering the Black Condition." France 24. June 16. http://www.france24.com/ (accessed January 30, 2010).

Sassen, Saskia. 1991. *The Global City: New York, London, Tokyo.* Princeton, N.J.: Princeton University Press.

———. 1998. *Globalization and Its Discontents.* New York: New Press.

———. 2004. "Global Cities and Survival Circuits." In Barbara Ehrenreich and Arlie Russell Hochschild, eds., *Global Woman: Nannies, Maids, and Sex Workers in the New Economy.* 254–274. New York: Holt.

Sasser, Bill. 2006. "Locking out New Orleans' poor." Salon.com. June 12. http://salon.com/news/ (accessed September 6, 2007).

Schäfer, Wolf. 2007. "Lean Globality Studies." May 28. *Globality Studies Journal* 7. http://www.stonybrook.edu/globality/ (accessed March 6, 2011).

Schnoebelen, Jill. 2009. "Witchcraft allegations, refugee protection and human rights: A review of the evidence." Research paper #169, UNHCR. January 10. Geneva: Policy Development and Evaluation Service. Available at http://www.unhcr.org/ (accessed November 20, 2010).

Schofield, Hugh. 2005. "Paris fires highlight housing shortage." BBC News. August 30. http://news.bbc.co.uk/ (accessed February 2, 2010).

Scott, Rebecca J. 2005. *Degrees of Freedom: Louisiana and Cuba after Slavery.* Cambridge, Mass.: Belknap Press of Harvard University Press.

Segesvary, Victor. 2001. *From Illusion to Delusion: Globalization and the Contradictions of Late Modernity.* Lanham, Md.: University Press of America.

Seanad Éireann. 2005. Adjournment Matters. "Asylum Applications," volume 179. March 24. http://debates.oireachtas.ie/seanad/ (accessed August 21, 2011).

Sen, Amartya. 1999. *Development as Freedom.* Oxford: Oxford University Press.

Shadare, Wole. 2005. "258 Nigerians deported in two months." *Nigerian Guardian.* October 12. http://nm.onlinenigeria.com/ (accessed July 22, 2008).

Sharkey, Patrick. 2007. "Survival and Death in New Orleans: An Empirical Look at the Human Impact of Katrina." *Journal of Black Studies* 37: 482–501.

Sherman, Arloc, and Isaac Shapiro. 2005. "Essential facts about the victims of Hurricane Katrina." Center on Budget and Policy Priorities, September 19. http://www.cbpp.org/ (accessed August 30, 2007).

Shirbon, Estelle. 2009. "Hint of ethnic statistics breaches French taboo." Reuters. March 17. http://www.reuters.com/ (accessed November 15, 2009).

Simon, Patrick, Malika Chafi, and Thomas Kirszbaum. 2001. Les Discriminations raciales et ethniques dans l'accès au logement social. May. Report. Paris: Groupe D'Etude et De Lutte contre Les Discriminations. http://www.ladocumentation-francaise.fr/rapports-publics/ (accessed December 1, 2009).

Simons, Stefan. 2007. "Sarkozy Stays Loyal to Increasingly Divisive Minister." *Der Spiegel International* (English). October 4. http://www.spiegel.de/international/europe/ (accessed March 15, 2010).

Sinha, Shalini. 1998. "The Right to Irishness: Implications of Ethnicity, Nation and State towards a Truly Multi-Ethnic Ireland." In Ronit Lentin, ed., *The Expanding Nation: Towards a Multi-ethnic Ireland.* 21–25. Dublin: Publication of the Ethnic and Racial Studies Program, Department of Sociology, Trinity College Dublin.

Smith, Michael P., and Luis E. Guarnizo. 1998. *Transnationalism from Below.* New Brunswick, N.J.: Transaction Publishers.

Smolar, Piotr. 2003. "Sarkozy face à la discrimination positive." *Le Monde.* November 15. http://www.lemonde.fr/ (accessed July 23, 2007).

Socialist Party News. 2005. "McDowell forced to back down on Kunle deportation." March 28. http://www.socialistparty.net/ (accessed September 6, 2007).

sos Racisme. 2009. "Sondage du CRAN: la diversion continue!" sos Racisme Press Release. April 29. http://www.sos-racisme.org/ (accessed November 20, 2009).

Spalding, Nancy. 2000. "A Cultural Explanation of Collapse into Civil War: Escalation of Tension in Nigeria." *Culture & Psychology* 6.1: 51–87.

Stanislavski, Constantin. 1989. *An Actor Prepares.* London: Routledge.

Stanton, William. 1982. *The Leopard's Spots: Scientific Attitudes toward Race in America, 1815–59.* Chicago: University of Chicago Press.

Steger, Manfred B. 2001.*Globalism: The New Market Ideology.* Lanham, Md.: Rowman and Littlefield.

Sublette, Ned. 2008. *The World That Made New Orleans: From Spanish Silver to Congo Square.* Chicago: Lawrence Hill Books.

Sullivan, Kevin. 2005. "How Could This Be Happening in the United States?" *Washington Post*. September 4. http://www.washingtonpost.com/ (accessed August 30, 2007).

Tagliabue, John. 2005. "Blacks in France fight equality bind." *International Herald Tribune*. http://www.iht.com/ (accessed July 27, 2007).

The Slate. 2001a. "Blacky Music Is Taking Over." September 2001: 15.

———. 2001b. "Racist Crossword." September 2001: 10.

Thomas, Debora A. 2004. *Modern Blackness: Nationalism, Globalization, and the Politics of Culture in Jamaica*. Durham, N.C.: Duke University Press.

Thomas, Dominic. 2006. *Black France: Colonialism, Immigration, and Transnationalism*. Bloomington: Indiana University Press.

Thompson, Robert Farris. 1984. *Flash of the Spirit: African and Afro-American Art and Philosophy*. New York: Random House.

Thompson, Vincent Bakpetu. 2000. *Africans of the Diaspora: The Evolution of African Consciousness and Leadership in the Americas*. Trenton, N.J.: Africa World Press.

Tissot, Sylvie. 2007. "L'invention des 'quartiers sensibles.'" *Le Monde Diplomatique*. August. http://www.monde-diplomatique.fr (accessed January 27, 2010).

Tissot, Sylvie, and Franck Poupeau. 2005. "La spatialisation des problèmes sociaux." *Actes de la recherche en sciences sociales* 159 (September): 5–9.

Tocqueville, Alexis de. 1835. *Democracy in America*. Charlottesville: American Studies Program, University of Virginia. http://xroads.virginia.edu/~HYPER/DETOC/home.html (accessed June 19, 2008).

Tossa, Mustapha. 2007. "France: Le charme rompu de Rachida Dati." *Aujourd'hui La Maroc*. http://www.aujourdhui.ma/ (accessed January 21, 2010).

Tracy, Marshall. 2000. *Racism and Immigration in Ireland: A Comparative Analysis*. Dublin: Publication of the Ethnic and Racial Studies Program, Department of Sociology, Trinity College Dublin.

Ugba, Abel. 2009. *Shades of Belonging: African Pentecostals in Twenty-first century Ireland*. Trenton, N.J.: Africa World Press.

Ukeje, Charles. 2001. "Youths, Violence and the Collapse of Public Order in the Niger Delta of Nigeria." *Africa Development* 26.1 and 26.2: 337–366.

United Nations General Assembly. 1960. Declaration on the Granting of Independence to Colonial Countries and Peoples. http://www.unhcr.org/ (accessed January 20, 2006).

United Nations High Commissioner for Refugees. 1983. The Problem of Manifestly Unfounded or Abusive Applications for Refugee Status or Asylum. Report. October 20. Geneva: UNHCR. http://www.unhcr.org/ (accessed March 25, 2011).

———. 2002. "Congo and DRC: Identity cards for refugees and asylum seekers." UNHCR. November 22. http://www.unhcr.org/ (accessed February 5, 2009).

———. 2004. "Ireland grants refugees and asylum seekers right to vote." UNHCR News Stories. April 30. http://www.unhcr.org/ (accessed April 2, 2010).

———. 2010. UN High Commissioner for Refugees, Protecting Refugees. Report. Geneva: UNHCR. http://www.unhcr.org/ (accessed March 25, 2011).

United Nations Human Rights Council (UNHRC). 2009. Report by Mr. Doudou Diène, Special Rapporteur on contemporary forms of racism, racial discrimination, xenophobia, and related intolerance. Addendum: Mission to United States of America. April 28. http://www.unhcr.org/refworld/ (accessed July 1, 2009).

U.S. Army Corps of Engineers. 2011. "Katrina Claims Information." U.S. Army Corps of Engineers, Team New Orleans. January 27. Available at http://www.mvn.usace. army.mil/oc/katrina_claim.asp (accessed August 24, 2011).

U.S. Census. 2010. "Profile of General Population and Housing Characteristics: 2010, New Orleans city, Louisiana." United States Census Bureau. http://factfinder2 .census.gov/ (accessed August, 23, 2011).

USCRI. 2000. "U.S. Committee for Refugees World Refugee Survey 2000—Ireland." U.S. Committee for Refugees and Immigrants. June 1. UNHCR. http://www.unhcr .org/refworld/ (accessed April 18, 2010).

Van Dijk, Teun A. 1992. "Discourse and the denial of racism." *Discourse & Society* 3.1: 87–118.

Van Eeckhout, Laetitia. 2009. "Diversité: une majorité de Français favorable aux en- quêtes statistiques." *Le Monde.* April 28. http://www.lemonde.fr/ (accessed De- cember 8, 2009).

———. 2010. "Un rapport consensuel sur les statistiques ethniques." *Le Monde.* Feb- ruary 5. http://www.lemonde.fr/societe/ (accessed February 6, 2010).

Van Hear, Nicholas. 1998. *New Diasporas: The Mass Exodus, Dispersal and Regroup- ing of Migrant Communities.* Seattle: University of Washington Press.

Vernet, Henri. 2009. "Identité nationale: le débat trouble les Français." *Le Parisien.* December 21. http://www.leparisien.com/ (accessed January 20, 2010).

Vertovec, Steven. 1997. "Three Meanings of 'Diaspora' Exemplified among South Asian Religions." *Diaspora* 6.3: 277–299.

———. 1999. "Conceiving and researching transnationalism." *Ethnic and Racial Stud- ies* 22.2: 447–462.

———. 2001. "Transnationalism and identity." *Journal of Ethnic and Migration Stud- ies* 27.4: 573–582.

Walker, Adrian. 2005. "'Refugees' in their land." *Boston Globe.* September 5. http:// www.boston.com/ (accessed July 30, 2007).

Walker, David. 1993. *David Walker's Appeal.* Baltimore, Md.: Black Classic Press.

Walsh, Anne-Marie. 2006. "Probe into alleged landlord racism." *Irish Independent.* February 7. http://www.irishindependent.ie/ (accessed January 12, 2010).

Ward, Tanya. 2001. *Immigration and Residency in Ireland.* Dublin: Publication of City of Dublin Vocational Education Committee (CDVEC). Available online at the Irish Center for Migration Studies website: http://migration.ucc.ie/ (accessed July 25, 2011).

Warren, Bob. 2006. "Rental Policy Called Discriminatory." *Times-Picayune.* Septem- ber 27. http://www.nola.com/ (accessed July 13, 2009).

Waters, Malcolm. 1995. *Globalization.* London: Routledge.

WDSU. 2008. "Group Trying to Redevelop Pontchartrain Park." WDSU. October 20. http://www.wdsu.com/news/ (accessed June 30, 2009).

Webster, Paul, Rory Carroll, and Pierre Tran. 2002. "A New French Revolution." *Guardian Observer.* April 28. http://www.observer.co.uk (accessed April 29, 2002).

Weil, Patrick. 1996. "Nationalities and Citizenships: The Lessons of the French Experience for Germany and Europe." In David Cesarani and Mary Fulbrook, eds., *Citizenship, Nationality, and Migration in Europe*. 74–87. New York: Routledge.

———. 2009. *How to Be French: Nationality in the Making since 1789*. Raleigh, N.C.: Duke University Press.

Weil, Patrick, Alexis Spire, and Christophe Bertossi. 2010. "EUDO Citizenship Observatory Country Report: France." April. European Union Democracy Observatory. Florence, Italy: European University Institute. Available at http://eudo citizenship .eu/docs/CountryReports/France.pdf (accessed August 25, 2011).

White, Elisa J. 2002a. "The New Irish Storytelling: Media, Representations and Racialized Identities." In Ronit Lentin and Robbie McVeigh, eds., *Racism and Anti-Racism in Ireland*. 102–128. Belfast: Beyond the Pale Publications.

———. 2002b. "Forging African Diaspora Spaces in Dublin's Retro-Global Spaces: Minority Making in a New Global City." *City: Analysis of urban trends, culture, theory, policy, action* 6.2: 251–270.

———. 2009a. "Paradoxes of Diaspora, Global Identity and Human Rights: The Deportation of Nigerians in Ireland." *African and Black Diaspora: An International Journal* 2.1: 67–83.

———. 2009b. "'You're Very Welcome': Considering the African Diaspora, Race and Human Rights in Contemporary Ireland." *Journal of Irish Studies* 24: 15–26.

Willett, Cynthia. 1998. *Theorizing Multiculturalism: A Guide to the Current Debate*. Malden, Mass.: Blackwell.

Williams, Leslie, and Coleman Warner. 2007. "N.O. may idle housing in east: Multifamily sites worry neighbors." March 8. http://www.nola.com/ (accessed July 14, 2009).

Winters, John D. 1991. *The Civil War in Louisiana*. Baton Rouge: Louisiana State University Press.

Xclusive. 2009. "What is Xclusive?" *Xclusive* website. 2006–2009. http://www.xclusive .ie/ (accessed April 10, 2010).

Yadan, Thomas. 2007a. "Combattre les discriminations." *Evene*. March. http://www .evene.fr/ (accessed January 20, 2010).

———. 2007b. "La cécité républicaine." *Evene*. May. http://www.evene.fr/ (accessed January 20, 2010).

Young, Cathy. 2006. "Katrina's racial paranoia." *Boston Globe*. January 16. http://www .boston.com/ (accessed August 30, 2007).

Young, Robert J. C. 2001. *Postcolonialism: An Historical Introduction*. Oxford: Blackwell.

Zafirovski, Milan. 2007. *Liberal Modernity and its Adversaries: Freedom, Liberalism and Anti-Liberalism in the Twenty-first Century*. Leiden: Brill.

INDEX

abolitionists, 32–34

About Adam, 68

"Action Plan for New Orleans: The New American City," 201–202

An Actor Prepares (Stanislavski), 80–81

actors, African, 65, 77, 79–84, 276, 288n4

Adebari, Rotimi, 47

Adigun, Bisi, 65, 72, 81, 83–84, 86

African Americans, 104; African views of, 24–25. *See also* African Diaspora community, New Orleans; Hurricane Katrina; New Orleans

African Diaspora communities: black identities, 25–26; as challenge to prior socio-cultural formations, 47, 147–149, 243; class distinctions within, 70–71, 145–146, 197–198, 212; democracy, relation to, 13–14; as distant localities, 11; equality restricted for, 19; interrogations/exposures of social regression, 2, 16–18, 20–21, 41, 177–178, 201, 227, 231, 263–266; liminal space, 19; limits on freedom, 274–275; non-monolithic, 26, 71, 143, 148; presence of, 33–34, 47

African Diaspora community, France: citizenship and, 217–221, 224–225, 227; interrogation of social re-

gression, 217; myth of, as noncitizens, 225, 260. *See also* citizenship, France; Paris *banlieues,* 2005 protest

African Diaspora community, Ireland, 283n2; beliefs about other groups, 115; businesses, 61–62, 66–67; children's experiences, 91–93, 97–98, 106, 108, 115–116; class status among immigrants, 145–146; community-building, 142–149; financial assistance within community, 124–125; friendships, 91–92; housing, 55–60, 67; inaugurals, 64–67; infantilization of, 57–58; inter-ethnic relations, 127, 130–131, 141, 145–149, 148; interrogation of homelands, 146–147; IT workers, 96–98, 107; loss of autonomy and, 105–108; outsiders, 113–114; potential permanence of, 54, 62, 86, 143; public places, discomfort in, 140–141; resident status, 22, 55–56, 86, 111, 120, 124–125; royalty, 111, 146; socio-cultural landscape and, 147–149; space and, 60–62; theater projects, 76–84; young age of immigrants, 124. *See also* asylum seekers, Ireland; employment, Ireland; Parnell Street community ("Little Africa," Dublin)

African Diaspora community, New Orleans: Frenchness of, 186–187; limited return of, 184; middle class, African American, 196–197, 200–201, 206–210; pre-Katrina statistics, 183; race, class, and removal, 206–210. *See also* Hurricane Katrina; New Orleans

"Africans in Eighteenth-Century Ireland" (Hart), 31–32

Africans Magazine, 65, 71

Afro-Caribbeans, 55, 287n9

Afro Celt Sound System (musical group), 84

After Optimism? Ireland, Racism, and Globalisation (McVeigh and Lentin), 49

Ahern, Bertie, 169, 176

Ahern, Dermot, 260

Albrow, Martin, 11–12

Aliens Act (Ireland, 1935), 36

Aliens (Amendment) Order of 1946, 36

Allen, William G., 33, 284n4

Amara, Fadela, 237–238

American Civil War, 187–188

American Dream, 189; 1970s New Orleans, 208; marred by racism, 197, 201; modernity and, 198–199; post-WWII fantasies, 206, 210; segregated housing, 196–197. *See also* United States

Amnesty International, 96, 106, 287n6, 290n7

Anglo-Saxons and Celts: A Study of Anti-Irish Prejudice in Victorian England (Curtis), 44–45

Angola, 100–101, 147

Angolan Community Association, 138

Annual Return of Registered Aliens, 52

Anny-Nzekwue, Peter, 71, 84

"anomalies" of modernity, 2, 21, 82, 170, 181, 189, 274–275

anti-colonial movements, 43

Anti-Deportation Campaign, 89–91

anti-immigrant commentary, 69

Anti-Racism Campaign (ARC), 138

anti-racist groups: France, 243–245, 249–250; Ireland, 65, 89–91, 138, 153, 290n3

Appadurai, Arjun, 9

Army Corps of Engineers, 213

arts community, Ireland, 68, 173–175

ascribed differences, 8–9

assimilation, 16, 160; color-blind model, 228, 229, 262; French ideas, 184, 217–218, 220–221, 227–228, 237, 257, 268, 282

Association of Refugees and Asylum-Seekers in Ireland, 140

asylum applications, Ireland, 51–54; "application refusal," 90, 98; approval, 102; "fast track" procedures, 51, 155, 169, 290n7; fear of rejection, 55–56; "humanitarian right to remain," 91, 98, 157, 172–173, 286n1; "manifestly unfounded track," 90; "unfounded," 153

asylum seekers, Ireland, 16, 22; aged-out separated children, 162–163, 172; black presence reduced to, 51–53, 147, 223; daily "sign-ins," 155; denied social welfare, 58; "double-speak" about, 168–169; gradations of skin color, 77; identity cards, 63; imprisonment, 90, 153, 163, 171; isolation of, 56–59, 67; precarious position of, 154; represented in theater projects, 77–78; stories, 89–91; underground aspect, 128–129. *See also* African Diaspora community, Ireland; Nigerians, deportation of

Athlone community (Ireland), 175–176

The Autobiography of Louis Hughes, Thirty Years a Slave; from Bondage to Freedom, the Institution of Slavery as Seen on the Plantation and in the Home of the Planter (Hughes), 59–60

Backsher, Lucia, 209–210
Badon, Austin, 208
Baka Beyond (musical group), 84
Baker, Richard, 184, 193
Baldwin, James, 263
Balzano, Wanda, 46
Baudrillard, Jean, 13
Beck, Ulrich, 6–7, 8–9
Bed and Breakfast accommodations, for asylum seekers, 56–60
Beddoe, John, 44
belief, loss of, 7–8
Benna, Zyed, 217, 266, 276
Berlin, Isaiah, 20
Berrigan, Ginger, 210
Besson, Eric, 252, 258
Biafran war, 130, 145, 292n8
Bibliothèque Elsa Triolet, 270–271
Billig, Michael, 74
Black Actors Workshop, 65, 77, 79–84, 276, 288n4
Black Baby boxes, 34–35, 76, 77
Black Baby identity, 158, 162, 281
"Black Day at Black Rock," 68
Black European Studies conference, 268
"Black or Black Irish" category, 54
Black Skin, White Masks (Fanon), 221–222
Blitzer, Wolf, 182
Boston Globe, 182
Boucher-Hayes, Philip, 176
Bradford, Calvin, 210
Breen, Claire, 58
"Bring Back New Orleans" Commission, 193, 201–204
Brown, Jacqueline Nassy, 45
Brown University study, 198, 202
Burton, Joan, 164–165
Bush, George W., 181, 184–185, 210, 229, 280–281

Cafferty, Jack, 182
Canal Plus, 227
capabilities, 20

Capo, Bill, 201
Casey, Noel, 176
Catholicism, Irish, 34–35
Cavendish Row (Upper O'Connell Street), 88
Center for the Care of Survivors of Torture, 173–174
Césaire, Aimé, 231
charities, Irish, 34–35, 76, 77
Chase, Edgar, III, 228
Chevigny, Marie-Noelle de, 233, 265–266
children: adult asylum seekers depicted as, 154, 162, 168–169; aged-out separated asylum seekers, 162–163, 172; as asylum seekers, 158–159, 162–163; deportation of, 173, 175; "exceptional orphans," 158–159, 162; experiences in Ireland, 91, 92–93, 97–98, 106, 108, 115–116, 176
Chonaill, Aine Ní, 69
Christianity, 160, 175
Cissé, Makhete, 258
cities, global, 13, 47
citizenship, 41; Ireland, 54, 285n1; *jus soli,* 54, 220–221, 286n12; United States, 188–190, 195
citizenship, France: African Diaspora community in France, 217–219, 224–225, 227; application for, 220–221; "inassimilability" of African immigrants, 224; myth of blacks as noncitizens, 225, 260
city, global, 47, 190
City Planning Commission (New Orleans), 203
civil rights, France, 226
civil rights movement, United States, 181
civilization, discourse of, 6, 38, 40–41
clash of civilizations, 13
class: distinctions within African Diaspora communities, 70–71, 145–146, 197–198, 212; race and, 206–210
Clinton, Bill, 280

127–128, 131, 137, 142, 275; import/
export businesses, 127, 128, 131; informal (off the books), 124; professionals, 107, 144–146; prohibition
of, 59, 169; work permits, 50, 52, 61,
284n1
end of progress, 8, 10, 11–12
Equal Status Act 2000, 55
equality: curtailed for asylum seekers, 58–59; eighteenth-century notions of, 2; freedom and, 18, 21; of
freedom, 21; as potentiality, 3, 13–14;
as racially specific, 179; restricted for
African Diaspora, 19
Equality and Law Reform, 90
Equality Authority, 52, 55
Equiano, Olaudah, 26
Eternity (hangout place), 124, 125–128,
135
Etzioni, Amitai, 229
European Economic Area (EEA), 50
European Economic Community (EEC),
37
European identity, 156–157
European Union (EU), 37, 45, 50; au-
thorities for investigating discrimi-
nation, 232; Dublin Conventions,
223–224
European Union Equality Directives, 55
Eurostat report, 246
evolution, concept of, 234

"Fair City" (soap opera), 72, 288n4
Fair Housing Act of 1968, 196, 207–
208, 209
Family Unity and Employment Op-
portunity Immigration Act of 1990
(United States), 157–158, 161, 174
Fanon, Frantz, 221–222
Federal Emergency Management
Agency (FEMA), 185, 212
Fela Kuti, 133–134
Fillon, François, 257–259
Fireside, Harvey, 189–190

firsts. See inaugurals
Flatley, Michael, 83
Fleet, Ian, 268
Flynn, Rosanna, 177
Foner, Eric, 20
Forum Café Bar, 65, 66–67, 112, 122–
124, 132
Fourteenth Amendment, 189
Fourth of July, 17–18
France, 13; 1974 ban on immigration,
222; African immigrants, 217, 218,
223–224; anti-racist groups, 243–
245, 249–250; Aulnay-sous-Bois,
266–273; burqa ban debate, 256, 257;
color-blind model of assimilation,
228, 229, 262; Constitution, Article
1, 242; core belief system, 234; criminalization discourse, 217, 225, 266;
desire to remove blacks, 220; discrimination authority, 232–233; diversity statistics, 234–235, 242–252,
267, 276; documentation, 217, 253–
254, 261, 276; egalitarianism, 16,
217–218, 237, 240, 261–263, 271; employment, 232, 233, 245–246, 249,
265–266, 271; gender discrimination,
245, 248; Haitian earthquake and,
278–280; identity of blacks checked,
217, 253–254, 261; "inassimilability"
of African immigrants, 224; migration to, 222; Muslim communities,
218, 223–224, 228, 257–258; national
identity, 221–222, 224, 230, 242, 251–
260, 295n9; ongoing colonization,
234; Parliament, lack of black representation in, 230; political appointments, 237–241; positive discrimination, 227, 229–230, 236; racialization,
185; republican values, 218, 221, 235–
237, 243, 253–254, 257–258, 263, 277,
279; Rights of Man concept, 189,
233, 234, 252, 279; sans papiers individuals, 225, 226, 276, 294n1; statistical data not recorded, 218, 220,

Hannerz, Ulf, 9, 14
harmonizing formula, 7
Hart, William A., 31–32
Healy-Rae, Jackie, 289n5
Henry, Thierry, 259
Héran, François, 242, 249, 251
Heritage Magazine, 61, 65, 70–71
Hesse, Barnor, 39
Hibernian Anti-Slavery Society, 32
Higgins, Joe, 161–162, 164, 170–171
High Authority for the Fight against
    Discrimination and for Equality
    (HALDE), 232–233, 251
homelands, interrogation of, 146–147
Hot Press, 73
House, Jim, 223–224
housing, Ireland, 55–60, 67, 91–93, 148;
    alternative, 104; conditions, 93–96;
    cooking prohibited, 57, 91, 93, 95,
    102; Dundalk, 117–119; flats, 91, 102,
    116–117, 124, 132–133; food strikes, 93,
    94, 106, 277; Kilkenny hostel, 93–96;
    opposition to Dispersal Scheme, 58;
    protests at, 93, 94–95; rent supple-
    ments, 56, 60
housing, New Orleans: blood-relative
    ordinance, 209; diversity, meanings
    of, 206–207; fair housing violations,
    196, 207–208; federally assisted,
    202, 204–205; home ownership, 199,
    208–210, 212–213, 267, 275; inter-
    section of race and class, 206–210;
    middle-class African Americans,
    206–208; "mixed-income," 202–
    204, 207, 226; multi-family housing
    moratorium, 209–210; "neighbor-
    hoods of choice," 206–207; pre-
    storm values and discrimination,
    199–200, 204, 275; rebuilding per-
    mits limited, 202, 203; rentals, 205;
    socio-geographic hierarchy, 187, 208,
    209, 267. *See also* New Orleans
housing, Paris, 217; apartment fires, 225,
    260; Aulnay-sous-Bois, 266–273;

banlieues, 2005 protest, 185, 217–220,
    222, 225–227, 266; housing condi-
    tions as racial conditions, 224–227;
    Maghreb families, 225–226; renewal
    plan, 269–270, 271–273. *See also*
    France
Housing Authority of New Orleans
    (HANO), 202, 205
Hughes, Louis, 59–60
human rights violations: Ireland, 54, 58,
    90, 106–107, 156; Nigeria, 155–156
humor, 73–76, 86
hunger strikes, Ireland, 95, 106, 169, 277
Huntington, Samuel, 13
Hurricane Betsy (1965), 195
Hurricane Katrina, 16, 40, 179–216;
    civil negligence suit, 213; French re-
    porting on, 179; inegalitarian pro-
    vision of disaster services, 183–184;
    "left to die" rhetoric, 182–183; lo-
    cation of bodies, 183; media com-
    mentary, 180–182; post-Katrina
    studies, 183–184, 198; range of socio-
    economic impact, 195–196; "selling
    Louisiana to the French," 184–186;
    slavery images, 180–181; slow re-
    sponse time, 179–181; survival nar-
    rative and, 191; UNHRC report, 213–
    216; victims as "refugees," 181–182,
    216. *See also* African Diaspora com-
    munity, New Orleans; New Orleans;
    United States

idealism, 41–42
ideas, movement of, 12
identification cards, 63–64, 288n14
identities, 25–26, 142; Creole, 187, 189;
    discursive spaces and, 277; Euro-
    pean, 156–157; French, 221; Irish na-
    tional, 46, 51–52, 54, 68–69, 149; new
    Irish, 84–87; white, 156–157. *See also*
    national identity, France
Igbo people, 111, 122–123, 125, 128, 142
Imagbe, Jay Ugi, 64

immigrants, African: loss of prior socio-economic status, 92–93, 98–99, 106, 125, 145; official status of, 50–51

immigrants, Dublin, 15–16, 22–25, 35

immigrants, France, 217, 218, 222–224; anti-immigrant discourse, 254–256

Immigration Act 1999 (Ireland), 163, 294n4

Immigration Act 2003 (Ireland), 155

Immigration Control Platform (ICP, Ireland), 69

"The Impact of Katrina: Race and Class in Storm-Damaged Neighborhoods" (Logan), 198, 202

imprisonment of immigrants, 90, 153, 163, 171

inaugurals: France, 227, 265; Ireland, 64–67, 68, 72, 276; New Orleans, 276

Incitement to Hatred Act 1989 (Ireland), 289n7

inclusion: criteria for, 49, 70, 169; modern concepts of, 158–161

individualization, 8–9

industrialization, 1, 7

Indymedia Ireland, 69

integration: France, 222–223; Ireland, 147–149, 158–160, 176–177; New Orleans, 206; retrogression and, 177

The Interesting Narrative of the Life of Olaudah Equiano, or Gustavus Vassa, the African (Equiano), 31

inter-ethnic relations: Ireland, 127, 130–131, 141, 145–149, 148; New Orleans, 207

International Federation of Association Football (FIFA), 260

International League against Racism and Anti-Semitism (LICRA), 243

International Organization for Migration, 166

Ireland: anti-racist groups, 65, 89–91, 138, 153, 290n3; bilateral readmission agreement, 50–51, 154–156, 290n7; blacks as temporary, 33, 49, 72; Celtic Tiger phenomenon, 45, 89, 284n6; censuses, 52, 84, 149; at core of postcolonialism, 42–43; documentation, 63–64, 90, 129, 146–148; early references to blacks, 31; economic globality, 38–39; as economically progressive, 48–49; European Union status, 45; Haitian earthquake and, 281; immunity to racism, perception of, 33–34; incomplete decolonization, 43–46; increased black presence, 33–34; inter-county bigotry, 86; interracial sexual relationships, 31–32, 35, 72, 134, 291n11, 291n13; as multi-diasporic site, 47; national identity, 46, 51–52, 54, 68–69, 81, 149; naturalized citizens, 285n1; as negatively racialized, 1, 3, 43, 85; new Irish, 84–87; outmigration to Liverpool, 45; perceived as homogeneous, 15, 46, 48, 49, 68; permanence of blacks in, 54, 62, 86, 143; refugees, reluctance to accept, 36–37; resistance to globality, 39; as retro-global society, 2–3, 37–38, 47–49, 54–55, 66–68, 86, 147; slavery in, 31–32; subaltern status, 3, 38, 44, 46; as "Third World" nation, 43. *See also* asylum applications, Ireland; Dublin; housing, Ireland; inaugurals; Nigerians, deportation of; space

"Ireland: Pluralism or Prejudice?" conference, 140

Irish Americans: hostility to abolitionism, 32–33; immigration legislation and, 156–157, 161, 174; negatively racialized, 85

Irish Diaspora, 35, 36; musical representation of, 84–86; resident in Ireland, 52–53; Saint Patrick's Day and, 156

Irish Examiner, 73

Irish Free State, 36

Irish Independent, 64, 167

116, 120, 143–144; polyandry, 111–112; polygamy, 121–122; professionals and, 144–145; resident status and, 116–117, 285n1; weddings, 109–116, 120, 142

Martin, Diarmuid, 167

Marx, Karl, 7

McAleese, Mary, 71

McDowell, Michael, 153–155, 162–170

McGrath, Paul, 73

McGuinness, Eithne, 77–78

McManus, Liz, 177–178

McVeigh, Robbie, 34–35, 49

media representation, France, 219–220

media representation, Hurricane Katrina, 181–182

media representation, Ireland, 68–70; Afro stories and agency, 76–84; class, 70–71

Mégret, Bruno, 248

Metro Éireann, 22, 66–67, 68, 70–71, 94; "Guess Who's Coming for the Dinner," 78–79

Middle Congo (Republic of Congo), 99, 146

Middle East, pro-democracy uprisings, 5

Minister for Justice, Equality and Law Reform, 153

Ministry for Immigration, Integration, National Identity and Development Partnership (France), 252

Mississippi River Gulf Outlet, 213

Mix-Cité, 242, 248

mobility, freedom of, 172, 183, 187

modernity: "anomalies" of, 1–2, 21, 82, 181, 189, 274–275; contemporary presence of earlier notions, 39–40, 177–178; contingent on inequalities, 1–3, 40, 67–69, 108, 172, 186, 219; core values of, 3–5, 10–12, 14–15; deportation as counter to, 172–173, 177–178; "double-speak," 168–169; duality of, 7, 12, 40; embraced and negated, 67; Enlightenment roots, 3, 5–6, 17, 296n12; failings of, 19, 40, 48, 162, 181, 183, 276, 279–280; freedom, equality, and democracy as integral to, 3–14; ideological impact on discourse and policies, 4–5; inclusion, concepts of, 158–160; interrogation of, by African Diaspora, 2–3, 16–18; measurement of, 1–2; multiple modernities, 4, 14; "new," 8–9; non-Eurocentric, non-Western-centric, 6, 9–10; past, distancing from, 11, 40, 45, 157, 262–263, 280, 282; persistence of myth in face of inequality, 280–282; as potentiality, 3, 13–14, 277–278; poverty and, 21, 172; progress rhetoric, 1–2, 19, 68–69; protest, themes of, 4–5; racialization and, 39–41, 44, 49, 54; reflexive, 6–8; "retro," 180–181; self-monitoring, 6; sense of loss, 179; stages of, 6, 9

Le Monde, 179, 250

Mono (television program), 65, 72, 81

Monshengwo, Kensika, 84

Moore Street (Dublin), 60, 65–66, 88–89, 290n2

Moore Street Mall (Dublin), 62

Morano, Nadine, 239

Morial, Ernest N., 190

Morial, Marc H., 182, 190

Morning Ireland, 173

Morrison, Bruce A., 157–158

Morrison scheme, 157–158, 161

Mouvement National Républicain, 248

Movement Against Racism and for Friendship among Peoples (MRAP), 230–231, 243

multiculturalism, 39, 48, 72, 214–215

multiple modernities, 4, 14

Mumba, Samantha, 73–75, 76

music, 105, 113; Celtic-and-African-influenced, 84–86; Nigerian, 133–134

"Muslim Communities in France" (House), 223–224

Nigeria, 46, 138; bilateral readmission agreement, 50–51, 154–156, 290n7; corruption, 139–140

Nigerians, 46; asylum applications, 51; conflated with asylum seekers, 223

Nigerians, deportation of, 16, 51, 61; children in hiding, 173, 175–176; confiscation of mobile phones, 154; as counter to modernity, 172–173, 177–178; depicted as children, 154, 158–159, 162; economic dimensions, 169; educational achievement and, 159–160; Olukunle Elukanlo case, 153–173, 177; *refoulement* potential, 156, 163, 164, 167, 170–172; safety concerns, 51, 155–156, 171–172; St. Patrick, references to, 174–175

Noirs de France (Yade), 260

Nord-Pas-de-Calais, 246

Norris, David, 88

North Africa: French colonies, 222, 223, 231; pro-democracy uprisings, 5

North African communities (*Beur*), 26

North Great George's Street Preservation Society, 88

Le Nouvel Observateur, 244

Nouvelle Orleans, 186–187

Nussbaum, Martha, 20

Nwanze, Iyabo, 175, 177

Obama, Barack, 19, 242, 280–281

O'Connell, Daniel, 32, 283n3

O'Connell Street (Dublin), 68, 290n2

O'Donoghue, John, 154

Odunsi, Elizabeth, 175–176

Office of the Refugee Applications Commissioner (ORAC), 51, 155, 293n3

Okenla, Gabriel, 61

Onyejelem, Chinedu, 65, 68

optimism, 3, 5, 10–12, 49

Othello (Shakespeare), 80

otherness: New Orleans and, 215; racialized, 35, 37–38; "where are you cialized, 35, 37–38; "where are you

from?" phenomenon, 86, 105, 114, 124, 136–137

"outsider inside" role, 89, 175

Oxygène, 269, 272–273

"Paddy's Lamentation" (De Jimbe), 84–86

Palmerstown Community School, 153, 161, 167, 170

Pan African Organization, 61, 104

parallel society concept, 218

Paris, 16, 25, 40; Aulnay-sous-Bois, 266–273. *See also* France

Paris *banlieues,* 2005 protest, 185, 217–220, 222, 225–227, 276; criminalization discourse, 217, 266; equality discourse and, 243; Germany, effect on, 268; Irish commentary on, 218–220, 266–267; national identity debate and, 252, 257. *See also* African Diaspora community, France

Parnell Street community ("Little Africa," Dublin), 23–24, 60–61, 65–66; transformations, 88–89. *See also* African Diaspora community, Ireland

passports, German, 128–129, 143

past, modernity's distancing from, 11, 40, 45, 157, 262–263, 280, 282

paternalism: France, 237, 239, 261; Ireland, 76, 81, 84, 158

Pathak, Avijit, 3–4

Pavee Point (Travellers' Centre), 52

peace, global, 41–42

perception, 11

Perry, James, 208, 209, 294n1

pessimism, 7, 10

Le Petit Robert dictionary, 230–231

Pierce, Amos, 201

Pierce, Ron, 201

Pierce, Wendell, 200–201

Pitt, Brad, 212, 294n2

Playboy of the Western World (Adigun and Doyle), 83–84

ELISA JOY WHITE is Associate Professor of Ethnic Studies at the University of Hawai'i, Mānoa, and holds a Ph.D. in African Diaspora Studies from the University of California, Berkeley. Her publications examine a range of areas, including the African Diaspora in Ireland, Black Europe, ethnicity and new media, human rights, and immigration policy.

Lightning Source UK Ltd.
Milton Keynes UK
UKHW010353040920
369273UK00013B/26